VIOLENCE AND SOCIAL ORDERS

All societies must deal with the possibility of violence, and they do so in different ways. This book integrates the problem of violence into a larger social science and historical framework, showing how economic and political behavior are closely linked. Most societies, which we call *natural states*, limit violence by political manipulation of the economy to create privileged interests. These privileges limit the use of violence by powerful individuals, but doing so hinders both economic and political development. In contrast, modern societies create *open access* to economic and political organizations, fostering political and economic competition. The book provides a framework for understanding the two types of social orders, why open access societies are both politically and economically more developed, and how some twenty-five countries have made the transition between the two types.

Douglass C. North is co-recipient of the 1993 Nobel Memorial Prize in Economic Science. He is the Spencer T. Olin Professor in Arts and Sciences at Washington University in St. Louis, where he served as director of the Center for Political Economy from 1984 to 1990, and is the Bartlett Burnap Senior Fellow at the Hoover Institution at Stanford University. A member of the American Academy of Arts and Sciences and a former member of the Board of Directors of the National Bureau of Economic Research for twenty years, Professor North received the John R. Commons Award in 1992. The author of ten books, including *Institutions, Institutional Change, and Economic Performance* (Cambridge University Press, 1990) and *Understanding the Process of Economic Change* (2005), Professor North has research interests in property rights, economic organization in history, and the formation of political and economic institutions and their consequences through time. He is a frequent consultant for the World Bank and numerous countries on issues of economic growth.

John Joseph Wallis is professor of economics at the University of Maryland and a research associate at the National Bureau of Economic Research. He received his Ph.D. from the University of Washington in 1981 and went on to spend a two-year postdoctoral fellowship at the University of Chicago. During the 2006–7 academic year, he was a Visiting Scholar at the Hoover Institution and a Visiting Professor of Political Science at Stanford. Professor Wallis is an economic historian who specializes in the public finance of American governments and more generally on the relation between the institutional development of governments and the development of economies. His large-scale research on American state and local government finance, and on American state constitutions, has been supported by the National Science Foundation.

Barry R. Weingast is the Ward C. Krebs Family Professor in the Department of Political Science and a Senior Fellow at the Hoover Institution at Stanford University. He is also a Senior Fellow (by courtesy) of the Stanford Center for International Development. Weingast received his Ph.D. from the California Institute of Technology in 1977. Prior to teaching at Stanford, Professor Weingast spent ten years at Washington University in St. Louis in the Department of Economics and the School of Business. The recipient of the Riker Prize, the Heinz Eulau Prize, and the James Barr Memorial Prize, among others, he has also worked extensively with development agencies such as the World Bank and the U.S. Agency for International Development. Professor Weingast coauthored *Analytical Narratives* (1998) and coedited *The Oxford Handbook of Political Economy* (2006). His research focuses on the political foundations of markets, economic reform, and regulation, including problems of political economy of development, federalism and decentralization, and legal institutions.

Violence and Social Orders

*A Conceptual Framework for Interpreting Recorded
Human History*

DOUGLASS C. NORTH

Washington University in St. Louis

JOHN JOSEPH WALLIS

University of Maryland

BARRY R. WEINGAST

Stanford University

CAMBRIDGE
UNIVERSITY PRESS

CAMBRIDGE UNIVERSITY PRESS

Cambridge, New York, Melbourne, Madrid, Cape Town, Singapore, São Paulo, Delhi

Cambridge University Press
32 Avenue of the Americas, New York, NY 10013-2473, USA

www.cambridge.org
Information on this title: www.cambridge.org/9780521761734

© Douglass C. North, John Joseph Wallis, and Barry R. Weingast 2009

This publication is in copyright. Subject to statutory exception
and to the provisions of relevant collective licensing agreements,
no reproduction of any part may take place without the written
permission of Cambridge University Press.

First published 2009

Printed in the United States of America

A catalog record for this publication is available from the British Library.

Library of Congress Cataloging in Publication data

North, Douglass C.
Violence and social orders : a conceptual framework for interpreting recorded human history /
Douglass C. North, John Joseph Wallis, Barry R. Weingast.
p. cm.
Includes bibliographical references and index.
ISBN 978-0-521-76173-4 (hardback)
1. Violence – Economic aspects – History. 2. State, The – History. 3. Social control – History.
I. Wallis, John Joseph. II. Weingast, Barry R. III. Title.
HM886.N67 2009
306.301 – dc22 2008040965

ISBN 978-0-521-76173-4 hardback

Cambridge University Press has no responsibility for the persistence or
accuracy of URLs for external or third-party Internet Web sites referred to in
this publication and does not guarantee that any content on such Web sites is,
or will remain, accurate or appropriate. Information regarding prices, travel
timetables, and other factual information given in this work are correct at
the time of first printing, but Cambridge University Press does not guarantee
the accuracy of such information thereafter.

This book is dedicated to our wives Elisabeth, Ellen, and Susie

Contents

Preface

Every explanation of large-scale social change contains a theory of economics, a theory of politics, and a theory of social behavior. Sometimes, as in the materialist theory of Marx, the theories are explicit. Often, however, they are implicit, and even more often theories of economics and politics are independent. Despite a great deal of attention and effort, social science has not come to grips with how economic and political development are connected either in history or in the modern world. The absence of a workable integrated theory of economics and politics reflects the lack of systematic thinking about the central problem of violence in human societies. How societies solve the ubiquitous threat of violence shapes and constrains the forms that human interaction can take, including the form of political and economic systems.

This book lays out a set of concepts that show how societies have used the control of political, economic, religious, and educational activities to limit and contain violence over the last ten thousand years. In most societies, political, economic, religious, and military powers are created through institutions that structure human organizations and relationships. These institutions simultaneously give individuals control over resources and social functions and, by doing so, limit the use of violence by shaping the incentives faced by individuals and groups who have access to violence. We call these patterns of social organization *social orders*. Our aim is to understand how social orders structure social interactions.

The conceptual framework articulates the internal logic of the two social orders that dominate the modern world and the process by which societies make the transition from one social order to another (the original social order preceding these was the foraging order characteristic of hunter–gatherer societies). After sketching out the conceptual framework in the first chapter, we consider the logic of the social order that appeared five to ten millennia ago: *the natural state*. Natural states use the political system to regulate economic competition and create economic rents; the rents order social relations, control violence, and establish social cooperation. The natural state transformed human history; indeed, the first natural states developed new technologies that resulted in the beginnings of *recorded* human history. Most of the world still lives in natural states today.

Next we consider the logic of the social order that emerged in a few societies at the beginning of the nineteenth century: *the open access society*. As with the appearance of natural states, open access societies transformed human history in a fundamental way. Perhaps 25 countries and 15 percent of the world's population live in open access societies today; the other 175 countries and 85 percent live in natural states. Open access societies regulate economic and political competition in a way that uses the entry and competition to order social relations. The third task of the book is to explain how societies make the transition from natural states to open access societies.

We develop a conceptual framework, not a formal or analytical theory. Our desire was to write a book that is accessible to social scientists and historians of many types. The three social orders identify three distinct patterns in human history. We show how the second and third social orders are structured, why they work the way they do, and the logic underlying the transition from one social order to another. We do not present a formal model that generates explicit empirical tests or deterministic predictions about social change. Instead, we propose a conceptual framework that incorporates explicitly endogenous patterns of social, economic, political, military, religious, and educational behavior. The challenge is to explain how durable and predictable social institutions deal with an ever-changing, unpredictable, and novel world within a framework consistent with the dynamic forces of social change. There is no teleology built into the framework: it is a dynamic explanation of social change, not of social progress.

We interlace historical illustrations with the conceptual discussion to provide enough evidence that these patterns actually exist in the world. In the case of the transition from natural states to open access societies, we show that the forces we identify can be retrieved from the existing historical record. We are not writing a history of the world. The history provides examples and illumination rather than conclusive tests of our ideas. The examples range from the Neolithic revolution to Republican and Imperial Rome to Aztec Mesoamerica to the Middle Ages to the present. Some specialists in the times and places we study will argue that we have lifted these examples out of context, and we have. However, our intention is to put these examples in a new context, to provide a new framework for interpreting the course of human history over the past ten thousand years, and to open new ways of thinking about the pressing problems of political and economic development facing the world today.

Acknowledgments

Although this has been a collaborative effort from the very beginning, John Wallis's role deserves special mention. He wrote the first draft and rode herd on the project as it evolved through many subsequent drafts. This project benefited from the input, support, and comments of a great many people and institutions, and it is a pleasure to acknowledge our debts.

The Hoover Institution at Stanford University provided invaluable support on many dimensions, without which this book would not have been produced. Since 1995, Hoover has sponsored North as a Senior Fellow, allowing him to be in residence each Winter quarter; and for the critical year of writing this book, he was in residence for both Winter and Spring quarters (AY07–08). Wallis was a Visiting Scholar in residence for the 2006–7 academic year and visits each winter. Weingast has been a Senior Fellow at Hoover since 1990. David Brady, Hoover's Deputy Director for Research and Program Development, generously supported the project with various funds. Silvia Sandoval of the Hoover Institution tirelessly and cheerfully provided several years' worth of research assistance. The Bradley Foundation provided generous support for Wallis and Weingast at the Hoover Institution.

Weingast thanks the Ward C. Krebs family, which has generously funded his chair in the Department of Political Science. He is also grateful for support of two grants from Stanford University: one from the Freeman-Spogli Institute for International Studies and the other from the President's Fund.

The World Bank has been generous and active in support of this project. Steven Webb has taken the lead in all of our activities at the Bank. We presented early ideas in several forums at the Bank. Two grants enabled us to bring together a group of scholars to begin writing case histories applying the framework to modern developing countries and finance two meetings of the group at the Bank. Jean-Jacques Dethier, François Bourguignon, Ed

Campos, and Phillip Keefer gave us valuable comments and encouragement. Brian Levy has been a steady supporter and inquisitor and helped organize the case studies. Mushtaq Khan has been particularly generous with his time and ideas. Joel Barkan, Alberto Diaz-Cayeros, Francis Fukuyama, Carol Graham, Paul Hutchcroft, Nicolas Meisel, Gabriella Montinola, Patricio Navia, Jacques Ould-Aoudia, Robert Peccoud, Jong-sung You, and a number of World Bank staff participated in the two case study meetings.

The Mercatus Center at George Mason University sponsored a two-day seminar in January 2007 at Stanford University, enabling us to get comments on all aspects of the early manuscript. Thanks for the comments, criticisms, and suggestions of the seminar participants go to Randy Calvert, Gary Cox, James Fearon, Rui de Figueiredo, Avner Greif, Stephen Haber, Philip Hoffman, Margaret Levi, Jan de Vries, and Steven Webb. Mercatus also sponsored Weingast as a Visiting Scholar in March 2006. We gratefully acknowledge the Mercatus staff for their support and activities: Brian Hooks, Mercatus Director, and Rob Herrit, Claire Morgan, and Frederic Sautet. Mercatus's Courtney Knapp was especially helpful. Paul S. Edwards, former Director of Mercatus, encouraged us from the beginning of this project. He also served as facilitator of the two-day seminar.

James Robinson arranged for us to present the manuscript at an Eric M. Mindich Encounters with Authors Symposium at the Institute for Quantitative Social Science at Harvard University in October 2007. The discussants, Steve Ansolabehere, Robert Bates, Niall Ferguson, Jeffry Frieden, Edward Glaeser, and Claudia Goldin, gave us extensive comments that helped guide our revisions. We also received many comments from those who attended these meetings, including James Alt, Thad Dunning, Naomi Lamoreaux, Noel Maurer, Robert Margo, Aldo Musacchio, Dani Rodrik, Ellis Goldberg, Kenneth Shepsle, and David Stasavage.

Mathew McCubbins arranged for a two-day seminar at the University of California at San Diego in January 2008, at which Gary Cox, Peter Gourevitch, and Stephan Haggard provided helpful comments.

Several universities and institutions afforded us with the opportunity to share our work through seminars, and we value the feedback we received at Brown University; Holden Village; the Mercatus Center at George Mason University; the Foundation for Teaching Economics; the National Bureau of Economic Research Program in the Development of the American Economy (NBER-DAE) Summer Institute; Stanford University (twice at the Center for Democracy, Development, and the Rule of Law and once in the Department of Economic History); the University of California campuses at Berkeley, Los Angeles, and San Diego; the University of Maryland; the University of

Kansas; Washington University; the World Bank; and Yale University. We also thank the participants in two Economics 613 classes at the University of Maryland and two Political Science 362 classes at Stanford.

Many of our colleagues read parts or all of this work, and our appreciation goes to them for the many conversations, comments, and feedback. They include Eric Alston, Lee Alston, Terry Anderson, Lee Benham, Roger Betancourt, Ruth Bloch, Randy Calvert, Gregory Clark, Roger Congleton, Karen Cook, Robert Cull, Larry Diamond, Alberto Diaz-Cayeros, Richard Epstein, James Fearon, Price Fishback, Page Fortuna, Sebastian Galiani, Judy Goldstein, Peter Gourevitch, Avner Greif, Stephen Haber, Stephan Haggard, Jac Heckelman, Jessica Hennessey, Paul Hinderlie, Ethan Ilzetski, Phil Keefer, Amalia Kessler, Mushtaq Khan, Dan Klerman, Steve Krasner, David Laitin, Steven LeBlanc, Margaret Levi, Brian Levy, Gary Libecap, Peter Lindert, Lili Liu, Beatriz Magaloni, Mathew McCubbins, Michael McFaul, Petra Moser, Ramon Myers, Roger Noll, Wally Oates, Josh Ober, Emily Owens, Sunita Parikh, Eleonora Pasotti, Sarah Perlman, Claire Priest, Jonathan Rodden, Joshua Rosenblum, Jean-Laurent Rosenthal, Andy Rutten, Richard Scott, Kenneth Shepsle, Mary Shirley, Michael Smith, Steve Snyder, Kathryn Stoner-Weiss, Jon Sumida, Don Sutherland, Alan Taylor, Werner Troesken, Jeremy Weinstein, and Tom Weiss. We also benefited from the support of Randy Robinson, Bruce Schmidt, and Alicia Newsholme.

Lauren Barr, Adam Levine, Mary Paden, Scott Parris, and Dona Hightower Perkins helped us travel the distance from a manuscript to a book.

We owe a special debt to two people for their advice, support, and friendship throughout this project. The first is John Raisian, Director of the Hoover Institution. In addition to the support noted earlier, Hoover provided a fertile intellectual and working environment that helped our project in innumerable ways. Second, Steven Webb of the World Bank has helped us with this project since its inception; has collaborated on joint work applying our framework to developing countries; and has sponsored various grants, workshops, and conferences at the World Bank helping to further this research.

Finally, we acknowledge the debt to our families for having to put up with us while we focused all too much attention on this work. Thank you Elisabeth; Ellen, Dexter, Dan, Towne, and Page; and Susie and Sam.

ONE

The Conceptual Framework

1.1 Introduction

The task of the social sciences is to explain the performance characteristics of societies through time, including the radical gap in human well-being between rich countries and poor as well as the contrasting forms of political organization, beliefs, and social structure that produce these variations in performance. Recorded human history began with the first social revolution – the Neolithic, agricultural, urban, or first economic revolution – and the appearance of the first large permanent groups of individuals between five thousand and ten thousand years ago. The second social revolution – the industrial, modern, or second economic revolution – began two hundred years ago and continues today. Changes in the organization of groups played a central role in this revolution as well. As Coleman describes it, "It is the corporate actors, the organizations that draw their power from persons and employ that power to corporate ends, that are the primary actors in the social structure of modern society" (1974, p. 49). The two social revolutions resulted in profound changes in the way societies were organized. The central task of this book is to articulate the underlying logic of the two new patterns of social organization, what we call *social orders*, and to explain how societies make the transition from one social order to the other.

In order to understand why emergent features of modern developed societies, such as economic development and democracy, are so closely linked in the second social revolution, we are interested in the basic forces underlying patterns of the social order. Social orders are characterized by the way societies craft institutions that support the existence of specific forms of human organization, the way societies limit or open access to those organizations, and through the incentives created by the pattern of organization. These characteristics of social orders are also intimately related to how societies

1

limit and control violence. Because social orders engender different patterns of behavior, individuals in different social orders form different beliefs about how the people around them behave. Violence, organizations, institutions, and beliefs are the elements of our conceptual framework.

All of human history has had but three social orders. The first was the *for-aging order*: small social groups characteristic of hunter–gatherer societies. Our primary concern is with the two social orders that arose over the last ten millennia. The *limited access order* or *natural state* emerged in the first social revolution. Personal relationships, who one is and who one knows, form the basis for social organization and constitute the arena for individual interaction, particularly personal relationships among powerful individuals. Natural states limit the ability of individuals to form organizations. In the *open access orders* that emerged in the second social revolution, personal relations still matter, but impersonal categories of individuals, often called citizens, interact over wide areas of social behavior with no need to be cognizant of the individual identity of their partners. Identity, which in natural states is inherently personal, becomes defined as a set of impersonal characteristics in open access orders. The ability to form organizations that the larger society supports is open to everyone who meets a set of minimal and impersonal criteria. Both social orders have public and private organizations, but natural states limit access to those organizations whereas open access societies do not.

The transition from the natural state to an open access order is the second social revolution, the rise of modernity. Although elements of the second revolution have spread everywhere, especially technology, most contemporary societies remain natural states. The transition entails a set of changes in the polity that ensures greater participation by citizens and secures impersonal political rights, more transparent institutions structuring decision-making processes, and legal support for a wide range of organizational forms, including political parties and economic organizations. The transition entails a set of changes in the economy that ensure open entry and competition in many markets, free movement of goods and individuals over space and time, the ability to create organizations to pursue economic opportunities, protection of property rights, and prohibitions on the use of violence to obtain resources and goods or to coerce others. Although evidence from the past few decades is mixed, over the past two centuries, political and economic development appear to have gone hand in hand.[1]

---

[1] Lipset (1959) asked why sustainable democracy seemed to require economic development. Przeworksi, Alvarez, Cheibub, and Limongi (2000) examined the correlation quantitatively and found substantial evidence that while episodes of democracy have occurred at

Simple evidence of the strong pattern of correlation between political and economic development is shown in Table 1.1. The table lists the thirty richest countries, measured by per capita income in 2000, and each country's rank in the Polity IV measures of democracy. The democracy measure combines information on the quality of political institutions: political access, political competition, and constraints on the executive branch.[2] Of the thirty richest countries, the income of four is based primarily on oil, and they have the worst democracy measures. Another five countries are too small to be included in the Polity data set. Of the remaining twenty-one countries, all but France and Singapore are tied for the highest rating of political institutions. The table shows that high income and good political institutions are closely related. If we consider economic performance in greater detail we find the same relationships. Lipset (1959) considered a set of factors he called the "development complex," what we think of as the open access pattern: income, education, urbanization, as well as car ownership, telephones, radios, and newspaper subscriptions (he was writing in the 1950s) and found strong correlations among all these measures and democracy.

An underappreciated feature of the different patterns of social orders relates to why poor countries stay poor. Economic growth, measured as increases in per capita income, occurs when countries sustain positive growth rates in per capita income over the long term. Over the long stretch of human history before 1800, the evidence suggests that the long-run rate of growth of per capita income was very close to zero.[3] A long-term growth rate of zero does not mean, however, that societies never experienced higher standards of material well-being in the past. A zero growth rate implies that

---

all income levels, sustainable democracy is primarily a feature of high-income countries. Whether there is a causal link between democracy and economic development, and if so which way the link runs, has remained an open question. Barro (1996, 1999) gives an economic analysis of the question. For an overview of the modernization hypothesis literature and the latest empirical results on the relationship and development, see Acemoglu, Johnson, Robinson, and Yared (2007). Economic historians have also considered the problem of development over the long run; Landes (1999), North (1981, 1990, 2005), and Rosenberg and Birdzell (1986).

[2] "The Democracy indicator is an additive 11-point scale (0–10). The operational indicator of democracy is derived from codings of the competitiveness of political participation (variable 2.6), the openness and competitiveness of executive recruitment (variables 2.3 and 2.2), and constraints on the chief executive (variable 2.4)..." (Marshall & Jaggers, 2005, p. 13).

[3] See Clark (2007b) for the most recent explication of the argument about long-term growth before 1800. Economic growth before 1800 did occur, but on the extensive margin of population growth rather than on the intensive margin of rising per capita income, see Fogel (2004, pp. 20–2).

Table 1.1. *Income per capita in 2000 and Polity IV ranking*

Rank	Country	Per capita income, 2000	Polity IV rank	Oil
1	Luxembourg	48,217	–	
2	Bermuda	35,607	–	
3	United States	34,365	1	
4	Norway	33,092	1	
5	Qatar	32,261	156	oil
6	United Arab Emirates	32,182	141	oil
7	Singapore	29,434	109	
8	Switzerland	28,831	1	
9	Netherlands	26,293	1	
10	Denmark	26,042	1	
11	Austria	25,623	1	
12	Sweden	25,232	1	
13	Kuwait	25,135	135	oil
14	Hong Kong	25,023	–	
15	Ireland	24,948	1	
16	Australia	24,915	1	
17	United Kingdom	24,666	1	
18	Canada	24,616	1	
19	Iceland	24,339	1	
20	Brunei	24,308	–	oil
21	Macao	24,224	–	
22	Germany	24,077	1	
23	Japan	23,971	1	
24	France	23,672	33	
25	Belgium	23,524	1	
26	Italy	22,487	1	
27	Israel	22,237	1	
28	Finland	21,302	1	
29	Puerto Rico	21,211	–	
30	New Zealand	20,423	1	

Sources: Real per capita income in 2000 dollars from Heston, Summers, and Aten (2006). Polity IV "Democracy" ranking from Marshall and Jaggers (2005). The Democracy ranking goes from a value of 10 to 0 in integer values. All of the countries tied for first, ranking of 1, have a value of 10. Those tied for second, like France, have a ranking of 33. There are 159 countries in the Polity IV data set. The Polity IV data set does not include small countries. Countries without Polity IV data are listed as –.

every period of increasing per capita income was matched by a corresponding period of decreasing income. Modern societies that made the transition to open access, and subsequently became wealthier than any other society in human history, did so because they greatly reduced the episodes of negative growth. The historical pattern of offsetting periods of positive and negative

Table 1.2. *Growth rates in good and bad years by per capita income in 2000*

	Per capita income in 2000	Number of countries	Percentage of world population	Number of years observed	Percent positive years	Average positive growth rate	Average negative growth rate
(1)	< $20,000	153	87%	5,678	66%	5.35%	−4.88%
(2)	> $20,000	31	13%	1,468	81%	4.19%	−3.49%
(3)	> $20,000 No Oil	27	13%	1,336	84%	3.88%	−2.33%
(4)	All	184		7,146			
(5)	Over $20,000	31	13%	1,468	81%	4.19%	−3.49%
(6)	No Oil	27	13%	1,336	84%	3.88%	−2.33%
(7)	$15,000 to $20,000	12	2%	491	76%	5.59%	−4.25%
(8)	$10,000 to $15,000	14	2%	528	71%	5.27%	−4.07%
(9)	$5,000 to $10,000	37	16%	1,245	73%	5.25%	−4.59%
(10)	$2,000 to $5,000	46	53%	1,708	66%	5.39%	−4.75%
(11)	$300 to $2,000	44	14%	1,706	56%	5.37%	−5.38%

Sources: Heston, Summers, and Aten (2006). "Real GDP per capita (Constant Prices: Chain series)" and their calculated annual growth rates for that series "Growth rate of Real GDP per capita (Constant Prices: Chain series)" were used. Countries were first sorted into income categories based on their income in 2000, measured in 2000 dollars. Average annual positive and negative growth rates are the simple arithmetic average for all of the years and all of the countries in the income category (zero growth is treated as a positive growth rate) without any weighting. The Penn World Tables include information on 188 countries, but only growth rates on 184 countries. The sample runs from 1950 to 2004, although information is not available for every country in every year. The "No Oil" category of income over $20,000 excludes Qatar, United Arab Emirates, Kuwait, and Brunei.

growth episodes is easier to see in the modern world, where we have better data.[4]

Table 1.2 uses the same data on real per capita income in the year 2000 used in Table 1.1, taken from the Penn World tables. The data cover 184 countries between 1950 and 2004 for which annual growth rates can be calculated. The table breaks down countries by income intervals from rich to poor, and for each income class we calculated the share of all years that countries experienced positive growth in per capita income and the average growth rate in years with positive and negative per capita income growth. The first three rows of the table separate the world into countries with

---

[4] No one knows what annual per capita income was for any period of time before the early nineteenth century, so the assertion in the text that the recent growth in developed countries is due to the elimination of negative growth episodes is merely an assertion, but one that accords well with what we know about economic performance in the past.

incomes more than and less than $20,000. Because the four oil-producing countries (Kuwait, Brunei, Qatar, and United Arab Emirates) in the high-income group have very volatile incomes that fluctuate with the price of oil, we report the more than $20,000 group in two ways: with (row 2) and without (row 3) the oil countries. Countries with less than $20,000 in income experience positive growth in only 66 percent of the years for which data are available, compared to positive growth in 84 percent of the years in the rich non-oil countries. The poorest countries in the sample, with incomes between $300 and $2,000 per year (row 11 of the table), experienced positive growth rates in only 56 percent of the years.

Strikingly, the richest countries are not distinguished by higher positive growth rates when they do grow. In fact, the richest countries have the lowest average positive growth rates by a substantial amount. Income in non-oil countries with incomes of more than $20,000 grows at an average rate of 3.88 percent in years when income is growing and falls by an average rate of 2.33 percent when income is shrinking. In contrast, incomes in countries with less than $20,000 income grow at an average annual rate of 5.35 percent when income is rising, but shrink at a rate of 4.88 percent when income is falling. When they grow, poor countries grow faster than rich countries.[5] They are poor because they experience more frequent episodes of shrinking income and more negative growth during the episodes.[6] Countries below $20,000 income do not exhibit a strong relationship between income and positive growth rates. The same is not true for the relationship between income and negative growth rates. When incomes are falling, they fall much faster in poorer countries, as shown in the last column of Table 1.2. The poorest countries experience both more years of negative income growth and more rapid declines during those years.

A third common pattern that differs across social orders concerns organizations. In open access societies, access to organizations becomes defined as an impersonal right that all citizens possess. In contrast, natural states limit access to organizations and third-party enforcement. The organizations that can be formed are often limited in complexity and size as well as limited to social elites. Natural states therefore have a much more limited

---

[5] Part of the high growth rates in poor countries when they are growing may be attributed to "catch-up," that is, the countries can grow more rapidly because they are simply recovering from a negative shock. The pattern of negative shocks cannot be explained by catch-up, however.

[6] Rodrik (1999), Ramey and Ramey (1995), and Mobarak (2005) provide more sophisticated empirical confirmation of this basic fact.

civil society.[7] Organizations are, in part, tools: tools that individuals use to increase their productivity, to seek and create human contact and relationships, to coordinate the actions of many individuals and groups, and to dominate and coerce others. Societies differ in the range and availability of organizational tools.

Fukuyama (1995, p. 10) places special emphasis on organizations in his definition of social capital: "the ability of people to work together for common purposes in groups and organizations." In his view, the ability to form organizations explains both the development of modern polities and economies: "The concept of social capital makes clear why capitalism and democracy are so closely related. A healthy capitalist economy is one in which there will be sufficient social capital in the underlying society to permit businesses, corporations, networks, and the like to be self-organizing . . . The same propensity for spontaneous sociability that is key to building durable businesses is also indispensable for putting together effective political organizations" (1995, pp. 356–7).

The importance of groups and organizations to the operation of modern liberal democracies has been a mainstay of the enormous literature on civil societies. A rich and varied network of groups and organizations provides both a check on the activities of government and an environment in which individual values of tolerance, participation, and civic virtue can be nurtured. We build on both of these aspects of civil society. We deviate significantly by emphasing that most organizations in all societies function with the explicit support of the state. We argue that most organizations, even simple ones, rely on third-party enforcement of agreements and relationships between the organization's members, or agreements between the organization and outside actors. The state most often provides third-party enforcement. Open access to organizations is a major and underappreciated distinction between natural states and open access orders. Impersonally defined access (rights) to form organizations is a central part of open access societies.

Table 1.3 gives an estimate of the distribution of one specific type of organization across countries by income. In this case, it is formal trade and business organizations, data gathered and published by the K. G. Saur Company underlying the analysis of Coates, Heckelman, and Wilson (2007).

---

[7] The importance of civil society and open access to organizations has been most notably argued by Putnam 1993, 2000, but the notion goes back at least as far as Hegel (1991/ 1820), pp. 220–74. See also Lipset (1963), O'Donnell and Schmitter (1986), Rosenblum (1998), Tocqueville (1969 [1835]), and Widner (2001).

Table 1.3. *Income and organizations*

Income per capita in 2000	Number of countries in income range	Number of organizations Total in income range	Number of organizations per country Average per country	Number of organizations per million residents Average per country	Share of organizations Worldwide in income range	Share of population Worldwide in income range
	(1)	(2)	(3)	(4)	(5)	(6)
$300 to $2,000	41	1,238	30.2	2.8	3.3%	18.0%
$2,000 to $5,000	38	1,430	37.6	4.5	3.8%	40.4%
$5,000 to $10,000	34	2,338	68.8	16.7	6.3%	20.0%
$10,000 to $15,000	15	714	47.6	21.2	1.9%	2.6%
$15,000 to $20,000	8	708	88.5	26.9	1.9%	1.6%
Over $20,000	28	30,976	1106.3	63.6	82.8%	17.3%
All	164	37,404	228.1	19.3	100%	100%

Sources: The number of interest groups is taken from Saur, as combined by Coates, Heckelman, and Wilson (2007). Numbers in the table were based on worksheets underlying their paper. Income from Heston, Summers, and Aten (2006).

There were 37,404 such organizations in the 164 countries for which we could match income data to Saur's counts. The poorest countries, with incomes of less than $2,000 per year, had an average of 30 organizations and 2.8 organizations per million inhabitants (columns 3 and 4 in the table). Countries with more than $20,000 in annual income had an average of 1,106 organizations and 64 organizations per million inhabitants. The number of organizations per million persons increases steadily as incomes rise (column 4). Countries with less than $10,000 income included 78.4 percent of the population in the sample (column 6), but possessed only 13.1 percent of the organizations in the sample (column 5). Countries exhibit a marked correlation between the number of organizations and the extent of economic and political development.

Table 1.3 covers only a small fraction of the organizations in a country. Developed open access countries have significant numbers of formal organizations. On the public side, for example, the United States in 1997 had 87,504 formally organized units of government (1 national, 50 states, 3,043 counties, 19,372 municipalities, 16,629 townships and towns, 13,726 school districts, and 34,683 special districts).[8] On the private side in 1996 there were 1,188,510 tax-exempt organizations (654,186 religious and charitable institutions, 139,512 social welfare organizations, 31,464 war veterans organizations, 80,065 taxable and nontaxable farmers cooperative organizations, 77,274 business leagues, and 91,972 fraternal benevolent societies). Although Robert Putnam (2000) has documented a decline in U.S. civic engagement, there is approximately 1 formal not-for-profit organization for every 160 people.[9] The for-profit sector in 1997 contained 23,645,197 organizations (17 million proprietorships, 1.7 million partnerships, and 4.7 million corporations) – 1 formal business corporation for every 60 people; 1 formal-sector business organization for every 13 people.[10] The numbers are impressive, particularly considering that the entire country had somewhere in the neighborhood of two hundred formal business incorporations between 1776 and 1800.[11]

---

[8] Figures taken from *Historical Statistics*, Vol. 5, p. 5–10, Table Ea1–9.

[9] *Historical Statistics* (2006), Vol. 2, pp. 2–859–861, Tables Bg-65–101. These organizations are formal in the sense that they are registered with the Internal Revenue Service to obtain tax-exempt status, although not all of them are formal corporations. These figures undercount the total number of not-for-profit organizations, many of which have not registered for tax-exempt status.

[10] *Historical Statistics* (2006), Vol. 3, pp. 3–496–498, Tables Ch1–18.

[11] See the tables in *Historical Statistics*, Vol. 3, pp 3–531–549 on incorporations in the nineteenth century and the introductory essay by Lamoreaux, pp. 3–477–494.

Table 1.4. *Size of government expenditures as percentage of GDP and by level of government*

Per capita income 2000	Number of countries	Central government percent of GDP	Number of countries	All government percent of GDP	Subnational government percent of all govt.	Average population) (000s)
	(1)	(2)	(3)	(4)	(5)	(6)
$300 to $2,000	9	29%	7	31%	4%	7,884
$2,000 to $5,000	17	26%	16	27%	5%	99,625
$5,000 to $10,000	20	25%	17	33%	13%	39,943
$10,000 to $15,000	11	32%	9	40%	16%	13,796
$15,000 to $20,000	8	31%	7	33%	6%	14,317
Over $20,000	22	37%	19	53%	30%	31,024
All	87	30.28	75	37.29	14%	42,274

Sources: Income, Heston, Summers, and Aten (2006), "Real GDP per capita (Constant Prices: Chain series)." Government as share of GDP from IMF: Government Financial Statistics. Note that not all countries report subnational government expenditures and only countries with reported expenditures, even if those expenditures were zero, are included in columns 3, 4, 5, and 6. Government expenditures as a percentage of GDP were taken directly from the IMF data, and reflect the average percentage of GDP over the period 1995–2000, calculated for years for each country for which there were data.

The number of formal government organizations raises the last element of the social order patterns: larger governments (see Lindert, 2004). Table 1.4 gives government expenditures as a percentage of Gross Domestic Product (GDP) for those countries with both income and government expenditure data. Because reliable data on the size of government expenditures are more difficult to collect, the samples are smaller in Table 1.4 than in the other tables. The table, nonetheless, reveals a strong relationship between the size and structure of government across income classes. As column 2 shows, income and the size of the central government are not related. However, when we include information on subnational governments – states, cities, counties, provinces, and so on – in column 4, a positive relationship between income and government size clearly emerges. Indeed, the strongest pattern is the positive relationship between income and the size of subnational governments, both as a share of total government expenditures (column 5) and as a share of GDP. High-income countries create and sustain a much denser network of subnational government organizations.[12] Governments in high-income countries are bigger because they provide more public goods, including highways and infrastructure, education, public health, and social insurance programs. They also provide these services impersonally to all citizens. As the striking study of corruption in India by Bertrand, Djankov, Hanna, and Mullainathan (2007) shows, natural states cannot issue something as seemingly simple as a driver's license on an impersonal basis.

Again, the biggest difference in the pattern of government size and structure occurs between countries with more than $20,000 in income and those with less than $20,000 in income. The relationship between income and development is most marked at the very top of the income scale in those countries that have made the transition to open access orders.

There are two basic social patterns in the modern world. The open access pattern is characterized by:

1. Political and economic development.
2. Economies that experience much less negative economic growth.
3. Rich and vibrant civil societies with lots of organizations.
4. Bigger, more decentralized governments.

---

[12] Physical and demographic size also have an effect on the number of sublocal governments, so Table 1.4 provides average population for countries in each class. For India, with more than one billion people, subnational government expenditures are 38% of all government expenditures. If we controlled for population size, the relationship between income and size of government would be even more marked.

5. Widespread impersonal social relationships, including rule of law, secure property rights, fairness, and equality – all aspects of treating everyone the same.

The limited access pattern is characterized by:

1. Slow-growing economies vulnerable to shocks.
2. Polities without generalized consent of the governed.
3. Relatively small numbers of organizations.
4. Smaller and more centralized governments.
5. A predominance of social relationships organized along personal lines, including privileges, social hierarchies, laws that are enforced unequally, insecure property rights, and a pervasive sense that not all individuals were created or are equal.

All societies are subject to random and unpredictable changes in the world around and within them. Changes in external factors like climate, relative prices, and neighboring groups as well as changes in internal factors like the identity and character of leaders, internal feuds and disputes, and relative prices all contribute to persistent alterations in the circumstances with which societies must cope. The variations in the economic performance of limited and open access societies over time reflect the inherent ability of the two social orders to deal with change. The conceptual framework is not a static social equilibrium, but a way of thinking about societies that face shifting constraints and opportunities in all times and places. The dynamism of social order is a dynamic of change, not a dynamic of progress. Most societies move backwards and forwards with respect to political and economic development. There is no teleology implied by the framework. Nonetheless, the framework illuminates why open access societies are better than natural states at dealing with change.

The persistent patterns across societies suggest that modern social development involves simultaneous improvements in human capital, physical capital, technology, and institutions. Because changes in these elements happen at roughly the same time, quantitative social scientists have been persistently frustrated in their attempts to identify causal forces at work in the midst of a sea of contemporaneous correlation.[13] As the recent

[13] The economics literature contains a wealth of studies attempting to sort out the independent influence of different factors as causal forces in economic development: see Acemoglu, Johnson, and Robinson (2001, 2002, 2005); Glaeser, LaPorta, Lopes-de-Silanes, and Shleifer (2004); Knack and Keefer (1995, 1997); Rodrik, Subramanian, and Trebbi (2004).

investigation of the modernization hypothesis by Acemoglu, Johnson, Robinson, and Yared (2007) demonstrates, the simultaneous relationship between democracy and high income appears not to be causal in a formal statistical sense, but reflects the influence of an omitted factor. We believe the omitted factor; is the pattern of social relationships in the open access order.

Too often, social scientists in open access societies implicitly rely on the convenient assumption that the societies they live in are the historical norm. In contrast, we argue that the default social outcome is the natural state, not open access. Until two hundred years ago, there were no open access orders; even today, 85 percent of the world's population live in limited access orders. The dominant pattern of social organization in recorded human history is the natural state. We use that appellation rather than the more literal limited access order to remind us that, unlike the *state of nature* described by Hobbes in which the scale and scope of human organization are extremely small and there is no state, the natural state emerged as a durable form of larger social organization five to ten millennia ago. The natural state has lasted so long because it aligns the interests of powerful individuals to forge a dominant coalition in such a way that limits violence and makes sustained social interaction possible on a larger scale.

1.2 The Concept of Social Orders: Violence, Institutions, and Organizations

All societies face the problem of violence.[14] Regardless of whether our genetic makeup predisposes humans to be violent, the possibility that some individuals will be violent poses a central problem for any group. No society solves the problem of violence by eliminating violence; at best, it can be contained and managed. Violence manifests itself in many dimensions. Violence can be expressed in physical actions or through coercive threats of physical action. Both violent acts and coercion are elements of violence. The relationship between violent acts and coercion involves beliefs about the actions of others, and we pay considerable attention to whether threats of violence are credible and the conditions under which the use of physical violence

---

[14] We are aware that societies are not actors. *Societies* do not deal with anything; individuals do. Nonetheless – and where it will not be confusing – we will sometimes use the language of reification and metonymy in the term *society* as convenient shorthand for the more cumbersome construction: the aggregate of individuals collectively dealing with a range of individual decisions in such a way to produce common and shared beliefs about choices, consequences, and outcomes.

will result in response from other individuals or from the state. On another dimension, violence may be the action of a single individual or the action of organized groups ranging from gangs to armies. Our primary concern is with *organized violence*; the use of violence or threats of violence by groups. Because threats of violence may be used to limit the use of actual physical violence, there is no simple way to measure the level of violence in a society. A person threatened by physical attack may be as influenced by violence as a person who is actually subjected to physical force. On a few occasions, we specifically deal with the frequency with which physical violence is used. However, in most cases our concept of violence encompasses the use of both threats and actions. We are careful to specify whether dispersed control over violence leads to threats of violence playing a central role in the social order, or whether control over violence is consolidated and thus many relationships are carried out without the threat of violence. Limited and open access orders differ fundamentally with respect to these dimensions of violence and the organization of violence.

There are important elements of social scale in the control of violence. Managing violence through repeated personal contacts can sustain only the formation of small groups of people, perhaps twenty-five to fifty individuals. Individuals in a society of small groups learn to trust one another by acquiring detailed personal knowledge, this includes the proclivity of each individual to be violent; and includes the belief that through repeated interaction the ongoing relationships create an interest. In larger groups, no individual has personal knowledge of all the members of the group or society, and so personal relationships alone cannot be used to control violence.[15] Some form of social institution must arise to control violence if societies are to develop larger groups. Whereas it is possible to imagine a larger society of peaceful individuals, such a society will not persist if the only way to control violence is through personal knowledge and repeated personal interaction.

Because individuals always have the option of competing with one another for resources or status through violence, a necessary corollary to

---

[15] Estimates of the typical size grouping range as high as 150 people. Dunbar (1996), pp. 69–79, finds a strong relationship between the ratio of brain size relative to body size and the size of the animal groups. Animals living in bigger groups require larger brains to process social information. On the basis of the brain size to body size ratio and other factors, Dunbar argues that the basic human group was roughly 150 people. The modal size of hunter–gatherer groups reported in Kelly's survey (1995) is twenty-five, pp. 205–32. For our purposes, the key insight is that permanent groups larger than several hundred people did not appear until ten thousand years ago.

limiting the use of violence within a social group is placing limits on competition. All three social orders are competitive, but they limit competition in different ways.[16] Ways of dealing with violence are embedded in *institutions* and *organizations*, concepts we need to clarify. *Institutions* are the "rules of the game" (North, 1990, pp. 3–4), the patterns of interaction that govern and constrain the relationships of individuals. Institutions include formal rules, written laws, formal social conventions, informal norms of behavior, and shared beliefs about the world, as well as the means of enforcement. The most common way of thinking about institutions is that they are constraints on the behavior of individuals as individuals; for example, if the speed limit is sixty miles per hour, how fast should I drive? However, institutions also structure the way individuals form beliefs and opinions about how other people will behave: for example, if the speed limit is sixty miles per hour, how fast will other drivers drive? Framed in this way, we ask what types of institutions can survive given the interaction of the institutional constraints, people's beliefs, and their behavior (Greif, 2006; Weingast, 2002)? This complex set of questions suggests why institutions span formal laws, informal norms of behavior, and the shared beliefs that individuals hold about the world.

The same institution produces different results depending on the context. Consider the institution of elections. Elections produce different results in a society with open political competition than in a society with limited political competition. The institution of elections does not inherently produce democracy. Elections require institutions and organizations along with beliefs and norms before they produce an open access order with democratic competition for political power.[17]

In contrast to institutions, *organizations* consist of specific groups of individuals pursuing a mix of common and individual goals through partially coordinated behavior. Organizations coordinate their members' actions, so an organization's actions are more than the sum of the actions of the individuals. Because they pursue a common purpose in an organization

---

[16] The use of repeated personal interaction in small groups appears to result in significant regulation of competition. Hunter–gatherer groups are aggressively egalitarian. The leaders and the best hunters, often not the same individuals, do not enjoy a larger share of consumption goods because of their prowess. Competition over consumption is suppressed to coordinate the incentives of the group. Violence plays an inevitable role in social discipline, including disciplining an over weaning leader. See Boehm (1999).

[17] This view contrasts with the most common approach in the literature on democracy, which counts a country as democratic if it has elections and has had at least one partisan turnover. See Przeworski et al. (2000). Our view corresponds more closely to that of Dahl (1971).

and because organizations are typically composed of individuals who deal with each other repeatedly, members of most organizations develop shared beliefs about the behavior of other members and about the norms or rules of their organization. As a result, most organizations have their own internal institutional structure: the rules, norms, and shared beliefs that influence the way people behave within the organization (Greif, 2006).

We differentiate two types of organizations. An *adherent organization* is characterized by self-enforcing, incentive-compatible agreements among its members. These organizations do not rely on third parties to enforce internal agreements. Cooperation by an adherent organization's members must be, at every point in time, incentive-compatible for all members. *Contractual organizations*, in contrast, utilize both third-party enforcement of contracts and incentive-compatible agreements among members (as Williamson, 1985, argues for the firm). In contrast to members of adherent organizations, third-party enforcement of contracts allows members in contractual organizations to precommit to a subset of arrangements among themselves that may not otherwise be incentive-compatible at every point of time. Our framework and history revolve around the development of institutional forms that can support complicated and sophisticated contractual organizations, both inside and outside of the state.[18]

Modern open access societies often limit violence through institutions. Institutions frame rules that deter violence directly by changing the payoffs to violent behavior, most obviously by stipulating punishments for the use of violence. People are more likely to obey rules, even at considerable cost to themselves, if they believe that other people will also obey the rules.[19] This is particularly true with rules about the use of violence. An individual has an incentive to shoot first and talk later when he fears that the others will fail to follow the rules and refrain from using violence. In order for a formal rule – an institution – to constrain violence, particularly violence among individuals with no personal knowledge of one another, some organization must exist within which a set of officials enforce the rules in an impersonal manner. In other words, formal institutions control violence only in the presence of an organization capable of enforcing the rules impersonally.

---

[18] For an overview of the economic theory of organizations see Milgrom and Roberts (1992) and for the sociological theory of organizations see Scott (2001).

[19] As Levi emphasizes in her studies of how contingent consent undergirds social participation, perceptions and beliefs in fairness, equality, or impersonality must be part of the equation: *everyone* has to be treated the same and this equality must apply to both the costs and benefits of social participation. "Third-party enforcement ensures that *others* are complying; an individual can then choose to comply with more certainty that she is not a sucker" (Levi, 1997, p. 213).

The larger the size of the society, the larger the set of enforcers who must somehow be organized. Theoretically, arguments can take one of two paths at this point: the state can be treated as a single actor or as an organization of organizations. Most social scientists abstract from the organization of the enforcers, treating them as a single entity, and focus on the relationship between the enforcement entity and the rest of society. As Weber's famous maxim goes (1947, p. 156), the state is that organization with a monopoly on the legitimate use of violence. Collapsing the identity of the state into a single actor makes it easier to explain how the state deals with the larger society by analyzing the constraints and incentives facing the state defined as the "ruler."[20]

Economists and social scientists concerned with understanding how the state develops and interacts with the larger society have modeled the state as a revenue-maximizing monarch, a stationary bandit, or a single-actor "representative agent."[21] By overlooking the reality that all states are organizations, this approach misses how the internal dynamics of relationships among elites within the dominant coalition affect how states interact with the larger society. Systematic rent-creation through limited access in a natural state is not simply a method of lining the pockets of the dominant coalition; it is the essential means of controlling violence. Rent-creation, limits on competition, and access to organizations are central to the nature of the state, its institutions, and the society's performance. Limiting the ability to form contractual organizations only to members of the coalition ties the interests of powerful elites directly to the survival of the coalition, thus ensuring their continued cooperation within the coalition.

The difficulty with a single actor approach to the state is that it assumes away the fundamental problem of how the state achieves a monopoly on violence. As we shall see, this process is central to how individuals and groups behave within a society and how a coalition emerges to structure the state and society.

We take the other path. Rather than abstracting from the problem of bringing together powerful individuals to manage violence through some

---

[20] Prominent examples include North (1981), Olson (1982, 1993), Barzel (2001), Levi (1988), Wintrobe (1998), Bueno de Mesquita et al. (2003). For specific applications of single-actor models of the state to the problem of violence see Bates, Greif, and Singh (2002). Tilly (1992, p. 34) has a self-conscious discussion of the problem of reification and metonymy when considering the state; nonetheless he does not explore the implications of collapsing the state into a single actor for his understanding of the rise of national states.

[21] Brennan and Buchanan's (1980) state as leviathan, North's (1981, Chapter 3) neoclassical theory of the state, and Olson's (1993) roving and stationary bandits, are three well-known examples.

organized effort, we begin with the problem of structuring the internal relationships among the individuals who make up the organization of (potential) enforcers. The first problem in limiting violence is to answer the question: How do powerful individuals credibly commit to stop fighting? Our answer forms the basis for this book and, we believe, a new conceptual framework for the social sciences. Controlling violence depends on the structure and maintenance of relationships among powerful individuals.

1.3 The Logic of the Natural State

The natural state reduces the problem of endemic violence through the formation of a dominant coalition whose members possess special privileges. The logic of the natural state follows from how it solves the problem of violence. Elites – members of the dominant coalition – agree to respect each other's privileges, including property rights and access to resources and activities. By limiting access to these privileges to members of the dominant coalition, elites create credible incentives to cooperate rather than fight among themselves. Because elites know that violence will reduce their own rents, they have incentives not to fight. Furthermore, each elite understands that other elites face similar incentives. In this way, the political system of a natural state manipulates the economic system to produce rents that then secure political order.

The dominant coalition contains members who specialize in a range of military, political, religious, political, and economic activities. It is, however, easier to understand how a dominant coalition functions if we begin with military specialists and then return to the full coalition.[22] Imagine a world where violence is endemic and the population is made up of many small groups with no well-organized governments or military forces. Some individuals specialize in violence, but all individuals must stand ready to defend their rights by force of arms. The violence specialists may provide protection to a small group of clients, but the biggest threat facing the specialists is one another. If they try to agree to disarm, the first specialist to put down his or her arms risks being killed by the other. Thus, it is an equilibrium outcome for both specialists to remain armed and continue fighting.

In order for one specialist to stop fighting, he or she must perceive that it is in the other's interest not to fight, an expectation that both specialists

---

[22] The following discussion is not intended to describe how natural states arose historically; we do not possess sufficient historical information to trace the specific development of the first natural states.

must share about each other. Only if the cost of fighting or the benefit from not fighting is tangible and clear to both specialists will they believe that not fighting is a credible outcome. The stylized solution involves the two specialists agreeing to divide their world into two parts, one controlled by each specialist, and then to recognize each other's rights to control the land, labor, resources, and trading within their sphere. The specialists do not disarm, but if their land, labor, and resources are more productive in the absence of violence then this arrangement creates an additional cost to fighting; herein lies the solution to the credible commitment to nonviolence. If each violence specialist captures a larger economic return (a rent) from the land, labor, and resources he or she controls when there is peace and if those rents are large enough, then it is possible for both specialists to credibly believe that the other specialist is better off by refraining from fighting. A *rent* is a return to an economic asset that exceeds the return the asset can receive in its best alternative use.[23] To the violence specialists, the rents from peace are the difference in the returns their assets earn when they do not fight compared to the returns they earn when they do fight. Although one specialist may be tempted to defect today, his or her repeated interaction makes it in his or her interest not to fight over the long term.

To be credible, the commitment requires that the violence specialists be able to mobilize and gather their rents, which are produced by the remainder of the population. Mobilizing rents, in turn, requires specialists in other activities. It is here that we move away from the simple ideas about violence and back toward a more reasonable depiction of the logic of the natural state. In the earliest societies of recorded human history, priests and politicians provided the redistributive network capable of mobilizing output and redistributing it between elites and non-elites.[24] In a natural state, each of the nonmilitary elites either controls or enjoys privileged access to a vital function like religion, production, community allocation of

---

[23] If a person is willing to work at a particular job for $10 an hour, but not for $9.99 an hour, and is paid $15 an hour, she receives a rent of $5 an hour. Rents depend not only on observable returns, such as the $15 an hour, but also on the value of the best alternative foregone. In this case, the equivalent of the $9.99 the person could have gotten by working another job or consuming leisure. Because the value of the best alternative is never observed, measuring rents requires particular circumstances in which choices are made. What makes rents different from observable returns is that they accrue only to persons doing the specific activity. So the rents from peace accrue to the violence specialists only if they are not violent.

[24] We consider the formation of the earliest state, all of which were theocracies, in Chapter 2; also see Steckel and Wallis (2006).

resources, justice, trade, or education.[25] Because the positions, privileges, and rents of the individual elites in the dominant coalition depend on the limited entry enforced by the continued existence of the regime, all elites have incentives to support and help maintain the coalition. Failing to do so risks violence, disorder, and the loss of rents.

Elite organizations generate and distribute rents to the coalition. Among the most valuable sources of elite rents is the privilege of forming organizations that the state will support. By devising ways to support contractual organizations and then extending the privilege of forming those organizations to their members, the dominant coalition creates a way to generate and distribute rents within the coalition as well as a credible way to discipline elites because elite organizations depend on the third-party support of the coalition. The ability of elites to organize cooperative behavior under the aegis of the state enhances the elite return from society's productive resources – land, labor, capital, and organizations.[26]

The incentives embedded in these organizations produce a *double balance*: a correspondence between the distribution and organization of violence potential and political power on the one hand, and the distribution and organization of economic power on the other hand. The idea of the double balance suggests not only that all of the social systems in a society must have an internal balance of interests but also that the political, economic, cultural, social, and military systems must contain compatible systems of incentives across the systems if a society is to remain stable.

Because the dominant coalition in any natural state is an adherent organization, peace is not inevitable: peace depends on the balance of interests created by the rent-creation process. Violence and civil war are always a possibility. Military specialists do not disarm; indeed, they must maintain their military strength both to balance one another's power and to overawe their respective clients. Dispersed military power is part of the logic of the natural state. In this way, the threat of violence becomes part of the arrangement that controls the actual use of violence.

---

[25] The various elite functions are often integrated, and critical individuals in the coalition may play more than one role, as did the kings in the ancient Chinese states who were simultaneously the military leader, the political leader, and the chief shaman (e.g., Chang, 1983, pp. 35, 45).

[26] Most elite organizations are not purely political or military, but integrate economic, religious, judicial, and other functions. A good example is the feudal manor, which is an organization that enables the coordination of production, justice, landownership and use, education, and religion.

Natural states are stable, but not static, and no dominant coalition is permanent. Societies face unexpected shocks and changes that can destabilize the internal relationships within the dominant coalition. Internally, policies and decisions made by leaders result in unintended consequences that change the circumstances facing the coalition. Leaders and coalition members are never completely sure of the full implications of their actions, and periodically they make serious mistakes. Externally, unpredictable changes in relative prices, climate disasters, bumper crops, technological change, and newly hostile neighbors are part of the world. All societies are subject to random and unexpected shocks. In natural states, the changes may affect the distribution of violence potential and require a renegotiation of the distribution of privileges and rents within the dominant coalition as well as changes in the membership of the coalition as new powerful interests arise and old interests weaken. If particular violence specialists grow stronger relative to the others, for example, they are likely to demand a larger share of privileges and rents. If these negotiations fail – when the groups with violence potential misjudge one another's capabilities – violence is likely, including civil wars (e.g., Biafra against the rest of Nigeria, Bangladesh against the rest of Pakistan), ethnic violence (e.g., the former Yugoslavia, Rwanda), or coups to prevent particular policies of democratically elected governments (e.g., those in Chile 1973 and Spain 1936).

Despite their fundamental similarities, natural states differ in many ways. Their history is rich and variegated and, as we discuss in Chapter 2, natural states appear in many different manifestations. We develop a simple taxonomy of natural states that reflects the ability of different types of natural states to support organizations. *Fragile* natural states are unable to support any organization but the state itself. *Basic* natural states can support organizations, but only within the framework of the state. *Mature* natural states are able to support a wide range of elite organizations outside the immediate control of the state. The ability to support organizations – to structure human interaction – is an important determinate of the economic and political development within the natural state.

1.4 The Logic of the Open Access Order

Open access orders control violence through a different logic than the natural state. These societies create powerful, consolidated military and police organizations subservient to the political system. All open access societies satisfy the Weberian assumption: their states possess a monopoly on the legitimate use of violence. Consolidation of violence carries the danger of the state using violence for its own ends. As a result, the logic of controlling violence in the open access order involves three elements: 1) consolidated organization of military and police forces is subject to the control of the political system; 2) the political system must be constrained by a set of institutions and incentives that limit the illegitimate use of violence; and 3) for a political faction or party to remain in power, it must enjoy the support of economic and social interests, broadly defined. Open access in the economic system prevents the political system from manipulating economic interests and ensures that if a political group abuses its control of the military it loses office. These three elements of a state monopoly on violence must develop within an institutional framework that makes commitments to limit the use of violence and maintain open political and economic entry credible. Control of violence in the larger society occurs through deterrence – the threat of punishment by the state – as well as by depriving nonstate organizations that use violence access to enforcement of organizational supports.

Control of the political system is open to entry by any group and contested through prescribed, and typically formal, constitutional means. All citizens have the right to form organizations, and they use the services of the state to structure the internal and external relationships of their organizations to individuals and other organizations. The ability to form organizations at will without the consent of the state ensures nonviolent competition in the polity, economy, and indeed in every area of society with open access.[27] The ability of political actors to use organized military or police power to coerce individuals is constrained by the ability of economic and other actors to compete for political control. When embedded in a constitutional setting with institutions that provide credible incentives that protect various rights, open access and democratic competition prevent illegitimate uses of violence.

---

[27] As we discuss in detail throughout the book, in an open access society the state supports organizations by enforcing both the internal and external arrangements of approved organizational forms, such as corporations. In this sense, approval of the state is required for all legitimate organizations. Open entry occurs when state approval is given to any group that meets some minimum requirements. In Britain, for example, open entry into the corporate organizational form occurred in 1844 through a process of "registration" under which a group that wanted to form a corporation filed the appropriate forms at an administrative office of the government. Open entry requires the explicit recognition of the organization by the state, *and* the state extends recognition to all who want to form an organization. We discuss these details in Chapter 5.

An open access order exists only if a large number of individuals have the right to form organizations that can engage in a wide variety of economic, political, and social activities. Moreover, the right to form an organization has to be defined impersonally. *Impersonality* means treating everyone the same. Equality is impossible without impersonality.

An important argument in our conceptual framework is that impersonality grows out of the structure of organizations and the ability of society to support impersonal organizational forms (i.e., organizations with their own identity independent of the individual identity of the organization's members). In the legal terms that came to characterize impersonal organizations in the Western tradition, these are *perpetually lived organizations*: organizations whose existence is independent of the lives of their members.[28] Perpetually lived organizations must have an impersonal identity. The Romans had organizations that were legal persons capable of bearing rights and duties. Only over the last five centuries did the identity of the organization truly become independent of the identity of its members.

Competition in an open access order, therefore, differs from competition in natural states for another critical reason beyond limitations on competition through violence. Open access societies are capable of sustaining impersonal relationships on a large scale through their ability to support impersonal, perpetually lived organizations, both inside the state and in the wider society. Impersonality fundamentally changes the nature of competition. Impersonal markets and impersonal exchange are not just a theoretical ideal in economics; they are a feature of open access societies.

Individuals and organizations pursue rents as vigorously in an open access society as they do in a natural state, but impersonal economic and political competition result in the rapid erosion of rents. Joseph Schumpeter (1942) described this process of innovation and change in the economy as "creative destruction." Innovation itself is a source of rents. An important form of economic competition occurs through the development of new products and services rather than lower prices or higher quality. Organizations form to exploit new opportunities and pursue the rents associated with innovation. Open entry and access to sophisticated economic organizations are prerequisites for creative destruction and a dynamic economy.

---

[28] A perpetually lived organization is not an infinitely lived organization; it is an organization whose "life" is independent of the lives of its members, so a modern corporation is a perpetually lived organization. Because a modern partnership must be reorganized on the death of a partner, it is not perpetually lived.

Schumpeter's approach has an important implication for political behavior. If the constellation of economic interests regularly changes because of innovation and entry, politicians face a fundamentally different world than those in a natural state: open access orders cannot manipulate interests in the same way as natural states do. Too much behavior and formation of interests take place beyond the state's control. Politicians in both natural states and open access orders want to create rents. Rent-creation at once rewards their supporters and binds their constituents to support them. Because, however, open access orders enable any citizen to form an organization for a wide variety of purposes, rents created by either the political process or economic innovation attract competitors in the form of new organizations. In Schumpeterian terms, political entrepreneurs put together new organizations to compete for the rents and, in so doing, reduce existing rents and struggle to create new ones. As a result, creative destruction reigns in open access politics just as it does in open access economies. Much of the creation of new interests is beyond the control of the state. The creation of new interests and the generation of new sources of rents occur continuously in open access orders.[29]

Many scholars emphasize the dangers of rent-seeking politics in open access societies (e.g., Bhagwati, 1982; Buchanan, Tollison, and Tullock, 1980; Krueger, 1990; Olson, 1965, 1982). These studies fail to appreciate that, although all governments attempt to create rents, not all governments do so to the same extent because not all operate within the same social order. Although open access does not eliminate rent-creation, it significantly constrains the kind of rent-creation that creates negative effects for society. Rent-creation that benefits only a narrow interest is not impossible; it is simply much less likely to occur in an open access society than in a natural state. Conversely, rent-creation that benefits large and encompassing groups – that is, rent-creation that is productivity enhancing rather than limiting – is much more likely to occur in an open access society than in a natural state.

Again, the basic insight reveals the existence of a double balance: open access and entry to organizations in the economy support open access in politics, and open access and entry in politics support open access in the economy. Open access in the economy generates a large and varied

---

[29] The process of rent-creation and rent-destruction is more complicated than the simple examples used here suggest; see Khan (2004, 2005) and Khan and Jomo (2000) for a sophisticated discussion of rent-creation. Baumol (2002) emphasizes the link between thriving markets and innovation.

set of organizations that are the primary agents in the process of creative destruction. This forms the basis for the civil society, with many groups capable of becoming politically active when their interests are threatened. Creative economic destruction produces a constantly shifting distribution of economic interests, making it difficult for political officials to solidify their advantage through rent-creation. Similarly, open access in politics results in creative political destruction through party competition. The opposition party has strong incentives to monitor the incumbent and to publicize attempts to subvert the constitution, open access in particular. While the opposition in natural state electoral systems may have similar incentives, the lack of open access and limits on competition weaken the ability of the opposition to counter an incumbent's efforts in comparison to those in open access orders. Put simply, party competition works far better in the presence of open access than in its absence.

1.5 The Logic of the Transition from Natural States to Open Access Orders

The big question then is how natural states make the transition to open access societies. Two obstacles stand in the way of understanding the transition. First, the transition begins in the natural state and must therefore be consistent with natural state logic. However, if that is true how does the transition get started? An explanation of the transition must show how conditions arise within a natural state that are consistent with the logic of the natural state and simultaneously put elites in a position where it is in their interest to move toward *impersonal* intra-elite arrangements.

The second obstacle is explaining how intra-elite impersonal arrangements translate in open access orders into a larger share of society. One way of asking the question is, why would elites ever choose to give up their position in society and allow non-elites into full participation? Framing the question in this form is problematic: it carries the implications that elites are giving something up, and it is not clear that elites ever do that.[30] We frame the question about the transition in a different way. Why do elites transform their unique and personal privileges into impersonal rights shared equally among elites? And how do elites secure their rights against each other? Creating credible protection for elite rights holds the promise of expanding

---

[30] This is the approach taken by Acemoglu and Robinson (2006), which stresses how elites, threatened by revolution or civil unrest, use institutions such as democracy to make credible commitments to non-elites.

output: for example, securing elite rights to form organizations directly produces more developed economies and polities. When elites create greater open access to political and economic organizations for themselves, they sometimes have incentives to expand access along several different margins into the non-elite population.

The transition, then, has two stages. First, a natural state must develop institutional arrangements that enable elites to create the possibility of impersonal intra-elite relationships. Second, the transition proper begins when the dominant coalition finds it in the interest of elites to expand impersonal exchange within the elite and institutionalize open elite access to organizations, effectively creating open access for elites. We call the conditions that may evolve in a natural state that enable impersonal relationships among elites the *doorstep conditions*. The doorstep conditions represent institutional and organizational support for increased impersonal exchange, as well as institutions consistent with the logic of the natural state that can be used in the transition to support open access orders.

The three doorstep conditions are:

Doorstep Condition 1. Rule of law for elites.
Doorstep Condition 2. Perpetually lived forms of public and private elite
    organizations, including the state itself.
Doorstep Condition 3. Consolidated political control of the military.

In combination, the doorstep conditions create an environment in which impersonal relations within the elite are possible. Rule of law for elites extends the range of contracts and relationships among elites and allows mutual dependency to exist that could not survive without some form of legal protection. Perpetually lived organizations create more powerful elite organizations that can undertake a wider range of economic and political activities than nonperpetually lived ones. Perpetually lived organizations also contain an irreducible element of impersonal identity. Consolidated control of the military removes the need for elites to maintain alliances among elite groups tied to military factions, which are activated in situations where violence breaks out. Impersonal elite organizations can utilize impersonal exchange by utilizing the identity of the perpetually lived organization rather than the personal identity of the organization's members. Once elite relationships become impersonal relationships, new possibilities begin to open up. If a society on the doorstep creates and sustains new incentives for elites to successively open access within the elite, then a transition proper ensues. Nothing inevitably impels societies on the doorstep to make the transition.

In the transition proper, elites transform their personal privileges into impersonal rights. All elites are given the right to form organizations, whether those organizations are political, economic, or social. At that point, the logic holding the dominant coalition together has changed from the natural state logic of rent-creation through privileges to the open access logic of rent-erosion through entry. Elite factions find it profitable to allow wider access, but they also want to ensure that their rights are protected.

Historic transitions occurred within relatively brief periods, typically about fifty years. Britain, France, and the United States appear to have been on the doorstep in the late eighteenth century and made the transition to open access between 1800 and 1850, or in the case of France, by 1880. Although they have not completed the transition, both South Korea and Taiwan's experience seems to parallel that of Europe, taking approximately fifty years. Some of the countries on the periphery of Europe have made a quicker transition, notably Spain after the death of longtime dictator Francisco Franco in 1975. All of these countries developed new economic and political institutions that secured open access for economic organizations through a general incorporation procedure; secured open access for political organizations through the development of articulated and competitive party organizations and broadening of suffrage; and secured open access to legal enforcement of rights through changes in their legal systems. These changes occurred within relatively narrow windows of historical time. Of course, the events leading up to these changes had taken centuries as the countries developed institutions, beliefs, and organizations that could sustain a transition.

1.6 A Note on Beliefs

All individuals form beliefs about the way the world works. Beliefs result directly from the nature of human consciousness in an uncertain world.[31] People know they are alive, and they know that what they do now can affect what happens next, even if they do not know exactly what will happen next. As a result, people are consciously intentional. We are concerned with the subset of beliefs that we call *causal beliefs*, which concern the causal connections between actions and outcomes in the world around us.

Social scientists have only a limited understanding of what goes on inside of people – what motivates, pleases, angers, and scares them. We take these

---

[31] Hayek (1952) was one of the first social scientists to explore the implications of belief formation for human behavior.

individual and idiosyncratic features of individual *preferences* as given. Interests arise from the interaction of preferences, alternatives, and causal beliefs. When economists claim that individuals are rational and act in what they perceive to be their self-interest, hackles rise in the rest of the social sciences. What is in the perceived best interest of individuals is a complicated amalgam of their preferences over different outcomes, the alternatives that they face, and their beliefs about how their actions will affect the world around them. People are intentional; they are trying to accomplish the best outcomes with their limited resources and choices, but how they behave depends critically on how they believe the world around them actually works. Because the world is too complicated for human understanding to master fully, no belief system can be a completely accurate depiction of the world around us.

We do not answer the deeper question of where causal beliefs come from.[32] The two main channels of belief formation are individual experience and education. Human beings are genetically programmed to learn in both ways. Human cultures, in part, are common information passed on through education, whether formal in the sense of classrooms or informal in the sense of parents and others teaching social norms to children. Neither way of forming beliefs is completely reliable, in part, because the beliefs we draw from experience are inaccurate models of the world around us.

Many beliefs about how other people will behave can be verified observationally, but they are not necessarily universally true: not all people behave in the same way.[33] From an individual's perspective, causal beliefs about those people with whom we interact repeatedly, beginning with the family, are more certain than beliefs about those with whom we have less interaction. At many points, beliefs about how people behave in the larger groups and aggregates shade into areas governed by knowledge from education, rather than experience, and from faith. Most causal beliefs about human behavior can, at least in principle, be confirmed or disconfirmed by experience in the set of social interactions, organizations, and networks in which individuals are embedded. The confidence that our causal beliefs are accurate – that they actually explain causal patterns in human behavior and can thus serve as a guide to intentional behavior – is a function of how close the beliefs fit our

---

[32] See North (2005) for an in-depth consideration of the problem of human cognition, belief formation, and integrating beliefs into economic models of social behavior.

[33] At another level, we also know that our beliefs about how other drivers behave are not universally true. In Britain they drive on the left side of the road. China has traffic laws completely incomprehensible to an American driver.

actual experience. Because experience is limited, all beliefs are necessarily incomplete.

Greif (2006) develops a powerful way of thinking about how beliefs form in specific institutional settings. He defines an institution as a set of *institutional elements*: rules, norms, beliefs, and organizations. He makes wonderful use of the idea of institutional elements in his concept of an equilibrium, showing how "institutions generate behavior." Greif limits admissible beliefs about how the world works to those that are consistent with the actual behavior induced by the institution. The confirmation of beliefs closes Greif's equilibrium system. Behavior – actions taken by individuals or organizations – generated by the incentives created by institutions must lead to beliefs that are consistent with the behavior. For Greif, institutions, behavior, and beliefs form the three legs of a self-enforcing equilibrium. Beliefs flow from actions, and because beliefs are, in part, about the consequences of actions, they are at the service of intentionality.

We differ from Greif in two respects. The first is a matter of language. Where Greif folds organizations into institutional elements and, for most of his book, discusses institutions without explicitly identifying organizations, we distinguish organizations and institutions and focus as much on one as the other. The second difference is substantive: we treat beliefs in a larger and more general, but less rigorous, way as resulting from larger cultural, educational, and religious organizations and not in the limited sense of beliefs immediately supported by modeling one particular subset of interactions in the society.

1.7 The Plan

The book follows the framework laid out in this chapter. Chapters 2 and 3 delve into the logic of the natural state and consider detailed examples of how institutions and organizations develop in the natural state. Chapter 4 focuses on the logic of open access orders. Chapters 5 and 6 consider the two parts of the transition. Chapter 7 concludes the conceptual framework, including a series of implications for the future of social science.

TWO

The Natural State

2.1 Introduction

A natural state manages the problem of violence by forming a dominant coalition that limits access to valuable resources – land, labor, and capital – or access to and control of valuable activities – such as trade, worship, and education – to elite groups. The creation of rents through limiting access provides the glue that holds the coalition together, enabling elite groups to make credible commitments to one another to support the regime, perform their functions, and refrain from violence. Only elite groups are able to use the third-party enforcement of the coalition to structure contractual organizations. Limiting access to organizational forms is the key to the natural state because limiting access not only creates rents through exclusive privileges but it also directly enhances the value of the privileges by making elites more productive through their organizations.

Every state must deal with the problem of violence, and if we begin thinking about the state by positing a single actor with a monopoly on violence, we assume away the fundamental problem. All states are organizations, involving multiple individuals who cooperate to pursue a common goal even as they retain their individual interests. In natural states, powerful elites are directly connected to the organizations they head. The resources elite organizations bring to the dominant coalition strengthen relationships within the coalition. Increasing specialization and division of labor, including specialization in violence, come with increasing size of societies. Because the application of violence requires organization, violence specialists typically head or are embedded in organizations.[1] The organization of the dominant

---

[1] It may be more accurate to say that members of the dominant coalition are leaders of organizations made up of many specialists, including specialists in violence, whether the leaders themselves actually are violent.

coalition then is a matter of organizing organizations, and the state is an organization of organizations.

Throughout recorded history, the cessation of violence (peace) is not achieved when violence specialists put down their arms, but rather peace occurs when the violent devise arrangements (explicit or implicit) that reduce the level of violence. Even when one actor within the dominant coalition is designated king or is in fact more powerful than the others, that actor is never more powerful as an individual than the coalition of his peers. The king or ruler only becomes powerful if he or she heads a powerful coalition. Remaining king depends on maintaining a dominant coalition that can best all rivals. Rulers are just one of many relevant actors in the dominant coalition. Focusing on the dynamic relationships of the players in the dominant coalition allows us to explicate and understand the logic of the social order and the conditions underlying all social organizations in a natural state.

The natural state is *natural* because, for most of the last ten thousand years, it has been virtually the only form of society larger than a few hundred people that has been capable of securing physical order and managing violence. Natural states encompass a wide variety of societies, however, and we have no wish to imply that they are all the same. Mesopotamia in the third millennium B.C.E., Britain under the Tudors, and modern Russia under Putin were all natural states, but very different societies. The limited access order is not a specific set of political, economic, or religious institutions; it is a fundamental way of organizing society.

We begin by laying out the features that all natural states share and then the dimensions in which natural states differ. The latter task produces a typology useful for thinking about the variety of natural states through time and also the conditions under which a natural state is capable of moving into a transition to an open access order. Just as we distinguish the three social orders by how they structure and support organizations, we also distinguish types of natural states by how they structure and support organizations, including the state itself. Then we turn to a series of historical examples that illustrate how different natural states are structured and develop. We also ask how the first societies managed to create larger, sustainable social units. Anthropologists have long debated the origin of "pristine states" in history; we do as well. We next study the problem of creating a more complicated natural state. As extended illustrations, we use the rise of the Aztec Empire in fifteenth-century Mesoamerica and the restoration of order under the Carolingians in eighth- and ninth-century Europe. Then we look at the development of ideas about the corporate structure of the state and the church in medieval Europe, as well as one example from seventeenth-century France. The discussion initiates our inquiry into the nature of perpetually lived organizations, an organizational innovation critical for our understanding of open access orders and the transition.

2.2 Commonalities: Characteristics of Limited Access Orders

All natural states share common characteristics. We are ultimately interested in understanding how societies develop the capacity to sustain impersonal rights. Open access orders require that a significant part of the population be treated equally, which necessarily involves treating everyone impersonally without regard to their identity as individuals. To understand how impersonal social relationships evolve we must first understand how larger societies develop that can sustain personal relationships and how personal relationships tie elites to the dominant coalition. These questions lead us into considerations of personality, social networks, and the manipulation of interests. We follow with a few technical notes about the size of a natural state's coalition and the extent of trade, specialization, and division of labor.

2.2.1 Persons, Personality, Impersonality, Identity, Patronage, and Interest

In foraging societies, face-to-face interaction among individuals in small groups created personal knowledge, trust (or distrust), and coordination. The limited access order builds on personal relationships and repeated interaction: a hierarchy of personal relationships among powerful individuals at the top of the social order. However, in larger societies, individual relationships cannot be based solely on personal knowledge and trust; they must be reinforced by the web of interests created by the social order. To create stable relationships, individuals must know with whom they are dealing, even if they do not know each other personally.

Societies do not jump directly from personal to impersonal relationships; rather, it is a long process of development that begins in a natural state. On one end of the spectrum, personal relationships are characterized by repeated and idiosyncratic interactions, whereas on the other end of the spectrum impersonal relations are characterized by intermittent and standardized interactions. In other words, all personal relationships are, in some way, unique while large classes of impersonal relationships are the same. In between the two extremes are relationships where the identity of the individuals is uniquely defined, but regularities in interactions between individuals arise.

What then is a person? Every person has two parts. Individual attributes make up one part of every person, including physical size, stature, and appearance, as well as the less tangible characteristics of intelligence, attitude, industry, and ability. The socially ascribed attributes of position, power, privileges, rights, and duties make up the other part of every person. Who we are combines these internal and external parts of our personality. Society recognizes both aspects of personality. When someone is named chief, elected class president, or appointed as department chair, the nature of his or her interpersonal relationships changes: his or her individual identity remains unchanged but his or her social identity changes.

By our nature, each individual's internal characteristics are unique. However, an individual's external social characteristics may be unique or those characteristics may be shared with a large group of other individuals. In modern open access societies, for example, the external characteristics of citizens are defined in impersonal terms as a set of social characteristics that apply to everyone who meets certain objective criteria.

Formally, we define a person as composing two interrelated parts: an internal individual persona and an external social persona. The development of impersonal relationships has to do with social persona. As long as social personas are unique across individuals, impersonal relationships are impossible. Impersonality arises as social personas become standardized.

Personality is more complicated than these two aspects. As far back as Roman times, for example, Western law recognized a legal person as any entity capable of bearing rights and duties. What makes an entity a legal person depends on who or what the law decides can bear rights and duties. Slaves and children were not legal persons according to Roman law. A legal person need not be a human being. An incorporeal entity, such as a town or a church, is capable of bearing rights and duties and thus is a legal person. Organizations, therefore, can be legal persons under the right conditions.[2] The personality of an organization is always a social persona, defined and supported by the larger society.

In natural states, most relationships within the dominant coalition are personal rather than impersonal. Status and hierarchy tend to be defined in terms of a social persona that is unique to individuals, even if those personas share similarities within broader classes. The notion of nobility in Western

---

[2] As Coleman argues in *Power and the Structure of Society* (1974, pp. 12–13), "In law there are, in fact, two major kinds of persons: physical persons of the sort that you and I know, indeed are what the law calls 'natural persons,' and 'juristic persons.' The difference between a legal person and a natural person is a staple of legal history."

Europe is one example. A class of nobles existed. The nobility, however, was further differentiated into dukes, earls, and other grades, and within the grades most nobles possessed unique social identities based in part on the unique privileges each held.

Take a specific but abstract example. The Duke of X possesses certain privileges, rights, and duties that fall on whichever individual corporeal being holds the title, Duke of X. The social persona of the duke includes the formal rights the duke can exercise by virtue of his unique ducal powers and properties. As an individual, the Duke of X possesses his unique features as a human being – his stature, appearance, social grace, ambition, intelligence, focus, and ability to work. His identity as a person encompasses both senses: the duke as a unique individual and the duke as the holder of an office.

The social persona of powerful individuals intertwines inextricably with the organizations that they head or represent. Powerful elites are identified as both individuals and with their organizations. This close relationship between the personal identity of an organization's leadership and the power of the organization forges the interests that hold natural states together. Powerful members of natural states possess the privilege of forming organizations that the larger society supports and recognizes. How sophisticated and well defined those privileges and obligations are depends on the sophistication of the larger society. Defining the relationship between a person's individual persona and social persona presents one of the most complicated problems a social order has to solve. The alleged quip of Louis XIV, "L'état, c'est moi," captures the essence of the problem. Are the official powers of the king vested in the king as an individual or in the king's social persona, in his dignity, in the office he holds?

In a phrase we will hear again, the question can be framed by asking whether the king is above, below, or identical with the law. Is the ability to change the law the prerogative of the king as an individual person, or is the king bound by the constraints of his social persona? The distinction between the king, duke, pope, or bishop as an individual and the king, duke, pope, or bishop as a social persona became so important in medieval Europe that a formal way of thinking about the individual and corporate aspects of personality developed. Kantorowicz captured this distinction between the individual and social persona in his book, *The King's Two Bodies*.[3] Whereas the question of a king being above or below the law applies only to the highest levels of society, the question of whether a leader is above or below the organization he heads applies throughout the entire

---

[3] The relationship between individual identity and office is treated at some length in Kantorowicz (1997[1957]), Coleman (1974, 1990), and Maitland (2003).

society. If the privilege of using the organization lies with the identity of the individual leader rather than the organization itself, then the society is based on personal relationships. As societies gradually begin to develop ways of privileging organizations as legal persons (entities), irrespective of the personal identity of the leaders, they become capable of sustaining more complicated organizational structures.

As more powerful and sophisticated human organizations, including the state, develop, so does the associated problem of wielding an organization's power. Is the church's power at the individual whim of the pope? Does the mayor represent the city? If the mayor errs, must the city pay? These questions are complicated ones, but their answers go straight to our central proposition about social orders: how a social order structures organizations determines the pattern of social interaction within a society. The fact that all organizations must be led by individuals ties the notion of personality and the relationship between individual and social persona directly into the concept of a social order.

The concepts of personality and identity help clarify the position of non-elites in limited access orders and illustrate how the organization of a natural state is reflected throughout the entire social order. The stark way we presented the conceptual framework in the opening chapter may seem to imply that non-elites have no way to obtain or enforce property or security, but some protections for non-elites, their persons and their property, exist in most natural states. Non-elites are not masses of undifferentiated individuals who are treated impersonally. Protection is extended through patronage or clientage networks. The heads of patron–client networks are powerful elites who dispense patronage to clients, provide protection for some aspects of their clients' property and persons, and negotiate arrangements among elite networks that limit violence if the negotiations are successful. The organization of the network leaders is the dominant coalition of the society. The social identity of non-elites is closely tied to the identity of the patronage network in which they are located: a non-elite is the king's man or the duke's man, a Tutsi or Hutu, or any of the millions of group identities that shape human societies.

Natural states include many organizational forms other than patron–client networks, but it may help to think for a moment of natural states as just composed of patron–client types of organizations.[4] In natural states, relationships are personal. Nevertheless, because natural states include societies

---

[4] Kinship groups, ethnic groups, bureaucracies and other forms of social networks may be organized along patron–client lines, but they need not be. We use patron–client networks as a stand-in for many types of social networks.

with millions of people, personal relationships do not mean that everyone knows everyone else. A hierarchy of elite relationships exists in which small groups of powerful elite individuals know one another through direct personal contact and experience. These circles of elite relationships interlock: all elite individuals know and are associated with other elite individuals above and below them in the social hierarchy. Sometimes elite hierarchies are highly centralized, with a pyramid structure vertically descending from a central king or court. Other natural state hierarchies are much flatter, with more horizontally linked networks of elites.

Natural state elites sit at the top of, but are also embedded in, patron–client networks that extend down into the rest of society. The intra-elite hierarchy roughly corresponds to the hierarchy of the organizations they represent. The most important source of rents binding the interests of the elites together is the rents that flow from their organizations. Patron–client networks combine elements of adherent and contractual organizations. They are simultaneously informal networks grounded on the maintenance of personal relationships between elite leaders and their clients, and more formal organizations where network leaders are able to access third-party enforcement of intra-network conflicts by calling on the dominant coalition.

Patron–client networks not only structure the creation, gathering, and distribution of rents that can limit violence; the networks also structure and organize violence itself. When violence breaks out, it is typically among networks of elite factions. Violence works both within and across patron–client networks. The ability of patrons to mobilize their power in aid (or threat) of network members enables them to maintain the network. The patrons' privileged position within the dominant coalition enables them to protect their clients from injuries caused by clients of other patrons (whether that protection is legal or physical) and their ability to distribute rewards and levy punishments among their clients. The ability of a patron to protect his or her clients depends, in part, on the ability of the patron's clients to inflict violence on the clients of other patrons. The ability to threaten and use violence is an inherent part of the relationships between elite patrons in the dominant coalition, and between patrons and their clients.

The rewards (rents) for being at the top of the patronage system are typically far higher than those for the patron's lieutenants, which are again far higher than for the rank and file.[5] The rewards of limiting access within the

---

[5] Criminal gangs and organizations illustrate the differential returns to members at different levels of the network. Levitt and Dubner (2005) explain why so many drug dealers live

patron–client network create strong incentives for cooperation within the network. Upward mobility within a natural state usually occurs through channels of patronage networks. A talented individual may rise to a position of power through industry and ability. Indeed, a slave in Rome could become a member of the elite. Natural states are limited access societies, not closed access societies. However, the need to rise through patron–client networks ensures that these societies remain limited access social systems.

Natural states include many other forms of organization beyond patron–client networks, and such networks often provide the connections between elites and non-elites. We assume throughout the book that some types of patron–client networks are in place in most natural states.[6] From the viewpoint of modern open access societies, patron–client networks appear inherently corrupt. Everything is personal. Whom an individual knows and who they are matter more than what they do. Such an attitude toward natural states, seemingly justified from the viewpoint of an open access society, misses the role that personality, personal relationships, and patronage networks play in containing violence within a natural state: personal relationships and rent-creation provide the incentive systems that contain violence and allow cooperation in a natural state. The inherently personal nature of all relationships in a natural state expresses the fundamental logic underlying the limited access social order.

Personality and identity express themselves in another common aspect of all natural states: the creation and manipulation of interest to ensure social order. If we think of a simple patron–client relationship, where the patron promises to provide protection and the client promises a share or fixed amount of output, the commitments of both the patron and client to

---

with their mothers: most drug dealers are lieutenants or rank and file, and they cannot afford to live on their own.

[6] A wide range of excellent case studies of patron–client networks exists. Keefer (2004) and Keefer and Vlaicu (2005) examine patron–client networks in modern developing countries. James Scott's (1972, 1987) work demonstrates the importance of these networks in Asia for ordering society and providing a modicum of non-elite security and protection. Kettering (1986) describes how elite patronage networks provided an important part of the structure of government in France, a subject we return to later in this chapter. Alston and Ferrie (1985) describe how a patronage network enabled Southern whites to dominate and protect Southern blacks in the late nineteenth and early twentieth centuries, and how those networks were broken down by the expansion of social welfare services in the 1960s. Syme's (1938) history of the Roman civil wars leading to the end of the Republic focuses on patronage networks as the major unit of analysis. In the next chapter we document the importance of patron–client networks in medieval England. Patron–client networks can be based on kinship, ethnicity, geography, religion, criminal activity, or other factors. They are ubiquitous in natural states.

each other can be credible if they have a long-term relationship. The client can believe the patron will provide protection, because the long-term value of the client's payments exceeds the cost of protection to the patron, and the patron can believe the client will continue to deliver the payment because the value of protection exceeds the cost of the payment. This requires a personal relationship between the client and patron, a social arrangement in which they are identified with each other. These types of arrangements, throughout society, are more credible and thus easier to sustain if the personal relationships between parties are sustained by social identities that link individuals to each other through organizational ties. Clients have more confidence in patrons if the patrons are embedded in a larger set of social arrangements where the patron's ability to enjoy a stream of rents from his or her clients is part of what makes the larger arrangement sustainable. In that case, if the patron defaults on his or her clients the patron not only loses the stream of payments from the clients but may also lose the benefits from being part of the larger coalition. The benefits elites receive from heading their networks are part of what make arrangements within the dominant coalition credible, and in turn generate even more benefits for elites. All this depends on identifying who gets the benefits: limited access identifies privileges, creates rents, and provides credibility to personal relationships throughout the society.[7] Natural states create and manipulate interests to ensure social order.

The pervasiveness of natural state limits on the ability to form organizations can take the form of a postulate or prediction:

All natural states limit access to organizational forms.

Similarly, natural states control economic opportunities by controlling the organizations and individuals who trade:

All natural states control trade.[8]

The creation of interests within natural states extends throughout society, well beyond the range of economics and politics. Many natural states treat

---

[7] In contrast, in open access societies long-term relationships are still important, but they are embedded in a social structure in which the social identity of individuals does not matter because all individuals are defined in the same terms (i.e., they possess the same privileges or rights).

[8] Natural states always control who trades, and may also control the places they trade and the prices at which they trade.

the organization of religion as a source of rents within the dominant coalition. All of the earliest human civilizations were theocracies, governed by priest–politicians. No doubt an institutionalized state religion reflected the society's beliefs and helped the authorities maintain social control, but the traditional explanation fails to see deeper into the social consequences of organized religion. The authority to lead worship or to found a church is often a closely guarded privilege of a few elites within the dominant coalition. Organized religion generates important rents that the dominant coalition uses to provide stability within the dominant coalition. A state religion provides a way to constrain elites and non-elites.

Most belief systems, religious or otherwise, involve ideas about the structure of organizations, institutions, and human interactions. Beliefs not only shape individual choices but they also shape organizations and institutions. In several of the historical examples that follow, we show how the practice of Christianity affected the development of organizations and institutions within European society. Contested issues always had a purely theological side, but the issues also contained implications for how the church and the larger society should be organized. Theology and practicality intermingled. The ability to influence beliefs was not independent of the ability to influence opportunities.

2.2.2 Size, Boundaries, Trade, and Specialization

Natural states face two problems concerning size – the size of the dominant coalition and the physical size of the society – and a third problem that growing social size creates in the form of gains from specialization. First, taking the physical size of the state as given, how big should the dominant coalition be? Natural state coalitions face a fundamental trade-off. Expanding the coalition without increasing rent-generating activities adds members and increases the coalition's ability to survive against internal and external threats. However, it also dissipates rents, which both lowers the value of being in the coalition and reduces the ability of members to punish the coalition by withdrawing their support. Because of this rent-dissipation, natural state coalitions are naturally self-limiting in size. Too large a coalition is unstable. The dominant coalition must be constantly aware of the danger that a subset of the existing coalition will attempt to displace the rest and take control of the state.

Natural states are stable as social orders but not static in terms of their makeup. Although a dominant coalition always exists, the identity and internal arrangements of the coalition constantly change as the world changes.

Relative prices, demographics, economic growth, technology, and a host of other variables alter continuously in ways that affect the power and position of various elites. As these changes advantage and disadvantage members of the coalition, their relative bargaining positions change. Adjustments in the distribution of privileges and rents must therefore take place to reflect the new balance of power. Because privileges are often inherent in the social identity of powerful elites, it may be difficult to make minor marginal adjustments within the coalition. Yet if minor adjustments fail to take place, then members who believe their power exceeds their share are likely to demand more and, if they fail to receive their due, they may fight for more privileges. For this reason, the actual structure of dominant coalitions in natural states is inherently unstable. The dominant coalition regularly changes size and composition by weeding out weaker members and by incorporating new strong members and, rearranging the entire composition of the coalition.

Limited access orders face another decision about size on the extensive, geographic dimension.[9] A natural state can become larger by incorporating new territory, or a natural state can become smaller by breaking up into several pieces. For most of recorded human history, changes in boundaries and borders were a significant source of change in the structure of the dominant coalition. Until two centuries ago, all societies tended to have somewhat fluid external boundaries. The structure of the dominant coalition is in part an alliance of elites that exerts control over diverse geographic units. Neighboring states must decide whether to ignore each other, fight, ally, integrate, or destroy each other. Whether they ally or unite depends in part on their ability to create credible arrangements between the dominant coalitions in the two societies.

The forces leading natural states to integrate on the geographic dimension exhibit a similarity to those on the intensive dimension: bigger states command more military resources and are therefore more secure. Yet bigger states offer more opportunity for conflict within the coalition. The interaction of the forces mirrors a similar balance and conflict within the natural state: How big should the dominant coalition be?

Successful natural states often capitalize on their ability to produce a larger social surplus and to mobilize resources for the use of the state, such as financing military expansion at the expense of their neighbors. Successful

---

[9] An important theoretical issue affecting the size of states that we do not consider is economies of scale in violence, which change over time. See Bean (1973), North (1981, Ch. 3), and Alesina and Spolaore (2003).

expansion is not the result of military prowess alone, however. Successful expanding states depend on a mix of military, political, economic, and religious factors that make integration of new territories possible. Better ability to coordinate the different elements of their societies – the political, economic, religious, educational, and military systems – gives successful natural states the means to be successful in many dimensions, not just in the military dimension. We illustrate this point with the Carolingian and Aztec examples later in the chapter.

Increasing the size of society creates a third problem for natural states, a problem rooted in an opportunity: the schizophrenic relationship of natural states to specialization and division of labor. Increasing trade and promoting specialization and the division of labor raise productivity and increase the surplus available to elites. As a result, natural state coalitions have incentives to promote trade. However, increasing specialization and division of labor often requires opening entry and access, and doing so dissipates rents, thus threatening the stability of the dominant coalition. Both forces operate in a natural state and, over time, produce ebbs and flows of access and entry. At some times, natural states increase trade and entry at some margins; at other times they restrict trade and entry at others.

2.3 Differences: A Typology of Natural States

Our framework draws a sharp distinction between natural states and open access orders. The distinction does not imply, however, that all natural states are the same. The enormous variation among natural states today ranges from failed states such as Sudan and well-functioning states with the trappings of democracy such as Mexico. Historically, natural states include ancient Rome, Mesopotamia, Egypt, Greece, Mesoamerica, China, the Indus River civilizations, feudal Europe, the Aztecs, and the Incas. How can we call all of these societies natural states and still appreciate the differences among them? Most economic and political development in human history occurred within natural states; how do we explain how natural states develop while still remaining natural states?

In order to draw out the difference among natural states, we characterize three types: fragile, basic, and mature. No sharp borders delineate the different types. Natural states differ primarily in the structure of their state and in the sophistication of the organizations they can support. The most important organization in a natural state is the state itself or, more accurately, the web of relationships within the dominant coalition. Following the idea of double balance, societies capable of supporting complicated private organizations have complicated and sophisticated public organizations. Societies incapable of governing themselves are also incapable of supporting strong private organizations. Although we draw implications about violence and robustness for the different types of natural states, the types are not defined by outcomes but by their institutional structures. We explain the variety of natural states by looking at the sophistication of organizations inside and outside of the state.

In a *fragile natural state,* the state can barely sustain itself in the face of internal and external violence. Contemporary examples include Haiti, Iraq, Afghanistan, Somalia, and several other places in sub-Saharan Africa. In a fragile natural state, commitments within the dominant coalition are fluid and unstable, often shifting rapidly, and dependent on the individual identity and personality of the coalition members. The coalition is fragile in the sense that small changes in the situation of the coalition members – changes in relative prices, any number of shocks from climate, neighboring peoples, disease, and so on – can upset the coalition. Shocks can easily lead to violence and the creation of a new coalition. Alternatively, shocks can lead to rearrangements within the coalition.

A fragile natural state is capable of containing violence, but all politics is real politics: people risk death when they make political mistakes. The coalition successfully provides order when the political interests of coalition members are balanced by their economic stakes in the existing order – the double balance. In a fragile natural state, not only is war politics by other means, economics is politics by other means. Wielding power within the coalition is the critical element in economic success, while the distribution of economic privileges is the key to creating incentives for stable relations within the coalition. Resources can be gained by military conquest, and within the coalition, resources can be gained by political success.

Because of their fluidity, fragile natural states are also characterized by simple institutional structures. Members of the coalition cannot credibly commit to rules or constitutions when the month-to-month reality of balance within the coalition is in flux. This does not mean that fragile natural states fail to perceive the potential benefits from institutional structures: members of the dominant coalition would like to implement rules and laws to limit violence. In reality, however, pervasive uncertainty about outcomes prevents the elite from credibly committing to observe the rules or laws in many possible circumstances. For similar reasons fragile natural states cannot support many, if any, private elite organizations.

Patron–client networks dominate the organizations within fragile natural states, and they are usually networks capable of using violence. The instability of fragile natural states prevents these societies from developing durable forms of public law: public law stipulates and governs the behavior of the state. Fragile natural states also have difficulty constructing and enforcing private law: private law governs relationships among individuals that the state will enforce.[10] Durable arrangements last through time. What law does develop is a mix of public and private law: simple laws that govern the relationships among individuals based on social identity and stipulate a set of rules that patrons can use to make decisions. For example, the legal codes in force in the Germanic nations in early medieval Europe, such as the Salic law, consist largely of schedules of compensation for injuries and violations of a variety of types. The *Pactus Legis Salicae*, the Salic code, includes 15 *Solidi* cases, such as stealing a castrated pig or cutting off another man's middle finger; 35, 45, and 62.5 *Solidi* cases, such as shooting a man with a poisoned arrow that misses; 100 and 200 *Solidi* cases, such as killing a free girl; 600 *Solidi* cases, such as killing a long-haired boy or a count; and 1,800 *Solidi* cases, such as murdering a long-haired boy or a count.[11] The penalties serve two purposes: one is a deterrent to violence, and the other is a way of settling feuds among families and groups by substituting a fixed monetary payment for retributive violence.[12] These fragile societies cannot sustain a legal system with complicated rules about organizational structures, public or private.

In contrast to fragile natural states, *basic natural states* sustain a durable and stable organizational structure for the state. The movement between fragile and basic natural states is gradual and marked by an increasing ability to structure durable arrangements within the organization of the state. Basic natural state institutions are largely public law institutions: institutions that structure aspects of the state, its internal relations, and its relations with members of the dominant coalition.

These public institutions serve several purposes. They provide standard solutions to recurring problems: succession of the leader, succession of elites, determination of tax and tribute rates, and division of the spoils of conquest. All of these problems afford an opportunity for violence and

---

[10] Justinian's Code drew the following distinction between public and private law: "There are two aspects of the subject: public and private. Public law is about the organization of the Roman state, while private law is about the well-being of individuals." Public law provided order for the structures of government and their interrelations.

[11] Drew (1991), pp. 159–63. In addition, see Rivers (1986) for the Salic law and Drew (1973) for the Lombard laws.

[12] Berman (1983) emphasizes the peaceful settlement or evasion of blood feuds.

renegotiation within the dominant coalition and are, therefore, potentially dangerous. Institutionalizing the decision process alleviates, but never completely eliminates the danger. Public institutions also enable the creation of some common beliefs about behavior among elites. Widening the set of commonly held beliefs among elites broadens the range of credible commitments that the dominant coalition can sustain.[13] Finally, public institutions provide elites with organizational forms, both in the public and private sphere, which they can use to contend with one another.

The origin of the Roman Republic illustrates all three of these aspects of public institutions. From its founding in 753 B.C.E., the city of Rome had been governed by kings. In 535, Sextus Tarquin, the son of King Lucius Tarquin Superbus, raped Lucretia. Lucretia's husband Lucius Tarquinnis Collatinus and Lucius Iunius Brutus (the king's nephew) vowed vengeance, returned to Rome, and expelled the king (Livy, 1998, Book I, Chapters 57–60). Rather than establishing one of themselves as king, Brutus and Collatinus were elected by the Senate to the newly created office of consuls, with the understanding that two new consuls would be selected by the Senate from the patriciate every year. Brutus and Collatinus validated the institution by stepping down as consuls at the end of their year. As a public institution, the creation of the consulship transformed the succession problem in the Republic, and it created a set of common beliefs among elites about the nature of political leadership.[14]

The Roman institutions utilized shared beliefs within elites. Membership in the Senate was limited to patricians who had previously held magisterial offices. Senate membership was determined by rule rather than the pleasure of a group or individual. Consuls possessed wide, but limited consular power. Consular power was further limited by the requirement that consuls step down at the end of each year. The process of senatorial consensus required that individual senators act collectively to discipline any consul who violated the limits. The primary function of consuls was leading the army outside of Rome. The ability to create effective executive control

---

[13] Greif shows how a supportable set of beliefs can develop within an institution if the beliefs are consistent with the behavior the institution induces. Successful public institutions create common knowledge, and therefore common beliefs, about how the formal or informal rules will be implemented. The common beliefs can sustain an institution that would otherwise not work. These shared beliefs become focal points, as described by Schelling (1960).

[14] The problem of succession returned with a vengeance at the end of the Republic and ultimately led to the Imperium.

of their armed forces under the consent of the Senate gave the Romans an organizational advantage. Because consuls controlled armies, however, individual senators had to believe that their colleagues would collectively act to exercise their responsibilities to discipline a wayward consul. If a consul brought his army into Rome, as both Sulla and Julius Caesar did, the Senate as a body could not resist the military power of the consul. The balance of interests within the Senate was upset, and the enemies of the victorious consul could pay dearly. Institutions and shared beliefs were all necessary elements in making the Roman organization of government function. Nothing made it inevitable that consuls would step down; indeed the Roman Republic ended when consuls became so powerful as army leaders that the Senate could not balance their power, and powerful leaders were declared "consul for life."

As in Rome, the institutions of a basic natural state structure organizations. The second fundamental feature of the basic natural state is that only organizations with direct connections to the state possess durability. Elite privileges are closely identified with the state, and an individual who wishes to pursue a complicated activity that requires a sophisticated organizational structure will use the state as the vehicle for organization. The balance of the interests created by elite organizations maintains order within the elite, and if order is sustained, it generates believable or credible expectations that arrangements will be repeated in the future. In fragile natural states, these organizations are highly personal, but as basic natural states begin to develop, public law, written or unwritten, may shape the formation of more complex organizations. Basic natural state institutions are not capable of supporting private elite organizations outside the orbit of the state's own organizational structure. So basic natural states do not support a rich civil society because few (perhaps no) organizations exist that compete with the state.[15] How public law grows varies enormously from society to society, and here, as always, it is important not to draw too many conclusions from any single experience.[16]

---

[15] Again, the ability of the basic natural state to support private organizations is not a zero/one outcome. As basic natural states develop, they become more capable of supporting private organizations.

[16] In Nazi Germany, for example, all organizations were either state organizations or had very close relations with the state. The tendency in twentieth-century socialist and communist countries has been to embed every organization within the ruling party. In late twentieth-century China, for example, the strict central control over the formation of state institutions was loosened in the 1980s with the creation of township and village enterprises. Local party

Public law in Europe during the Middle Ages developed support for elite organizations within, but not beyond, the framework of the state. The organizations themselves were under the control of powerful members of the dominant coalition. The privilege of heading an organization constituted an important part of a powerful member's social persona. Bishops, for example, headed religious organizations. By virtue of their office, bishops held a formal place in the structure of the state. Appointments of bishops, as we discuss later, were a critical area of conflict and compromise within the religious–political coalition that governed Europe in the Middle Ages. In basic natural states, the formation of organizations remains within the orbit of the state.

How well basic natural states perform and survive is likely to depend on building state organizations that serve broader segments within the elite. When state organizations serve smaller groups of elites and a small subset of the dominant coalition, the rents the organizations create are more vulnerable to appropriation by the rest of the coalition. If, however, specialized state organizations emerge to serve several different members of the coalition, the new organizations are likely to survive.

Finally, the range of social arrangements that can be sustained by a basic natural state is limited because the state is not perpetually lived and only exercises limited control over violence. We have used the term *durable* to indicate arrangements that last through time. Perpetual lived arrangements are fundamentally different. A *perpetually lived organization* is one where the identity of the organization is independent from the identity of its individual members.[17] All states are organizations, and perpetually lived states are ones where the identity of the organization is independent of the identity of the individuals who make up the organization. Basic natural states develop public institutions internal to the state, and out of those institutions it is possible to develop common beliefs about the expected life of the state; that is, about the credibility of the state to make commitments about the future. A basic natural state has a limited ability to make credible commitments through time. A basic natural state may have durable institutions, but the basic natural state is not perpetually lived.

---

organizations were given more discretion to pursue alternative economic arrangements. The results have been astounding in terms of economic growth.

[17] The use of *perpetual* does include an element of time, because the organization lives beyond the lives of its members, but perpetual life does not imply infinite life. A perpetual organization can be created to live to a specific and limited time period as we see later in the case of a variety of types of corporations.

The third type of natural state is a *mature natural state.* A mature natural state is characterized by durable institutional structures for the state and the ability to support elite organizations outside the immediate framework of the state. Both characteristics distinguish the mature natural state from the basic natural state, but to reiterate, the differences are of degree rather than of kind. At the limit, a mature natural state is able to create and sustain perpetually lived organizations, but that is not a common feature of mature natural states.

The institutions of mature natural states must emerge simultaneously to develop more sophisticated public and private organizations and more highly articulated public and private law. Private law provides individuals with an understanding of the relationships among individuals that the lord (or his agent or eventually the courts) would enforce and so provides individuals with a framework to reach agreements within the law's bounds. A well-articulated body of public law specifies the offices and functions of the state and the relationship between the offices and functions, and provides for methods of resolving conflicts within the state and, by extension, within the dominant coalition. The public law may be written or unwritten, but it must be embodied in state organizations, such as a court, capable of articulating and enforcing the public law.[18] The durable public institutions of a mature natural state are capable, in normal circumstances, of lasting through changes in the makeup of the dominant coalition.

Unlike basic natural states, the institutions of mature natural states are able to support elite organizations that are not intimately tied to the state. Public law helps here as well, particularly in combination with the idea of legal personality. Legal persons are capable of bearing rights and responsibilities. As discussed earlier, an individual may or may not be a legal person, and organizations can be legal persons. Because so much of private law and legal history focuses on the law as a method for ordering the relationships among individuals or among entities, it is easy to overlook the dramatic implications that legal personhood has for the support of the internal structure of organizations. To function efficiently, contractual organizations need an external party to enforce their internal arrangements and their external dealings with individuals, other organizations, and the state. Official legal recognition of an organization as a legal person for external purposes also opens the door to formal legal recognition of internal organizational agreements as enforceable in the courts. Municipalities, for example, can sue

---

[18] Myerson's (2008) recent work on governance stresses this aspect of the ruler's "court."

and be sued, and the relationship of the mayor to the city can come under purview of the law.[19]

Intra- and inter-organizational contracts require both a form of legal system for administration of contracts and a system to protect these organizations from expropriation by the state and by other members of the dominant coalition. That is, a form of rule of law for organizations must emerge in mature natural states. Because rule of law cannot emerge by fiat, it is easily undone, and many attempts to create it in basic natural states fail. The institutions providing these services must be embedded in the state in a way that they are protected from the frequent natural state dynamics whereby privileges are regularly rearranged among members of the dominant coalition so that the rule of law is eroded.

In Roman law, a variety of organizations – *collegia, universitas, municipium* – were all sanctioned by the law as organizations capable of bearing rights and responsibilities. The Roman experience highlights both the way mature natural states deal with organizations and the impossibility of drawing a hard and fast line between basic and mature natural states. The creation of organizations under Roman law remained a matter of public law: that is, formal organizations had to be recognized by the state as organizations. However, as the Republic matured, access to organizational forms became easier for the upper classes. The de facto independence of Roman organizations, supported by the development of Roman law, provided the stability and incentives for rapid economic and political expansion. The ability of wealthy individuals to mobilize their resources and power through organizations provided the magistrates and Senate with independent incentives to maintain Roman rights.

The same wealth creation that fueled Roman growth, however, was a source of instability over the long term. As the Republic grew, the provisioning of armies and the administration of the empire required a multiplication of offices and concentration of military power in the hands of leaders who were potential threats to the independence of the Senate. In 88 B.C.E. Sulla led his armies into Rome; in 49 B.C.E. Julius Caesar did the same, both claiming to restore Roman rights against a tyranny. After a century of civil war, the Republic effectively ended with the elevation of Octavianus to emperor as Augustus Caesar. Many of the formal, public law institutions remained under the Principate, but with much different functions and outcomes than under the Republic. Was the empire a mature or basic natural state? The answer is that the Roman Empire over the next

---

[19] Wallis, Weingast, and North (2006) discuss these issues in greater detail. For the Roman history, see Duff (1938).

four hundred years moved back and forth along the dimensions of social organizations that define basic and mature natural states.

2.4 Privileges, Rights, and Elite Dynamics

The example of Republican and Imperial Rome provides clear evidence that no teleology pushes societies to move along the progression from simpler to more complex natural states. No forces inevitably move societies along the continuum from fragile to basic to mature natural states. Societies appear as capable of regression as progression.[20]

The logic of the natural state offers some insight into why the forces operating on limited access societies do not produce an inevitable progression from simpler to more complex forms of social organization. The forces of double balance are an important element of development within the natural state. In order for the public organizations of the state to become more sophisticated, private-sector organizations must develop. The development of public and private organizations must proceed together, including the degree of specialization and division of labor within and among organizations, the ability to own and transfer real estate and movable wealth, the ability to monitor and record the activities of the organization, the degree to which external third-party enforcement of agreements is used and, in large enough organizations, the ability to provide internal third-party enforcement.

As basic natural states emerge from fragile natural states, support for organizations is vested in powerful members of the dominant coalition. Elites have strong interests to promote trade and specialization and division of labor. They also have strong interests to define their privileges with respect to one another as elites. Initially these privileges are fluid, the result of the dynamics of the coalition. However, if a coalition stabilizes, the creation of public law institutions can in part be a mechanism for resolving elite conflicts. Our third proposition or prediction is that:

The origin of legal systems lies in the definition of elite privileges.

Legal systems initially develop to enforce unique and personal elite privileges, including the privilege to form organizations. The organizations

---

[20] Over the last decade, for example, Bolivia, Venezuela, and Russia all seem to be regressing as they nationalize, control, or outlaw once-independent organizations. In the 1930s, Nazi Germany regressed from a mature to a basic natural state as it forced previously independent organizations into the orbit of the state.

formed by elites often contain elements of both public and private organizations; for example, the manor in medieval England or the town in medieval Germany. Early legal forms can be credible among elites because they individually possess the power and incentives to discipline each other, through extralegal means if necessary. The existence of a court or laws for elites does not imply rule of law or unbiased enforcement. Powerful individuals will probably receive more favorable treatment (as reflected in the Salic law). If, however, a privilege is held by all elites, then not only do the incentives of all elites align to maintain that privilege but also the shared nature of a privilege makes it possible to transform the privilege into a right. For example, in medieval England, as we will see in Chapter 3, major lords all possessed the right to hold their own manorial courts. Their rights created a shared interest in maintaining those courts (sometimes in opposition to or in competition with the king's courts).

As elites form more powerful organizations, it becomes more credible for elites to believe that arrangements defined by the internal rules of the dominant coalition will be followed. More powerful elite organizations provide elites with both the ability to discipline the coalition and incentives to support the shared institutions that support their organizations. An important consequence follows when private elite organizations have some degree of independence from the state and freedom of action, even if it is limited. When elite organizations have an enhanced ability to discipline (or reward) the state for violating (honoring) its commitments, then natural states are better able to credibly commit to more sophisticated public organizations as well. This is the virtuous side of the logic of the natural state. If and when limited elite rights to form organizations emerge, basic natural states move closer to mature natural states. Mature natural states cannot develop without more sophisticated private organizations.

The process of converting elite privileges into elite rights secured by a balance of political and economic interests does not happen automatically, however, because there is an equally powerful and persistent reason for elites to convert rights into privileges. The dominant coalition holds together only if the balance of economic and political interests can be maintained. If circumstances change, and they always do, there may be incentives to shift resources or privileges to elements within the coalition in order to maintain balance. It may be difficult, if not impossible, however, to make small marginal changes to arrangements. If a faction within the coalition becomes more powerful, it maneuvers to get more rents or it threatens to fight or leaves (and perhaps returns to fight). Intra-elite relationships are always more or less dynamic, and are never static. As natural states develop, they do not reduce the uncertainty or dynamism of the dominant coalition. Instead, they manage to secure more sophisticated public and private elite organizations that sustain a wider range of adjustments to changing circumstances that do not require transforming elite rights back into elite privileges. When such dramatic adjustments are required, natural states often suffer partial or complete breakdowns in the dominant coalition, and civil war, rather than legal adjustments, can be the result. In those circumstances, mature natural states can quickly move back toward social arrangements typical of a basic or even a fragile natural state.

2.5 Origins: The Problem Scale and Violence

The discovery of agriculture and the domestication of plants and animals began the Neolithic revolution ten thousand years ago. The growth of cities, new production technologies, and new forms of social organization transformed human societies over the following five thousand years. Archeological evidence reveals the emergence of groups of larger than several hundred people for the first time in human history. Regardless of the causes of the Neolithic revolution – climate change, genetic change, the discovery of agriculture, or a new social technology – we need to understand how societies managed to become substantially larger beginning five to ten thousand years ago.

Larger societies required new ways to manage and control violence. Basic social units in foraging orders (bands or family groups) were typically groups of twenty-five to fifty individuals. Larger social units (tribes or local groups or big-men collectivities) range up to five hundred people. For each of these ways of organizing social interaction, increasing size produces increasing intragroup conflict and what Rappaport called the "irritation coefficient": "sources of irritation . . . increase at a rate greater than population size. If population increase were taken to be linear, the increase of some kinds of dispute . . . might be taken to be roughly geometric" (1968, p. 116). The increasing violence and disorder with group size, *ceteris paribus*, conform to the generally observed positive correlation between the level of violence and size of population in modern societies.[21]

The numbers twenty-five and two hundred recur in anthropological research. The modal size of the basic foraging social group appears to be

---

[21] Johnson's (1982) notion of scalar stress suggests that human cognitive limits begin to be reached when six or seven items have to be attended to simultaneously, so that six groups of six people, 36 people, or six groups of six, 216 people, might be natural sizes for groups.

around twenty-five people (Kelly, 1995, pp. 209–16). Agglomerations of bands or family groups were often around two hundred people. Service's (1971) categories of band, tribe, chiefdom, and state correspond to groups of roughly this size, with perhaps one thousand as a modal unit for chiefdoms. Johnson and Earle (2000, p. 32) transform Service's categories into family groups (including the family/camp and family/hamlet), local groups (both acephalous and big man), and regional groups (both chiefdoms and states). The size of these different societies is bounded at the upper range by problems of managing violence.[22] Although the evidence is contested, small societies seem to experience high levels of violence (Keely, 1996; LeBlanc, 2003; Steckel and Wallis, 2006).

Although new archeological evidence is accumulating, evidence about what happened five or ten thousand years ago is too limited to make inferences about social organization in the Neolithic societies. However, three sets of available evidence are relevant to the question of social organization and scale. Ethnographic studies of small-scale societies in anthropological research abound and suggest similarities in organization of societies that increase in size from local to regional polities, or from tribes to chiefdoms.[23] Related work includes the literature on the structure of "pristine" societies, the first large-scale civilizations to arise in different parts of the world that appear to have done so without external influence (Trigger, 2003). Finally, we have evidence on the incidence of human-induced violence in New World societies based on archeological evidence of skeletal remains (Steckel and Rose, 2002).

Johnson and Earle (2000) draw together evidence on nineteen ethnographies of societies at different scales. Of particular interest is the transition between local and regional groups, or between big-man societies and chiefdoms. In big-man societies, an individual or family leads the group and enjoys more wealth but is subject to considerable constraint from the larger group. The big man leads by building a personal following. The big man usually possesses the key privilege (or performs the function) of controlling trade between his group and other groups.

---

[22] Johnson and Earle (2000, p. 246) provide a table with population breakdowns across 19 of the ethnographic cases consistent with size breaks at 25/30, 200/250, and 1,000 (although the fit is not perfect, as one would expect). Service (1971) discusses size categories and types. Dunbar (1996) suggests that the optimal size of a human group, based on studies of brain size and group size in primates, is about 150. Bandy (2004) studies the fusion–fission process in Mesoamerican societies.

[23] Earle (1997, 2003), Johnson and Earle (2000).

The emergence of chiefdoms involves a more complicated form of political economy of social organization. Earle identifies three types of power – economic, military, and ideological – and argues that chiefdoms emerge when "the material flows of the political economy provide the wire that binds the sources of power together" (1997, pp. 207–8). In Earle's words:

In chiefdoms, control over production and exchange of subsistence and wealth creates the basis for political power ... Economic power is based on the ability to restrict access to key productive resources or consumptive goods ... Control over exchange permits the extension of economic control over broader regions, ... The real significance of economic power may be that the material flows through the political economy can be used by the chief to nurture and sustain the alternative power sources ... (1997, p. 7).

The coalition, which the chief heads and that always controls trade, is distinct from the common people through some form of social identification (an important function of ideology). Violence and coercive power are inherent elements of larger social groups, but the groups are held together not only by the threat of coercion but by mutual interests (Earle, 1997, p. 106). The creation of elites requires the social construction of social personas. The emergence of chiefdoms, of societies of more than one thousand members, appears to be associated with institutions that reflect the logic of the natural state.

State is a term of art with a specific meaning in anthropology, but less so in political science and economics. States are distinguished from chiefdoms by size and structure and include formal administration of government. For anthropologists, states do not appear until populations rise into the hundreds of thousands.[24] In contrast, what we define as the natural state arises as societies reach populations of one thousand or more, and new forms of integrated political and economic organization develop to limit violence. As Earle recognizes, "The fundamental dynamics of chiefdoms are essentially the same as those of states, and ... the origins of states is to be understood in the emergence and development of chiefdoms" (1997, p. 14). We add the logic of natural state to the approach of Johnson and Earle: the key link that constrains military power is embedding the individuals who direct military power in a network of privileges. By manipulating privilege, interests are created that limit violence.

The emergence of social hierarchy in early societies results directly from the creation of privileged elites. Ancient civilizations do not afford us a

---

[24] For recent investigations into the archaeology and anthropology of pre-modern states see Smith (2004), Farghar and Blanton (2007), and Blanton and Farghar (2008).

direct view of early developments at the dawn of the Neolithic revolution, but they do give us a clear picture of early natural states. All these societies were theocracies.[25] All had interlocking sets of religious, economic, political, military, and educational elites; indeed, in many the highest leaders were simultaneously priests, warriors, and kings or princes. As Service (1975) argued, any state that rules by coercing subjects and rivals must continually risk war against both its own subjects and its rivals. Successful societies "wage peace," in Service's evocative phrase. Securing peace prepares the ground for beliefs to grow up in the population at large about the legitimacy of the system. Those beliefs are consistent with positive incentives for powerful individuals to maintain the peace, in contrast to societies where a balance of terror is all that ensures order. Ideology, both in material culture and in the religious and educational organizations of elites, interlocks with the logic of the social order.

The implication is that chiefdoms and states exhibit the characteristic organization of natural states, and they should therefore experience lower levels of violence than the foraging order. Using recently developed forensic techniques for inferring the existence of human-induced violence from skeletal evidence, Steckel and Wallis (2006) show that the rate of human-induced violence in a sample of New World individuals declined as the size of the population increased. Individuals living in small foraging groups had significantly higher rates of human-induced trauma. We summarize the results in the appendix to this chapter.

The anthropological evidence suggests that the increasing scale of human societies is associated with the emergence of social organizations implied by the logic of the natural state. The political economy of chiefdoms expresses the logic of the natural state. All of the pristine ancient civilizations were societies with strong theocratic hierarchies in which limited access to economic, political, military, and religious functions played a key role in identifying the social persona of elites. The evidence from skeletal remains suggests that, as the scale of societies increased, human-induced violence declined.

---

[25] Service includes Mesopotamia, Egypt, the Indus River, China, Mesoamerica, and Peru. Trigger excludes the Indus River civilization, and includes the Aztecs and Incas of the fifteenth and sixteenth centuries and the Yoruba and Benin peoples of West Africa in the eighteenth century. Trigger does not require civilizations to be "pristine" in the sense of being the first civilization to develop in its part of the world (2003, pp. 28–9). Freid (1967), Feinman and Marcus (1998), and Yoffee (2005) offer alternative frameworks for interpreting early civilizations and more recent anthropological work on the origins of "archaic states."

2.6 Natural State Dynamics: Fragile to Basic Natural States

How do fragile natural states move toward basic natural states? How does a society whose major accomplishment is holding the dominant coalition together become transformed into one where the state establishes durable institutions and under the spreading umbrella of state support develops economic, educational, and religious organizations that sustain the integration of the society into a larger geographic and cultural entity?

Two historical examples illustrate how a basic natural state forms out of a fragile natural state: the Mesoamerican Aztec Empire (1428–1519) and the European Carolingian Empire (751–840). Each empire was founded in a society living in the shadow of historical greatness, where disintegration and decline had occurred over several centuries. Each empire experienced a quick rise to power, yet lasted a relatively short time. Their key similarities relate to the way in which the dominant coalitions structured their internal relationships and how they used military, economic, political, religious, and educational institutions and organizations. Each empire built on existing social materials, and each borrowed extensively from preexisting institutions, making small modifications in them that dramatically changed the way the social order performed. Finally, in each empire the state was the only framework within which organizations could be supported. These were truly basic natural states.

The Aztec Empire. Mesoamerica had seen three large civilizations rise and fall: the coastal Olmec from about 1500 to 300 B.C.E.; Teotihuacan in the Valley of Mexico from about 100 to 750 C.E.; and the loosely organized Toltec society from roughly 900 to 1200 C.E. Each empire was followed by a period of disintegration. In the thirteenth and fourteenth centuries, the Valley of Mexico was composed of competing city-states and fragile alliances.[26] One of many migrant ethnic bands, the Mexica, settled on the island of Tenochtitlan in Lake Texcoco. The lands around the lake were fertile, and the area was a center of military and political conflict over control of the region. In the late fourteenth century, the most powerful local alliance was headed by the Tepanecs, which included the Mexicas in their alliance.

---

[26] The large literature on Aztec society is continually growing and changing. We have drawn on Smith (2001, 2003), Smith and Montiel (2001), Lockhart (1992) Carrasco (1999), Conrad and Demarest (1984), Berdan (1982), Berdan et al. (1996), Blanton (1996), and Brumfiel (1987), Hassig (1988), among others.

The basic units of Mexica society were the *altepetl* and the *calpulli*. The *altepetl* were ethnic states that were primarily organizations of people controlling a given territory. The *calpulli* were the constituent parts of the *altepetl*, whose land was owned by nobles who granted use of the land to *calpulli* members. The *calpulli* served as the unit of organization for schools, temples, and military units.[27] The Mexica aristocracies, the *pipiltin*, were the first families of the *calpulli*, and higher political leaders, the *tlatoani* (ruler) were drawn from the *calpulli* leadership. Integration into the Tepanec alliance gave the Mexicas an opportunity to develop their own elites, to serve in military campaigns, and to acquire administrative and military skills. The Mexicas petitioned the city of Culhauacan and the Tepanec alliance to provide them with a prince of Toltec blood. The first *tlatoani*, Acamapichtli, came to Tenochtitlan around 1370. Whether he came because of a request or was imposed on the Mexicas by the Tepanecs is not clear.

The death of a powerful Tepanec leader in 1426 was followed by a period of confusion. In the power void, a coalition of three city-states – the Triple Alliance of Tenochtitlan, Texcoco, and Tacuba – defeated the Tepanecs in 1428. The Triple Alliance became the Aztec Empire (Smith, 2001). The Triple Alliance was always a coalition. Despite the relative ascendance of the Mexica Aztecs within the coalition, it remained an alliance until the Spanish arrived in 1521. The southern valley was divided into three regional states, each governed by one part of the coalition. The alliance turned its military forces to the conquest of other city-states in the southern part of the valley by the 1430s.

The Aztec leaders immediately began distributing land from conquered areas to leading elites, particularly military leaders.[28] The land went to the *tlatoani*, the military warriors, and the principal members of the *pipiltin* aristocracy. A new leadership group was formed called the Council of Four, which consisted of all members of the Imperial family, who exercised executive power within the state and determined succession upon the death of the emperor. Religious and government offices were restructured to reflect the new order. A tight relationship among wealth, conquest, and land developed in which a small dominant coalition mobilized the economic resources of the society to provide both social order and the wherewithal to continue a program of conquest.

---

[27] Lockhart (1992), pp. 14–20; Conrad and Demarest (1984), p. 23, Zorita (1963), pp. 105–11 on land tenure and pp. 135–51 on schools; Carrasco (1999), pp. 16–21 on *calpulli*.

[28] Hodge (1996) describes the Aztec methods of governance.

Three features of the Aztec system are of interest. The first is the use of religion. Aztec religious beliefs were rooted in the larger Mesoamerican religious tradition. Aztecs held that the sun god daily battled his way across the sky against his brothers the stars and his sister the moon. In order to triumph in this battle, the sun needed to be strong and vigorous, for which he required the *chalchihuatl*, the precious liquid, the blood of man (Caso, 1958, pp. 12–13). Failure to nourish the sun would result in the destruction of the earth. The expanding use of human sacrifice fueled the expansionary military goals of the Aztecs, and it provided an ideological framework that justified the labor of the masses even if they did not participate fully in the gains (the earth would be destroyed): the religious structure permeated the way in which the dominant coalition defined itself. The last feature is critical. Because changes in status within the Aztec society were associated with ritual sacrifices, the religious structure identified who was powerful. The religious structure held the same position for the *pipiltin* aristocracy and for the merchant class (which we discuss in a moment).

The second feature is that access to the political-religious structure required access to education. The Aztec *calpulli* traditionally included a temple and a school, the *telpochcalli,* where male youths were taught the skills that would make them warriors. A parallel system of schools for the elites, the *calmecac,* instilled the same warrior skills and values, but also taught the students how to read "sacred books, the arts of painting, of counting the days and years, of placing the festivals of the gods, of chanting the hymns, and of understanding the demands made by the supernaturals" (Leon-Portilla, 1963, pp. 134–52). Education in a *calmecac* was an essential prerequisite for admission to the higher reaches of elite status. The combination of religion, education, and politics created a dominant coalition with a strong identity, clear shared beliefs with strong educational roots, and limited access.

The third feature is that the Aztecs limited access to economic activity by empowering a specific group of merchants, the *pochteca*. The *pochteca* possessed exclusive privileges to trade in long-distance and luxury goods, organized in guilds, with their own elaborate social ranks signified by special privileges in dress and behavior.[29] The Aztec Empire's fiscal system ran on a

---

[29] Conrad and Demarest (1984), pp, 50–1; Hodge (1996), pp. 43–4; Brumfiel (1987); and Blanton (1996), pp. 47–84. Blanton's conclusions, pp. 83–4, are particularly relevant to our argument. For the role of *pochteca* in the outlying provinces of the empire see Berdan (1996), pp. 115–35 and more generally Berdan's analysis of the role of trade in the Aztec system in Berdan (1982, 1985, 1987) and Smith (2003).

combination of tribute and market taxation. Local markets for agricultural products were under the control of local elites, but control of long-distance movement of goods was either directly under the control of the state in the form of tribute payments or indirectly under the control of the state through *pochteca* networks and formal regulation of markets for long-distance and luxury goods (Hodge, 1996). The Aztec Empire possessed a market economy, but the state harnessed the market economy to the needs of the political system.

The Aztec Empire created sophisticated organizational structures in politics, trade, religion, education, and the military. Reflecting the essence of a basic natural state, none of these organizations existed outside of the state.

The Carolingian Empire. Carolingian history, institutions, organizations, and culture differed from that of the Mexica. Nonetheless, striking similarities exist between the two cases. Both the Carolingians and the Aztecs harnessed the productive power of organizations. As with the Aztecs, the Carolingians built organizations only within the framework of the state. Both were basic natural states.

The decline of the Roman Empire in the west was associated with a series of barbarian migrations beginning with the Goths in 376 and continuing through 476 when the last emperor fell. Relatively small barbarian populations, in comparison with the Roman population, moved into and eventually controlled strategic areas of the empire (Heather, 2006). By the eighth century, barbarian kingdoms occupied most of Western Europe, with a few vestiges of Roman authority in Italy in the Papal States and in the Exarch at Ravenna.[30] The Catholic church remained an important influence, both in Italy and throughout the parts of Western Europe that had converted to Christianity.

The chaotic and ever-changing political map of Europe from 476 to 750 tracked kingdoms of Visigoths, Vandals, Franks, Lombards, Saxons, and Frisians; the invasions of Moslems; and the political machinations of the eastern Roman Empire (Geary, 1988). The Kingdom of the Franks was just one of several kingdoms when Charles Martel, then Mayor of the Palace, subdued his competitors for power within the Franks, conquered Frisia, and repulsed the Saracen invasion of Provence at Tours in 732. Charles died in 741, leaving the state between his two sons Carloman and Pippin. When Carloman retired to a monastery in 747, Pippin III took unified command of the Kingdom of the Franks.

---

[30] See Hodges and Whitehouse (1983), Hodges (1989), McCormick (2001), Heather (1996, 2006), and Geary (1988) for a review of the evidence.

In the meantime, the pope had his hands full in Italy. The Lombards had occupied much of northern and eastern Italy, and the Lombard king was attempting to deal with rebellious Lombard dukes in Benevento and Spoleto. The Byzantine Empire was fighting the Moslem expansion throughout the eastern Mediterranean and trying to maintain a foothold in Italy in the form of the Exarch at Ravenna. The pope still nominally acknowledged the Byzantine emperor, and the emperor still nominally acknowledged the pope as the first personage in the church, but East and West continued to be split by doctrinal disputes. The pope faced (at least) a four-cornered struggle for power within Italy.

As with the Aztecs, the beginnings of the Carolingian rise to power lay in an alliance. Charles Martel had cooperated with the pope in the face of the Saracen invasions. Despite an existing Merovingian king, the pope agreed to recognize Pippin as King of the Franks in 751. Pippin cemented the alliance by coming to the aid of the pope in Italy, sending an army to deal with the Lombards who had taken an army to the walls of Rome. In 754, "the Pope solemnly renewed the consecration which Boniface had bestowed upon Pippin, and, on penalty of excommunication, forbade the Franks ever to choose a king who was not descended from Pippin" (Pirenne, 2001[1954], p. 225).

By recognizing Charlemagne (Pippin's son) as emperor in 800, the pope decisively broke with the Eastern Empire and the Eastern emperor. By pledging themselves as protectors of the Catholic church everywhere in the world, the Carolingians gained entry to all of Christian Europe, an entry that Charlemagne made masterful use of. Through diplomacy and war, Charlemagne built a political coalition based on control of land and personal obligations. Military service and land tenure became closely linked, forming the origins of the feudal system.

Carolingian integration utilized natural state mechanisms. A coalition of military specialists was tied economically to the land through vassalage. Charlemagne granted land to powerful individuals in return for personal service and obligation (Bloch, 1961; Ganshof, 1968, pp. 50–2). Another coalition of traders was built up by promotion of long-distance trade under the protection and direction of the emperor.[31] Trading emporia were established at Quentovic and Dorestad. Contentious relations between Charlemagne and the Danes, for example, arose in part by Charlemagne's desire

---

[31] This was nothing new. Long-distance trade was always subject to political control; indeed, given the dangers of long-distance trade it was not feasible to trade without explicit political guarantees of protection and passage. See the discussion of "Emporia" in Hodges (1989), pp. 47–65.

to control and maintain the trade with the Eastern Empire and the Abbasid Caliphate (Hodges and Whitehouse, 1983, pp. 111–22, 171).

The alliance with the church was an integral part of the Carolingian economic structure. Long-distance trade was centered in a few cities and in a number of monasteries. By mobilizing wealth through the coinage of silver and the movement of interregional goods within the empire along rivers to approved trading centers, the Carolingians generated an economic surplus at the service of the Carolingian coalition (Hodges and Whitehouse, 1983, p. 171). The evidence that trade did grow in Europe during the eighth and ninth centuries now appears overwhelming, and it was a trade controlled by the state (McCormick, 2001).

Finally, Charlemagne encouraged the development of an elite educational system, again in alliance with the church. The Carolingian literary renaissance was ecclesiastic (Ullmann, 1969). The expansion of literacy, the dissemination of books, and the development of a literary elite were concentrated almost exclusively within the church and its ecclesiastical structure. The emphasis on Latin as the written language of the empire at a time when it had ceased to be the spoken language of most of the population highlights the elite nature of the educational system: because only elites learned Latin, elites alone had access to the state or ecclesiastical administration, courts, and business.

The Carolingian Empire was a basic natural state. From our modern perspective, the alliance of church and state may appear strange and forced, and our attention is drawn first to the political, military, and economic arrangements of the Carolingians. The defining characteristic of a basic natural state, however, is an inability to support organizations outside of the state.

The Carolingian natural state coalition combined many social elements – political, military, religious, economic, and educational – into a coalition of interlocking interests that for a short time existed in one large geographic entity, the Carolingian Empire. However, even after the political entity broke into smaller pieces, this structure helped order most of Europe for the next six centuries. Despite being composed of many organizations and actors, a key distinction made in most histories of Europe is between the church and the state. As we have emphasized, in basic natural states, organizations all exist within the framework of the state, so disentangling the connections between church and state in medieval Europe illuminates how a basic natural state can be structured and opens a window into understanding how Europe eventually developed the institutions and organizations characteristic of a mature natural state.

Figgis described the key to understanding medieval society:

> In the Middle Ages the Church was not a State, it was the State; the State or rather the civil authority (for a separate society was not recognised) was merely the police department of the Church. The latter took over from the Roman Empire its theory of the absolute and universal jurisdiction of the supreme authority, and developed it into the doctrine of the *plenitudo potestatis* of the Pope, who was the supreme dispenser of law, the fountain of honour, including regal honour, and the sole legitimate earthly source of power, the legal if not the actual founder of religious orders, university degrees, the supreme "judge and divider" among nations, the guardian of international right, the avenger of Christian blood. All these functions have passed elsewhere, and the theory of omnipotence, which the Popes held on the plea that any action might come under their cognizance so far as it concerned morality, has now been assumed by the State on the analogous theory that any action, religious or otherwise, so far as it becomes a matter of money, or contract, must be matter for the courts (Figgis, 1923, p. 4).

What did Figgis mean when he said that the church was the state? On one level, the actual provisions of public services that we associate with states were undertaken both by the church and by secular political organizations. The church was primarily responsible for education and social welfare (of a variety of types including poor relief, hospitals, disaster relief, and food storage). The church shared responsibility for the provision of justice with secular authorities. The ownership and management of land, both in land's generalized legal characteristics defined through courts and in the day-to-day operation of operating political units, were also shared by the church and secular authorities. After the tenth century, the church ceded police and military power to the secular princes.

On another level, the church occupied critical nodes in the organization of political power, just as secular lords occupied critical nodes in the organization of religious authority. The Electors of the Holy Roman Emperor, for example, included the archbishops of Mainz, Trier, and Cologne. The archbishops and bishops of England were members of the House of Lords. The church constituted the first estate in France and, down to the revolution, maintained an interdependent fiscal relationship with state finance. Symmetrically, Charlemagne encouraged his feudal retainers to organize, support, and defend religious institutions. Proprietary churches under the control and support of a secular donor were sufficiently common that attempts to reform the system led to clashes between church and secular leaders, the most spectacular of which was the Investiture Crisis that we consider in detail in the next section. Archbishops and bishops were appointed by kings and lesser lords. Just as the archbishops and bishops exerted significant fiscal and political influence on the secular powers, so too the secular powers exerted influence over the church. We cannot make much sense out of European history from Charlemagne to the Reformation without acknowledging the close interlocking and interdependent nature of ecclesiastical and secular elements of the dominant coalition.

The interdependence of secular and ecclesiastic authority created recurrent constitutional issues within the church, within the state, and in their interactions. The church needed to define and maintain a vertical structure of authority between the church in Rome and the church throughout Europe. At each horizontal level within the church, a structure of authority had to be sustained, including the pope and the College of Cardinals in Rome; at the level of bishops, their dioceses, their cathedrals, and the college of canons; and at the level of the individual parish, abbey, monastery, and convents. Because the churches and her officers were large landowners playing central roles in the allocation of privileges within local secular states, the constitutional structures at the individual levels corresponded closely to political and other secular institutions and organizations.

2.7 Moving to Mature Natural States: Disorder, Organization, and the Medieval Church

The Aztec and Carolingian histories are starting points for understanding how mature natural states develop. Both civilizations grew out of environments where multiple small social units competed with each other for power, resources, and security. It was a world where conditions changed frequently, rulers were deposed, cities despoiled, and populations displaced. This, of course, is the normal world for most of human history. Even within Aztec Mesoamerica, large parts of the population lived outside the empire and faced ongoing warfare and confusion. Similarly, although the Carolingians united part of Europe for a time, at the death of Louis the Pious in 840, the empire was permanently dismembered so that by 900 Europe faced conditions similar to those of 700. There was nothing inevitable about the increasing scale of society under the Aztecs or the Carolingians, or about the decrease in scale and increasing disorder of Europe after 840.

All natural states face the problem of maintaining their dominant coalitions by granting elite individuals and organizations economic and political incentives to cooperate with one another. In basic natural states, all organizations – political, military, economic, religious, and educational – are integrated closely into the structure of the dominant coalition. For convenience, historians and social scientists often identify the military organization as the "state," but as Figgis argues for Europe, the church was as much a part of the state as the military leadership. How does a society manage to develop institutional support for elite organizations outside the immediate framework of the state? Beyond that, when independent elite organizations come into existence, how is it possible to endow them with perpetual life?

The essence of a natural state is personal relationships. The legal system cannot enforce individual rights if every individual is different, if every relationship between two individuals depends uniquely on their identity within the dominant coalition. Following their Roman origins, in Europe both public and private law evolved.[32] Private law structured a limited number of relationships between individuals who are recognized as persons in the law. Not all legal persons enjoyed equal protection under the law; and the law recognized more than one category of legal persons, such as kings, nobles, and freemen. Public law structured relationships among and within organizations, including the most important organization in society, the state.[33] Public law entities were typically idiosyncratic. Each public law organization possessed rights and bore unique responsibilities, consistent with the logic of the natural state.

The combination of the public law that creates and sustains organizations designated as legal persons and the private law rules about how persons relate to one another creates the possibility for a rule of law for organizations. The interaction of public law organizations with the rest of society is determined by both public law (to the extent that the organization possesses special privileges) and private law (to the extent that the organization functions as a legal person).

The close integration of church and state organizations under the Carolingians posed a fundamental structural problem. Charlemagne's coronation did not answer the question of whether the pope created the emperor or the emperor created the pope. Under the original institutions by which the Catholic church became the state church of the Roman Empire, there was no confusion. The Catholic church was grounded in the Roman law, particularly the law as codified by Justinian: *Ecclesia vivit iure Romano,* or "the Church lives according to the Roman law" (Ullmann, 1975, p. 54). Justinian's Code opens with the law by Theodosius the Great that made the Christian religion the sole religion of the empire. In Roman law, the

---

[32] This explanation is clearly influenced by the development of European law, and may not be applicable to other societies, but it is a starting point.

[33] These distinctions and the argument in this section are developed in Wallis, Weingast, and North (2006).

emperor was the source of law and above the law. The emperor was above the law both as an individual person and in his social persona.

In the years after the fall of the empire, the church played an increasingly central role in the provision of order. Here was the problem: the pope's legal foundation was the emperor. If the pope created an emperor and recognized him as the emperor in law, then the church's legal foundation stemmed from the emperor as the *kosmokrator* – the ruler of the world – and as the *pantokrator* – God's earthly representative. How could the pope create an emperor, when the emperor could then create a pope? Was the pope or the emperor the *pantokrator*?

Charlemagne was crowned emperor by the pope. With respect to the church, he came to the defense of the pope in his struggles with the Lombards. He promoted the construction of cathedrals and support of the monasteries. He made large grants of lands to the church and to specific churches and monasteries. He issued diplomas and charters that formally granted immunity from specific taxes and regulations to individual churches and monasteries (Ganshof, 1968, pp. 45–50). Charlemagne acted within the framework of the law accepted by him and the church. Charlemagne also encouraged other nobles to found churches and arrange for their continued support. The practice developed into the establishment of proprietary churches where the patron appointed the priest or the bishop in return for the patron's continued support.

The division of the empire in 840 and the subsequent disruption of Western Europe by another wave of Saracen and Viking incursions removed the question of papal or imperial supremacy from active consideration for a time. However, the issue did not disappear. The origin of legal systems is defining elite rights and structures, and the existing law for the alliance of church and state in medieval Europe had a fundamental contradiction at its root. After the return of peace in the eleventh century, the issue came to a head in what is known as the investiture crisis.

Gregory VII became pope in 1073. He was a Cluniac monk and a reformer dedicated to eliminating two sources of corruption within the church: simony (the sale of church offices for money) and concubinage (priests marrying or living with women) (Ullman, 1972b, pp. 129–31). As with many reformers, Pope Gregory was concerned that the church had become too intimate a part of the worldly dominant coalition. Reform of simony struck directly at the proprietary church system whereby local lords selected local bishops and priests. In 1075, Gregory declared that only the church could select bishops and priests. The proprietary system was an integral part of the basic natural state in Europe promoted by Charlemagne. Gregory's reforms had serious implications for both the structure of the church and the larger society.

At its most visible level, the investiture crisis was about patronage and the structure of patron–client networks within the dominant coalition: Would the pope or the secular lords appoint bishops, archbishops, and other members of the ecclesiastic hierarchy? Traditional views of the crisis pit the church against the state, the pope against the Holy Roman Emperor Henry VI. However, the crisis was a broader conflict within the dominant coalition.[34] The conflict was officially resolved in 1222 when a more complicated procedure for selecting and investing bishops was developed in which the church nominated, but the emperor/king approved, candidates.

The fascinating reaction came not from the secular lords, but within the church. The pope declared himself not just the Bishop of Rome, but the Vicar of Christ.[35] When the pope asserted his right to appoint bishops and archbishops he claimed a much greater position than the first bishop among essentially equal bishops; the pope claimed direct authority over all the powerful lords of the church. Because most bishops held their lands, and thus their wealth, as vassals of secular lords, the bishops had conflicting allegiances and interests. The pope's attempt to extend a more direct control over the entire administration of the church was a direct threat to the working alliance that most bishops and archbishops had with their secular lords. Papal appointment would have significantly reduced the independence of both the bishops and the kings. Papal appointment would have restructured the entire dominant coalition within Europe.

In order to function, the church needed two interdependent constitutional structures: one for vertical relationships among the levels of the church, and another for horizontal relationships at the different levels. The horizontal constitution structured ecclesiastical dioceses and other corporate entities of the church (abbeys, monasteries, universities, and orders). The constitutional relationship between a bishop and his college, for

---

[34] It was more than a conflict between a secular power and an independent church, although the emperor and pope did battle. The pope excommunicated Henry IV, which hurt Henry with his German supporters. Henry went barefoot in the snow to petition Gregory at Canossa. The pope relented and restored Henry to the communion, but in the meantime the pope had thrown his support behind another candidate for the empire. When Henry regained his position in Germany, he again opposed the pope, who again excommunicated him.

[35] The title had been claimed by kings before the crisis; after all, the king was the protector of the faithful in his kingdom.

example, affected the internal workings of the cathedral and diocese, in general when and to what extent the bishop had to seek the counsel or explicit consent of the cathedral college to make specific decisions. It also affected the external relations between the diocese and the external world in terms of the freedom and responsibilities that the bishop exercised as a representative of the diocese. Finally, it concerned the process of selecting bishops when a vacancy occurred and the exercise of a bishop's functions while the office lay vacant (Tierney, 1955, pp. 106–31).

Had the investiture crisis been solely about the appointment of bishops by the pope or the emperor, only the last aspect of the horizontal constitution would have been affected. However, lay investiture also affected the economic and social status of the bishop, because the proprietary church system gave the bishop and the diocese control over land and resources that the secular lord was pledged to honor. The constitutional structure of a bishop's diocese and its relationship to the secular authority therefore came directly into the matter.

The other major constitutional issue concerned the vertical relationship among the pope, the church in Rome (including the College of Cardinals), and the archbishops and bishops: How were the parts of the church to interact? How much independent authority did Rome have over the rest of the church? This debate occurred within the church itself, but involved the entire structure of power within European society. At issue was whether the pope as an individual had discretion over the entire church, or whether there existed some group within the church who had the power to depose a pope, as in the case of a heretical pope. The argument that the supreme authority in the church rested not with the pope, but with a general council, was put forward by theorists later known as conciliarists.[36] In terms of identity and personality, was the social persona of the pope above or below the law? Was the social persona of the bishop above or below the corporate identity of the diocese and cathedral college?

These questions were never answered definitively in the Middle Ages, although several positions were intensely debated. What emerged from the investiture crisis was a significant innovation in the church as an organization. Important steps were taken that led toward the establishment of

---

[36] One can immediately see how debates about the constitutional structure of the church played a critical role in debates about the constitutional structure of European society as a whole, and as a result, in the political theory of the Middle Ages. See Tierney (1955), Ullman (1972b, 1975), and Kantorowicz (1997[1957]) for an introduction to this enormous literature.

self-constituting bodies within the church. The corporate identity of the diocese was strengthened, although it was never completely detached from the identity of its bishop.

The innovation that changed the corporate identity of the church was a new agreement about the ownership and alienation of church property. From the thirteenth century onward, it became general practice to acknowledge that ownership of church property did not reside with the individual person of the bishop, nor did it reside with the social persona of his office. Specifically, the bishop took an oath not to alienate the fiscal resources of the church without the consent of the cathedral college. Presaging the modern debate about ownership, control, and fiduciary responsibility, the developing canon law began to identify the interests of the church as a corporate body with respect to real property. By privileging the corporate interest in property, the body of the church, the *congregatio fidelium* – the body of the faithful (as represented by the cathedral canons) – had obtained leverage with the bishop as leader and a control over the bishop as the representative of the corporation in the wider world. Formalization of the process of consent and consultation between the bishop and the cathedral chapter created an organizational structure that gave an independent life to the corporate body.[37] This structure extended further into the structure of the church when popes also began including promises not to alienate church property as part of their coronation oaths.

The seeds of an elite organization independent of the state are visible in these new arrangements: a congregation or cathedral whose corporate identity was created by and associated with the property of the corporate group. In the thirteenth century, the church was not about to set individual churches free. The bishops were too critical and powerful an element in the political balance of the age, and the dominant coalition was not about to strip the bishops of their source of rents. By identifying the corporate identity of the individual cathedral with the body of property that generated the bishop's rents, however, the law began moving the organization of the

---

[37] "The inevitable starting point for such inquiries was the accepted fact that, when a prelate appeared in a court of law on behalf of his church, it was not his own possessions that he defended; he did not possess legal *dominium* over the ecclesiastical property entrusted to his protection; his status, therefore, had to be defined as that of one who represents the interests of another party. The canonists often discussed the question where actual *dominium* did reside and usually agreed that, while God himself was the ultimate owner of all the goods of the church, *dominium* over them in an earthly sense belonged to the ecclesiastical community. Hugguccio attributed it to the *congregatio fidelium*" (Tierney, 1955, p. 118).

church out of the structure of the state. The cathedral college became, in a limited but important sense, a self-constituting corporate entity. The diocese began to take on a form of legal personality independent of the grant of such personality by a pope, bishop, or king.

Just as the Carolingians and the popes cast their agreements in the classical forms of Roman law, so too did Gregory VII claim that his policies were lawful. The investiture crisis heightened the interest of Roman and canon law within the church. Moreover, Gregory's claims against the secular lords stimulated the development of civil law studies. The new ideas about the corporate identity of the church were embedded in the public law of the church and of the state. As we consider in Chapter 5, Kantorowicz shows that the secular lords also began swearing not to alienate common property in their coronation oaths.

The next major constitutional crisis occurred in 1378. The papacy had been located in Avignon for seventy years and was in the process of returning to Rome when the reigning pope died. The College of Cardinals initially elected Italian Bartolmeo Prignano as Pope Urban VI. A few months later, the College of Cardinals declared that they had been forced to elect Urban under duress and wished to change their mind. The College then elected a French pope, Clement VII, who promptly returned his papacy to Avignon. The church was stuck in another constitutional anomaly: it had two popes.[38] Because the investiture crisis had not settled the issue of who had the ultimate power of decision over the church in a time of crisis, the pope or a general council, the church faced a serious dilemma.

The issue was not resolved until a general council, called with the assistance and influence of the French king and the Holy Roman Emperor, met at Constance in 1414. The Council of Constance affirmed that a general council had authority over the pope in critical matters and resolved that councils would thereafter meet on a regular basis. The conciliarists triumphed, and a new constitutional structure for the church was decreed. The schism produced a concrete articulation of the church as a corporate body, independent and potentially self-governing. In a crisis, ultimate authority in the church rested with the body of the faithful, the *congregatio fidelium*, as represented by a general council. The councils were composed of elites – archbishops, bishops, abbots, and cardinals – and in no sense was there representation of the typical churchgoer. However, an identifiable corporate entity had been recognized.

---

[38] For a history of the Great Schism see Ullman (1972a).

The great schism was a constitutional crisis. Although the locus of the crisis lay within the church, it spread to larger European society through the identification of factions within the church with factions in European politics. The close parallels between canon and civil law would bring the innovations of the Council of Constance to the larger structure of the dominant coalition within Europe. Churches were developing a corporate identity outside the umbrella of the state, following a principle actuated at the Council of Constance.

Ironically, the constitutional provisions of the Council of Constance, although firmly embedded in the canon law, did not prevent the resurrection of a powerful papacy. The popes soon ceased to call regular councils. The pope remained not just the head of the church, but as God's representative on earth he remained above the law of the church. The effective concentration of power in the papacy and the church in Rome would be a powerful force leading to the reformation after 1520. If the decrees of the Council of Constance were in fact canon law, then a pope above the law was unconstitutional. Resolution of this issue did not come easily to the Catholic church.

2.8 Mature Natural States: France and England in the Sixteenth, Seventeenth, and Eighteenth Centuries

The previous section focused on the church because in the legal and political environment of medieval Europe, organizational changes in the structure of the church immediately applied to the wider society. The problem of guaranteeing elite organizational independence was not solved by the church, however. These are subtle questions. For our last examples, we turn to France and England after the sixteenth century.

Increasing support for the corporate identity of elite organizations proceeded steadily in France in the seventeenth and eighteenth centuries. Few French corporations functioned like a modern business, however. Corporate identities were created for courts, municipal governments, and financial offices within the government. The corporations were central institutions in the development of the French economy and polity. France was a nation of independent and diverse geographical units, each with unique histories, institutions, and relations with the central government. The corporations provided an important element by which the dominant coalition was able to cement relationships across the nation through the explicit creation of limited entry corporate privileges. The crown created rents that could then be shared with the corporate office holders, and, in turn, the sale and taxation of corporate offices provided an important source of royal revenues. The rise of corporate groups was tied closely to the fiscal structure of the French crown.[39] In return for creating corporate privileges, the crown sold offices within the corporation to elite individuals. Office holders could sell their office or transfer it to descendants under a complicated set of rules.[40]

Cities and towns were key corporations. Bossenga's (1991) study of the city of Lille offers a window into the inner workings of corporations in the dominant coalition in seventeenth- and eighteenth-century France. In 1667, Louis XIV conquered Walloon Flanders and accepted the keys to the city of Lille. After negotiations with the city leaders, Louis confirmed the city's ancient rights and prerogatives, and signed a capitulation treaty detailing the privileges the city was to enjoy. Upon the ascension of Louis XV in 1726, Lille's privileges were again confirmed, this time after the payment of 703,300 livres, a payment the town felt was a violation of the very privileges it was purchasing. In 1774, Louis XVI ascended to the throne, and although he did not press Lille for a monetary payment, he was not much interested in swearing mutual oaths or honoring the ancient privileges of the city (Bossenga, 1991, pp. 1–4).

As with most cities, Lille possessed ancient privileges that endowed the city with a corporate identity vested in its leading citizens. Leadership was not selected by election, but by membership in the corporation of municipal government. The corporate privileges and identity were durable, but subject to the lives and personality of the city's mortal overlords. In some dimensions, the city was a perpetual organization. Membership in the municipal corporation came with a significant social persona, but the identity of the city itself as a corporate entity was independent of the individuals who made up the corporation. The city could borrow money at lower rates than the king. When under fiscal duress, the king forced loans from the city largely by offering new offices in the municipal corporation for sale. The town council was forced to buy the new offices with borrowed funds. The

---

[39] Although France often comes off badly in comparisons with Britain in the study of economic and political development in the eighteenth and nineteenth centuries, the recent research of Lamoreaux and Rosenthal (2004, 2005), and their wider research with Guinanne and Harris (2007), consistently shows that France was organizationally more sophisticated with respect to business corporations than Britain or the United States through much of the nineteenth century. We return to their work in Chapter 6.

[40] Doyle (1996), Kwass (2000), and Root (1994) explain how the French utilized corporate privileges and Collins (1995) gives a more general background on France in the early modern period.

crown also imposed financial responsibilities on the city, both in kind for expenditures on troops and barracks and in money as the town was required to remit a share of its taxes to the center (Bossenga, 1991, pp. 22–46).

Municipalities like Lille were halfway down the path to perpetual life. Some aspects of the corporate identity of Lille were perpetually lived, others were subject to the will of the king; and the entire corporation was potentially dependent on the personal goodwill of the sovereign. The recognition that Lille possessed ancient privileges was a tacit acknowledgment that Lille possessed a corporate identity of its own, an identity not directly dependent on the crown. In normal times, the city and the king would negotiate changes in their arrangements, but in times of duress the king possessed the ability to change the agreement unilaterally by manipulating several dimensions of the corporate structure, like the number of offices in the corporation. The king could and did recognize the city of Lille and its ancient privileges, but he was subject to continually changing circumstances both inside and outside of France. Thus, the king could not credibly commit to honor his agreements with Lille, and he broke them when circumstances compelled him to do so. The same conditions held for thousands of cities, towns, courts, and corporate entities throughout France. In one sense, France in 1700 was the most corporately organized society the world had ever seen to that point in history. Nevertheless, the needs of France as a mature natural state, a coalition of interests subject to forces continually in flux, prevented those corporations from taking on a perpetual life of their own that was completely independent of the crown.

The evolution of corporate entities in England followed a different path than in France. England also had a long history of chartering municipalities and, within them, craft guilds. These formal chartered entities possessed economic privileges and limited access in several different dimensions.[41] In the mid-sixteenth century, England began chartering joint-stock companies, the largest of which engaged in overseas trade and colonization. The first was the Russia Company, followed by the Virginia Company, the East Indies Company, the Massachusetts Bay Company, and the Hudson Bay Company, among many others. These were all natural state creations: organizations controlled by elites who enjoyed, in this case, the explicit legal support of

---

[41] For municipal charters and governments see Webb and Webb (1908). The interpretation of medieval craft guilds underwent steady revision in the twentieth century, beginning with the collections of charters in Ballard (1913) and Ballard and Tait (1923) through Scott (1917), Thrupp (1948), Munro (1977, 1990), Swanson (1988, 1989, 1999), and the recent work of Richardson (2001, 2004). The literature has moved from treating urban guilds as monopolies to economic entities with a much more varied set of privileges.

the state. Commercial and trading interests had always been a part of the dominant coalition in England, but in the seventeenth century, the growing importance of commerce, both domestic and international, engendered a shift of emphasis within the coalition, away from landed interests and toward commercial and manufacturing interests. These adjustments were not accomplished without bloodshed and disorder.

Two aspects of the seventeenth-century English struggles are worth noting. First, these struggles were not simply between parliament and king, as so many histories suggest, but a struggle between the elements in the dominant coalition – particularly commercial interests – which sought more power and new rules to benefit its interests. Second, many of the new rules sought by the commercial constituency were in the form of greater rights and impersonality. Paralleling the demands of earlier landed elites who sought to restrict the king's ability to adjust the dominant coalition through redistributing rights in land, the subject of the next chapter, the new commercial constituency sought greater security from arbitrary decisions by the king to adjust the coalition to changing circumstances.

Similar to France, it was difficult to institutionalize the impersonal aspects of organization. In a very important sense, aspects of the seventeenth-century claims of the king's arbitrary action parallel our observations about the Roman emperor and the popes being above the law. As heads of natural states, all of these rulers used their powers to maintain the natural state coalitions. From a modern, constitutional perspective of an open access order, this behavior looks arbitrary; but from the perspective of the natural state, this behavior is a logical consequence of natural state coalition maintenance under changing circumstances.[42]

2.9 Natural States

The progression of natural states involves increasing more complex societies, requiring increasingly complex institutions that support more complex organizations. In all natural states, economics is politics by other means: economic and political systems are closely enmeshed, along with religious, military, and educational systems. The close interrelationship between the church and the state in medieval Europe from Charlemagne through the sixteenth century illustrates the futility of drawing hard and fast

---

[42] Our perspective helps explain the behavior of the king prior to the Glorious Revolution, which North and Weingast (1989) took as given.

lines around governments in natural states and calling them the state. Power is dispersed in natural states.

We have stressed the importance of institutions that enable the organization of elites as the primary element in moving from fragile to basic to mature natural states. Organizations in fragile natural states are usually closely tied to powerful individuals. The emphasis on personal identity begins with the identification of specific individuals with specific privileges in a dominant coalition. The dominant coalition is the organization of organizations that powerful elites are associated with. As societies move toward basic natural states, these identities become less associated with specific individuals and more with social personas that become associated with powerful organizations. As societies move from fragile to basic natural states, these organizations become clearer and better defined. Organizations begin to become institutionalized. This process initially occurs simultaneously in the public and private sector; indeed, it is a primary reason that governments in most limited access societies appear so corrupt to observers from open access societies: Most important basic natural state organizations are closely associated with the (private) individual identities of the elites who inhabit them. These organizations span the boundary of public and private, personal and social.

In mature natural states, credible institutions evolve that provide organizations a measure of rule of law. As more complex organizations develop, both inside and outside of the formal government, the distinction between public and private organizations begins to appear. The first steps toward Weberian states or governments with consolidated, monopoly control over the military occur in mature natural states. Sustaining some amount of rule of law for elite organizations appears to be incredibly complicated to pull off and is the beginning of the doorstep conditions.

No teleology pushes states through the progression from fragile to basic to mature natural states. The dynamics of natural states are the dynamics of the dominant coalition, frequently renegotiating and shifting in response to changing conditions. If adjustments lead to more power and rents based on personal identity, institutions become simpler and organizations less sophisticated, and the society moves toward the fragile end of the progression of natural states. If adjustments lead to more power based on durable agreements, institutions become more complex and organizations become more sophisticated, and societies move toward the mature end of the progression. No compelling logic moves states in either direction. As governments becomes more sophisticated and institutionalized across the natural state progression, they also become more resilient to shocks. Mature natural states are more stable than basic natural states, which are more stable than fragile ones.

We define the progression of natural states – fragile, basic, mature – in terms of the organizations they can support. Paralleling this increasing organizational sophistication is an increasing institutional sophistication. Growth in state capacity is equally important as that of private organizations. Creating more sophisticated and complex organizations therefore requires that the state becomes more sophisticated and complex; it must be capable of greater tasks and a greater range of credible commitments that create durability and predictability, including the emergence of the rule of law.

Basic natural states are richer in organizations and more institutionally complex than fragile natural states. They have greater specialization and division of labor among organizations and institutions, often including organizations specializing in trade, education, religion, production (e.g., mineral extraction), and taxation. These societies often also have a range of other institutions, such as succession rules for determining the next ruler when the current one dies; institutions for dividing spoils of conquest; and perhaps an official forum in which nobles formally negotiate with the ruler, such as a cortes or parliament. Basic natural states also tend to differentiate public from private law.

Mature natural states are yet more institutionally complex than basic ones. To support a wider range of private organizations, these societies must develop institutions to better support private organizations, including a form of legal system for administration of intra- and inter-organizational contracts and more secure commitments to protect private organizations from expropriation by the state and the dominant coalition. In other words, a more complex rule of law must emerge in mature natural states. Because rule of law cannot be improved by fiat – which is too easily undone – many attempts to enhance and extend the rule of law in basic natural states fail. The institutions providing these services must also be embedded in the state and society in a way that protects them from the rearrangement of privileges among members of the dominant coalition.

One of the principal institutional issues that emerged in this chapter concerned the problem of constraining personality: putting the king under the law. At the level of societies, the head of the dominant coalition – whether the pope or the Catholic Church, the emperor of Rome, or the king of a European state – reflects the realities of these natural states: the ruler is often above the law. This allows him or her to adjust the rules, privileges, rights, and laws to suit the needs of the coalition as the fortunes of various elites rise and fall. Elites gaining power must be granted more privileges and rents while those losing power also lose privileges and rents. The ruler is not free to make these decisions at his discretion, but must instead attempt to maintain a coalition to support the natural state. Failure to do so risks coups, civil war, and other forms of disorder.

The ruler is not the only person above the law; in many natural states, this problem extends down through the institutions and organization of society. How are the powerful personalities of elites to be constrained within institutional structures that subject and commit them to the organizations of which they are a part? How the bishop is constrained by the cathedral college, the duke by his manorial court, or the corporate leader by his corporate bylaws are critical reflections of the entire social order.

The issue of constraining the ruler plagued the West for two millennia. A major feature of this chapter's cases involved the emergence of a dual identity of the leader – the personal and the social identity – whereby the social identity began to embody a series of duties and constraints for the ruler (Kantorowicz, 1997[1957]). We return to this issue on several occasions in later chapters.

APPENDIX: SKELETAL EVIDENCE AND EMPIRICAL RESULTS

Richard Steckel and Jerome Rose invited a large group of physical anthropologists, economic historians, demographers, and medical historians to document and analyze the history of health in the Western hemisphere using data from archaeological skeletons (Steckel and Rose, 2002). Anthropologists contributed data on several skeletal indicators of health for individuals who had lived at sites scattered from South America to southern Canada. The combined data set includes 12,520 skeletons from 65 localities representing populations who lived from 4,500 B.C.E. to the early

Table 2.1. *Expected probabilities of violent trauma*

Group	Expected probability (%)	% male	Sample size
Pre-Columbian, hunter–gatherer	13.39	47.13	715
Pre-Columbian, city	2.70	48.63	183
Early post-Columbian, village	9.48	44.43	673
European-American, city	7.25	59.88	496
African-American, city	18.53	49.90	511

Source: Western Hemisphere database (Steckel and Rose, 2002).

twentieth century. Some sites were deleted from the statistical analysis and some skeletons lacked estimates of age or did not have the requisite bones for study of trauma.

Table 2.1 shows estimates of the incidence of violent trauma based on evidence of head or weapon trauma in a sample of 3,431 adult Native Americans. The estimates controlled for age, elevation of the site, and time period, as well as whether the skeleton was located in a mobile group, village, or city (Steckel and Wallis, 2006). Surprisingly, both the lowest and highest rates occurred in urban areas, natives who lived in pre-Columbian cities versus blacks who lived in nineteenth century cities. Violence in pre-Columbian hunter-gatherers was nearly twice that of European Americans. Trauma was lower among village tribes in the early post-Columbian period, and lowest in the pre-Columbian cities (although) the somewhat low proportion of males among the dead suggests the level may be underestimated by burial of men in other locations). The skeletal evidence is clear: the shift from hunting-gathering societies to sedentary urban societies was accompanied by a marked reduction in the level of human induced violence.

THREE

The Natural State Applied

English Land Law

3.1 Introduction

The logic of the natural state draws attention to the way the dominant coalition manipulates the economy to provide incentives for powerful individuals not to use violence. Land is the primary asset in agrarian societies. Access, use, and the ability to derive income from land therefore provide a rich set of tools with which to structure a dominant coalition and its relationship to the wider economy. As De Soto (1989, 2000) and the larger development literature emphasize, establishing well-defined and easily transferrable property rights to land remains a significant problem in many parts of the world today.[1]

If access to land plays a role in balancing interests within a dominant coalition, then there are implications for the clarity of property rights with respect to land in developing societies. Clear property rights make land more valuable, but they may also reduce the ability to use land as a tool to structure elite relationships in natural states. As a result, elites have conflicting interests in making land rights more secure. In fragile natural

---

[1] The export of English land law to the American colonies is a centerpiece of most economic histories of the New World. English land law provided an institutional and legal basis for a relatively equal distribution of freehold land in the American colonies, while Spanish and Portuguese land law led to the creation of large estates and unequal distribution of land throughout what would become Latin America. Hughes (1976, 1977) emphasized the importance of the English inheritance for American development. North (1988) and North, Summerhill, and Weingast (2000) emphasized the contrasting institutions brought from metropole to colonies in British North America versus Spanish America. Acemoglu, Johnson, and Robinson (2001, 2002, 2005), La Porta et al. (1998), Glaeser and Shleifer (2002), and Engerman and Sokoloff (2005) all studied the importance of initial conditions, including the distribution of land and land law, and adoption of national legal systems for subsequent growth and development.

states, the flexible redistribution of landownership and control can serve as a tool to balance interests within the coalition, especially as the balance of power shifts among prominent members. In basic natural states, landownership typically stabilizes, but control of land remains within the direct framework of the state. In mature natural states, landownership may move beyond the direct control of the state and perhaps become truly impersonal.

The development of English land law has long been central to English political history, the development of the legal system, and the rule of law. By placing the institutions regulating the ownership, use, and transfer of land in the context of governance structures, we track how the English utilized control of land to stabilize their dominant coalition and how, over time, more sophisticated institutions and organizations emerged with respect to land. This process allows us to trace the emergence of impersonal elite rights and exchange in land, including aspects of the rule of law. Land is not the only development that mattered in English history, and we are not claiming that land law explains all of English development. Yet the importance of land in the English feudal system, where political relationships were tied to landownership and use, places land law at the core of English political history.

The idea that secure ownership of land provided the basis for stable political and constitutional development over the centuries between the Norman Conquest in 1066 and the Glorious Revolution of 1688 is a staple element of traditional Whig history. Whig history interprets English history as the natural and inevitable development of a constitutional structure capable of providing limited government and, ultimately, open access. In his classic book *The Whig Interpretation of History*, Herbert Butterfield (1965[1931]) singled out the teleological implications of nineteenth-century Whig historians who portrayed English development as the inevitable triumph of rights over tyranny and despotism. In the late nineteenth century, Whig historians coined the term *bastard feudalism* to describe political developments where personal and monetary ties grew up to hold together the fabric of aristocratic social relations, including the mobilization of armies. Bastard feudalism's rise in the thirteenth and fourteenth centuries constituted the most significant deviation from the Whig path, when political power and the interaction of the crown and aristocracy began to be governed by relationships that were not mediated by control of land.

The historical chronology, the evolution of the land law, and the history of bastard feudalism fit neatly into the framework of the natural state and the movement from a fragile, basic, to mature natural state at various points in its history. Property rights in land did become more secure in England, and for most people they were very secure. However, for the most powerful individuals, ownership and tenure in land remained subject to conflicts within the dominant coalition. Without the Whig teleology, and by looking deeper into the nature of property rights in land, the structure of institutions and organizations governing land in England falls into periods corresponding to the three types of natural states.

3.2 Chronology

The invasion of England by William the Conqueror in 1066 created an unusual political situation for Europe at the time: a geographically integrated political entity with military control vested in one easily identifiable group, the Normans. Faced with the need to quarter his army and maintain control of the population, William and his staff created a feudal political system in which major political and military figures held land directly from the king; in return, they owed knight-service, homage, and fealty to the king as their personal lord. By 1086, there were roughly fifteen hundred such tenants in chief.[2]

Distribution of land within the powerful elements of William's ruling coalition was essential to the success of the new government. The initial distribution of ownership and tenure did not require evicting the land's existing occupants. New landlords were simply installed over the existing structure, and they, in turn, were owed service, homage, and fealty by their tenants (Simpson, 1986, p. 5). Powerful lords subinfeudated their lands; that is, they made new feudal grants to lesser lords and knights who owed the greater lord military service, homage, and fealty.[3] The basic unit of governance and of landholding was known as a *manor*. Manors were often the holdings of individual knights, but manors could be held directly by tenants in chief or the king himself. Manorial land was worked directly by the lord using wage or unfree labor on his own land, his demense, or by freeholders and by villeins (a type of unfree labor) on their own plots of land held of the local lord. Powerful lords controlled multiple manors,

---

[2] "This triumph of order was made possible by the Conquest, and by the high degree of administrative efficiency attained by King William's staff." Simpson (1986), p. 3–4.

[3] Appendix I to this chapter contains a glossary of technical terms involving land use. In addition to the sources cited in the notes and text that follow, we consulted Bean (1989), Bellamy (1973), Bernard (1985), Elton (1977, 1991), Gray (1963), Habbakuk (1958), John (1960), Milsom (2003), Pollock and Maitland (1899), Stenton (1963[1932]), Thorne (1959), Vinogradoff (1908), and Waugh (1986).

as many as one hundred. Local lords and knights held their manors from more powerful lords.

Initially, ownership of land reverted back to the king on the death of a tenant. The logic for the arrangement was unimpeachable: the king required powerful and capable military tenants (as did the major lords). The personal identity, individual persona, of powerful lords mattered to the king. As long as armies were raised through feudal levies, the king had to have the power to place able commanders on major landholdings. Therefore, the grant of land from the king to a military retainer was a personal one. In knight's or military tenures, the tenant held the land in return for providing military service. The children of existing commanders might be capable, but perhaps not. Because major lords fulfilled their obligations to the king by raising their own armies, secured by grants of land, the logic of personal relationships held throughout the land system: granting land to a militarily ineffective tenant weakened the coalition (Simpson, 1986, p. 16–17). The personal and military nature of the obligations surrounding landownership led to the security of any specific lord's property depending on his favor with the king and his place within the coalition. Alliances and power within the coalition were closely related to landholdings.

In the early days after the Conquest, England was a fragile natural state. Property rights in land were only secure for those closely connected to the dominant coalition, and even for them rights were not secure enough to ensure a person's ability to determine who would enjoy his land after his death. Personal relationships and identity within the dominant coalition were closely associated with the ownership and use of land. The rents from landownership were deliberately limited to a small group.

The second stage in land law development began with the formalization of heritability. Powerful members of the coalition quickly sought the ability to confer the ownership of their lands on their heirs. The Coronation Charter of Henry I in 1100 recognized, in principle, the idea that tenants in chief should not have to buy back their lands from the king, but could enter into them on the payment of a just and lawful relief.[4] Over the course of

---

[4] Simpson (1986, p. 17), describes the movement from fragile to basic natural state arrangements with respect to land: "Immediately following the Conquest, the principle of heritability, especially in the case of land held by military tenure, was not established. To allow an heir to inherit military lands irrespective of his ability as a knight was open to obvious objection, so we find that the military tenant is originally thought of as having something in the nature of a life interest only, his heir having, at best, a strong claim to succeed him. This claim, if it was recognized, could only be exercised if he were willing to buy back the land from the lord for a large payment. However, Henry I in his coronation charter

the twelfth century, the presumptive right of the legal male heir to enter immediately "into such seisin as his father had on the day that he died . . . " was established.[5] The idea that the male heir would eventually inherit his father's land, even though the king or landlord would take the land in hand for a time after the father's death, consolidated through the twelfth century. The Coronation Charter settled the idea of inheritance, but not the issue of when the heir actually became seised of his title. By the end of the twelfth century, it had been established that the heir possessed his title immediately upon the death of his ancestor.

However, the security of immediate inheritance did not eliminate the privileges possessed by a lord on the death of a tenant. The tenant was still required to pay relief to the lord, and if the heir was a minor, the lord was entitled to take the child as his ward and to administer the lands of the ward until the child reached the age of majority. The nominal monetary amounts to be paid for relief eventually became fixed for barons in the Charter of 1215. The unpredictable element in this wardship procedure was the return of control over the land to the lord during the minority of the legitimate heir. Because money reliefs were fixed in nominal monetary terms, they declined in value over time. However, the incidents of wardship were fixed in the use of the land, so as land increased in value (and price) wardships increased in value commensurately. Lords were very jealous of the rights of wardship and relief.

Inheritance differed for the tenants in chief in a significant way: the king retained the right to take back possession of their lands into his hands until all of the reliefs and fines were paid by the heir. Unlike lesser individuals, the tenants in chief did not enter into legal title to their property immediately upon the death of their ancestor (Clanchy, 1965, pp. 107–9; Milsom, 1976, pp. 162–3). When all the requirements were fulfilled, the king's ministers delivered the land to the legal heir, a process called *livery*. If the heir was under age, the king administered a wardship. These feudal incidents remained important to the king and tenants in chief into the seventeenth century.

Securing the process of inheritance raised other issues. Land could be inherited but land could not be devised by will. Landowners could not divide

---

(1100) enunciated the rule that the heir need not buy back the land, but take it up on payment of just and lawful relief, and this amounts to recognition of the right of the heir to inherit, or perhaps to be regranted the lands. Much difficulty was experienced in fixing an appropriate sum."

[5] We discuss seisin in greater detail in the next section. In brief, seisin is the person in physical possession of the land, but in a feudal context, this is not as simple as it seems.

their land among their children or make bequests of land at their death. A formal set of rules governed inheritance. In most English jurisdictions, land went first to the direct lineal male descendant, primogeniture, and then direct female descendants. If there were no lineal descendants (children or grandchildren), land then passed through collateral lines (again with a preference for male over female lines). Landowners could divide land between their heirs during their lifetimes by gift or sale, but they could not at death. Although inheritance was clear in principle, in practice who inherited land could be extremely complicated when collateral descent was involved.

Land could initially be transferred between individuals by two methods, subinfeudation and alienation. First, an existing tenant or lord could create new tenants by devising new feudal arrangements (subinfeudation). Because of subinfeudation, most large landholders in England were simultaneously tenants and lords and, very important for understanding how land law worked, most pieces of land had multiple layers of owner/tenants. Second, a tenant could alienate land to a new tenant who would assume the obligations of service and incidents of the old tenant. Typically, this was done with the permission of his lord.[6] The Act of *Quia Emptores* in 1290 halted subinfeudation and the multiplication of tenures. The act forbade further subinfeudation, but allowed for the alienability of tenures held in *fee simple* (*feodo simpliciter*) without permission of the lord. The tenure of *fee simple* in medieval England was not the same as *fee simple* tenure in the modern United States. *Fee simple* land was alienable and not encumbered by conditions. Encumbered land was held in *fee tail. Fee simple* and *fee tail* are discussed at greater length later. The act guaranteed the interests of the lord by ensuring that the new tenant "shall be forthwith charged with the services for so much as pertaineth or ought to pertain to the said chief lord . . . "[7] *Fee simple* became the prominent form of land tenure for freehold land. Feudal incidents could still apply to land held in *fee simple* (Simpson, 1986, p. 56; see also p. 13). Land held under fixed and certain incidents, often a monetary payment, was held in *free and common socage.*

---

[6] "In Glanville's time [thirteenth century] it is doubtful whether a tenant was entitled to alienate his holding without the consent of his lord; to be on the safe side it was wise to secure the lord's consent to a gift, but it was not perhaps essential if the gift was a reasonable one which did not seriously affect the lord's interest" (Simpson 1986, p. 54). In the twenty-first-century usage, alienation refers to sale. In medieval England, all land transfers used the language of "gifts," so the seller was the "donor" and the buyer the "donee." This was true initially whether the gift involved compensation or not.

[7] Digby (1897), pp. 236–8. Digby provides the original Latin text of the land laws and judicial decisions regarding land, as well as English translations.

Another important distinction was drawn between land held in free and unfree tenures. Freehold land was held in feudal or seignorial tenures where a direct relationship existed between the lord and the tenant – the kind of relationship that justified wardship on the part of the lord to protect his interests in the land and the interests of an heir in his minority. Unfree tenure, typically *villeinage*, applied to tenures where the tenant was bound to the lord's service. The distinction between freeholds and unfreeholds (which later evolved into copyholds) was clear in the legal system. Land held in freehold was protected against the actions of manorial courts held by local lords and its landholders had access to the royal courts. Landowners who held in an unfree tenure or copyhold did not enjoy any protection in the royal courts until the late fifteenth and early sixteenth centuries.[8]

Remember that in the English system of land tenure multiple individuals held interests in the same piece of land. At the highest tenure levels, the tenants in chief held all their lands in freehold, although most of their lands were held in knight's or other military tenures. Many of the tenants of the tenants in chief also held land in freehold tenure. All of these individuals had recourse to the royal courts to resolve disputes over land. At the bottom of the social ladder, the villeins and copyholders did not have access to the royal courts. They could look for justice with respect to landholding only in the manorial courts of the lords from whom they held their lands.[9]

By the late twelfth or early thirteenth century, English land law had developed characteristics of a basic natural state. At the top of the landholding structure were a small number of landholders who held large (acreage) holdings in freehold tenures, followed by a slightly larger number of landholders who held smaller but still substantial (acreage) holdings. Below the major and minor lords was a significantly larger group of freeholders and yeomen holding in freehold. At the bottom were a very large numerical group of individuals with very small (acreage) holdings and tenuous ownership or no landholdings at all. A dual legal system operated where powerful freeholders could contend for land, protect their property, or attempt to

---

[8] The distinction between freehold and copyhold rights was often not clear on the ground. At the level of individual manors, who owed what services to the lord and who had what rights to which pieces of land became jumbled over time. For the confusing attempts to formally define freehold see Simpson (1986, pp. 72–4); Milsom (1969, pp. 12, 22, and 132–6); and Digby (1897, pp. 48–52, 136–57, and 161–74). For villeinage in general see Vinogradoff (1905, 1923).

[9] It is not clear that tenants invariably enjoyed less security in manorial courts. Local lords had incentives to create clear and secure rights for their tenants as well, and manorial courts often adopted rules and procedures of the royal courts.

seize others' property by legal maneuver in the royal courts; the remainder of the population possessed more ambiguous and limited ownership enforceable only in customary manorial courts.

The large landholders dominated both the society and the government. This dominance rested firmly on their control of land. The significant organizations of production, governance, and salvation were all tied to the feudal manor; control over land amounted to control over manors, and control over manors amounted to control over government. Because of the decentralized nature of the royal administration in medieval England, most of the day-to-day functions of government were carried out in local administrations, initially by justices of the peace or sheriffs, as well as by the officials of the manorial courts and the manors themselves. Reflecting the definition of a basic natural state, control over the fundamental organizations of English society was all vested within the structure of the state. The state in England, however, extended well beyond the formal bureaucratic institutions of royal authority.

The third stage in land law development began in the late fifteenth century and extended through to 1660. The signal change was the extension of title protection to copyholders in the royal courts. Traditionally, when an unfree tenant desired to sell his interest in land to another, he needed his lord's permission. The old tenant submitted his land to the lord, who then admitted the new tenant. A "copy" of the agreement was kept on the rolls of the local manorial court, thus copyhold (Simpson, 1986, p. 170). The lord remained the freeholder of the land; the lord was seised in his title. Copyholders did not own a freehold, and so even though the copyholder possessed secure ownership, he did not enjoy the ability to protect his title in the royal courts.

This began changing at the end of the fifteenth century when a new way of proving title developed in the royal courts. A *termor* was a tenant for a term of years. Even if the termor was a free man, his land tenure was not as a freeholder, and thus he did not have recourse to the royal courts to defend his property. Trespass, however, was a charge against the peace of the king and could be brought as a civil action by any individual in the royal courts. The use of trespass to establish title opened the door for copyholders to use the crown courts to protect their claims on land. By 1467, the common law courts put forth the idea that trespass could be used to protect the rights of copyholders against overly aggressive landlords (Simpson, 1986, p. 162). In 1499, the King's Bench held in *Gernes v. Smyth* that termors could bring the action of *eiectio firmae*, a writ of trespass, to recover his "term"; that is to eject the trespasser and recover the use of his land. The question of whether trespass had occurred hinged in part on the question of title: courts had to decide if the termor had better title than the trespasser. Because the termor had a lease, not a freehold title, the court's decision depended on the quality of the landlord's title because it was the lord who was seised in his title. If the lord's title was better than the trespasser's title, the trespasser was ejected from the land.

Thus, the use of ejectment to determine title developed over the sixteenth century. By the early seventeenth century, the rules for such cases were firmly established, and ejectment became the preferred way of proving title allowing copyholders to obtain relatively secure title defensible in the royal courts. There were still elements of freehold tenure they did not possess; the lord was still the freeholder and in most cases retained residual rights to mines, minerals, and timber and the right to vote associated with the land (Simpson, 1986, pp. 168–9). Nonetheless, the security and alienability of rights in English law had improved markedly over this period.

The second major change over the sixteenth century was the development of ways to avoid duties and obligations to lords on the death of a tenant. As early as the fifteenth century, the creation of the "use" was a way to evade the death duty obligations of the land laws. In the early sixteenth century, the Tudor kings attempted to stamp the evasions out. What happened instead was the establishment of the evasion as institutional elements in English law.

The most common way of getting around obligations at the time of death and allocating land among one's heirs was the "use."[10] Suppose A held land in *fee simple* from L, the lord. A could convey the land to B to the use of A for his life and then to the use of C (A's heir) and to C's heirs and assigns. B became the trustee and held the title, but A had the use of the land. When A died, the use of the property went to C, without any incidents payable on A's death going to L. Moreover, even if C was a minor when A died, there was no wardship. By naming a suitable number of people trustees and renewing their numbers periodically, it was possible to devise property according to the wishes of the owner, and to do so in a way that escaped incidents to the landlord on the death of a tenant. The "trust" created by uses were upheld and enforced by the Chancery courts in equity rather than the common law courts. The trust was a flexible institutional form. Significantly, the trust was an early form of organization that had private law roots; individuals could form trusts at will.[11]

---

[10] The following example is from Simpson (1986), p. 175.

[11] After it was developed to serve in land law, the trust formed the seed that would grow into a form of perpetually lived business organization outside the direct control of the state,

The use denied landlords wardship and other feudal incidents, and in 1536 parliament passed two pieces of legislation, the Statute of Uses and the Statute of Enrolments, to close off the loophole (Simpson, 1986, pp. 171–207). The intention of the statutes was to vest ownership of the legal estate of the land deeded for use with the grantor, the *cestui que use*, or A in our example. The Statute of Enrolments required that such transfers be recorded. Because of a technicality in the way the statute was drawn, however, it was possible and perfectly legal for a conveyance of interest in land to be made in a way that did not fall under the requirements of the Statute of Enrolments. These secret conveyances defeated the Statute of Enrolments and vitiated the intent of the Statute of Uses (Simpson, 1986 pp. 188–90).

In 1540, Henry VIII bowed to the inevitable and consented to the Statute of Wills, which allowed landowners to devise by will two-thirds of their land held in knight-service and all of their land held in socage.[12] Henry did not lose by the concession, however, because those using the ability to devise by will under the statute still owed feudal dues. The process of collecting and administering these dues was formalized by the creation of the Court of Wards and Liveries, which Henry created in 1540 as well.[13] Disputes over trusts were adjudicated in the Chancery's courts. For this reason, a trust was more likely to be established when large and valuable landholdings were at stake. For that same reason, the lawyers continued to apply their ingenuity to the establishment and defense of trusts. The legal principles with respect to uses and trusts were clear and settled by the early seventeenth century. In the course of the English Civil War (1641–49) and Restoration (1660), the crown and parliament reached a series of agreements that effectively eliminated wardship and similar feudal incidents by abolishing military and knight's tenures and restricting tenants in chief to the tenure of free and common socage.

As late as the early seventeenth century, ownership of land in England remained heavily skewed toward the powerful nobility and major gentry, but the law under which the land was held had become characteristic of a mature natural state. Rule of law for elites had developed with an extensive set of

---

a subject we return to in Chapter 6 (Maitland, 2003). Trusts develop out of the use and appear as a formal legal mechanism in the seventeenth century.

[12] Socage and free and common socage are defined and discussed in the next section.

[13] Simpson (1986, p. 191–2); Bell (1953, pp. 13–15). As Bell makes clear, Henry VII initiated a policy of extracting as much as possible from wardships and his son Henry VIII was continuing the policy of his father. The crown earned revenue from selling wardships rather than administering the land directly.

institutions governing, regulating, and enforcing property rights in land capable of supporting impersonal exchange among elites. The institution of the use to devise land by will and avoid feudal incidents blossomed into the trust, a nascent form of perpetually lived organization that would play a major role in later developments. Landownership moved further outside the direct orbit of the state and became steadily more impersonal. Over the course of the seventeenth century, a mature natural state emerged in England. To understand why, we briefly turn to the law and then to politics.

3.3 The Courts, Legal Concepts, and the Law of Property

As the saying goes, possession is nine-tenths of the law. In England, ownership of land was rooted in possession of land and possession was "seisin": "the person seised of land was simply the person in obvious occupation, the person 'sitting' on the land" (Simpson, 1986, p. 40). The problem with simple notions of occupation or possession in a feudal system is that multiple individuals have claims over the land. Who is seised of what? Milsom argues that the original use of seisin was as a verb to indicate what the lord did when he granted land to an individual: "A tenement is not a lawyer's long word for a parcel of land, but what a tenant holds of a lord for service. A tenant is not just one physically in possession but one who has been seised by the lord. The lord seises the tenant of his tenament... " (1976, pp. 39–40). Nevertheless, to be seised gradually became a condition rather than an action. To be seised of land, therefore had elements of both proprietary interest and of possessory fact, but far from simple elements. A landlord could be seised in his title to freehold land even if he let it to a tenant for years; the tenant for years was not seised of the land, even though the tenant physically possessed the land. To be disseised, however, was to suffer displacement by the entrance of an intruder onto your land. The simple physical presence of an intruder on land established the intruder's presumptive claim to seisin, because the intruder established his seisin as soon as he came into possession of the land.

Actions in the courts to establish title appear in the earliest years after the Conquest.[14] An early decision held that, according to the custom of the realm, no man needs answer in any court for his freehold land unless commanded to do so by the king's writ. Glanvill, writing around 1187–9, described that "When anyone claims to hold of another by free service and

---

[14] For an introduction to the English courts and the actions relating to land see Maitland (1968).

free tenement or service, he may not implead [sue] the tenant about it without a writ from the lord king or his justices. Therefore he shall have a writ of right, directed to the lord of whom he claims to hold" (Clanchy, XII, 2, 1965, p. 137). A *writ* was a judicial order by the king that directed the king's agent to investigate the claim of a freeholder and to protect his property in the royal courts. The writ of right depended on the proof of title by the oldest and best evidence of seisin, and "the mode of trial appropriate to the Writ of Right has been trial by battle."[15]

An alternative method had been introduced by the mid-twelfth century: the *Assize of Novel Disseisin*. In novel disseisin, a landowner could claim that he had been disseised of his property by the entry of a disseissor. In novel disseisin the issue was not over the ultimate best title to the land (as in a writ of right), but the seisin of the displaced owner with respect to the seisin of the disseissor. The displaced owner (the disseisee) must complain to the court in a timely manner; thus it must be a new or "novel" disseisin. The court would immediately put the disseisee back into possession of the land if a jury of twelve good and lawful men of the neighborhood – the assize – answers yes to the question was the disseisee unjustly put out of his tenement.

The advantages of novel disseisin to parties in dispute were readily apparent. The process was much quicker than a writ of right. By the end of the twelfth century, novel disseisin was widely used to establish and defend title to land (see Maitland, 1968; Simpson, 1986). The structure of the writ placed a great deal of weight on seisin, and the overlapping claims of lords and tenants required a new sophistication in the concept. By the time of Bracton, 1220–30, it was well understood that the lord and the tenant were both seised of property, but that the property that each possessed was different. The lord owns the seignory and the tenant the land itself, so their claims to seisin were not in conflict.

Eventually, seisin in intangible property was recognized. The delineation of rights through the concept of seisin and the articulation and separation of elements of those rights, including rights to incorporeal things and obligations, were fundamental achievements of English land law. However, we must keep in mind that, even as these legal concepts were crystallizing in the twelfth and thirteenth centuries, the concepts were serving a relatively small set of elite landholders whose access to courts was defined by their freehold and social status. These elites did not seek to implement the ideal

---

[15] Maitland (1963[1908]), p. 21. By the late twelfth century few battles were actually fought.

system of property rights sought by twenty-first-century economists, but ones that served their ends and that solved their immediate problems. The next question before them was the nature of alienability.

As noted earlier, the language of land transfers utilized the terms of gift and transfers, and all alienations of land were treated as gifts and transfers. During the thirteenth century, alienability of land took two distinct courses: with or without conditions. Two pieces of parliamentary legislation implemented the distinction: *De Donis Conditionalibus* (*De Donis*) in 1285 governed alienation with conditions and regulated the fee tail (*entail*), and *Quia Emptores* in 1290 governed alienation without conditions and regularized the notion of fee simple and, eventually, free and common socage.

Traditional Whig history portrays the common law courts as always on the side of greater alienability, of supporting a market for land through the creation of clear and transferable titles to land. However, the powerful interests dominating England saw advantages in greater alienability when it suited them and, at other times, the advantages of tying up land so that alienability was virtually impossible. *De Donis* dealt with cases where land was given or sold conditionally; for example, a parent gifting land jointly to a son, his newly married wife, and their heirs with the right of reversion to the person donating (selling) the land if there was no male issue from the marriage (see Digby, 1897, pp. 222–30). The condition requiring a male heir meant the grant was not a grant in fee simple because not all of the fee had been granted: something had been retained by the grantee (Dibgy, 1897, pp. 224–5).

In contrast to fee tail, land held in fee simple was heritable and alienable. Once land is granted in fee simple, "no further limitation of the estate is possible, for the grantor has alienated his whole interest, which is eternity" (Simpson, 1986, p. 89). After *Quia Emptores* in 1290, the conditions under which unconditional alienability of fee simple occurred were clear. Eventually, the tenure of free and common socage would enable alienation of land without any continuing obligation of feudal service on the part of the buyer.[16]

---

[16] " ... today it is still the law that all land must be 'held', and since it must be held by some tenure we say it is held in free and common socage. This is only another way of saying that it is just held, for socage which is free (of services) and common (in the sense of special customary incidents), had no positive characteristics" Simpson (1986, p. 13). As Hughes (1977) stresses, the fact that the original Virginia Company charter issued in 1606 limited land tenure in Virginia to free and common socage had enormous implications for the subsequent development of the American colonies. The English tenure of free and common socage is what Americans today call "fee simple." American fee simple, therefore, differs from medieval English fee simple.

We are accustomed to think of fee tail (*entail*) as a method by which descent of land was restricted to family lines. Although this was certainly a way in which fee tail could be used, fee tail was a much broader category of tenure and contract in which not all of the simple fee was transferred to the tenant. Any conditionality put the tenant in the position of holding in fee tail. What complicated fee tail was the ability of the grantor to retain reversionary rights. Before *De Donis* reversionary rights existed, but they could not be sold or transferred to another individual because they were merely possible rights. After the statute, it was possible to create reversionary rights and then alienate the reversionary rights (Digby, 1897, pp. 225–6). *De Donis* and the subsequent interpretations of the statute as authorizing conditional grants of land in perpetuity made it possible to write much more complicated contracts for landownership.

Neither *De Donis* nor *Quia Emptores* were imposed on an unwilling nobility by an overreaching monarch. Both acts – and the tenures they modified – were the result of interests operating with the natural state's dominant coalition. Powerful lords in England wanted the opportunity to alienate land in a way that created free and clear title, and they wanted a way to alienate land with complicated conditions. The acts established the means of doing both.

English land law's deceptively simple structure hid an enormous complexity. Land law was secure and followed a rule of law: rules that were clear. However, the combination of inheritance rules that mandated transmission of land through collateral lines and the possibility of creating conditional grants and sale of land meant that the security of an individual title was a relative concept. A grant of land conditional on the issue of a male heir with the right of reversion might pass steadily for generations until the lack of an appropriate heir suddenly caused the land to revert, perhaps back to a long-dead individual decades or centuries removed from the present. Conditions need not be limited to male heirs, and the confusion caused by collateral inheritance in the closely interbred English aristocracy created opportunities for mischief.

At the same time, never forgetting that multiple individuals had claims to most land in Britain, the actual occupiers of land could enjoy relatively secure title that they could pass on to their heirs (under the limitation of the inheritance law). Most of the mischief was located at the higher levels of English society, where the aristocracy was seised in title not to the physical possession of land, but to the right to derive a stream of rent from the land's tenants. The conflicts over higher level titles to land – land wars – were a pervasive element of bastard feudalism.

The last important legal change in the shape of land tenures was finalized in the Statute Abolishing Tenures in 1660, whose formal title was "An Act taking away the Court of Wards and Liveries, and Tenure in Capite, and by Knight-Service, and Purveyance, and for settling a Revenue upon his Majesty in lieu thereof" (Digby, 1897, pp. 396–400). Remember that the king had not surrendered his right to take in his hand the lands of tenants in chief (*tenants in capite*) on the death of a tenant, although that right had been extinguished for other lords in the twelfth century. The 1660 statute required that all tenures of military service or of knight's service be converted into free and common socage; it abolished the Court of Wards and Liveries; and it extinguished the ability of the king to take land into his hands. The 1660 act confirmed earlier acts in 1645 and 1656, following efforts to abolish feudal dues and compensating the crown with other revenues that date to as early as 1612.

The changes begun in the early seventeenth century and formalized in 1660 brought the land law to a form where institutions characteristic of a mature natural state were possible. Almost all freehold tenures of land had been converted to fee simple or to free and common socage. Landownership of the basic units of social and economic organization, the manor, was now subject to the impersonal forces of alienation and sale within the elite. Ownership of large landholdings was still critical to membership in the dominant coalition. The largest landowners were not only the most powerful politically but they were also the most likely to structure and develop their own trusts, organizations supported by the Chancery Courts but beyond the direct and immediate reach of the state. In order to understand the implications of these changes, we need to turn our attention to politics.

3.4 Bastard Feudalism

Over time, the land law changed the legal characteristics of ownership, alienation, and inheritance. Given the importance of land in English society, we should be able to see how the allocation of land and the income from land affected and reflected power within the dominant coalition. First we consider the categories into which the landowners can be placed, and then we review the evidence on their holdings and their survival.

The aristocracy divided into two main categories. The nobility was required by their station and title to give their counsel to the king when requested. Those who became the peers of the realm were always a small number:

Between 1150 and 1350 the nobility were tenants-in-chief of the crown: either earls, never much more than a dozen in total, or the barons (or leading men), who numbered two hundred or more and varied greatly in wealth. This state of affairs was of course a continuation of conditions which had existed since 1066. Not very different were the leading mesne tenants or honorial barons. After 1350 the nobility became ever more select and stratified. Some particularly well-endowed barons were grouped with the earls rather than the rest even in the late twelfth century. Whilst all the barons were noble and eligible to attend parliament as peers under Edward I (1272–1307), in practice many were seldom or never summoned and only a hundred at anyone time. By 1388 a mere 48 barons had become parliamentary peers, who had established a hereditary right to a summons, and the rest were shut out (Hicks, 1995, p. 5).

The *gentry* were the nonnoble part of the aristocracy. The term "gentry" did not exist in 1150, but by 1413 it had come into common use and was formally recognized. The gentry were the most numerous of the aristocracy. The distinction between the nobility and gentry is often overdrawn (Hicks, 1995, pp. 7–8). Gentry and nobles came from the same families, were raised and educated in the same manner, shared the same expectations, but some were lucky and some were not. The lucky included first-born males or the younger brother of an older brother who died before having a son. Those gentry with an ennobled, childless rich uncle were lucky. Luck was not everything; some gentry attained their nobility through skill, valor, or service. The difference between the nobility and gentry, the greater and lesser aristocracy, and that between the greater and lesser landowners all parallel one another. At certain times and places, as when a parliament was called, the distinctions had real meaning. However, the boundary between the two groups was fluid.

How much land did the aristocracy own? The problem of landownership and use presents a conundrum in English history. The finely developed sense of seisin and of proprietary and possessory rights is part of the problem. Most parcels of land in England between the twelfth and seventeenth centuries were simultaneously owned by more than one person. Seisin of title could be held by multiple individuals with different claims to use or derive income from land. Land could be farmed by villeins, freemen, villeins working on the lord's demense, or wage labor working on copyhold, freehold, or demense lands. Land could be farmed by a termor or a leasee, operating on a long- or short-term lease. Disentangling who owned and who operated the land is not easy.

We describe how the details of landownership can be estimated in the appendix to this chapter. Because of the uncertainty about exactly who owned and used land at any particular point in time, none of the estimates bears up under the weight of a detailed questioning. Nonetheless, the research supports the following conclusions:

- A small number of powerful noble individuals, who were both large landowners and politically important counselors of the king through the House of Lords and in council, numbering somewhere between fifty and two hundred, controlled roughly 20 percent of the land and a similar share of income.
- A group of powerful gentry, the greater knights if you will, numbering somewhere between two hundred and two thousand, controlled substantial amounts of land, but may or may not have been called to parliament. Later, they were likely to have been elected to serve in the Commons. Whether they controlled more or less land and income as a class than the magnates is not clear, and their relationship to the nobility varied over time.
- A third group of lesser gentry, numbering between five thousand and eight thousand, enjoyed landholdings and income far above the lot of commoners, but substantially below the holdings and income of the greater lords.

The population of England between 1200 and 1600 ranged between 2.5 and 6 million, peaking in the early fourteenth century before the Black Plague, representing between roughly 500,000 and 1,200,000 families.[17] The 6,000 to 10,000 families of nobles and gentry represented approximately .5 to 1 percent of all the families in England, a limited access elite indeed. Appendix Table 3.1 gives Cooper's estimates of landholding by class in 1436. The three groups together held roughly 45 percent of the land, the king another 5 percent and the church an additional 20 percent. In all a very small group in the population held claims to 70 percent or more of the land in England. This does not mean that the other 99 percent of the population was crowded on to 30 percent of the land, but that income and privileges associated with landholding in England were concentrated in a very small group of political, military, economic, and religious elites.

These elites were neither closed nor static, but exhibited considerable movement up and down, with some permeability at the bottom. McFarlane's numbers on "extinctions" of peerages in Appendix Table 3.2 bears out the conclusion and indicates something of the mechanisms involved. McFarlane counted as a peer all those nobles who had been called to parliament within a twenty-five-year period, beginning in 1300. A peer became extinct if he

---

[17] See Clark (2007b) for a review of recent population estimates. The figures on families are simple extrapolations from the population estimates assuming five people per family.

died without a lineally descended male heir. Extinction did not necessarily mean the end of the title, but it did require a movement of the title, and typically land, to a collateral line of the family. In other cases, peers could be attainted (convicted of treason), which eliminated all of the civil rights and property of the peer and his family. The lowest extinction rate in the quarter-century intervals between 1300 and 1475 was 24 percent, the highest 35 percent. Because mortality was high and survival problematic, the elite were always permeable.

Mobility within the aristocracy could be abrupt and dramatic and depend on happenstance. Richard Duke of York (a major figure in the Wars of the Roses) was the son of the Earl of Cambridge. His father was executed as a traitor and, by virtue of being attainted, left little provision for his son. A few months later, Richard's uncle, Edward Duke of York, died without issue in 1415. Had Richard's Uncle Edward died before his father, Edward's title and property would have been lost and Richard would have received nothing. However, because his uncle died after his father, Richard inherited everything from Edward and became Duke of York. The death of Richard's maternal uncle, Edmund Mortimer, Earl of March and Ulster, also without issue, left Richard the richest landowner in Henry VI's England when he came of age in 1432. Richard's story was spectacular in scale, but not unusual in process (McFarlane, 1973, pp. 185–6).

Despite constant change, the families of the aristocracy were sufficiently stable over time that, of the sixty-two leading landowners in the parliament of 1640, one-half "had descendants or kin who owned 3,000 acres or upwards in 1874" (Tawney, 1941, p. 2). England's dominant coalition was very much like the stylized dominant coalition we sketched in Chapter 2. It was small and enjoyed privileged access to valuable resources and activities. The aristocracy dominated the military, the church, and the government, and when colonial expansion began in the sixteenth century, they dominated the positions of importance in the chartered colonial companies and the large trading companies.

The aristocracy was a stable group, but its membership was not static. Entry from below was limited, but possible. Formally, an aristocrat's position within the hierarchy depended on land. An individual's mobility within the elite hierarchy depended in part on changes in the value of his holdings and privileges, but also in part on his ability, intelligence, hard work, friends, and luck. Military forces were raised through feudal tenures, and tenants holding in knight's tenure were obligated to provide military service to their lords. Household members, retainers, and their landed tenants made up the body of men that a lord could call on for military service in wartime as well as for other service in peacetime. These groups of men were termed *affinities* or, later, *connections*. They were patron–client networks. The networks worked to the interest of the lord and the retainer. Moreover, because a lord's political position depended in part on his ability to deliver and command men on demand, a lord who commanded more men was in better position to reward those men.

The aristocracy as a whole was made up of greater and lesser nobles and their families, linked to each other along well-understood lines of patron–client networks. The aristocracy sat atop patron–client networks that extended downward through the gentry and into the greater English society. Land tenure arrangements gave a formal and legal structure to the networks.

As we have seen, only a hundred or so magnates exerted significant influence in national politics. The individual identity of these great magnates was not fixed by title and inheritance, although it was certainly easier for an earl's son to play a prominent role in society than the son of a country justice. Men of ability and talent competed within the coalition for dominance; not even kings were immune to elimination if their capabilities were inadequate to the challenges they faced. Within this world, social personas reflected the unique and valuable privileges in the control of each major player.

The magnate's access to rents, however, provided the incentive for lesser lords and ambitious men to ally themselves to a powerful lord. Men of humble origins could obtain access to the system by climbing onto its bottom rungs. Successful household service could lead to an opportunity to distinguish oneself in battle or conflict, draw the eye of a lord, and move upward. Talent and ability were rewarded, but only within the framework of existing social organizations. The English hereditary aristocracy was the dominant coalition in a limited, but not closed, access social order.

The patronage networks of medieval England were made up of men connected by land and money. What Plummer first called bastard feudalism in 1885 in his introduction to Fortescue's *Governance of England* (1885) was more complicated than a simple idealized feudal system where ties between lord and servant were secured only by land. McFarlane (1981, p. 23) notes that Plummer used the label bastard as a term of abuse: "misbegotten, debased, corrupted, degenerate"; McFarlane suggests that instead we think of another meaning of bastard: "of having the appearance of, somewhat resembling." McFarlane contended that bastard feudalism was really land-based feudalism by other means, an integral part of the social order in medieval England. Money was not inherently corrupt; it was another way of ordering relations among men.

The complaints of Plummer, Stubbs, and other nineteenth-century historians about the corrosive effect of bastard feudalism ran along two lines. First, even at the time of the Conquest, England did not have consolidated control of its military forces. By dispersing his army throughout the countryside William was able to control the population, provide order, and create incentives that aligned powerful lords with the interests of the king through the discretionary distribution of land. However, as the king's ability to allocate and reallocate land declined with the strengthening of inheritance law, William's descendants found the dispersal of military power more of a threat than a consolation.

By the thirteenth century, the process of raising an army directly via a levy of feudal retainers had become too cumbersome. In Edward's first Welsh War of 1276–7, he could have claimed the services of seven thousand knights. Instead, he called on the feudal service of 375 knights, extracted a monetary payment in lieu of service – scutage – from the rest, and raised further troops by other means. The Hundred Years' War with France was fought with a military force raised by kings and lords commanding the services of men through two other methods than the granting of land. One was to take men directly into the household of the lord.[18] The other method of tying lords and men was the retainer.[19]

Powerful lords assembled groups of men, bound to their lord's interests through grants of land, money, and influence, and then used those groups for their own military purposes as well as the king's. The origin of livery lay in outfitting a lord's retinue with common uniforms.[20] By the fourteenth

[18] At its peak, the king's household included seven hundred knights who received payments in monetary fees and robes that were supplemented in wartime by wages, keep, and compensation for dead horses. The household members gained, from their proximity to the king or a greater lord, influence over action and policy at court and the chance to shine in wartime. Henry I created three earls from his household (Hicks, 1995, pp. 21, 19–48). Household members typically performed services during peacetime, including attendance on the lord, administrative duties, and humbler functions within the manor.

[19] Retainers could be for the short term, such as a military retainer for service in a specific war, or longer term, such as a retainer to provide legal service for the remainder of the solicitor's life. A network of retainers provided lords with the ability to call on services when they needed them. Although individuals often held retainers from several lords at the same time, retainers tended to remain loyal to their lords.

[20] We have already mentioned the other type of "livery," the process by which title to land was delivered to a person. The Courts of Wards and Livery created by Henry VIII was concerned with the delivery of title to wards when they came of age. The second type of "livery" was a uniform worn by feudal retainers. Laws limited the ability of lesser lords to issue livery, and restrict the tenants in chief to liverying only certain of their retainers.

century, powerful lords were in command of private armies made up of household members, retainers, and tenants. The armies were called for the king's service as well as the lord's. These armies threatened the domestic peace, a concern of the king, and created the problem of overly powerful subjects. We return to this question shortly, for the problem of overly powerful subjects, or "under weak kings" (as McFarlane termed it), is a central issue in how we frame the political problems facing England.

The second line of argument that the historians used to indict bastard feudalism was the use of connections and influence by powerful lords to sway the course of justice. The root of the problem was the use of influence in the courts to obtain favorable decisions from juries in actions, such as novel disseisin, over the title to land. Given the complicated nature of title enforcement, particularly after the death of a landholder without a lineal heir, a lord with the slimmest of claims to title might gamble and enter into land literally by taking an armed band onto the property (forcible entry). By entering, the lord established seisin through possession. He then had to defend his seisin as the defendant in an action of novel disseisin.[21] A lord confident of controlling or influencing the court might find an adventure against a neighbor a profitable, if risky, undertaking.

Powerful lords used multiple methods to influence the courts and juries, including riot and forcible entry, illegal retaining and livery, maintenance, embracery, and conspiracy. Forcible entry, riot, and conspiracy related to attempts to enter onto land and establish seisin. Maintenance and embracery were ways in which lords brought influence to bear on courts and juries. The prevalence of these practices is well established in the historical record, as are attempts to stamp out the practice through statutes. Legislation dates from at least Richard II (1377–99) regarding livery and maintenance and continues unabated and largely ineffective through the fifteenth and sixteenth centuries.[22]

Attempts to obtain land were rarely conducted completely outside the framework of the law; claimants typically had some shred of evidence on their side to support their claim. If our earlier discussion of novel disseisin, inheritance law, and alienability law and practices seemed tedious, the pay-off is here. English land law was clearly about property rights in land in

---

[21] "It was a foolhardy and indeed a rare man of lesser standing who decided to bring a suit against a magnate who had unjustly deprived him of land" (Bellamy, 1989, pp. 57–8).

[22] Bellamy (1989) has a thorough treatment of the relationship of bastard feudalism and the laws, and the long and initially fruitless attempts to curb judicial intimidation and influence.

the fourteenth century: the rules were well known and well understood. Unfortunately, the rules did not always result in clear and obvious decisions about who actually possessed seisin to land, particularly in complicated inheritance cases in which previous generations created a patchwork of claims through conditional alienations and grants in fee tail. When ambiguity about title to land mixed with a patronage network built around military service and a court system subject to influence and intimidation, the outcome was not rule of law in any modern sense.

Land wars within the aristocracy occasionally broke out into civil war and overt violence. However, the continuing conflicts over land between aristocrats were often carried out within the courts. There the social persona of the individual lords affected the outcome. Control over land meant control over local government. Land remained a major marker of success and indicator of relative status within the dominant coalition.

3.5 Bastard Feudalism and the Impersonalization of Property

Two aspects of bastard feudalism illuminate how control of resources and functions within a natural state can be used to structure a coalition. One is the heart of the nineteenth-century Whig criticism: that the use of money to structure relationships was inherently corrupting. The other goes back to the fundamental point that no states are single actors, that all states are organizations of organizations. The English story is not just the king versus the barons. In the case of English feudalism, organizations started with landholding and powerful individuals identified as landowners after the Norman Conquest, but steadily moved to more complicated organizational forms within and outside of the state.

Traditional Whig history makes the struggle to constrain the arbitrary power of one man central to the development of representative institutions by which the governed grant their consent to be governed. The privilege of holding court was valuable in post-Conquest England. When the king moved into the business of adjudicating land disputes in the twelfth century when he gave freeholders access to the royal courts, the manorial lords suffered a loss of revenue in the form of fines and court costs from cases that left their courts and moved to the royal courts. In traditional terms, this was a struggle between the aristocracy and the crown. As Coss argues (1989, p. 41), for example, the loss of revenue was potentially just the tip of the iceberg: royal incursion into local affairs threatened the social position of the nobility and gentry: "If certain latent possibilities had been allowed to develop and crystalize, they [the nobility and gentry] would have been faced with the prospect of social extinction." The reaction of the lords against the king to defend their privileges strengthened the lords at the expense of the king.

As McFarlane pointed out, this way of thinking about the problem was not productive. When armies were no longer raised through feudal levies, but instead through personal military contracts with powerful subjects financed through more general taxation and scutage, the balance between royal and baronial interests was no longer maintained solely by the land. With the rise of bastard feudalism, lords began to substitute monetary payments for direct military service. The increasing importance of other sources of power and rents, including trade and commerce, meant that land became less central and less critical as a measure of power within the dominant coalition. As conditions changed in English society, the allocation of power within the coalition had to change as well. It was a fiction to focus solely on the land as the stabilizing and balancing interest in the coalition, except perhaps in the relatively short period immediately after the Conquest when England was a fragile natural state.

Most of these changes were reallocations of power within the dominant coalition, for example in the form of land wars. The adjustments took place constantly whether the crown was involved or not. Given the institutions of medieval English society, political order depended on the formation of a durable organization, an alliance of interests that usually included the king. On some occasions, however, the king was a relatively weak and ineffectual member of the ruling coalition; at other times, the king was eliminated altogether.

Going beyond McFarlane and his students, we can see that England in the Middle Ages was a basic natural state governed by a dominant coalition whose rents were generated by limiting access to land, prayer, fighting, and justice. Elites held the coalition together through an interlocking set of personal relationships based on land but bolstered by relationships based on monetary exchange. This is the essence of bastard feudalism. To repeat, the significant organizations of production, governance, and salvation were all tied to the feudal manor: control over land amounted to control over manors. Control over the fundamental organizations of English society was all vested within the structure of the state. Powerful lords controlled more than one hundred manors apiece, and some of the most powerful lords were bishops. The hundred men at the top of the dominant coalition continuously worked out the arrangements that held English society together. Through its fascinating complexity, English land law enabled limited access to land at the higher and politically more important levels of aggregation and moved toward more open access at the level of small individual tenants who held alienable tenures from greater lords, then gradually lost their conditions of feudal service and moved to cash transactions.

History, culture, and institutional inheritance mattered enormously. The origins of the land law in the fragile natural state created after the Conquest created opportunities, difficulties, and contradictions. When land reverted to the lord on the death of the tenant – whether a tenant in chief or a minor freeholder – the redistribution of land could be used to maintain the coalition at the national and local level. However, once a measure of stability had been attained, no one had a distinct interest in maintaining the reversion system. If tenants were willing to pay for more secure land rights, the landlords could also be better off by granting them those rights in return for more service. Over the course of the twelfth century, inheritance through lineal descendants became the rule. However, heritability came in the form of strict settlement on lineal heirs. Seisin was not devisable by will. Moreover, at the very top of the hierarchy, the king never surrendered his right to take the lands of the tenants in chief back into his hand at their death. Land was only one of the many valuable assets and functions that English society used to consolidate and order their basic natural state, but it was a central one.

Secure and transferrable property rights in land were valuable for their own sake. At the very least after 1295 and *Quia Emptores*, part of the institutions of English land law were moving toward secure ownership of land. More secure property rights in land, however, developed in a manner that still left ambiguity about exactly who owned what property at times of death and transfer. From our modern-day perspective, the ambiguity appears as a flaw in the system. Yet from the perspective of England as a basic natural state, ambiguity facilitated the dominant coalition's need to use control over land to structure and adjust the distribution of political and economic power as circumstances changed. Landownership in the medieval English system was not only inherently personal but it also embodied the personal relationships that held the dominant coalition together. To reallocate power within the dominant coalition, the system required some flexibility to transfer control over land among members of the elite as individuals gained or lost power. Who controlled power in the English state was most visibly apparent by who controlled land, particularly as the control of land translated directly into control of government functions at the local level. If elite property rights in land had been defined without ambiguity – and therefore if land distribution could be altered only by sale or grant – then the English system of government would have lost an important degree of flexibility. The irregular reallocations of land through land wars (with or without violence) within the system of English land law reflected the changing political power of individuals within the coalition and were an integral part of what made the system work. Unfortunately, the system did not always work smoothly and, on several occasions, broke down into civil war. These wars were over more than just land; they typically concerned power, prestige, honor, and revenge as well. Nevertheless, control of land was the central mechanism by which power was attained and exercised (Bellamy, 1989, p. 35). The greatest of these, the Wars of the Roses, occurred in the latter half of the fifteenth century (Pollard, 1988).

This complicated history illuminates why no teleology or inevitable forces move societies toward more mature institutions. The complexity of land transfer at time of death, including the costly possibility of wardship if the male heir was a minor, created incentives for the lords to work around the legal problem. No inevitable forces moved to make this system more rational and transparent. *De Donis* was as logical a development for powerful landowners as *Quia Emptores*. Whereas *Quia Emptores* clarified ownership, *De Donis* enormously complicated ownership.

Whether the development of the use and trust to evade death duties was a positive or negative innovation depended on your position, and here as well there was no inevitable movement toward more efficient arrangements. Although the king suffered a loss of revenue from uses so did the major lords because they too held rights of wardship with their own tenants (Bell, 1953, p. 1). As individuals, lords (major or minor) had incentives to avoid the death charges by creating uses. However, as a group, the king and parliament suffered a reduction in revenues as uses sapped a revenue source of the king and the tenants in chief.[23] In 1536, the crown and parliament together supported an attempt to suppress uses in the Statute of Uses. As we have seen, the attempt failed. However, the act's passage suggests that both the royal and aristocratic elements of the dominant coalition of England in 1536 were quite willing to suppress what appears to us to be a fundamental

---

[23] Because the Chancery courts were willing to enforce use agreements in equity and because the crown derived revenues directly and indirectly from the Chancery, the king had another competing set of fiscal incentives to allow uses to develop. The fiscal interests of the king and the major lords were not symmetric, however. How much a transfer of feudal obligations in tax obligations affected individual lords depended on their relationship with the king and with their tenants.

organizational improvement in English society. Likewise, the failure of the Statute of Uses cannot be laid at the feet of a penurious parliament unwilling to grant the king his revenues. Many members of the House of Lords had similar fiscal interests in abolishing uses as the king.

In response to the failure of the Statute of Uses, parliament passed the Statute of Wills in 1549. The continued ability to employ uses meant that most major landholders would evade wardship.[24] Allowing tenants in chief to devise their land by will clarified the state of land title on the death of a magnate. No longer did the Byzantine inheritance rules alone govern the descent of most land. Property rights in land suddenly got much clearer in the sixteenth century, and the incentives and opportunities for land wars were proportionately reduced.[25] Parliament did not intend the crown to lose revenues by the Statute of Wills; in the same year they endorsed the formation of the Court of Wardship and Livery to enforce the crown's right to wardship, an issue we return to shortly.

Similarly, the shift in the common way of defending title from novel disseisin to ejectment in the late fifteenth and sixteenth centuries had profound implications. Property rights for freeholders and copyholders became better defined and much more easily defended. The extension of similar rights to copyholders was equally important in clarifying ownership.

No one understood these implications at the time. Changes in the land law were not part of an overall scheme to improve the quality of property rights in land; they were the result of ongoing dynamics within English society. Simpson argues that the royal common law courts saw a possibility to capture some cases from the equity courts, which were willing to hear copyhold cases on the basis of equity (Simpson, 1986, pp 163–4). Again, it is a fiscal interest argument that led one set of courts to change its rules to capture some business from another set of courts.[26]

More secure and transparent ownership and transfer of land meant land became less useful as a tool for balancing interests within the dominant coalition. The changes in land law that began in the 1540s substantially reduced the fiscal advantages to kings and magnates from owning and holding land directly and enjoying their feudal incidents. Perhaps we should

---

[24] Simpson (1986, p. 191). It is interesting that Simpson falls back for his explanation on why events occurred to the fiscal situation of the king.

[25] Bellamy (1989, pp. 123–6). Suggests that cases of maintenance and forcible entry had declined in number and, more importantly, in the status of the defendants by the early seventeenth century. By then, the major lords had stopped using the courts to obtain land.

[26] For a more general analysis of the fiscal impact of jurisdictional competition on English law see Klerman (2007).

not be surprised, therefore, that this period witnessed a marked decrease in the amount of land owned by the crown. Although Henry VIII seized church lands, he also followed a policy of progressively selling the royal land-holdings, and Elizabeth continued divesting royal land. Historians almost invariably attribute this policy to fiscal crises facing the crown, but it seems clear that changes in fiscal returns to crown lands were also involved.[27]

The logic of the natural state suggests that the crown lands, while an important source of revenue, would be used in ways that stabilized the coalition beyond simple revenue maximization. Despite the focus on revenues and the idea that the sixteenth-century crown was using "a revived fiscal feudalism [that] squeezed wealth out of the landed classes" (Stone, 2002, p. 61), the issue of wardship that has arisen throughout this chapter and the Court of Wards and Livery under Henry VIII and Elizabeth provide a clear example of how rulers can create rents to coordinate the coalition rather than to maximize fiscal revenue. The court was established in 1540 and administered as a natural state institution: creating rents by limiting entry and then using the rents to secure the stability of the dominant coalition by giving the major players an incentive in maintaining the regime that generates the rents. Rents were not taken from the court in cash, however. When an estate passed into wardship and came under the purview of the court, the court sold the right to wardships, usually to friends and allies of the king. They then often sold the wardship to the mother of the ward. Because the prices of both sales were recorded, we can observe both the price that the court received for the wardship and the amount that the ultimate customer actually paid for the wardship.

Hurstfield investigated the operation of the Court of Wards and Liveries and came up with a surprising conclusion: the court was never run in a way that maximized revenue from wards and liveries. The king received only a quarter of the price paid for wardships.[28] Lord Burghley was master of the court from 1561 until his death in 1591, and he actually administered the court to benefit members of the king's coalition rather than to maximize revenues: "The significance of the feudal revenues in the Tudor period lies not in their direct yield to the state but as a method of payment, albeit indirectly and capriciously, to ministers and civil servants" (Hurstfield,

---

[27] For the Crown Estates see Hoyle (1992); for the aristocracy in general see Stone (1965, 2002); and for royal finances see Dietz (1964).

[28] "The profits of fiscal feudalism were, in essence, ambivalent... that the unofficial profits from fiscal feudalism, taken as a whole, were at least three times as high as the official ones. Contemporaries thought the disparity was much higher than this" (Hurstfield, 1955, p. 58); see also Hurstfield (1949, 1953).

1955, p. 59). When Burghley died, his son Cecil took over. Cecil began administering the court as an instrument for raising revenues, squeezing out the intermediaries. Although the annual revenues of the court rose by almost 50 percent in the 1590s, by the early 1600s the court had lost its political support in parliament and was headed for extinction. Used as an instrument of a natural state coalition, the court was politically viable. Used simply as a mechanism for extracting revenue, it had no place in seventeenth-century England, and was abolished. Thomas (1977) finds an exact parallel to Burghley's use of the Court of Wards and Liveries in the policy of leasing crown lands to favored servants on extremely favorable "reversionary" leases.[29] Land was always used this way by the crown.[30]

   Land gradually lost its role as a balancing item in the dominant coalition. Ownership of land was not completely secure from political manipulation until 1660. Estates would be confiscated and sequestered during the seventeenth-century civil war (Habakkuk, 1965). Nevertheless, most of those estates would be restored to their owners. By the end of the seventeenth century, landownership and the organizations associated with land had been moved outside the immediate control and manipulation of the state. On the dimension of land, England exhibited the institutions and organizations of a mature natural state.

3.6 The Typology of Natural States

This chapter is not an economic history of England between 1066 and 1660. Land was an important element of both the political and economic system of England over the entire period, and because of its importance in law, politics, and society, the history of land law, land allocation, land use, and the institutions regarding all three is easily accessible. However, there were dramatic and important changes in many areas of English society over these years. The commercial and monetized economy steadily developed, and the close connections grew between state finances and commercial exchange. The development of new forms of business organizations, particularly the business corporation, again with close associations with the crown and

---

[29] " ... the Crown gained a large amount of political support from its tenants. The purpose of this short article is to show that the Crown sometimes managed its lands not for the revenue or for the tenants, but as a source for casual supplements to the incomes of its servants. This was done by granting them leases in reversion on favourable terms" (Thomas, 1977, p. 67).

[30] "They [the Crown Lands] were much more than a source of rental income, but formed an important part of the Crown's armoury of patronage and rewards" (Hoyle, 1992, p. 1).

aristocracy, is a subject we return to in Chapter 6. Increasing productivity and new forms of organization and scale in agriculture were introduced (Allen, 1992; Clark, 2005, 2007b). The use of new public/private forms of organization in overseas colonies began (Tilly, 1992), including several types of corporate forms. The development of financial markets and financial market institutions came about (Dickson, 1967). Creation of a state church and then increasing religious tolerance, with lapses, began developing. These were all critically important developments, none of which we wish to slight.

Instead, we apply the natural state framework to medieval and early modern English history to show how an important asset was handled to secure and stabilize the dominant coalition and trace the evolution of the state from fragile to basic to mature through the land law. We began when William the Conqueror displaced the existing power structure and created a new fragile natural state. William managed a dominant coalition whose principal asset was land. As the fortunes of various elites rose and fell, he and his successors actively used land redistribution (especially on the death of landowners) to maintain the coalition.

Over the next few centuries, a basic natural state emerged, more stable than the fragile natural state. The basic natural state produced a series of differentiated organizations closely associated with the state in the form of the manor: a stable, rent-creating social structure that harmonized relations among local religious, military, economic, and political elites. As with the fragile natural state, the members of the basic natural state's dominant coalition experienced rising and falling fortunes, leading to power struggles and civil wars, including the Wars of the Roses but also international wars, such as the Hundred Years' Wars.

As a natural state, England was stable but not static. The society changed with circumstances. As the fortunes of the elite rose and fell, the coalition adjusted, sometimes imperfectly, and sometimes violently, including civil wars. Over time, the formal government evolved into a more complex form, in part because elites sought to take advantage of greater economic opportunities. Although England changed, it remained a natural state through the entire period.

By the end of the sixteenth century, ownership rights in land were relatively secure and impersonal. Similar changes had occurred on other dimensions of elite rights. As Maitland (1963[1908]) details, between the eleventh to the seventeenth centuries the legal system moved from a system based on trial by combat and ordeal to one based on evidence and legal process. In the late sixteenth century and through the seventeenth century, England moved from a basic natural state to a mature natural state. The signature feature of a mature natural state – organizations independent of the state – began to emerge in the form of trusts, merchant firms, business corporations, political associations, and religious groups.

Yet England faced new challenges. The growing security of land rights meant that one traditional method of adjusting the dominant coalition – redistributing land – was no longer available. The rise of a new source of wealth from commerce and trade caused a series of political problems, including new sources of economic and political power. No longer did the gentry rise up from wealth based solely on land. Indeed, the rise of new interests changed the coalitions based on land and other forms of wealth. As the dominant coalition attempted to adjust along new margins other than land, coalition members sought – in the same manner we emphasized earlier for land – more secure rights that would reduce the king's ability to adjust the coalition. The struggles of the seventeenth century can therefore be read in both constitutional terms and as a struggle within the dominant coalition of a natural state facing the rise of a powerful set of groups that, by virtue of being relatively new, find their interests are under-institutionalized.

APPENDIX

A Glossary of Technical Terms involving Land Use

Assize: a court, a trial session, a jury trial, or a judgment.

Attainment, attainder: the legal consequences of a conviction for treason or felony, involving the loss of all civil rights.

Copyhold: land tenure acquired at some point in the past from an unfree tenant and registered (by a copy of the agreement) at the local court.

Freehold: land tenure of free individuals.

Courts: Chancery, common law, equity, Royal.

Disseisin: loss of seisin.

Entail: see fee tail.

Fee: what the tenant held.

Fee simple: a tenure in which the fee transferred in the entirety to the tenant.

Fee tail: a tenure in which only part of the fee was transferred, often subject to contingencies.

Seisen/seised: In its most literal sense, "the person seised of land was simply the person in obvious occupation, the person 'sitting' on the land." (Simpson, 1986, p. 40). Seisin evolved over the centuries. Over

time, the person seised in title was in possession of the property, even
if the property was not physical occupation of the land, for example,
the right to an income stream from property. Eventually, seisin in
intangible property was recognized.

Socage; free and common socage: A more limited version of fee simple in
which a complete and unconditional transfer of tenure occurred and
the new tenant owed only "fixed and certain incidents" and had no
other obligations to the land lord.

Subinfeudation: an existing tenant or lord could create their new tenants
by devising new feudal arrangements.

Termor: a tenant for a term of years.

Uses: a method of transferring land to one person for *the use* of another.

Villeinage: an unfree tenure.

Writs: a form of legal action, issued by the king or a court, directed that
certain actions be taken following established legal forms (Maitland,
1968[1909], p. 4).

Writ of right: a writ directing that claims regarding seisin be resolved
(Maitland 1968[1909], pp. 18–90).

Estimating Landownership Concentration in Medieval England

An early estimate of land use was drawn from the Hundred Rolls of 1279 by
Kosminsky (1931). The Hundred Rolls covered a small sample, roughly 6
percent of England, and was probably not representative (Campbell, 2000,
p. 57). Kosminsky found that out of the half million acres of land, 31.8
percent was in demense, 40.5 in villeinage, and 27.7 percent in free land.[31]
That gives a rough idea of how land was distributed within manors. Lords
would derive income directly from roughly 70 percent of the land. Manor
estimates, however, tell us nothing about the overall distribution of land
because major lords held more than one manor, which complicates the
calculation of their total landholdings.

Appendix Table 3.1 is taken from Cooper (1983) and draws on the work
of Gray (1934). Gray used the income tax returns for 1436 to construct
estimates of income by type of landowner. Cooper converted Gray's income
estimates into acreage estimates by dividing total income by estimates of
average annual income derived from an acre of land of different types. The
table also reports the number of landowners in each category from Gray.

---

[31] Campbell (2000), pp. 57–8.

Table 3.1. *Income from and landholdings in 1436*

	Landed income, £	Persons	Millions of acres	Percentage of acres
Greater landowners	78,000	234	3–4	20
Landowners £5–100	113,000	7,000	4.5–5.5	25
Landowners under £5	100,000		3–4	20
Church	75–100,000	–	4–5	20–25
Crown	20,000	–	1–1.5	5

Source: Cooper (1983), Table 1, p. 19. The number of "persons" is taken from Gray (1934). Cooper's numbers draw on Gray (1934) and Thompson (1966).

Table 3.2. *Barons summoned to parliament, extinctions, and new summonses*

Date	Total called	New peers	Extinctions	Percent extinct
1300; 1300–24	136	60	51	26.02
1325	145	47	45	23.44
1350	147	29	50	28.41
1375	126	17	41	28.67
1400	102	11	40	35.4
1425	73	25	25	25.51
1450	73	22	24	25.26
1475	71	10	20	24.69

Source: Based on McFarlane (1973), pp. 175–6. The numbers are based on the *Complete Peerage* and were based on McFarlane's notes as reconstructed by the editors. A peerage became "extinct" when the peer died without a male heir (so the peerage itself might have continued in name, but through collateral rather than direct descent).

Table 3.3. *Gregory King's distribution of families by status*

Families	Type
200	Lords Spiritual and Temporal
1,500	Knights and Baronets
3,000 (or 3,800)	Esquires
15,000	Gentlemen
80,000	Freeholders at 50[l] per annum
200,000	Freeholders at 10[l] per annum
400,000	Farmers
100,000	Cottagers, day labourers, and paupers
300,000	Tradesmen and Professionals
1,100,000	Total

Source: Cooper (1983), p. 39.

Table 3.4. *Chamberlayne's estimates of income by class*

	Number	Average income, £	Total income, £
Peers	159	8,000	1,272,000
Baronets	749	1,200	898,000
Knights	1,400	800	1,120,000
Esquires and Gentlemen	6,000	400	2,400,000

Source: Cooper (1983), p. 32.

The largest landowners in 1436 numbered only 234. Of these, 51 great barons had landed income in total of £40,000 (an average of £768 a baron). The 183 greater knights with incomes over £100 had a total income of £38,000 (an average of £208 per knight). In aggregate, these landowners controlled roughly 45 percent of the acreage in England and 40 percent of the income from land in estates subject to the income tax. A greater baron might hold an estate of 8,000 to 9,000 acres or larger.[32] Gray (1934, p. 630) reports, "All together 7,000 men in England, non-noble in status, enjoyed income from lands, rents, and annuities ranging from £5 to £400, most of these being from £5 to £100." These 7,000 men controlled more than 70 percent of the land. The numbers are consistent with other estimates.

Hicks noted that only forty-eight barons had hereditary rights to be called to parliament in 1388. McFarlane reports that 102 barons were summoned to parliament in 1300 and another 34 had been summoned in or after 1295. Appendix Table 3.2 gives the numbers of individuals called to parliament by twenty-five-year intervals from 1300 to 1475. The greatest number was 147 and the lowest number 71, which is a rough estimate of the number of magnates, great landowners, and nobles over the two centuries.

Cooper also provides a distillation and interpretation of Gregory King's estimates of the distribution of families by type in the later seventeenth century, shown in Appendix Table 3.3. Chamberlayne's estimates of the number of Peers, Baronets, Knights, and Esquires and Gentlemen in 1692 are provided in Appendix Table 3.4.

---

[32] This paragraph is based on Cooper (1983), pp. 17–19.

FOUR

Open Access Orders

4.1 Introduction

Although open access orders are far more peaceful than natural states, social scientists take this peace for granted. No models explain why violence is generally absent, whether in the form of coups, riots, rebellions, or civil wars. These societies are Weberian: the government holds a monopoly on the legitimate use of violence, which is subject to clear and well-understood rules. In open access orders, political and social arrangements identify a set of military and police organizations that can legitimately use violence and a set of political organizations that control the use of violence by the military and police. Control of the government, in turn, is contestable and is subject to clear and well-understood rules.

Open access orders exhibit a virtuous circle linking the control of violence and open access. The political system limits access to the means of violence; open economic and social access ensures that access to the political system is open; credible prohibitions on the use of violence to compete maintains open economic and social access; and political and judicial systems enforce prohibitions on the use of violence. Similarly, open access to organizations in all systems sustains competition in all systems. Competition in all systems, in turn, helps sustain open access.

Standard views about how developed societies operate and sustain themselves typically focus on one system, either markets or democracy, without considering the other. Economics takes open access as given and explores its consequences; explanations for market stability usually focus on the equilibrium properties of the economy. Because economics provides no explanation of why and how the political system defines property rights, enforces contracts, and creates the rule of law necessary for markets, economics fails to explain an open access order's stability. Similarly, political science explanations focus on democracy, taking open access and political competition as given, exploring their consequences. Political science fails to explain why open access orders maintain stable democracy while most natural states cannot, how democracy in open access orders sustains a market economy, or why democracy in natural states typically fails to do so. Political science, therefore, fails to explain the open access order's wealth and productivity.

Drawing on the idea of the double balance, we show that open access in all systems is mutually reinforcing. Our argument has three parts. First, citizens in open access orders share belief systems that emphasize equality, sharing, and universal inclusion. To sustain these beliefs, all open access orders have institutions and policies that share the gains of and reduce the individual risks from market participation, including universal education, a range of social insurance programs, and widespread infrastructure and public goods.[1] Moreover, because these programs widely share the gains of the market economy in a manner complementary to markets, they reduce citizen demands for redistribution in ways that potentially cripple the economy.

Second, political parties vie for control in competitive elections. The success of party competition in policing those in power depends on open access that fosters a competitive economy and the civil society, both providing a dense set of organizations that represent a range of interests and mobilize widely dispersed constituencies in the event that an incumbent regime attempts to solidify its position through rent-creation, limiting access, or coercion.

Third, a range of institutions and incentive systems impose costs on an incumbent party that seeks to cement its position through systematic rent-creation and limiting access: imposition of systematic rent-creation yields a shrinking economy and falling tax revenue. Mobile resources leave the country, and the country's competitive position in international markets deteriorates. These reactions impose direct costs on a regime that attempts limited access and grants the opposition a competitive opportunity to attract votes to regain power.

---

[1] Bueno de Mesquita et al. (2003) show a similar result: in their approach, authoritarian governments tend toward private goods while democratic ones tend toward public goods. These scholars do not distinguish between democracies in open access orders and natural states, however.

An important property of open access orders is the seeming independence of economic and political systems. Economic organizations in open access orders do not need to participate in politics to maintain their rights, to enforce contracts, or to ensure their survival from expropriation; their right to exist and compete does not depend on maintaining privileges. Markets in open access orders therefore appear more autonomous than in natural states where all major market organizations must also serve political ends. The same logic holds for politics, which in open access orders appears to intervene – that is, constrain, control, and regulate – markets that seem to exist without action or support of the political system. This apparent autonomy is endogenous to open access, however.

An integral feature of the open access order is the growth of government. Incorporation of mass citizenry induces responsiveness to their interests (Acemoglu and Robinson, 2006). The widespread sharing in open access orders just noted entails large government. Public goods spending on education and infrastructure involves expensive programs, as do the various programs that provide social insurance, including unemployment insurance, old age insurance, disability, and health insurance. Governments in open access orders are therefore larger than those in natural states, and their actions and policies are more complementary to markets.

4.2 Commonalities: Characteristics of an Open Access Order

Open access orders differ widely, both over the 150 or so years of their existence and among themselves at any given moment in time.[2] Some are parliamentary systems while others are presidential; some are small trading states while others are large countries with complex, diversified economies. Nonetheless, all open access orders have a series of characteristics in common. First, all are characterized by a set of beliefs widely held among the population. These beliefs include various forms of inclusion, equality, and shared growth. All citizens are equal. All citizens have the ability to form organizations, to write contracts, to use the courts and the bureaucracy, and to access public goods and services. The specific nature of these beliefs differs across open access orders, with the Anglo-American countries tending to emphasize equality before the law and the East Asian countries tending to emphasize shared growth. The nature of these beliefs has differed over

---

[2] Throughout this chapter, we assume that an open access order exists. We treat the important question of the transition – of how natural states become open access orders – in Chapters 5 and 6.

time. In the open access orders of the mid- and late nineteenth century, beliefs of inclusion centered on incorporating the masses as citizens, with rights of political participation and equal access to the market and to the institutions of the state, including the courts. Prior to that time, as countries on the doorstep, these states limited access to many rule-of-law institutions to elites. During the transition, these countries widely increased rights and access. Inclusion in most post-World War II open access orders emphasizes a much wider sense of equality and equity, including a range of social programs that share the gains and lower the personal risk of the market economy.

Second, the eponymous characteristic, open access, is central to all open access orders. The civil society encompasses a wide range of organizations independent of the state. Open access also fosters competition in all systems, specifically in politics and economics. Systematic competition for control of the state means these states are democratic; systematic competition in the economy means that these states are market economies. All open access orders have constitutions, including institutions and incentive systems to sustain them.

Third, all open access orders are, largely, impersonal. These societies have the only type of governments that can systematically provide services and benefits to citizens and organizations on an impersonal basis; that is, without reference to the social standing of the citizens or the identity and political connections of an organization's principals. Programs for unemployment insurance actually deliver benefits to those recently unemployed rather than well-connected individuals or clients of powerful patrons. Food subsidies go to those individuals meeting the relevant characteristics rather than, as in the case of ration cards in India, being sold by corrupt bureaucrats to the highest bidders. An important feature of impersonality is the rule of law: rights, justice, and enforcement are rule bound and impartial. Economies in these states are also characterized by impersonal exchange.

Finally, open access orders cannot easily manipulate interests. Because open access orders deliver public goods for all citizens, it is harder for these states to force potential opponents to support the state by threatening to cut off important services if they fail to do so. Another part of the open access order's inability to manipulate interests arises because these states are characterized by limited government: their constitutions create what philosophers sometimes call a realm of private action beyond the reach of the government. Rights, for example, limit government action in ways that grant individuals freedom from political manipulation and harassment.

We summarize the characteristics of an open access order as follows. In addition to meeting the second two doorstep conditions – a perpetually lived state and consolidated political control over violence – an open access order has the following characteristics:

1. A widely held set of beliefs about the inclusion of and equality for all citizens.
2. Entry into economic, political, religious, and educational activities without restraint.
3. Support for organizational forms in each activity that is open to all (for example, contract enforcement).
4. Rule of law enforced impartially for all citizens.
5. Impersonal exchange.

As we discuss next, these characteristics have implications for the structure of the state and its institutions. The first characteristic requires that reality not be so far off from the ideal that beliefs in equality and inclusion cannot be sustained. Without some basis in reality, citizens in open access orders could not sustain beliefs in equality.

Characteristics 2 and 3 require that an open access order provide for open access to organizational forms in all walks of life and to anyone or group who meets a set of minimal, impersonal requirements. Open access for organizations in all activities means that open access orders have both political and economic competition markets and democracy. Stable democracy necessitates a range of self-enforcing limits on governmental activities in the sense that political officials have incentives to honor the rules (Przeworski, 1991; Weingast, 1997, 2006a).

Characteristic 4 requires a set of institutions that makes citizen rights impersonal, enforceable, and impartial across all citizens. Rule of law for all citizens, in turn, requires a perpetually lived state with the ability to maintain perpetually lived rights and organizations; and political control of the military requires that the state have a monopoly control over violence and be bound by appropriate rules governing the use of violence, especially against citizens. With respect to characteristic 5, all exchange in limited access order is dominated by personal knowledge. The big change in open access orders is impersonal exchange: people do not need to know one another anymore to exchange. As economic historians have long emphasized, impersonal exchange greatly expands the economic opportunities, allowing the economies of scale in modern capitalist economies (see Greif, 2006; North, 1981).

Each characteristic requires institutions to sustain it. The specific institutions providing for the doorstep conditions and various credible commitments differ from open access order to open access order. No simple template exists for specifying institutions that accomplish these tasks. We treat this topic in the next section.

Nonetheless, all open access orders have a common set of institutional elements. They have open access for organizations of all types, market economies that create a comparative advantage that generates a major portion of the society's wealth, and competitive elections with every citizen enfranchised. Other instituitons support rights, such as a free press, freedom of expression, freedom of religion and conscience, and the right to assemble. All open access orders have some form of division of powers and multiple veto points (Tsebelis, 2002), sometimes explicit, as in the American Constitution's separation of powers system, and sometimes implicit, as in the coalition governments of Europe with separate ministries, a prime minister, a cabinet within which coalition members negotiate and approve legislation, and parliament necessary to pass legislation. All open access orders also have judicial and bureaucratic mechanisms for enforcing citizen rights and contracts. And finally, they all have constitutions (whether official documents or small "c" constitutions) that provide for the limit condition – limiting the stakes of power so that everything is not up for grabs in the next election (Weingast, 2006a).

Open access orders prevent disorder through competition and open access. Consolidated, political control over violence combines with the rules governing the use of that violence to reduce and control access to violence. Constitutions and rule of law provide limits on governmental policymaking, thus limiting the ways in which citizens can feel threatened by the government that in natural states induce them to support the use of violence and extra-constitutional action to protect themselves. In addition, as we discuss in Section 4.5, competition is intimately involved in enforcing the constitution and rule of law that support these limits on violence.

4.2.1 Schumpeter's Insight

A final aspect of all open access orders is Schumpeter's notion of creative destruction, one of the most powerful descriptions of a competitive, open access economy. When Schumpeter wrote *Capitalism, Socialism, and Democracy* in the early 1940s, the economic theory of perfect competition among atomistic firms (i.e., firms too small to have market power) had come under sustained attack as unrealistic. Large and powerful economic organizations dominated the new economy, and their behavior did not match the textbooks. Despite this dominance, the economy produced historically unprecedented, sustained economic development. Schumpeter asked, How could large businesses that were supposed to choke off competition and growth nonetheless generate such spectacular productivity increases in a world that seemed ever more competitive?

Schumpeter solved the paradox by transcending the textbook notion of competition, focusing on competition in a world of large organizations, which he termed *creative destruction*:

> Capitalism, then, is by nature a form or method of economic change and not only never is but never can be stationary . . . The fundamental impulse that sets and keeps the capitalist engine in motion comes from new consumers' goods, the new methods of production or transportation, the new markets, and the new forms of industrial organization that capitalist enterprise creates . . . The opening up of new markets, foreign or domestic, and the organizational development from the craft shop to the factory to such concerns as U.S. Steel illustrate the same process of industrial mutation – if I may use that biological term – that incessantly revolutionizes the economic structure *from within*, incessantly destroying the old one, incessantly creating a new one. This process of Creative Destruction is the essential fact about capitalism. It is what capitalism consists in and what every capitalist concern has got to live in (Schumpeter, 1942, pp. 82–3, emphasis in original).

Schumpeter's entrepreneurs are both innovators and organizers who see new possibilities for products, processes, and markets and who take advantage of those opportunities by building new organizations and changing the structure of old ones. Schumpeter's creative destruction requires open entry and access to organizational forms. The natural state cannot support creative destruction because the creation of new economic organizations directly threatens existing economic organizations and their patterns of rents.

How does creative economic destruction affect politics? First, in the economy, it constantly changes the pattern of economic interests and therefore the pressures facing political officials; second, in the polity, political entrepreneurs continually adapt, advancing new ideas and creating new coalitions. As organizations form to pursue whatever ends they desire and creative destruction continually produces new patterns of interests within society, political organizations form to channel those interests into political action. Political entrepreneurs who lead political parties seek to advance new ideas and programs in ways that increase the likelihood of success over their rivals.

However, we are not home yet. How does political competition secure open access? Unleashing creative destruction in the political system by itself seems unlikely to secure the rights of losers (Przeworski, 1991). Effective political competition requires credible guarantees that losers will not be expropriated and that losing political organizations continue to enjoy access to future competition. What then credibly guarantees the rights of losers to continued political access?

4.3 Institutions, Beliefs, and Incentives Supporting Open Access

Officials in open access orders face a citizenry with shared beliefs that emphasize various forms of inclusion and equality. To be sustained, such beliefs must have a basis in reality. Open access orders implement these beliefs through a series of public goods and services that open opportunities to a large portion of the population (such as education, access to the courts, and infrastructure provision) and that share the gains of economic growth while lowering the risks to individuals of markets (such as various social insurance programs).

Open access orders also subject political officials to competition in both economic and political realms, which limits their ability to solidify their advantage through rent-creation (as we discuss later in Section 4.6). Where limited access orders use rent-creation and limited access to provide order and stability, open access orders use competition and open access. Individuals and groups may freely form organizations and enter into most economic, political, social, and other activities, subject to general rules applied impersonally, such as refraining from violence. Open access therefore results in a thick and variegated structure of organizations, often called the civil society. Political scientists and philosophers have long emphasized the importance of the civil society for open and democratic societies (Gellner, 1994; Lipset, 1963; O'Donnell and Schmitter, 1986; Putnam, 1993; Tocqueville, 1969[1835]; Widner, 2001). For our purposes, the civil society is relevant in two ways. First, open access is a necessary condition for a broad-based and active civil society. Restrictions on the ability to form organizations directly inhibit the civil society. Second, as emphasized in the literature, a civil society reflects a wide range of organizations that are easily adapted to political purposes when a government threatens an open access order. Organizations from garden clubs and soccer leagues to multinational corporations and nongovernmental organizations (NGOs) to interest groups and political parties all form pools of interest that can independently affect the political process. Rents in this system attract entry and competition, which erode these rents.

Institutions provide for the credible commitments that support the rule of law, including open access and competition. Here too beliefs are central, in the form of the consensus condition: that is, citizens in open access orders share beliefs about the appropriateness of central tenets of their constitution so that they help police the rules by withdrawing support from officials who seek to violate these tenets.

4.4 Incorporation: The Extension of Citizenship

Perhaps the most central feature of open access orders is the transformation of a society based on elites to one based on a mass citizenry. This transformation also combines beliefs in equality and open access to markets, the institutional apparatuses of rule of law, and mass political participation.

Incorporation of citizens encompasses different groups at different times. At the beginning of the first transitions, only a portion of native males became citizens, although some (such as the United States) had relatively liberal citizenship laws for male immigrants from some regions. Later these states widened suffrage for males and incorporated other groups, notably women, in the early twentieth century. The process of incorporation is ongoing today, as is evident with the struggles in Europe with Muslim immigrants and in the United States with more than a century-long struggle to incorporate African Americans.

Political incorporation under open access implies mass politics, including the development of perpetually lived political parties that compete electorally for citizens' votes. Along with political participation comes political responsiveness: as Bueno de Mesquita et al. (2003) suggest, political officials facing mass electorates respond by providing public rather than private goods.

Historically, open access orders have provided different types of public goods in a sequence. In the beginning of the first transitions, societies extended the rule of law from elites to all citizens, a process we discuss in Chapter 6. Next typically came infrastructure and the beginning of mass education. For example, transportation infrastructure often transformed large areas of traditionally organized, low-income, and self-sufficient peasant economies into specialized food producers in integrated regional, national, or international markets, greatly increasing efficiency of both production and incomes. Third, after considerable struggles, often violent, open access orders began to ensure labor against vicissitudes that result from participation in impersonal labor markets. Some policies focused directly on labor markets, such as policies allowing labor to form unions and bargain with employers. These policies were controversial and played out over several generations in both Europe and the United States. The other type of policies grew more slowly over the twentieth century and became especially important after World War II: social insurance programs that protect labor against a range of new set of uncertainties that arose with integrated markets in the late nineteenth and early twentieth centuries. These programs, which significantly reduced the individual risk of market participation, include unemployment insurance, accident insurance, health insurance, and old-age insurance.

To illustrate this process of policy responsiveness, consider the United States. At its founding, the United States was transitioning to an open access order. The country was geared toward elites based on property ownership. Nonetheless, access to the elite was relatively open because, in comparison with Europe, abundant land and scarce labor made access to property far easier in America than in Europe (North, 1961). As the United States expanded, new states and territories on the frontier competed for scarce labor. In Schumpeterian fashion, political entrepreneurs in these states sought to make themselves attractive to labor by innovating through providing an array of institutions and public goods, including secure property rights, rule of law, and universal white male suffrage. Often their competitive innovations forced older states to follow their lead.[3] Public goods provided by frontier states and territories included infrastructure granting citizens access to markets in the established state, including roads, canals, and, later, railroads, but also banks to finance the shipment of produce to markets.[4] Whereas many people moving to the frontier in 1800 did so as self-sufficient farmers, those moving in the 1840s typically did so as prospective market specialists in interregional or international markets. Universal education also expanded along the frontier. Finally, the frontier's extension of suffrage in turn forced the established states on the eastern seaboard to follow suit. By the 1840s, white males were enfranchised across the United States. Moreover, as we detail in Chapter 6, mass political parties organized for the first time to mobilize citizens' votes.

---

[3] Engerman and Sokoloff (2005) trace this history.

[4] An extensive literature studies this economic and political history. See Goodrich (1960), Heckleman and Wallis (1997), North (1961), Taylor (1951), and Wallis, Sylla, and Legler (1994).

Evolving rights of organized labor reflect another set of struggles in all open access orders, at times violent. In the United States as in Europe, union activity was met at times with legal suppression and state-sponsored violence. This situation changed dramatically in the 1930s in large part due to the Great Depression. Directly, the Depression put so many people out of work that industrial unionism took off. Indirectly, the Depression brought the Democrats to power who crafted their New Deal, including the National Labor Relations Act of 1935, granting workers the right to organize, to bargain collectively through unions, to take part in strikes, and to bring their disputes with firms to a new agency, the National Labor Relations Board, for resolution. Union membership increased dramatically, violence against organized labor virtually disappeared, and the government ceased to collude with firms to use violence against workers (Davis et al. 1972, pp. 223–7).

Extension to other groups came in the twentieth century, beginning with white women. During this period, many European immigrants of the late nineteenth and early twentieth centuries remained suspect, especially German, Irish, and Jewish immigrants. By the mid-twentieth century, these groups had been incorporated. In the 1960s, following major political and social confrontations, a series of steps were taken to incorporate African Americans with the Civil Rights Act of 1964 and the Voting Rights Act of 1965. Simultaneously, the national government created a range of new Great Society programs to serve these constituencies. The courts have been involved through policies such as school integration, equal protection, and affirmative action. Nonetheless, the process of incorporation of African Americans remains incomplete.

Another feature of political responsiveness is that as citizen incomes, values, and preferences have changed, so too has governmental policy. For example, throughout most of the nineteenth century, economic regulation in the United States was undertaken by the states rather than the national government. The system of federalism induced competition among states, including competition for solutions to common problems.[5] This system worked reasonably well, especially when much economic activity was local or regional. By the latter portion of the century, however, the increasingly integrated, national economy created several economic problems that states could not solve on their own; notably, problems with the extensive, integrated railroad network and antitrust. Both problems became

---

[5] The importance of federalism in sustaining open access (although not in that specific term) is the subject of Stepan (2004) and Weingast (2006b).

national political ones as citizens increasingly sought national action. The national government responded by producing the first two major national regulatory laws, the Interstate Commerce Act of 1887 regulating railroads and the Sherman Antitrust Act of 1890 providing for a national antitrust law.

4.5 Control of Violence in Open Access Orders

The logic of controlling violence in open access orders runs counter to the logic of the natural state. In a natural state, dispersed control over violence leads to the formation of a dominant coalition that manipulates access in the economy and society to sustain political arrangements within the coalition. Access to violence is open to anyone strong enough and well organized enough to use it. The natural state coordinates these individuals and groups through an interlocking set of rent-creating arrangements that limit access throughout the rest of society.

Open access societies strictly limit access to violence while ensuring open access to political and economic activities. Because the political system in an open access order does not limit economic access, it appears that the economy exists independent of the political system. As the neoclassical economic fiction holds, markets exist and then politics intervenes. This seeming independence of politics and economics in an open access society overlays a much deeper and fundamental connection. It is here that impersonality occupies center stage. Political control of a specialized military and police force involves formal institutions and agreements about how and when violence can legitimately be used. The resulting rules governing the use of violence in open access orders must be impersonal; that is, the agreements must be independent of the identity of the individual member of the military or police force and, equally important, independent of the identity of the political officials.[6] If the rules do not apply impersonally, the society is a natural state.[7] Citizens defend these rules by withdrawing support from

---

[6] The case of the American commander during the Korean War, General Douglas MacArthur, illustrates the role of impersonality and political control of the military. MacArthur sought greater autonomy and authority during the Korean War, forcing a confrontation with President Harry Truman. The confrontation ended when Truman removed him.

[7] Consolidated political control of the military in a mature natural state also involves formal agreements, but the agreements are not sustained by open access. Nonetheless, a mature natural state with consolidated control of the military often meets at least one of the doorstep conditions and is potentially in a position to make a transition to open access, as we discuss in the following chapters.

political officials who attempt to violate these institutions and agreements (Weingast, 1997).

Because open access orders authorize the police and military to use violence to regulate relationships among everyone in society, rules about the use of violence affect the larger society. One function of the judicial system in an open access society is to regulate governmental relations with the military and police; another function is to regulate the formal authority given to the police and military to intercede in private relationships. Societies in which the government can credibly and impersonally limit the use of violence in private relationships are also able to provide third-party support for nonviolent private relationships.

The seeming independence of economic, political, and military arrangements in open access orders reflects the underlying conditions that make an open access society more robust to dynamic changes. Political management of violence is based on impersonal rules and organizations, not, as in the natural state, on the manipulation of economic privileges. As a result, open access societies adjust to economic and social changes without necessarily making adjustments in the political arrangements dealing with violence.

4.6 Growth of Government

Big government in open access orders is not an aberration but an integral feature of these societies. As Table 1.1 in Chapter 1 shows, governments (at all levels) in rich countries with per capita income of more than $20,000 averaged 53 percent of Gross Domestic Product (GDP). In contrast, countries with per capita income of $2,000 to $5,000 averaged 27 percent, and those with $5,000 to $10,000 averaged 33 percent.

Several factors produce larger governments in open access orders. We have already mentioned that incorporation of mass citizenry results in political responsiveness[8] and that the policies implementing equality and sharing are intimately connected to the politics of sustaining an open access order. Social insurance programs – as opposed to populism, socialism, and other forms of more explicit, massive redistribution – are relatively low-cost ways of sharing the gains of the market without disrupting it. These programs become integral to open access orders in that by lowering individual risk these programs lower the cost to the individual of market participation and thus reduce the probability of an antimarket political reaction during

---

[8] Acemoglu and Robinson (2006) provide the most extensive study of this effect.

bad times. All these programs require substantial budgetary outlays and expansion of government.

Impersonality is a second factor underpinning the growth of government in open access orders. People in all states desire a range of public goods and services. Yet in most natural states, the political system is both less responsive and less capable of meeting these demands. The biggest difference, however, is a supply-side effect. Because open access orders can deliver policy benefits on an impersonal basis, they can provide a far wider range of public goods and services than natural states. The result is big government in the sense of a wide range of policies and in government spending as a portion of GDP.

Another feature of the growth of government is more subtle and involves what is sometimes called state-building. These states require a series of public goods and services that the government must provide to sustain open access, including the five characteristics listed in Section 4.2. All of these elements require an institutionally complex government capable of delivering policies in particular ways without deteriorating into corruption or the personalized natural state politics. They also imply the strong limits on government – the limit condition (Weingast, 2006a). Each of the conditions listed in Section 4.2 requires limits on the government that lower the stakes of power and that help make the society more stable and less subject to coups by incumbents who cannot stay in power by the ballot box and so set aside democracy. Institutions that limit the stakes of power also lower support for coups: they make democracy – especially the costs of losing elections – less costly.

Open access orders must therefore have a far more articulated institutional structure and process than natural states. The explicit process of governing is both more transparent and more elaborate; and open access orders are able to sustain greater numbers of veto players, including a separation of executive, legislative, and judicial functions. The process of creating sovereign commands is unambiguous and common knowledge: everyone knows how laws and regulations are produced, and these laws are impersonal rules that apply to everyone. All these institutions are protected by credible commitments, including the consensus condition protecting the basic rules of the political and economic systems.

The growth of government in all open access orders reflects the policies necessary to maintain the social order through sharing the gains of long-term economic growth. Creating and maintaining an open access order require that the society incorporate the mass of citizens and elections without so much redistribution that it cripples the economy. Because the masses participate, some form of redistribution is inevitable, and an important aspect of an open access order is incorporating the mass of citizens with low dead-weight cost. The set of programs listed earlier – public goods and social insurance programs – all share the gains of the market and help to prevent more massive redistribution. Many of these programs complement the market rather than interfere with it, notably, education, infrastructure provision, and social insurance that increases labor's investment in human capital. Both Iversen (2005) and Mares (2003) suggest another feature of this complementarity. Because social insurance programs reduce labor's risk from market vicissitudes, they induce labor to make industry- and firm-specific investments that improve productivity in these industries.

To illustrate this view, consider the small trading states among the open access orders of Europe, including Austria, Belgium, Ireland, Italy, the Netherlands, the Nordic countries, and Switzerland (Katzenstein, 1985; Rogowski, 1989). Each of these countries has a relatively small trading sector compared to its economy, which generates economic returns on the international market through specialization and comparative advantage. Domestic political arrangements in these states embody an exchange: political stability, moderation of labor's wage demands, and rules favorable to the international sector in combination with significant taxes that share the benefits of economic success, not through cash payments but through high levels of social insurance programs. The exchange is made credible by various political institutions – such as proportional representation and coalition governments – that protect the status quo bargain and hence the relevant investments from expropriation (Rogowski, 1987). Consistent with our argument in Section 4.3, the economy also constrains politics: because the trading sector must compete on international markets, expropriation or draconian taxes risk the international sector's competitiveness and have immediate feedback effects.

Another advantage of open access orders over natural states is that they can endow bargains and compromises that solve major problems with credibility. In corporatist countries of Europe, national wage bargaining allows compromises to solve budget problems: for example, labor defers wage demands in exchange for higher taxes on firms (Garrett 1998). In the antebellum United States, several compromises between the non-slaveholding or free North and the slaveholding South helped keep the country together. The balance rule afforded each region a veto over national policy through equal representation in the Senate. The veto allowed slaveholders to prevent antislavery policies. This veto gave Northerners incentives to cooperate in other areas of mutual gain, notably the economy (Weingast, 1998).

The ability to make credible commitments affords open access orders the ability to solve many ongoing political problems as they arise. Without the ability to make these credible bargains, individuals and groups would instead play their short-term maximization strategies and fail to resolve a range of problems.

4.7 Forces of Short-Run Stability

All open access orders face two problems of stability. The first concerns static stability – the institutions and incentives that create a self-enforcing open access order and that prevent the tendency to degrade into a natural state. The second concerns dynamics – how open access orders sustain themselves in the face of the numerous problems and crises that arise over time. This section treats the first topic while the next section treats the second subject.

Political officials in all states are tempted to use rent-creation to solidify their position and to alter the rules in ways that make it difficult for their opponents to compete. For open access to survive, officials must have incentives to resist these temptations. In this section, we show how competition in both the political and economic systems helps sustain the open access order. No one institution or set of incentives alone sustains an open access order; instead, the institutions and incentive systems supporting this social order are numerous and redundant (as Landau, 1969, and Mital, 2008, suggest for the U.S. Constitution).

4.7.1 Elections, Party Competition, and the Civil Society

Democracy in open access orders sustains competition among political parties for the exercise of power. Competition for power induces parties to offer competing visions for addressing the society's principal problems. As with other forms of competition, innovators who devise more attractive ways of dealing with problems have advantages over those who do not. Because new problems, issues, and crises inevitably arise, Schumpeterian competition reigns: parties must constantly try new ideas in their attempts to capture or retain power. As Riker (1982a, Chs. 1 and 9) emphasizes, electoral losers have especially strong incentives to innovate in their efforts to regain power. Failing to do so risks remaining out of power with an absence of personal and political rewards. To capture power, today's losers must devise new ways of combining interests, constituencies, and political support.

Franklin Roosevelt's creation of the New Deal following the 1932 election and Tony Blair's remaking of the British Labour Party in the mid and late 1990s illustrate this principle. Both leaders devised new programs for their parties in the face of successful opponents and lackluster success of their own parties. Roosevelt's triumph came after the 1932 election following the Republicans' long-term dominance of American elections since 1860 and especially since 1918. Addressing various problems associated with the Great Depression, Roosevelt's New Deal programs became very popular not only among Democrats but also among Republicans who were affected by unemployment or feared being so.[9] Their political success granted Democrats united political control of American national government for a dozen years, a block of time that they had not enjoyed since Jackson's election in 1828. Blair's success came in the wake of Margaret Thatcher's successful conservative turn of Great Britain, which began with her becoming prime minister in 1979. Using the label "New Labour," Blair moderated his party's goals, symbolized by his removing the clause in the party's constitution seeking the common ownership of the means of production. Labour renounced Keynesian-style management of the economy, nationalization of industry, and negotiated income policies, focusing instead on competitive markets and fiscal and monetary conservatism (Iverson, 2005, p. 253). Although Blair significantly increased health and education spending and raised the minimum wage, he maintained many of Thatcher's economic policies and continued coordinating foreign policy with the United States.

Party competition forces parties to compromise and to moderate interest group and constituency demands. Rent-creation cannot be the primary product of party competition in open access orders. Consider first-past-the-post electoral systems. These systems are subject to Duverger's law (Cox, 1997; Duverger, 1959; Riker, 1982b), so that they produce two major parties.[10] Successful parties in these systems are therefore large, encompassing organizations that combine a wide range of disparate groups and interests. A party cannot hope to win general elections with extremist positions or policies that fail to command support from a range of different interests, constituencies, and voters. Because parties need to gain the support of many interests, they must temper the (rent-creating) demands of each, lest the associated extreme positions hinder the party's electoral prospects.[11]

---

[9] Reflecting this aspect of the era, David Kennedy (1999) titled his Pulitzer-Prize-winning history as *Freedom from Fear.*

[10] Cox (1997) shows how this law generalizes in a natural way to other types of electoral systems.

[11] A related logic holds in proportional representation (PR) systems even though parties can be more narrowly focused on particular issues in these political systems, such as

The efficacy of party competition, however, depends on open access to organizations and the civil society. Organizations allow citizens whose interests are harmed to coordinate, act, and advance their interests, and elections are a low-cost means of affecting outcomes short of direct confrontations with governments (Fearon, 2006). Organizations also monitor the incumbents and respond when their interests are affected. They have incentives to collaborate with opposition parties when their interests are harmed by incumbents. As the literature emphasizes, successful democracy and the civil society go hand in hand (Lipset, 1963; Gellner, 1994; O'Donnell and Schmitter, 1986; Tocqueville, 1969[1835]; Putnam, 1993; Widner, 2001).

Interparty competition fosters intraparty moderation and cooperation in another way. Van Buren explained in the 1830s that without competition individuals and organizations that compose a party have only weak incentives to make the compromises necessary to maintain the party as an effective organization and electoral competitor (Hofstadter, 1969, Ch. 6, especially pp. 226–52). As organized political parties emerged in the first American party system in the early 1790s, each party sought to destroy the other. Americans in this era had no concept of the loyal opposition: one had never existed in any political system. When the opposition Federalist Party disappeared in the Era of Good Feeling (1816–24), the dominant Jeffersonian Party fell into several factions that failed to work well together. Demise of the opposition did not result in triumph.

Van Buren realized that the disparate factions within a party have incentives to compromise and accommodate one another only when winning required it. Hofstadter explains:

> Here it became evident that the party had lost ground not because of the presence of a strong rival party but because of its absence: without external pressure toward solidarity, internal disintegration was unchecked. *The lesson was clear: the divisive and agitating effects of personal factions were far more serious and far more to be condemned, than the open principled conflict of two great parties* (Hofstadter, 1969, p. 229, emphasis added).

With the rise of the second-party system (roughly 1832 to 1860) following the Era of Good Feeling, beliefs came into line with experience: by the mid-1830s, a new system of stable two-party competition emerged, and Americans' beliefs transformed from those reflecting the attempt of each

green parties. Because parties in PR systems typically do not win with a majority of seats, forming a government involves a coalition of parties. Compromise and moderation arise when forming a government. Being an attractive coalition partner typically requires that parties moderate their demands, lest they be unattractive coalition partners.

party to vanquish the other to the idea of a two-party system with a loyal opposition party.

The transformation in beliefs was central to sustaining party competition in open access orders. We now accept competition among parties as commonplace, but the idea of party competition, especially the idea of loyal opposition parties, had to be invented and sustained. Van Buren recognized a central piece of the incentives for sustaining these beliefs: competition from the opposition was necessary for the winner's success. Here too, we see that sustaining party competition results in limits on politics: the winners do not seek to destroy the opposition, nor is the goal of the opposition to take power and destroy the incumbents.

The pluralists revealed another aspect of this same logic of competitive politics. These scholars understood politics as a balance of power among interest groups (Truman, 1952). Dahl's classic pluralist text, *Who Governs* (1962), demonstrated that open access order democracies face many public issues and that no group can extract too much for fear of mobilizing a great many groups against it. Dahl observed that the set of groups and constituencies active or attentive differ across the many public issues. Groups that dominate one issue (say, developers concerned about local urban development) tend not to be major players in other issues (say education, welfare, agriculture, or defense).

This observation has an implication not understood in this literature. A problem with pluralist analysis and studies of interest groups more generally is that it takes the pattern of constituency and group activity as exogenous. Instead, the interests active on any issue are endogenous. If a group attempts to extract too much, then other groups who are normally not active on an issue are likely to begin paying attention and become active, with the potential to alter dramatically the political forces on this issue and hence the outcome. Taking an endogenous pluralist approach to group influence suggests that groups in open access orders have incentives to moderate their demands most of the time. Failing to do so risks mobilizing outsiders to become active in ways detrimental to the original group's interests. The endogenous approach suggests that a few open access order markets might be cartelized or protected, such as agriculture, and certain markets regulated to produce rents, such as airlines in mid-century United States. However, these markets are the exception, not the general rule.

The force of both the inter- and intraparty competition and the pluralist arguments is that rent-seekers in open access orders have strong incentives to look down the game tree, to temper their policy demands lest they tip groups currently inactive on their issue toward becoming active and upsetting the current policy equilibrium. Although many policies create rents, most markets in open access orders are not cartelized or subject to high levels of tariff protection. The two social orders differ significantly on this dimension.

Fiscal incentives represent another set of incentives against rent-creation in open access orders that complement political competition.[12] No matter what their goals, political officials in all governments need revenue to pursue them. This fiscal effect biases officials in favor of policies that enhance their revenue. Open access orders tend to raise revenue on broad taxes on economic activity, such as value-added taxes common in Europe or the general income tax in the United States. Dependence on taxes of this type means that the government's fiscal resources rise and fall with economic prosperity. Policies that shrink the economy diminish tax revenue.

The main implication is clear: widespread rent-creating policies destabilize an incumbent coalition. These policies significantly shrink both the economy and tax revenue, so the coalition cannot maintain the current pattern of benefits and must therefore cut back on expenditures, harming constituencies who benefit from these expenditures. The fiscal interests of political officials force them to be concerned with economic prosperity even if this is not their principal goal. Incumbents in open access orders have strong incentives to maintain prosperity, and the evidence suggests that failing to do so turns them out of office (Kramer, 1971; Tufte, 1978). Furthermore, as Bueno de Mesquita et al. (2003) suggest, the turn toward massive rent-creation is politically inefficient in mass electorates; political leaders do far better gaining votes with public goods (education, social insurance) than with private goods (rent-creation).

4.7.2 Market Competition

Thriving market economies also facilitate the stability of open access orders, democracy in particular, in a surprising number of ways. By studying democracy in isolation of markets, political scientists have missed these forces of political stability. Most obviously – and this effect political scientists have long known – competitive markets provide the most powerful means for long-term economic prosperity. Evidence from across a range of political systems shows that they are more stable when they are more prosperous and that incumbents are more secure in power when they provide for prosperity (Haggard and Kauffman, 1995; Kramer, 1971; Londregan and

---

[12] For explicit discussion of fiscal interest see Wallis, Sylla, and Legler (1994) and Weingast (2006b); for more general discussion of fiscal effects see Tiebout (1956) and Oates (1972).

Poole, 1990; Tufte, 1978). Because open access orders provide for thriving markets, they produce prosperity over the long term in ways that natural states cannot match.

More subtly in its effects for political stability, the price mechanism facilitates pluralism, civil society, and party competition. Prices in competitive markets reflect marginal cost. This means that a change in one policy domain ripples through the economy, for example, by changing prices in other markets. The larger the change in other policy domains induced by the original policy change, the bigger the likely response of interests from other domains back into the area of the original policy domain. Competitive markets therefore combine with open access to organizations to facilitate monitoring of governmental policies and coordination against adverse policies by the government. The absence of competitive markets inhibits this signaling and response effect.

Another feature of open access markets reflects the idea that this order widely shares the gains of the market economy: when one sector of the economy experiences significant improvements and expansion, the dynamic aspects of the economy mean that the effects are felt throughout the economy. If the expanding sector employs a significant portion of the workforce that raises wages, for example, then factor price equalization raises wage rates in other parts of the economy, resulting in a greater sharing of the gains of economic growth. Incomplete and heavily controlled markets in natural states inhibit this effect. The same effect holds for productivity gains produced by open access markets. As labor productivity increases, so too do wages.

International competition among open access orders represents another set of forces helping to sustain these societies.[13] First, an open access order that imposes rent-creation policies with high costs on the economy gives its international competitors a market advantage. This competition produces a feedback effect: the country must decide if the policy benefits are worth the economic price. This feedback effect is especially important in small trading states that finance much of governmental spending from taxes related to the trading sector. Because these effects are felt quickly, they help protect the competitive sector in small trading states.

For example, with market integration in Europe, an aging workforce, the growth of globalization, and the growth of service economies, many

---

[13] The effect of international competition requires international openness. Periods in which some open access orders insulated themselves from international trade dampened this effect.

European states have tempered their market controls, macroeconomic management of their economies, and aspects of social-welfare policies. Across Western Europe, social democratic parties have moderated their programs and outlooks from those of the 1970s and 1980s but also have been innovative in the adaptations of their programs to the new realities of the 1990s and the 2000s (Garrett, 1998; see also Berman, 2006; Prasad, 2006), as illustrated by the transformation of the Labour Party under Tony Blair. The Nordic countries – among the most innovative social democracies in the 1960s and 1970s – have experienced considerable reform. As Lindert (2004, Ch. 11) observes, much of the Swedish reform has focused on macroeconomic management and tax policy rather than on reform of the welfare state. Garrett (1998) makes a similar argument for Western Europe more broadly.

The second effect of international competition involves violence and war. As the two world wars and the Cold War of the twentieth century illustrate, external violence is a central if episodic aspect of the international environment. To survive, open access orders must have the ability to succeed, not only in economic competition but also in violent competition (Ferguson, 2002; Schultz and Weingast, 2003; Tilly, 1992). Without this ability, they risk succumbing to the ambitions of authoritarian states. Had the Nazis succeeded in World War II, for example, then open access orders would be unlikely to dominate the world today, and all of Europe might remain authoritarian.[14] The success of open access orders in World War II and the Cold War demonstrates the need for these states to maintain economic, military, and adaptive superiority, or else risk being taken over or dramatically challenged by aggressive, powerful natural states. This risk remains today, as international terrorism and the events of 9/11 emphasize.

Violent international competition also tempers policymaking in open access orders, especially during periods of intense competition. The European willingness throughout the Cold War to cooperate with the United States illustrates this. The Soviet armies to the east, including their dominance by force of Eastern Europe, not only fostered cooperation through NATO but U.S. aid also helped foster market reform in Western Europe. U.S. aid often depended on market reform; for example, the famous Marshall Plan after World War II required as a condition that the countries of Western Europe lower tariff barriers to one another, create a realistic plan for macroeconomic management, and join a new organization for economic cooperation called the Organisation for Economic Co-operation

---

[14] Ironically, it took an alliance between the open access orders (the United States and Great Britain) and a limited access order (the Soviet Union) to defeat Germany in World War II.

and Development (OECD). Aid focused on market economies for providing prosperity in part as a means of making socialism a less attractive alternative.

International military competition has two closely related effects. The first is economic: thriving markets in open access orders provide the resource base from which these societies sustain long-term international struggles with hostile rivals. Open access orders that compromise their economies also compromise their ability to survive against hostile international rivals. The second is institutional: open access orders have the ability to make credible promises. With respect to sovereign debt, this ability allows open access orders to borrow heavily in times of need. Borrowing leverages a society's resources so that it may spend well beyond what it can raise in taxes. Borrowing and paying back the bonds over a thirty- or fifty-year horizon allow the society to "tax-smooth"; that is, to distribute the economic burden of the conflict through taxes over a much longer period, thereby greatly lowering the total deadweight losses from taxes (Barro, 1979). This contrasts with natural states' more limited ability to borrow; these states must rely more heavily on current taxes to finance their wars. Because they tax more heavily in times of great need, the associated tax burden and deadweight economic losses are necessarily high. As Schultz and Weingast (2003) show, borrowing facilitated open access orders' success in several multigeneration conflicts with natural states, including the Anglo-French-American rivalry with Germany (from the late nineteenth century through the end of World War II) and the Cold War between the United States and its allies and the Soviet Union (from the end of World War II through the collapse of the Soviet Union in 1991).[15]

A closely related effect is political: to create thriving markets, especially in the areas of early modern Europe moving to the doorstep and then making the transition, states had to create various forms of credible commitments to establish rights and rule of law, first for elites, and then for the whole citizenry (North and Weingast, 1989). These institutions created the new constitutional institutions underlying the emerging open access

---

[15] Moreover, these international effects are not limited to the twentieth century. Over the last three to four centuries, the West has experienced four sustained rivalries for dominance. In addition to the two mentioned, we include the Hapsburgs' drive to dominate Europe, resulting in the Dutch Revolt (1570–1640s); and the more than the century-long Anglo–French rivalry that ended with the defeat of Napoleon (1689–1815). In all four of these competitions, the open access order (or its doorstep and transitioning precursors in the Dutch and British cases) succeeded, in part because it had more efficient systems for mobilizing resources for international conflict than do the more personalistic natural state systems (Schultz and Weingast, 2003; Tilly, 1992).

orders of Western Europe, providing for open access in both politics and economics.

4.7.3 Implications

All states, open access orders included, face pressures for rent-creation. Political officials are tempted to create rents as a means of solidifying their positions and locking out their opponents. However, access and competition work against attempts to create rents in an open access society. Absent a constitutional coup that dramatically and quickly changes the rules of the game, too much rent-creation by the incumbents gives the opposition a competitive advantage: economically, it typically leads to fiscal constraints and declining prosperity; and politically, it grants the opposition the Schumpeterian basis to launch effective campaigns against the incumbents as they have ruined the means of prosperity. Open access to organizations fosters this outcome, as the opponents of those gaining rents support the opposition in its attempts to undo the new rent-creation policies.

This outcome reflects the virtuous circle of competition and open access. Political and economic competition combine: governments that fail to provide prosperity and public goods and services valued by citizens are punished by shrinking economies, lower tax revenue, the exit of mobile factors, and opposition parties that seek to unseat them.

4.8 Forces of Long-Run Stability: Adaptive Efficiency

All societies face the problem of how to survive in the face of uncertainty, the never-ending set of new challenges, dilemmas, and crises. The sources of these challenges are varied: changes in relative prices, demographic change, macroeconomic crises, ethnic conflict, civil wars, technological change, and security conflicts with other states.

Competition in open access orders to address major social problems fosters adaptive efficiency, the ability of the society to survive in the face of an ever-changing array of problems and difficulties (Hayek, 1960; North, 2005; Ober, 2008). Schumpeterian competition provides political and economic entrepreneurs with incentives to devise better and more attractive solutions to their society's problems.

Open access orders exhibit dynamic stability for two reasons. The first follows from open access and competition, which promote solving new problems. Open access and the free flow of ideas generate a range of potential ways to understand and resolve new problems. The larger the problem faced by the society, the more extensive is both the debate about the nature of the problem and the set of potential solutions. Individuals and organizations affected by the problem have incentives to invest in creating and advertising new solutions to problems. Political parties, interest groups, and organizations all compete to solve major problems and address crises. Those in power seek solutions to help them remain in power. Opposition parties and their support groups have strong incentives to expose the weaknesses in the incumbent's proposals and to devise more attractive alternatives. The larger the problem, the more individuals and organizations are affected by it, and the more widespread public input and discussion. The free and open expression of ideas means that many ideas will be heard. In their quest to maintain or to regain power, competing parties will draw on this competition for solutions, seeking ideas that further their interests.

This process is far from perfect; indeed, it is often a mess. Nevertheless, in comparison with natural states, open access orders more readily generate a range of solutions to problems; they more readily experiment with solutions to problems; and they more readily discard ideas and leaders who fail to solve them. For example, parties in power attempt to devise a program that they believe addresses the problem in a way that matches the interests of their constituents. If this program fails to resolve the problem, citizens can vote out the incumbents and bring in the opposition. The more attractive the opposition's program, the more likely is partisan turnover. If the incumbent party biases its reaction to benefit its constituents rather than to solve the problem, it grants its opponents a competitive advantage in the next election.

This experimental process is imperfect, in part because of the fundamental uncertainty about the nature of the problem and in part because of voter ignorance. Nonetheless, experimentation provides the best opportunity for open access orders to persist. In comparison to the absence of open access or competition in authoritarian natural states and the more hobbled version of electoral competition in many natural states, competition to solve problems in open access orders works reasonably well. The aggregation of information and ideas in the open access's free society gives these countries strong advantages over natural states in searching for solutions to problems. Limited access in natural states places limits on the range of individuals, groups, and organizations that participate in devising and debating new solutions; they also have many fewer mechanisms to allow the replacement of ideas and leaders, so experimentation works less effectively in these societies.[16]

The second reason for dynamic stability is the ability of open access orders to provide credible commitments. Political conflicts arise in all societies, for example, between rich and poor, agriculture and industry, workers and firms, and among different regions. The ability to make credible commitments in open access orders combines with this order's ability to deliver impersonal benefits to widen the set of feasible solutions to conflicts. Open access orders therefore more readily address these conflicts without disorder. For example, students of Western Europe argue that explicit incorporation of labor allows credible commitment to policies that solve budgetary problems in times of fiscal stress. In contrast, Spiller and Tommasi (2007) in their study of Argentina show that this inability plagues natural states' ability to solve similar problems.

All open access orders have faced this type of political conflict, and all have provided for political solutions that alter policy in ways that accommodate, to varying degrees, both sides. These are often called "pacts" in the literature (Burton, Gunther, and Higley, 1992). For example, the United States solved four major crises in the nineteenth century with pacts: the Compromises of 1820, 1833, 1850, and 1877, all major changes in the rules of the game that resolved political crises. Similarly, the Revolution Settlement of the Glorious Revolution (1689) and the various Reform Acts in nineteenth-century Great Britain (the subject of Chapters 5 and 6) were all pacts that resolved political conflicts. In contrast, the more limited ability to make credible commitments in natural states makes the set of feasible compromises smaller. These states cannot as readily endow policy solutions with credible commitments, so pacts are less likely to succeed. Conflict is therefore more likely to result in disorder.

Several other features of open access orders also contribute to this order's greater resiliency to crises. First, entrepreneurs in market economies seek to discover and exploit new niches. Some problems faced by natural states never become problems for open access orders because markets emerge to solve or mitigate them. Second, open access orders face fewer problems than do natural states, in part because natural states face far more self-induced problems, such as macroeconomic imbalances that cause regime instability. Very few open access orders have experienced hyperinflation, whereas large

---

[16] Ober (2008) explores similar ideas to those in this paragraph in the context of democracy in ancient Athens.

portions of modern natural states have. Third, as we have noted, the ability to provide benefits on an impersonal basis means that open access orders can provide far more public goods than natural states. Here too the wider range of policy flexibility implies that an open access order can solve certain problems through policy changes.

4.8.1 Sources of Change in Open Access Orders

Open access orders exhibit many sources of change. The two reasons underlying dynamic stability – experimentation and credible commitments – combine with uncertainty and the never-ending set of new problems to imply that open access orders exhibit regular, if episodic change. In Chapter 2, we explained how natural states are stable but not static. They too face a never-ending source of new problems and challenges. Yet their more limited ability to address these problems – to generate appropriate solutions and to endow these solutions with credible commitments – means that the dominant coalition is much less stable. In comparison with open access orders, these societies exhibit far more disorder in the form of coups, political turmoil, macroeconomic instability, civil wars, and ethnic conflict. Our discussion in Chapter 3 of medieval England illustrated this process of the natural state being stable but not static.

The varying reactions to the Great Depression of the 1930s illustrate this point. Although the depression created political problems in every open access order, the reactions were far less severe than in many natural states. In Latin America, for example, several of the major states experienced political disorder and military coups, including Argentina and Brazil. Yet the major open access orders, such as Britain, France, and the United States, were able to experiment with new policies that responded to citizen interests without disrupting these orders.

The political history of every open access order is punctuated by crises and the forces creating or limiting the types of ways that society can address the crises: wars; mass markets for agricultural products; huge atomistic labor markets facing large firms; ethnic, racial, and religious issues; and recessions and depressions.

A second source of dynamics is Schumpeterian competition. This competition means that markets continually evolve, creating new firms, products, and patterns of consumption. This evolution changes the range of interests in society. These changes combine with the positive responsiveness of an open access order's political institutions to imply that policies will adjust as interests change.

4.9 Why Institutions Work Differently under Open Access than Limited Access

All natural states have some markets and a degree of the civil society; their governments face fiscal incentives and mobile factors of production; and many have elections and competitive parties. If these institutions are present in natural states, why do they produce different outcomes in open access orders? This issue is especially puzzling in the context of democracy because the tendency in both the recent academic literature and the popular press is to identify democracy with elections.[17]

The answer is that the same institutions work differently in the presence of open access and competition than under limited access and the absence of competition. Consider the political system. Many mature natural states have elections and party competition, and contemporary political scientists typically consider them democracies in the same way as the open access orders of Western Europe, the United States, and Japan. However, elections are not the same across this divide, and we cannot lump them together as a single category called democracy.

Mature natural states may have elections and party competition, but they lack a wide range of institutions that support open access democracy in ways that are simply missing in natural states.[18] Mature natural states do not have open access to organizations, so they typically have a weak civil society where a wide range of organizations can represent and mobilize the interests of their members. Many natural states impose restrictions on the competitive party process, making it difficult or impossible for the opposition to organize, field candidates, or use the press. Their limited ability to provide impersonal benefits means that natural states cannot sustain public goods and social insurance programs that share widely the benefits of the market economy in ways complementary to markets. These states are therefore much more subject to populism and policies that create macroeconomic imbalances and budgetary crises, as is common throughout Latin America, most recently in the 1998–2002 crises throughout the region. The economic effects in natural states differ from those in open access orders. For example, natural states tend not to rely on broad taxes on the economy so that the fiscal

---

[17] See, e.g., Przeworski et al. (2000) and Barro (1999) for standard views in political science and economics, respectively.

[18] More than a generation ago, Dahl (1971) provided a multidimensional definition of democracy, which he called *polyarchy*, listing a wide range of factors beyond elections necessary for successful democracy. This compares with the definition more common in the literature today.

interests of the government do not reflect the state of the economy in the same way as in open access orders.[19] Similarly, limited access inhibits market competition sufficiently that these states tend to insulate themselves from the effects of mobile resources and international competition. In short, natural states short-circuit the open access and competitive mechanisms that provide for the virtuous circle in open access orders so that, although they may have elections and party competition, these institutions do not work in the same way that they do in open access orders.

The inability to provide impersonal benefits has another debilitating effect on natural states. Not only does this mean that courts are typically corrupt, but that natural states cannot implement legislation allocating benefits according to impersonal criteria. In the open access orders, legislation provides details about how laws are administered; for example, that a person recently unemployed is to receive benefits of a certain amount for a certain duration. In these states, impartial, rule-of-law courts impose penalties on the executive for failing to implement the laws according to the provisions specified in the law. Not so in the typical natural state. Instead, corrupt courts do not constrain the executive; moreover, the legislature rarely – and rationally – undertakes the job of writing detailed provisions to constrain the executive, leaving the executive great freedom to allocate the funds as desired. Evidence from Latin America suggests that social programs serve immediate political goals, such as reelection, rather than their intended purposes.

These points combine with the central logic of the natural state. The natural state's use of privilege and rents to maintain the dominant coalition necessitates limited access that prevents an opposition civil society capable of policing the government. For example, many natural states grant governmental employees, unions, and teachers privileged positions with above-market wages and with various rights to jobs that insulate them from market forces. In contrast to social insurance policies of open access orders, this form of policy to benefit workers reduces the incentives to invest and even to work (indeed, the evidence in many of these countries is that employees in these categories often do not work at these jobs, but have second jobs). Many mature natural states pursue populist policies that are far more detrimental to their economies than are the social insurance policies of open access orders.

---

[19] For example, Putin in Russia focused on economic reform as a means of gaining economic resources necessary to become more powerful, but once it became clear that oil prices would continue to rise, he abandoned reform (Goldman 2008; Kurov, 2008).

Next, consider markets. Most natural states have some markets, but natural states systematically limit access to organizations and market activities. Rent-creation to maintain the dominant coalition means that many markets face very limited or no access and hence the absence of competition. Widespread privileges and rents also disrupt the price-signaling mechanism. Natural states limit the ability of new organizations to form, which mobilize citizens against the state. Limited access also means that new sources of rents are typically captured by the ruling coalition. In short, natural states combine the elements of markets, elections, and organizations in very different ways than do open access orders. These states lack the dynamic Schumpeterian character of open access orders.

Finally, consider beliefs. At the most general level, few natural states have widely shared beliefs in equality and inclusion. Their inability to provide impersonal benefits hinders the provision of public goods and services, so the reality matches the absence of such beliefs: a great many people are left out. Natural states cannot support policies that widely share the gains of economic growth. Instead, citizens, especially poor ones, are more likely to support populist policies that conflict with markets. A major reason for support among the poor for Venezuela's President Chavez is that the poor do not gain much from economic growth during the oil boom cycle that disproportionately benefits the elite.

At the level of specific beliefs – the consensus condition – open access orders have a far more extensive range and domain of application than natural states. This condition encompasses the constitution in open access orders, including various structure and process creating the limit condition. Even in mature natural states (as in Venezuela) or those far along the transition (as in Korea), polls show that citizens hold beliefs inconsistent with maintaining the constitution, including support for military coups under some circumstances and that authoritarians are better at solving some of society's problems.[20] Natural states may have elections, but they do not have extensive systems of rights or rule of law for most citizens, and restrictions on organizations prevent many interests from mobilizing.

Our argument that the same institutions work differently in natural states than in open access orders stands in contrast to several literatures. We have already mentioned that economists and political scientists fail to understand the personalistic, rent-creation basis of natural states that makes it difficult for them to produce many of the common public goods

---

[20] See Baloyra (1986) on Venezuela and Shin (2000) on South Korea.

and services associated with markets and economic growth. The literature on democracy provides another example. Modern students of democracy overemphasize elections as the singularly essential feature of democracy. Although obviously necessary for open access democracy, elections alone fail to capture the broader context of democracy. Most cross-country studies of democracy fail to make the distinctions we emphasize. Thus, Argentina, Brazil, Mexico, and Russia all have elections, but these elections do not make them open access orders.

To summarize, many natural states have some of the features and institutions of economic and political competition, but neither system works the same as in an open access order. Markets in natural states have far less access and are subject to far more explicit privilege and rent-creation, so they are significantly less competitive. Prices frequently do not reflect marginal costs. The same holds for electoral competition. Many natural states have elections and opposition parties, but they do not have open access competitive democracy, which works very differently. Restrictions on the competitive process (hindering the opposition's ability to organize and compete), limited access to organizations, and a stunted civil society all hinder the competitive process. Similarly, the absence of competitive markets also reduces the salutary effects of fiscal incentives and mobile resources facing governments. Natural states cannot create the virtuous circle of open access and competition.

4.10 A New "Logic of Collective Action" and Theory of Rent-Seeking

The theory of open access orders provides a new approach to the "logic of collective action," one that turns both Olson (1965, 1982) and public-choice theorists studying rent-seeking (Buchanan, Tollison, and Tullock, 1980) on their heads. Both sets of scholars emphasized the pernicious effects of organized interests. Olson's (1965) logic of collective action involves a bias in interest group formation: in comparison with diffuse interests, concentrated interests are more likely to form. He argued that this bias allows the former to capture policy benefits at the expense of the latter. Although Olson (1982) argued that encompassing groups could push the state toward greater benefits for citizens, he emphasized that interest group influence eventually hampers all states; echoing Thomas Jefferson, he suggested that countries needed periodic revolutions to counter the negative influence of interest groups. Similarly, scholars emphasizing rent-seeking hold that political officials respond to concentrated interests by providing policy benefits that create privilege, exclusion, and rents.

Undoubtedly, considerable policymaking in all open access orders reflects this logic.

Nonetheless, both approaches fail to capture the essence of open access orders. Competitive markets in open access orders survive, despite the continued growth in the number and size of large, well-organized interests. Europe, United States, Japan, and several commonwealth countries have all long been characterized by open access market economies. Neither Olson nor the public-choice, rent-seeking scholars can explain the long-standing survival of open access markets and competition in the face of organized interests that comprise the civil society. Nor can either approach explain why rent-creation is so much more central to natural states than open access orders.

Our framework suggests a different view. Organizations are the lifeblood of both political and economic competition. They are the vehicles through which economic and political entrepreneurs implement their ideas and affect the dynamics of the economy and the polity. Moreover, as we suggested in our endogenous approach to pluralism, Olson and the rent-seeking scholars ignore the idea of an equilibrium set of politically active groups. Yes, many active interest groups gain policy benefits and rents, but Olson's approach fails to understand the potential for a much wider range of interests to form in opposition to systematic attempts to dismantle an open access order through privilege and rent-creation. Olson also ignores the ability of political institutions to reflect the interests of unorganized groups. When too many rents threaten an open access order, the opposition party has Schumpeterian incentives to make this a central issue, publicizing this problem and advocating its eradication.

Most organizations seek rents, and some (especially a few pivotal constituencies, such as farmers) succeed in gaining policies that provide them with government-run cartels, subsidies, and rents. However, that side of the story misses that organizations are also the chief reason why the vast majority of markets are not cartelized despite producers being more concentrated than consumers and why the extension of privilege does not dominate open access orders and transform them into limited access orders. Without open access to organizations and the subsequent civil society, the citizen reaction underlying the consensus mechanism would not work nearly so well; policing the constitution and the society's structure and process would be far more difficult.

Indeed, one of the principal purposes of open access orders is to unleash the power of organizations. Galbraith (1956) provides an important insight into the operation of modern open access orders with his idea of the countervailing power of large organizations. All firms want privileges and policy benefits from the government, and most large firms are politically active today. Yet all have an interest in maintaining a level playing field and preventing their competitors, suppliers, and customers from gaining privileges at their expense. At the same time, the competitive process of rent-erosion represents a force in an open access order against privilege. The result is many new sources of rents from the Schumpeterian creative destruction process of rent-creation, rather than a political process of rent-creation through privilege and limited access.

4.11 Democracy and Redistribution

Models central to understanding democratic decision making in the political economy literature hold that democracy is redistributive. Meltzer and Richard (1981), long a standard, show that when the distribution of income is skewed, the median voter theorem allows low- and middle-income citizens to redistribute income to themselves from the rich. This model assumes a one-dimensional setting in which voters face the sole policy choice of income redistribution. Acemoglu and Robinson (2000, 2006) use a variant on this logic in their recent work on democratization, showing that elections are a method by which the wealthy elite commit to a redistribution of income to the poorer masses over time (see also Boix 2003). This approach to democracy as redistribution is widely influential in studies of redistribution, government spending, welfare policy, and the role of the state in the economy (e.g., Iversen, 2005; Wren, 2006).

Our approach differs. Democracy involves responsiveness to the citizenry. However, the Meltzer and Richard approach forces the framework into one dimension where the only choice is redistribution. This framework misses the essence of responsiveness in open access orders. Open access orders involve inclusion, equality, and impersonality. Policy responsiveness involves not soak-the-rich redistribution but public goods and services that are complementary to the market, which provides open access to all.[21] As we have emphasized, these policies involve mass education, financial and transportation infrastructure, and social insurance programs that in combination facilitate economic growth, increase human capital, and lower the risk to individuals from participation in markets. As Lindert (2004) emphasizes, it is not obvious that these programs are, on net, costly for

---

[21] Garrett (1998) provides a similar view in the context of democratic politics in contemporary Western Europe.

open access orders. The reason is in part the idea of complementarity. These programs are not mere transfers of income with deadweight losses, but are public goods that generate positive economic returns.

Most natural states cannot pursue impersonal policies, so they have trouble providing public goods, infrastructure, mass education, and social insurance programs. When they face high demands for responsiveness, too often it is in the form studied by Meltzer and Richard: direct transfers, such as those to government employees, teachers, and guarantees to labor. Various forms of populism in Latin America and Africa too often lead to macroeconomic imbalances, economic crises, and the collapse of regimes.

Open access orders avoid playing the zero-sum Meltzer and Richard game. Not only are elections more competitive in open access orders, but the ability of open access orders to provide impersonal policy benefits allows responsiveness to citizens to occur through a positive-sum game involving public goods.

An important aspect of the positive-sum game is institutional. To create and maintain equality and impersonality, open access orders create institutions and the rule of law that prevent discrimination. Constitutional provisions in the United States, for example, limit the ability of laws to discriminate against individuals, forcing laws to be general provisions that apply to broad classes of individuals.

As evidence for our perspective, consider the application of the Acemoglu and Robinson (2006) framework to the first transitions in the nineteenth century. One problem with their view is that the governments in all these states remained small in the nineteenth century, and they pursued few programs involving explicit redistribution. Government in these states cannot be interpreted as a deal to commit to transferring wealth from the rich to the poor. In a literal sense, Acemoglu and Robinson are wrong; however, they are right in a deeper one.

As part of the transition to open access orders, responsiveness meant inclusion: granting access of the citizenry to existing institutions of the rule of law, previously limited to the elite; initiating or expanding education to the masses; and opening access to the markets and organizations where once elites alone had privileges. Here, too, democratic responsiveness was not zero sum as envisioned by Meltzer and Richard. As we will see in Chapters 5 and 6, opening access was not forced on elites, but was in part driven by elites who found it in their interest to expand access. Again, the politics of inclusion and responsiveness involved a positive-sum game.

The literature on capitalism, democracy, and the welfare state also provides evidence for our approach. For example, Garrett (1998, p. 5) explains the positive-sum logic of the corporatist open access orders of Western Europe:

> Social democratic corporatist regimes are based on a virtuous circle in which government policies [such as social insurance programs] that cushion market dislocations are exchanged for the regulation of the national labor market by the leaders of encompassing trade union movements. The products of this virtuous circle include predictable patterns of wage setting that restrain real wage growth in accordance with productivity and competitive constraints, highly skilled and productive workers, cooperation between labor and business in the work place, and low levels of social strife more generally. These economic "goods" are attractive even to mobile asset holders generated by big government and high labor costs highlighted by neoclassical economics.

As another example, whereas the older literature on the welfare programs argued that the state forced these programs on an unwilling capitalist class, the more recent literature provides evidence that firms and business leaders cooperated in the creation of these programs (Estevez-Abe, Iversen, and Soskice, 2001; Garrett, 1998; Iversen, 2005; Iversen and Soskice, 2001; Mares, 2003; Swensen, 2002). At the heart of this new literature is the observation that the social programs induce workers to make firm- and industry-specific investments that have payoffs for both workers and firms. Working from a very different tradition and evidence, Fishback and Kantor (2000) show that the origins of workers' compensation programs in the American states required the cooperation of employers, insurance companies, and workers. The failure of any of these players to cooperate led to the failure of a state to adopt such a program. The lesson of these studies is that social welfare programs are not forced on the rich or employers, as in a zero-sum context, but emerge from a cooperative context in which both sides gain. These programs reflect open access orders and democracy within that order as facilitating complementarities rather than confrontation and zero-sum politics.

4.12 Adaptive Efficiency and the Seeming Independence of Economics and Politics in Open Access Orders

The defining feature of an open access society is open entry into politics and economics. On the political side, the extension of citizenry creates mass politics and political competition and is fundamental to opening access. In different eras, incorporation of citizens has extended to ever-larger sets of groups, beginning with native males, extending to native women, and later to broader groups. On the economic side, allowing access to organizational forms, enabling participation in credit and goods markets, and empowering individuals to enter any market in which they feel they can compete are fundamental to opening access.

Economic and political accesses are deeply connected. Political responsiveness in open access orders reflects shifts in economic interests. This, in turn, leads political officials to provide a range of public goods and services that respond to economic opportunities. Early in open access history, public goods focused on access to institutions and services that were traditionally the exclusive domain of elites, such as access to markets, rule of law, and the administration of impersonal justice. Open access orders of the nineteenth century also provided infrastructure, especially those providing access to markets (roads, canals, railroads) in Western Europe helping to transform vast areas of once traditionally organized, self-sufficient, poor peasant agriculture into market economies. Extension of mass education also began in this era. In the twentieth century, public goods extended to a wide range of local public goods, services, and social insurance programs that dampened the effects of market vicissitudes for individuals.

The approach in this chapter has new implications for understanding democracy. The dominant view identifies democracy with electoral competition. We disagree. Elections in natural states differ from those in open access orders in several ways. Open access affords a rich civil society, a free press, and open competition of an opposition, whereas natural states tend to limit each of these. The ability of open access orders to provide impersonal benefits allows them to offer a far wider array of public goods than natural states. These states use public goods to respond to electoral demands in ways that are more complementary to markets at lower cost than do natural states. In contrast to the Meltzer and Richard (1981) zero-sum game of redistribution, which characterizes many natural states, elections and responsiveness become a positive-sum game in open access orders (Garrett, 1998). Only open access societies can sustain democracy in the sense of a stable system for controlling political officials and responding to citizens.

This chapter also suggests a new "logic of collective action." Olson and other theorists of rent-seeking emphasize the pernicious effects of organized interests. These theories have no explanation for why open access orders have been sustained for generations. Taking the political system as a given, these approaches show that organized interests at the margin gain rents. By taking open access as a given, however, these approaches fail to see that organizations are a major reason for the system's stability. Organizations are tools that allow constituencies to mobilize when their interests are threatened and that help police the government when it threatens to violate constitutional principles.

The ability to provide a changing mix of public goods is just one manifestation of the open access order's ability to adjust to dynamic change, what Hayek (1960) and North (2005) have called adaptive efficiency. All societies face new challenges, dilemmas, and crises. Open access orders provide the best means of adapting in the face of these ongoing challenges. By virtue of open access, these societies generate a range of new ideas in the face of dilemmas. Political competition also provides those in power with strong incentives to adapt policy in ways that address the problem; failing to do so risks losing power. Reflecting Schumpeterian creative destruction, economic actors are quick to find and exploit new sources of profits in the changing conditions. New economic solutions change the incentives facing political actors. The political system also embodies creative destruction, as the political opposition has especially strong incentives to devise creative solutions to dilemmas (Riker, 1982a): providing more attractive solutions than those offered by the incumbent is an obvious route to political office. Open access orders are better than natural states at generating new ideas and at discarding bad ideas in the face of the omnipresent unfolding of new problems faced by all societies.

Adaptive efficiency in open access orders appears to be the result of independent economic and political systems. In a natural state, all big economic organizations are necessarily also political organizations because they cannot survive and protect their privileges without serving political ends. In contrast, most large economic organizations in the market economies of open access orders focus on market activities. As Rosenberg and Birdzell (1986) emphasize in their economic history of organizations in the West, economic organizations in open access orders do not have to serve political interests. In terms of our approach, economic organizations in open access orders need not be closely tied to political actors to maintain their rights or to ensure their survival from expropriation. Open access orders protect the rights of individuals and organizations and provide the rule of law, including the enforcement of contracts. Markets and other systems in open access orders, therefore, appear more autonomous than in natural states where all major market organizations must also serve political ends. The same logic holds for politics. Although political systems in open access orders support impersonal markets, markets seem to exist without action or support of the political system.

This seeming independence reflects equilibrium independence, however. In an open access order, political actions that affect economic interests result in economic organizations that become more politically active. Mobile resources and fiscal interests both directly constrain policymaking, if in ways sufficiently subtle that scholars often miss them. If political actors anticipate the potential reactions of economic actors, this deters the types of policies that would cause economic actors to become politically active. The extent to which economic actors appear to operate largely through economic organizations depends on this close, but not obvious, connection between economics and politics.

The seeming independence of the political and economic systems in open access orders also explains why open access orders exhibit a much higher degree of adaptive efficiency than natural states. The much greater degree to which economic arrangements can adjust independently of political arrangements gives open access societies much more flexibility in the face of dynamic change. Because open access orders successfully control violence, everyday political and economic decision making do not take place in the shadow of violence. The greater degree of independence of economics and politics can be deceptive and misleading. If we take the economy or democracy as a given, we miss the subtle but striking forms of interaction that sustain open access.

FIVE

The Transition from Limited to Open Access Orders

The Doorstep Conditions

5.1 Introduction

Societies do not leap from limited to open access. Transitions occur in two steps where first the relations within the dominant coalition transform from personal to impersonal, and then those arrangements are extended to the larger population. The transition begins in a natural state, so the initial steps must be consistent with the logic of the natural state and personal relationships. Impersonal elite relationships can develop within the natural state by changing formal rules that transform elite privileges into rights. When a natural state develops institutions, organizations, and beliefs that allow elites to treat each other impersonally, then that society is on the *doorstep*. In the second step, the transition proper, societies on the doorstep continue to transform intra-elite relationships. Creating institutions that formally protect impersonal elite identities and elite access to organizations enables the extension of the same rights to a larger segment of the population. We treat the transition proper in the next chapter.

Our emphasis on personality and impersonality flows from the importance of developing impersonal exchange and relationships in human history. Personal elite identities are closely related to organizations, and the connection between personality and identity allows us to deal directly with formation of beliefs. Viewing the dynamics of social orders as shaped by the way in which organizations and institutions are structured, the consequent focus on the state as an organization and the dynamics of intra-elite relationships within the coalition now pays dividends. Institutionalizing impersonal elite relationships once the doorstep conditions are attained requires modifications in the underlying structure of elite organizations, identities, and beliefs.

Focusing on intra-elite relationships within the dominant coalition follows directly on the logic of the natural state. However, as an answer to the question of why elites give up their privileges, it differs fundamentally from the emphasis of modern economics and political science. Acemoglu and Robinson's *Economic Origins of Dictatorship and Democracy* (2006) presents innovative, state-of-the-art thinking about the transition process and serves as a useful point of comparison to our approach. They formulate the transition question in terms of democracy:

To starkly illustrate our framework, consider a society in which there are two groups: an elite and the citizens. Nondemocracy is rule by the elite; democracy is rule by the more numerous groups who constitute the majority – in this case, the citizens. In nondemocracy, the elite get the policies it wants; in democracy, the citizens have more power to get what they want. Because the elite loses under democracy, it naturally has an incentive to oppose or subvert it; yet, most democracies arise when they are created by the elite.

This approach raises a puzzle: if democracy brings a shift of power in favor of the citizens, why would the elite ever create such a set of institutions (Acemoglu and Robinson, 2006, p. xi)? This question provides the framework for Acemoglu and Robinson's powerful and sophisticated analytical framework of the transition.

Characterizing Acemoglu and Robinson's framework as a more subtle version of a single-actor state model oversimplifies their approach, but does no fundamental injustice to their method. They focus on elites and non-elites and ask when elites find it in their interest to concede power to non-elites. Their answer, unfairly simplified, is that elites concede power when they fear they will lose it anyway and believe they will lose less by concession than through revolution. Much of Acemoglu and Robinson's sophistication lies in demonstrating how elite promises to share power with non-elites are made believable through democratic reforms, a concern we share.

We come at the same problem from a different perspective. In natural states, elites are not a unified group, but are composed of disparate groups that compete and cooperate, and sometimes go to war against each other. Because they are not unified, elites cannot intentionally decide to do anything, let alone decide to share power. Members of the dominant coalition are rarely so unified.

Consistent with the logic of the natural state, open access emerges as a solution to the existing problem of structuring relationships within the dominant coalition to ensure order. The first step occurs when some elites find that moving to more impersonal relations makes them better off without threatening the stability of the coalition. As conditions allowing impersonal relations among elites are created, elites may find it in their interests to secure their impersonal privileges through formal institutions, such as legislation, a legal system, and the extension of citizenship. Giving all elites the same privilege transforms that privilege into a right.

5.2 Personality and Impersonality: The Doorstep Conditions

Any explanation of the transition must begin with societies that are natural states. This imposes three specific logical requirements:

1. The institutions, organizations, and behavior of individuals in place at the beginning of the transition must be consistent with the logic of the natural state.
2. Changes in institutions, organizations, and behavior that occur during the transition must be consistent with the interests of members of the dominant coalition (but the results of those changes may be unintended).
3. The transition must occur in historical time through a series of reinforcing changes in institutions, organizations, and individual behavior such that incremental increases in access are sustained by the existing political and economic systems at each step along the way.

While all natural states create rents through personal privileges, natural states can support impersonal characteristics as well. In English land law, *freeholder* was an impersonal category based on land tenure that granted all freeholders the right to use the king's courts and, if they possessed enough land, the right to vote. The impersonal category of freeholder was embedded in a system where the rights of the tenants in chief were personal.

Natural states are dynamic and their internal structures undergo regular if episodic change. Regimes and dynasties rise and fall, relative prices adjust, climates fluctuate, neighboring competitors appear and disappear, and boundaries and borders shift. The wide variety of possible forms that can be taken by political and economic systems within a natural state produce different economic and political outcomes. Out of these shifting patterns, societies occasionally produce arrangements with a better chance of initiating the transition to open access. Historically in the West, societies in Athenian Greece, Republican Rome, and the Renaissance city-states of Northern Italy appear to have been on the doorstep of the transition, although all three failed to produce open access societies. All three societies are celebrated in Western history, and all managed to create an impersonal identity for elite members of the governing coalition: citizen.

Three facets of natural state societies are necessary to sustain impersonal relationships among elites. We call these the doorstep conditions because once the doorstep conditions are in place it is possible, but not inevitable, for impersonal relationships among elites to generate incentives to open access in the polity and economy.

The three doorstep conditions are:

DC #1. Rule of law for elites.
DC #2. Perpetually lived organizations in the public and private spheres.
DC #3. Consolidated control of the military.

Historically, the doorstep conditions built on one another in the first societies to move to open access. The creation of perpetually lived organizations for elites grew out of rule of law for elites. The creation of consolidated control over the military involved both elite rule of law and elite perpetually lived organizations. All three conditions are necessary to establish extensive impersonal exchange among elites. It is not clear, however, that the historical order of development is necessary.

DC #1) Rule of law for elites. The dominant coalition in every natural state is an adherent organization, a group of individuals bound together by mutual interests and threats. Their constant interaction inevitably gives rise to the possibility of regularizing behavior through rules, both informal and formal, governing specific relationships among the elite. Adjudicating disputes among elites is a fundamental part of sustaining relations among elites. All natural states accomplish this by identifying procedures for arbitration and mediation functions. In some natural states, these functions become formalized into a machinery of government and justice. As we stressed earlier, the origin of property rights and legal systems is the definition of elite privileges in the natural state.

Rule of law requires the establishment of a judicial system in which individuals with the appropriate standing have access to rules and procedures (usually including courts or bureaucracies) whose decisions are binding and unbiased, at least with respect to elites.[1] Rule of law is not, of course,

---

[1] We mean unbiased in the sense that the laws are applied fairly, not that the laws are fair. Natural state legal systems typically distinguish among different individuals on the basis of status; as we have seen, rule of law for elites in a natural state does not imply that all

a zero/one variable; the extent and dimensions of rule of law vary continuously and from society to society.

DC #2) Perpetually lived organizations in the public and private spheres. A perpetually lived organization lives beyond the life of its individual members. Because a partnership must be reformed on the death or withdrawal of any partner, a partnership is not perpetually lived. A corporation is a perpetually lived organization because its structure allows it to live beyond the life of the members who create it; no single member can dissolve the corporation at will. Organizations that exist at the pleasure of the king or leader are therefore not perpetually lived. Perpetual life is not eternal life, but a life defined by the identity of the organization rather than the identity of its members.

Durability of the institutional arrangements within an organization does not, in itself, grant an organization perpetual life. A perpetually lived organization requires a legal system capable of enforcing legal rules regarding organizations. In the eyes of the law, the organization must be a *legal person* capable of bearing rights and duties, and it must be independent of the identity of its individual members at any given moment. Perpetual life is a characteristic of both public and private organizations. Political, municipal, educational, fraternal, and religious corporations are numerically and substantively much more important forms of corporations than business corporations until the nineteenth century.

Perpetually lived private organizations cannot exist without a perpetually lived state. A mortal state cannot credibly commit to support perpetually lived contractual organizations; no successor state is bound to honor the organizations created by the old one. If a state cannot credibly commit to honor its agreements beyond the current dominant coalition, then it cannot commit to enforce the agreements of an elite organization whose life extends beyond the lives of its members. The second doorstep condition requires development of perpetual life for states as the most important elite organization.

The creation of perpetually lived organizations creates a form of impersonal exchange and relationships. Contracts and agreements become more secure because they are made with the organization, not with individual members of the organization. Those contracts also extend beyond the life of

---

elites are treated the same. Instead, rule of law for elites implies that all individuals of a certain class or standing are treated the same.

any individual member. For example, creating corporate business with tradable shares may provide incentives for elites to expand impersonal markets so they can increase the value of their shares.[2]

DC #3) Consolidated control of the military. The third doorstep condition is consolidated control of the military. As we have emphasized, natural states rarely have consolidated control of the military, although the Soviet Union was an exception. Instead, in most natural states access to the means of violence is dispersed throughout the elite.

Consolidated control of the military requires the existence of an organization with control over all the military resources of the country; that control over the various military assets is consolidated in that organization; and a set of credible conventions that determine how force is used against individuals and coalition members. The organization that controls the military is usually a political organization embedded in the larger structure of the government, such as the Defense Department in the United States. Societies experiencing a civil war, by definition, do not have consolidated control of the military. Societies in feudal Europe or the Ottoman Middle East did not have consolidated control of the military, as armed and dangerous elements of the population were spread throughout the dominant coalition.

Consolidated control of the military is a subtle problem. Nothing precludes a faction within a natural state from taking control of military resources. However, such a natural state is very likely to be a tyranny, not a society on the doorstep. Moreover, societies where a single faction dominates the military are unlikely to sustain consolidated control for long, because the factions and groups in the dominant coalition without the means to protect themselves have no reason to believe that the commitments made to them will be honored. In most natural states, the absence of consolidated control of the military is simply a fact of life.

Most natural states are organized through patron–client networks in which groups of nonmilitary elite members – traders, producers, priests, educators, and others – are allied with militarily potent members of their network. The dispersion of military power corresponds to the existence of multiple networks. Because agreements that reach across networks are vulnerable in times of violence, they are less likely to be undertaken. Identity within patron–client networks matters. Natural states with elite rule of law

---

[2] Jha (2008) studies this in the context of seventeenth-century England.

and support for elite organizations, but without consolidated control of the military, therefore limit the range of impersonal relationships among elites. Consolidated control of the military removes this source of risk and thus extends the range and scope of impersonal relationships among elites.

All three of the doorstep conditions are consistent with the logic of the natural state and arise historically within limited access orders. The establishment of laws and courts is the means by which the dominant coalition regularizes relations among elites. Perpetually lived organizations are a vehicle for limiting entry and generating rents in a systematic manner. Consolidating military power under control of the political system creates a monopoly on violence that reduces the frequency of violence in a state. Combined, the three doorstep conditions create the possibility of impersonal relationships within the elite, even though that was not necessarily the result elites intended.

5.3 Doorstep Condition #1: Rule of Law for Elites

Rule of law covers a wide spectrum of social, legal, and political arrangements that vary in many dimensions. Rule of law for elites in a natural state is not the same thing as rule of law in a modern open access society. It is not unbiased law covering a wide range of civil and criminal activities, applying to everyone equally within the society, and structuring public as well as private relationships. Throughout this chapter, the term *individual* is used to designate individual human beings and *persons* to indicate legal persons who may or may not be individuals.

Several legal systems made appearances in earlier chapters: the Roman law and its successors in the European canon and civil law, the Salic codes of the ancient Franks, and the land law of medieval England. The privilege of administering justice provides valuable rents to some elites in natural states. In early states, law was often administered in connection with religious authority. As societies develop more durable institutions for the state, the law formalizes how the dominant coalition uses its coercive power to discipline and punish individuals inside and outside of the coalition.

The administration of law must confront two conflicting aspects of reality within natural states. Most elites benefit, in principle, from well-defined rules enforced in an unbiased manner. Knowing the structure of relationships among private individuals (private law) and how relationships among individuals, organizations, and the state itself (public law) enhances the value of elite exchange and produces valuable information for all elites.

At the same time, elites know that political, economic, and military power are not distributed equally throughout the coalition. Formal laws that are inconsistent with the distribution of interests within the coalition will not be enforced for long, even if they remain on the books. One way to resolve these conflicting aspects utilizes differences in identity to construct a law that can be credibly enforced in the face of wide differences in the power and influence of members of society. Recall the examples of Salic law: Killing a lord involved a much greater penalty than killing a slave. Legal systems do not have to treat everyone the same, and the extent to which legal systems formally treat individuals differently creates differences in identity.

Indeed, legal systems vary on many dimensions. One is the scope of jurisdiction in terms of activities and functions that are regulated (land, property, crime, contract, and so on). Another is the scope of jurisdiction over individuals (in medieval England only freeholders had access to the king's courts for land disputes). A third dimension is the differentiation among categories of persons that the legal system recognizes, which can range from homogeneous (all persons the same) to idiosyncratic (each individual possesses unique characteristics). A fourth dimension is the extent to which enforcement of laws and rendering of decisions is unbiased.

Set aside questions about the scope and public or private structure of legal systems for a moment and focus only on categorical differentiation of legal persons and the extent of bias. In a fragile natural state, regardless of the categorical differentiation of legal persons, laws will be enforced in ways that meet the immediate needs of the dominant coalition. Fragile natural states are unlikely to have unbiased enforcement of laws, no matter how the law or persons are defined. As basic natural states emerge and develop more durable institutional structures for their states, they are likely to create paths of legal development that more or less differentiate among categories of legal persons.

Consider the distinction between public and private law. The definition of legal persons and the specification of the legal rights attached to specific legal persons are elements of public law. Chapter 2 introduced the European history of the king's two bodies; the idea that the king possessed a mortal, individual body and a corporate, immortal body (or person). The king's dignity, his corporate person, was a legal entity, uniquely defined, protected from insult or slight by *les majeste*, endowed with privileges and obligations that kings confirmed in their coronation oaths.[3] All manner

---

[3] At the end of his life the great English legal scholar F. W. Maitland struggled to understand the concept of the king as a "corporation sole" (2003, pp. 9–31). Maitland had become

of major personages possessed a social persona whose uniquely defined identity (and therefore personal rather than impersonal identity) contained the institutionalized elements of that person's social and legal standing, as well as the person's inherent privileges to economic, political, and military assets and other social functions.

In modern societies, public law includes various categories, including constitutional law, administrative law, and statutory law. In earlier societies, public law was constitutional law as well, but the constitution of the society was not defined in terms of relationships among abstract and impersonal actors – president, senator, prime minister, the bureaucracy, and citizens – but among live individuals such as kings, dukes, popes, and bishops whose identity was an amalgam of individual characteristics and social characteristics of their office. In modern open access societies, public offices have become impersonally defined and distinct from the individual identity of the person who occupies the office. In contrast, in earlier societies and in most natural states today, public law is unable to clearly separate the identities of public persons as specific individuals from the privileges they possess as office holders and from the organization they represent or head.

For example, when Charlemagne issued a diploma to an abbey granting it rights to certain revenues and exemptions from other taxes in perpetuity, he not only chartered an organization, he created a public person, the abbot, who possessed certain privileges and duties. The grants of rights and privileges to every abbey and abbot differed – they were inherently personal. The exact relationship between the abbot as an individual and the abbot as the office holder was also not perfectly clear.

Many important attributes of significant legal persons are organizational rather than individual. In Rome and Europe up to the nineteenth century, all formal organizations were public law entities: entities created by the state with a place fixed in the public order. Kings, dukes, earls, popes, and bishops possessed privileges that enabled them to form, govern, and direct organizations. The laws limiting the number of liveried retainers of the fourteenth-century English tenants in chief, for example, not only created a special privilege for powerful lords but also denied those right to all other lords.

What then of rule of law for elites? Elements of rule of law for elites arise when aspects of the law apply equally to all elites and are enforced without

interested in the work of Gierke (1958[1900]) who interpreted the law and history in terms of corporate entities. Kantorowicz (1997[1957]) solved Maitland's puzzle of the corporation sole by elucidating the concept of the king's two bodies.

bias. Rule of law for elites is not a zero/one variable; it can exist on some dimensions but not others. In English law, all freeholders enjoyed a shared, common right of inheritance. This right originated with the promise made by Henry I in his coronation oath of 1100 that on the death of a tenant, his heirs could enter into their inheritance after the payment of a just relief. Early English land laws created categorical differentiation among types of elites. Over a long period of five centuries, however, land law came to recognize only one type of elite landowner, the freeholder (who possessed political rights denied to the copyholder), and one tenure of land, free and common socage. With the passage of the Tenures Abolition Act in 1660, the English system finally possessed rule of law for elite land.

English land law is only an example of how rule of law for elites may develop, but it illustrates important implications of how rule of law for elites affects the transition. Rule of law for elites with respect to land created an environment in which exchanges of land among elites occurred without reference to the personal identity of the parties. Truly impersonal exchange over elite landholdings, particularly at the level of manors, was impossible as late as the sixteenth century. In the land wars, more powerful lords had an advantage in enforcing their rights in the courts; in effect, ownership rights varied with the power of the lord.

By instituting a common set of rights held by all elites, rule of law for elites created a common interest in defending those rights. A great deal of English history is written in terms of the tensions and conflict in the relationships between the king and nobility. By ignoring intra-elite disputes, historians overemphasize king–nobility disputes. Intra-elite competition dominated conflicts over land, not competition between the nobility and the crown. The Wars of the Roses, the largest land war in English history, was an intra-elite conflict. Intra-elite competition between the Chancery Courts and the Common Law courts, both royal courts, for jurisdiction and revenue produced many of the changes in English land law. Once all elite landowners possessed the same right, such as the right of inheritance and later the right to devise by will, the elite had a united interest to protect those rights, be it against the king or an element within the dominant coalition. The elites could collectively use the land more effectively because all elites had the same security of property. Ownership of land no longer gravitated to powerful individuals simply because they were politically powerful; it gravitated to individuals who would use ownership of the land most effectively. As long as landownership serves both a political and an economic purpose, it will serve its economic purpose less well than if ownership responds more closely to economic incentives.

The extension of rule of law for elites to a larger number of legal elements within society was the first doorstep condition for a society to reach in Europe.[4] The extension strengthens the ability of the coalition to enforce and protect those rights because consensus about rights is more easily reached when all elites possess the right. Identical rights are more easily defended than idiosyncratic privileges; a legal compromise of one elite's right becomes a precedent that compromises the rights of all elites. Putting some aspects of elite rights onto an impersonal basis enables elites to act on, contract, and exchange those rights in an impersonal manner. Separating personal identity from privilege is the first step in developing elite rule of law, and the first step in developing impersonal relations.

5.4 Doorstep Condition #2: Perpetually Lived Organizations in the Public and Private Spheres

Rule of law for elites creates some space for impersonal relationships among members of the dominant coalition, but until those relationships can be embedded in a matrix of more sophisticated public and private organizations, impersonality does not emerge historically. The capacity to form and support perpetually lived organizations has direct consequences for a society's ability to structure social relationships over time. The creation of legal personalities for organizations constitutes an essential element of perpetual life; it is inherently impersonal because it is defined without reference to any specific individuals. The creation of powerful organizations is consistent with the logic of the natural state, and therefore the effect of perpetually lived organizations on identity, personality, and impersonality plays a central role in moving societies to the doorstep conditions.

A note of caution. In developed, open access societies, the history of perpetually lived organizations is almost invariably told as legal histories of institutional forms: in private-sector organizations, business firms, churches, and other charitable institutions, corporate law structures perpetually lived organizations; in public-sector organizations, public law

---

[4] In modern natural states establishing rule of law for elites seems to be more difficult. As Haber et al. (2008) document, Mexico has established the possibility of perpetually lived organizations, but Mexico is still unable to guarantee rule of law for elites. Banks, for example, can be chartered corporations, but their life, while legally perpetual, is constantly threatened by the possibility of nationalization. Furthermore, those banks, even when owned by powerful members of the elites, are unable to get the courts to establish and enforce clear enough property rights in land to support mortgage lending.

contains the institutions of national and subnational governments.[5] The development of these organizations and institutions is typically explained in terms of functions, with little appreciation of the interrelated effects of organizations on both political and economic systems. The first societies to move toward open access invented the forms of perpetually lived public and private organizations because of a combination of political and economic forces, not simply to improve the functional characteristics of economic organizations or the functional characteristics of political organizations.

The creation of perpetually lived organizations poses two vexing historical problems. The first relates to beliefs. How do people come to believe that an organization will be perpetually lived when one has never existed? Consider an agreement with a perpetually lived organization (such as an insurance company) that involves a contract in which all the parties to the contract may be dead when the specified actions are to take place and all of the beneficiaries are yet unborn. How is it that all the currently living people come to believe that people yet to be born will honor the contract? Establishing the belief that commitments will be honored requires a long and incremental process of development.

The second problem is that a mortal state cannot credibly create a perpetually lived organization. The state is an organization of organizations and the development of natural states from fragile, through basic, to mature can be described in terms of the interaction between elite organizations within the dominant coalition. Political and economic development result from creating more sophisticated and durable institutions to structure elite relationships within the dominant coalition. Perpetually lived public organizations must coevolve with perpetually lived private organizations. Rule of law for organizations in a mature natural state does not imply that organizations are perpetually lived. The Romans developed rule of law for organizations, but they never solved the problem of perpetual life. By understanding why the Romans could not implement perpetually lived organizations, we gain insight into how later Europeans accomplished the feat.

In both a formal legal and real sense, the Roman emperor was above the law. Because the emperor was the source of all law, the law could

---

[5] In the case of England see Scott (1951); for America see Hurst (1980), Joseph Davis (1917), and John Davis (1961); for international comparisons see Lamoreaux and Rosenthal (2004). Even when the point in question is how political forces affect the development of perpetually lived organizations, the focus still remains on the development of institutional forms; for the United States see Cadman (1949), Wallis (2003, 2005); for England see Harris (2000); for France see Freedeman (1979).

not bind the will of the emperor, because he could simply change the law. The Romans could not figure out an identity and personality for the emperor where ultimate sovereignty did not reside with an individual. This problem extended throughout Roman society in any situation where a corporate body had to be represented by and act through individuals. The Romans developed a public law capable of creating organizations as legal persons, but they never figured out how to structure the relationship between a municipality or any other corporate entity – *collegia, universitas, municipium* – and the individual who spoke for the corporate entity. As Duff (1938) details, these issues clouded Roman law: Was the mayor liable for decisions he made on behalf of the city? And was the city liable for the decisions of the mayor?[6]

At its highest levels, the Roman Empire located sovereignty in a mortal individual, the emperor. The empire was capable of sustaining a range of durable institutions and organizations that constrained the emperor, structured the polity and the economy, and enabled the Romans to manage a far-flung empire for half a millennium. However, no organization within Roman society, no matter how durable, was beyond the reach of the emperor's will.

Perpetual life is not a zero/one variable. No organization is immortal and no organization possesses a life beyond the reach of the society in which it is embedded. Social orders support more or less perpetual life for their organizations on a continuous scale. Because emperors could not dissolve organizations without bearing costs, they were constrained by the institutional structure of the Roman system, but every emperor possessed the right and power to dissolve any organization at will.

Similar issues persisted within the church well into the Middle Ages. The crises within medieval society over investiture and the Great Schism did not result in a neat solution to the problem of perpetual life. The Council of Constance in 1414 gave ultimate authority in the church to the council, but the pope effectively co-opted the council's power. General councils were to be called every five years, but by the mid-fifteenth century, the popes had ceased to call them. The pope, like the Roman emperor, as an individual above the law was able to subvert the attempts by the Council of Constance to bind the pope by the law. Parallel problems extended down through the organizational structure of the church. The cathedral college had similar

---

[6] The recent examples of Enron and WorldCom suggest that modern open access societies continue to struggle when it comes to identifying the individual as opposed to the corporate identity of individuals within a perpetually lived organization.

problems defending itself against its bishop, as did a congregation with its priest.[7]

Europeans struggled with these questions well into the seventeenth century. Nonetheless, the outcome of the eleventh- and twelfth-century investiture crisis and the fourteenth- and fifteenth-century Great Schism produced changes in the institutional and organizational structure of the church. The outcome of the investiture struggle resulted in a focal interface for the relationship between the leader and the corporate body defined by the inalienability of collective property. The oaths of thirteenth-century popes, bishops, and kings required them to alienate the collective property of the church, the diocese, or the kingdom only with the consent of the corporate body. The body of economic assets held collectively by the corporation came to be known in the church as the *christus* and in the secular world as the *fiscus*. The *christus* and *fiscus* became the property administered by the leader/ruler/pope/bishop that was at the leader's disposal to use, but remained the collective property of the corporate body. The *christus* and *fiscus* formed the nexus around which perpetually lived organizations could form.

The Great Schism redefined the corporate identity of the church. At different levels of aggregation, the corporate body of the church was conceived of as the body of the faithful, the cathedral college, or the membership of a congregation. The formation of these corporate entities moved outside the formal structure of the state and became self-defining. The identification of the corporate body of a church congregation was no longer the privilege of the king or lord who created a proprietary church (the source of controversy in the investiture crisis) or the bishop in whose diocese the congregation lay. The whole body of the faithful, the *congregatio fidelium*, became a self-defining entity.[8]

Defining corporate identity in terms of the *fiscus* or *christus* engendered a persistent confusion, or difference of opinion, about inalienability and sovereignty. One aspect of the debate centered on the inalienability of

---

[7] Notice that we can view this problem in principal–agent terms: How does the corporate body (the church) get its agent (the pope) to act in its interests? The Europeans were clearly trying to work out elements of that problem. What makes this much more complicated than a traditional principal–agent problem is that the Europeans were simultaneously trying to work out who was the principal and who was the agent. Was the pope the principal, representing God on earth, or was he the agent, acting as the representative of the communion of saints and the fellowship of all believers? The same problems plagued European states.

[8] This did not, however, give a congregation or a diocese the ability to define itself at will.

sovereignty.[9] In the fifteenth and sixteenth centuries, as the powers of the kings increased relative to those of the pope, kings began asserting that their right to rule derived from God just as directly as the pope's sovereign rights (Figgis, 1923). If the sovereign powers and privileges of kings were God's gift, they were inalienable. Each king's will was sovereign, a king could not be bound by his predecessors, nor could a king bind his successors. Inalienable sovereignty implied, for example, that if one king sold land to a private individual, a subsequent king could seize the land back.[10]

Inalienable sovereignty put the pope or king above the law, beyond the reach of the corporate body of the *christus* or *fiscus*. As Figgis shows, the claims to divine and inalienable rights by kings stemmed from the conflict and contest between kings and popes, itself part of the struggle to separate church from state.

However, the claim of the kings to inalienable and divinely conferred sovereignty was inconsistent with the growing notion that inalienability meant "alienability with consent," as embodied in the notions of the *christus* and *fiscus*. Confusion also lay in the nature of the entities that revolved around the *christus* and *fiscus*. If the king was above the law, he then possessed ultimate sovereignty with respect to the *fiscus*. However, if the king could only alienate property with the consent of the corporate body, then the corporate body possessed ultimate sovereignty with respect to the *fiscus*. How did the king fit into the corporate body?

---

[9] See Kantorowicz (1997[1957]). Riesenberg (1956) has a clear discussion of how the "inalienability of sovereignty" spanned the church and state in the late Middle Ages. See also Figgis (1923, 1960) on the divine rights of kings and Tierney (1955) on the conciliar movement.

[10] The Duchy of Lancaster had been treated by the Lancastrian kings as personal, rather than part of the *fiscus* and thus inalienable without consent. "On his accession in 1399, Henry IV ordained with the consent of Parliament that all lands of the Duchy... were to be governed 'as though we had never achieved the height of royal Dignity'" (Kantorowicz, 1997[1957], p. 403). When the Yorkist Edward IV seized power he tried to treat the Duchy of Lancaster as his personal property. Parliament responded not by confirming Edward's claims, but by making the Duchy into a formal corporation, which the king, in his formal office, held as director of the corporation. In his commentaries in 1816, Plowden described the distinction neatly: "The three [i.e., the Lancastarian kings] held it in their Body natural separate from the Crown, and the fourth [i.e., Edward IV] is his Body politic in right of the Crown, and separated in the Order and Government of the Crown, and not otherwise" (as quoted in Kantorowicz, 1997[1957], p. 404). Maitland wrote about Plowden's comment "that I do not know where to look in the whole series of our law books for so marvellous [sic] a display of metaphysical – or we might say metaphysiological – nonsense" (Maitland, 2003, p. 35). Both Plowden and Kantorowicz have the better of Maitland on this question.

Kantorowicz (1997[1957]) explains how the notion of the king's two bodies developed as a solution to the inalienability problem. The king (or pope, bishop, duke, priest) possessed two bodies, identities ascribed to him by law and social practice. One identity was a personal, corporeal, mortal body that died; the other social identity an abstract, corporate, perpetual, incorruptible body that did not die. The office of the king, his dignity, was part of his corporate body. The distinction separates the private interests of the individual holding the office from the interests, rights, and duties of that individual in his role as an officer. The king's two bodies were two identifiable and separable legal persons.

Kantorowicz and the other scholars of medieval Europe who study political development grasped the idea that the corporate identity of the church or the state whose membership is impersonally defined in terms of participation and whose leadership is vested in offices or positions possessed a kind of perpetual life. The advantage of examining the struggles in the medieval church to define its organizational structure is that solving the problem of constraining its leaders required that the church define itself as a perpetually lived organization. Double balance suggests that the conceptual development of a perpetually lived sovereign had to be balanced by a perpetually lived corporate entity that consents to the alienation of the *christus* or *fiscus*. Yet no human beings have perpetual or immortal lives. For the general council to become a long-term constraint on the pope's decisions, both the pope and the general council had to become perpetually lived organizations. As the pope undermined the agreement, perpetuity was not established at this time. As so often happens, language leads us astray if we think of the problem only as a creating single, perpetually lived thing called the state. States are organizations of organizations. Creating a perpetually lived state, therefore, involves the creation of multiple, perpetually lived organizations connected in a dynamic relationship with one another.

We have already described how the development of a corporate entity to give its consent to the alienation of the *christus* or *fiscus* occurred over several centuries. There were advantages, however, to both the leader and the entire dominant coalition, of adopting an effective way of moving resources around among individuals, for example, by alienating them. The concept of the king's corporate body developed to create a sovereign as an impersonal entity possessing perpetual life (Kantorowicz, 1997[1957]). The current occupant of the office, the king in his corporeal body, could not unilaterally alienate (alter) the features of his corporate body. However, the king's commitment to honor his corporate responsibilities was not credible in and of itself because that commitment required the presence of a second corporate entity representing the *fiscus*.

With respect to alienating property, recognition of the *fiscus* formally put the king under the law, fundamentally changing the identity of the king and making the king's identity substantially more impersonal. Because the constraints on alienation applied to the king's corporate body, the constraints had to be perpetual: they applied regardless of the individual identity of the person who served as king. Symmetrically the consent-granting corporate body also had to possess perpetual life. Perpetual life for the consent-giving body was achieved by vesting the right to consent in a specific set of office-holders – such as dukes, earls, or bishops.[11] Critical to the process is the creation of at least two perpetually lived entities.

As a solution to the commitment problem, the consent-granting entity had to represent interests of officeholders and elites who would collectively manage and defend the king's corporate body against the arbitrary actions of an individual king who sought to act against the corporate interests. However, nothing was automatic about these arrangements or how they worked, as we saw when the pope failed to continue calling the general councils. If these arrangements fail, so too does the credible commitment.

The intimate connection between impersonality and perpetual life enables the organizational and institutional structure of the dominant coalition to credibly commit to such arrangements and develop sustainable beliefs about the identity and behavior of impersonal corporate actors within the coalition. Credible arrangements require that aspects of the leader's office pass unchanged to his successor in the office: these aspects of the leader's corporate body had therefore become impersonally defined. Similarly, membership of the corporate body had to be impersonally defined in terms of offices rather than individuals.

To modern minds, this solution may seem obvious: grant sovereignty to the corporate body and allow it to delegate some of its authority to an agent, such as the king. Yet a modern perspective comes from open access orders and does not work in a natural state. In the latter – that is, in all of human history up to this point in the fifteenth or sixteenth centuries – power had been always located in individuals because they were powerful

---

[11] The right to participate in the decisions of the corporate body was usually well defined within general dimensions, although who could participate was often a matter of negotiation. The most famous example is the Estates General in France in 1789.

individuals. The process of identifying powerful individuals and balancing their interests is an ongoing, continuous process at the heart of every natural state; it is the basic dynamic of natural states. Transforming aspects of the process into stable and durable institutional forms is part of creating a more stable natural state. Removing the personal element of individuality from some parts of the structure of the coalition, such as the agreements over alienability in the fourteenth century, required that impersonal organizational structures be put in place. This is the key connection between perpetually lived organizations and impersonal identities.[12]

When we read the histories of institutional forms written to explain the function that the institution serves, we often miss the critical interaction between different organizations as a way of sustaining social arrangements. It is not just that king and parliament (with variations) become perpetually lived organizations in different European societies that made for stable governance. Within a dominant coalition, powerful individuals represent and head organizations of their own. It is those elite organizations whose identity is gradually confirmed as perpetually lived (that is, organizations independent of the personal identity of their leaders) that must also develop if a perpetually lived state is to form. The development of powerful and sophisticated elite organizations not under the direct control of the state, therefore, was a necessary precondition for expanding the range of the state as an impersonal, perpetually lived organization. Separating the king's two bodies was critical to this process, because a perpetually lived impersonal sovereign had to be invented before the idea of the state as a perpetually lived organization could be realized.

The emergence of multiple, perpetually lived organizations inside and outside of the state created new possibilities for sustainable balance among the political, military, and economic organizations. The power of the state as a formal entity (the king's corporate body) could gradually be entrusted with more distinct control of military force if members of the dominant coalition with their own organizations consented to the use of the common economic resources possessed "by all" (the consent-granting corporate body) and to discipline of the use of military force by the state.

---

[12] A large literature exists in the sociology of organizations on the creation of corporate/collective actors and the social construction of corporate/collective identities. See Meyer, Boli, and Thomas (1987); Pederson and Dobbin (1997); and Meyer (1994). For an analysis of the European origins of corporate/collective organizations similar to the material covered here and in Chapter 2, see Coleman (1974, 1990). For a focus on the United States covering material in Chapter 6, see Roy (1997); Creighton (1990); and Perrow (2002).

The state as a formal government organization began to come into focus in the sixteenth and seventeenth centuries, the period of history in which the sovereign state emerges, as does a more complex economy. This emergence also coincides with the formalization of the parts of the dominant coalition as perpetually lived organizations, ultimately constraining the powers of the state and creating elite rights. Because the rights of elite organizations are possessed in perpetuity and do not adhere to individual identities, both the powers and privileges of the sovereign state and of elites must be defined impersonally.

The first societies to reach the doorstep conditions were Britain, France, the Dutch, and the United States. As these *first movers* reached the doorstep and access began widening in these societies, the corporate body of the sovereign state came to prominence. Over this period, the individual identity of the monarch faded in comparison to the corporate identity of the state. By the eighteenth century, the first movers had created a perpetually lived corporate state. By doing so, these societies not only constrained the powers of the king, they constrained the power of every individual leader of any state organization and began to restructure private organizations as well.

5.4.1 Moving toward the Doorstep in Europe and the United States: Impersonality in Public and Private Organizations

In natural states, the place of each organization within the state hierarchy is typically tied to the position and power of the elite individual (or individuals) who lead the organization.[13] The bureaucratic structure of a natural state becomes more complicated and sophisticated as a natural state matures, but it retains its personal nature. The development of perpetually lived state organizations leads to the identification of state organizations as legal persons with a life of their own. Government organizations cease to be defined in terms of the life or identity of their leader and instead become organizations that live on beyond the lives of their members.

State treasurers in the early United States are an example. From the American Revolution on, every state had a treasurer who was an officer of the state. Some were elected, but most were appointed. In almost every state, the treasurer's accounts, and the money in them, were legally the

---

[13] Bates (2001, pp. 66–8) illustrates this with his discussion of the Percy family in sixteenth-century England. Many elite organizations have multiple leaders who are part of the dominant coalition. We often use "leader" where "leader and leaders" would be more accurate.

property of the treasurer as an individual: they were not legally the property of the state. When a treasurer died in office, resigned, or was replaced, the accounts of the old treasurer had to be audited. It often transpired that the accounts of the old treasurer did not balance, embroiling the state in legal battles that could last for years. The new set of state accounts created with every new treasurer had to include an entry in which claims against the old treasurer were carried as unrealized assets of the state. In formal and sometimes financial terms, the treasury as an organization died whenever the treasurer died.[14]

The transformation of the state treasuries into organizations with perpetual life with accounts that did not die with the treasurer required a change in the organizational and institutional structure of the state. The development of treasuries as formal organizations did not eliminate the problem of fraud and incompetence. However, it did mean that significant financial operations could no longer be carried out by the treasurer as a private individual playing with the state's money. Risky financial operations by treasurers, previously the personal prerogative of the treasurer as an individual, could now more easily be placed off limits.

Dan Bogart's (2005a,b) work on parliamentary incorporation of turnpike trusts in the eighteenth century provides another illustration. The British began creating local governments with explicit perpetual life, the ability to levy taxes on local ratepayers, and to impose tolls on turnpike users. Bogart shows how these powers facilitated British development of the transportation infrastructure. Venal office holding in France, although usually not thought of in this respect, is in part a history of the creation of local government organizations. Among the most important organizations were courts and municipal governments, but thousands of other local governments (and, of course, local rent-creation arrangements) were also created and sustained in France (Bossenga, 1991; Doyle, 1996; Kwass, 2000).

For a society to move to the doorstep involves thousands of incremental changes such as these. The changes vary widely in content from society to society, and history and culture affect the specific changes that take place. In general terms, states begin transforming themselves from a hierarchy of

---

[14] The United States was no outlier. Mathias and O'Brien (1976) and O'Brien (1988) note the difficulty of reconstructing the British fiscal accounts before the nineteenth century because the accounts were the personal property of the Chancellor of the Exchequer and the many and various other officials who handled funds. The same was true in France, on a vastly larger scale, where financial offices were bought and sold (see Bonney, 1981).

organizations tied together through individual and personal connections to a hierarchy of perpetually lived, impersonal, and often more independent organizations. Britain, France, the Dutch Republic, and the United States developed methods for creating perpetually lived organizations within the state. Creating perpetually lived organizations and the institutional means to support them was part of what put these countries on the doorstep of a transition by the late eighteenth century.

The history of formal business incorporation is well known, and we examine it more closely in Chapter 6. The first British business incorporation was the Russia Company, formed in 1553 (Scott, 1951). In typical natural state fashion, the company was closely held by powerful friends of the government. The use of charters in Britain grew slowly in the sixteenth and seventeenth centuries. The Russia Company was followed by the Africa Company, the Merchant Adventurers, and the East India Company. The Virginia Company was chartered in 1606 to establish the first permanent British colony in North America. Eventually all the North American colonies received charters. The Dutch chartered their own East Indies Company, the VOC, in 1597 to exploit opportunities in the Portuguese-controlled Asian trade, the New Netherlands Company in 1614 to exploit North America, and the West Indies Company in 1621. In France, Colbert created the state-subsidized French East and West Indies Companies in 1664, plus a *Compagnie du Nord* (established in 1669) to compete with the Dutch in the Baltic. French companies existed before 1664, but the sources for French business corporations are more difficult to access.[15] In competition with Spain and Portugal (and each other), the British, Dutch, and French created colonial empires by licensing "merchants to organize colonial rule" (Tilly, 1992, p. 92).

These corporations were natural state entities created in response to changing economic opportunities. The corporate charters granted extensive and exclusive privileges to these companies in return for fiscal and (occasionally) military support for the government. The charters also explicitly recognized the sovereignty of the state in the expanded territory colonized by the corporations. The grant of a corporate charter represented an explicit political manipulation of economic access, creating exclusive privileged rights to resources and activities. Every corporation received a charter from the hand of the king or the action of a legislature. Each charter was considered separately; no hint of open access to incorporation existed yet.

---

[15] Dutch and French corporations are discussed by de Vries and Van der Woude (1997, pp. 382–410).

Natural states used these corporations to respond to new opportunities and to generate new sources of rents through creating new forms of exclusive privileges and limited access.

5.5 Doorstep Condition #3: Consolidated Control of the Military

Achieving consolidated control of the military appears to be the most difficult doorstep condition for a natural state to achieve. It is also difficult to define and understand. Consolidating control of the military involves severing the close links among economics, politics, and the military in natural states. Economic and political organizations undergo changes that mirror the changes in military organizations, and separation of functions and specialization of organizations occur throughout society. Consolidated political control of the military began developing in Western Europe in the seventeenth century, although consolidation was not complete until the eighteenth century. It involved bigger armies and navies, larger public treasuries to finance them, and bigger bureaucracies to collect revenues and run the armies and navies. The appearance of sovereign nation states in Europe, therefore, was closely associated with consolidating control of a standing professional army and navy and disarming the rest of the population. People have been thinking and writing about the emergence of modern nation states for centuries. The close association of nation states with the rise of modern societies tends to push the history of the transition back into the eighteenth century when nation states first established consolidated control of their militaries, rather than the nineteenth century when the transition proper occurs. We return to questions about the chronology of the transition proper in Chapter 6.

Consolidation of military power cannot be understood without confronting single-actor theories of the state. The image of a single commander in chief possessing the ability to direct the entire military power of a society appears to possess consolidated control. Because kings, dictators, and all types of leaders abound in human history, a single leader has been assumed to be available, and the problem then is to sufficiently constrain the leader so that he will not abuse his power. Nevertheless, natural states are always governed by coalitions of powerful individuals; only in exceptional conditions will one faction or group in the dominant coalition have an effective monopoly on violence. Even more exceptional is the condition when other groups in the coalition are satisfied and comfortable with not having access to military resources. Because consolidation of military power produces an

increase in specialization within the dominant coalition as well as consolidation of economic and political power, the process is particularly awkward
to explain with a single-actor model. Understanding how elite groups and
factions voluntarily agree to concede control of the military requires a
deeper understanding of the entire coalition, not just of a single military
leader.

What does political control of the military entail? It is not the presence
of a professional army. Professional armies with specialization in military
functions have been around for millennia. Nominal separation between
civilian and military authorities is also not enough. If active support of the
military forces is necessary to hold or obtain control of civilian government
institutions, then a society does not have political control of the military.
If military officers serve as officers (in uniform, as it were) in the civilian
government, for example as legislators or executives, then a society does not
have political control of the military. If the military as an organization enjoys
ownership of significant economic assets that it can alienate or acquire
without consent of the civilian authorities, then a society does not have
political control of the military. Finally, the selection of the high military
leadership must be under the control of the civilian authorities; armies who
select their own leaders are not under political control. These measures are
all matters of degree rather than absolutes, but they indicate that many, if
not most, societies in the world today do not enjoy political control of the
military. Many societies enjoy the appearance of civilian government but
live in the shadow of violence where the possibility that the military will
assume an active role in governance does not lie far below the surface.

By definition, when military force is consolidated the military authority
cannot be disciplined by the threat of military force from elsewhere in
society. That would require the existence of another military force and the
dispersed control of violence. In order, therefore, for a consolidated military
force under political control to refrain from using violence for illegitimate
ends, where *legitimacy* is determined within the framework of the dominant
coalition, the nonmilitary elite groups and organizations must be capable
of disciplining the military force through nonmilitary means. In order for
elite groups and organizations to concede control of military assets to a
single organization, they must believe they can collectively discipline the
military organization. Logic does not tell us where the nonmilitary means
of disciplining the armed forces resides or how it is developed, but the other
doorstep conditions do.

As the previous discussion of perpetually lived states illustrates, the emergence of multiple, perpetually lived organizations inside and outside the

formal state is a necessary prerequisite to sustaining any perpetually lived organizations. It is not possible to create just one perpetually lived organization – several have to be created simultaneously. Likewise, external control of the military involves the coevolution of perpetually lived organizations in the state and in the private sector. At the level of procurement and supply, which we consider in a detailed example later, interlocking arrangements between the private sector and the military are one way that perpetually lived organizations can be fostered.

The most intensely studied way in which the political and military relate is through the public treasury, or control over the *fiscus*. Increasing the size of the military usually carries significant military advantages at the cost of reducing the material well-being in the rest of society.[16] The institutions that determine the amount of resources allocated to the military are central to establishing political control of the military. In eleventh-century England, control of land and control of military power were intimately related. The essence of a natural state is linking control of military resources to economic resources and activities. Often, control of military, political, and economic resources are embedded in the same organizations linked together through the dominant coalition. If, however, elites develop more powerful organizations that specialize in economic (or other) functions, then an institutional arrangement, like alienation with consent, can provide a method for allocating resources to the military that can be controlled by nonmilitary elites.

This is where the other doorstep condition, rule of law for elites, enters the picture. Getting the leader of an organization under the law is an integral part of perpetually lived organizations. The example of subjecting the powers of the king to alienate the *fiscus* to consent of a corporate body was an integral part of getting the king under the law in Europe. Separating the decisions of when to fight and how much to spend on fighting, from the direction of military activity was central. A corporate military organization empowered military leaders with the authority to decide how to fight, but not when to fight or how much to spend on fighting. A separate corporate social organization possessed the power to decide when to fight and how much to spend on fighting. Separating the authority to make the two decisions produced political control of a consolidated military.

---

[16] The assertion about reducing the material well-being of the population must be tempered by the possibility that the existence of the military may produce gains in the form of increased security, or loot, booty, and expanded territory, or reduce losses through conquest and domination by an external force.

In natural states where the leader and other powerful members of the dominant coalition lead active organizations with combined military, political, and economic power, there can be no consent-giving corporate body with meaningful independent existence. Because personal charisma and individual identity can be critical to military leadership, establishing impersonal, perpetually lived organizations in the military can be particularly difficult. However, if perpetually lived elite organizations with substantial economic or social, but not military, power develop, it becomes possible, if extremely difficult, to fashion institutional arrangements in which control over the means of fighting and the decision to fight are separated from the actual conduct of fighting. The arrangements may be credibly enforced by lodging control in the consent-giving group of the resources for military activity. Without powerful nonmilitary elite organizations, it is difficult to see how such an arrangement can be sustained.

Of all the concepts in this book, consolidated political control of the military is the hardest to understand. The root of the problem is the paradoxical relationship of natural states with specialization and division of labor that we noted in Chapter 2. Natural states enable societies to manage larger numbers while dealing with violence. Although this allows natural states to capture greater gains from specialization, at the same time specialization also threatens rent-creation. Natural states are inherently limited, both in terms of access and in terms of the degree of specialization they can support. Political control of the military requires greater specialization within the dominant coalition (it does not require greater access, however). Moving toward greater specialization within elites is undoubtedly aided by stronger elite organizations, but the web of causal relationships is too tangled to sort out neatly.

The title of Charles Tilly's (1992) great book, *Coercion, Capital, and European States: 990–1992*, captures the importance of specialization within the coalition. Tilly traces the evolution of national states in Europe over a millennium, using variations in the initial character of political and economic institutions and organizations (i.e., the distribution of coercion and capital) to explain patterns of state formation. In Tilly's model, governments exist to make war, and their behavior is shaped by how best to mobilize, coordinate, and deploy resources to win wars. Implicit in Tilly is a logic of the use and control of violence, which Robert Bates makes explicit in his 2001 book *Prosperity and Violence* using examples from the same European history. Tilly draws heavily on the development of large-scale military organizations embodied in the military revolution studied by Geoffrey Parker (1996) and others. In sequence, we will look at Bates, Tilly, and Parker.

Bates (2001) describes how, in a world of persistent disorder and violence, individuals will privately supply coercion. However, purely individual provision of protection is both costly and fraught with incentive problems. Everyone has to fight to protect their persons, families, and assets; moreover, the individual provision of violence limits specialization and division of labor. One response to a violent world is kinship provision of coercion through the institution of the feud. Drawing on Evans-Pritchard's (1940) study of the Nuer, a confederation of tribes located in southern Sudan and western Ethiopia, Bates lays out the logic of deterrence. Coercion involves the use of violence or the threat of violence. Actual violence need not be used to alter behavior. Often, the most effective violence potential arises when it remains a threat rather than a reality. If kin group members are willing to punish anyone who injures a member of their kin group, a balance of coercion can result. "The very readiness of the Nuer to employ violence provides a reason, then, that violence so rarely takes place," Bates (2001, p. 45) writes. In the terminology of game theory, violence is an outcome that participants in the game do not expect to happen, so the actual use of violence is off-the-path behavior. As a result, the level of actual violence observed in a society captures only one dimension of how violent societies really are. Societies without high levels of observed violence may nonetheless experience very high levels of coercion through threats of violence.

The provision of security through the omnipresent threat of violent retribution "produces a peace that is fragile" (Bates, 2001, p. 47). Indeed, this logic supports the peace of a fragile natural state: few complex organizations, limited specialization and exchange, limited wealth, and a society ruled by elites whose influence extends through some form of patron–client networks. As we emphasized in Chapter 2, patronage networks serve as a way of identifying which individuals stand together in case violence breaks out.[17] In fragile natural states, the threat of violence permeates society. In the simplest societies, everyone must be prepared to be violent, and the military resources of the community are widely dispersed throughout the population.

In basic natural states, order becomes a more regular outcome as society becomes better organized and is more capable of suppressing violence among different groups and factions. In Bates's terms, the basic natural state is capable of using violence for constructive instead of solely destructive

---

[17] The work of Phil Keefer (2004) and Keefer and Vlaicu (2005) focuses on the role of patron–client networks as a mechanism for creating credible commitments in a variety of political settings.

purposes: "Rather than providing means for engaging in costly acts of redistribution, [coercion] becomes a means for promoting the creation of wealth" (2001, p. 50). In Service's (1975, pp. 297–8) terms, the state "wages peace." The logic of Bates's argument is straightforward: As long as the violence specialist receives more from defending his clients than he receives from expropriating them, he refrains from using violence. Because the violence specialist can expect to receive rents from his clients over a long period, the critical elements in his calculus are the benefit of expropriating today versus the loss of a stream of income over an indefinite future.[18] If the violence specialist gains more from doing good things (such as promoting the creation of wealth) than he does from doing bad things (such as expropriating wealth), then prosperity follows. Reducing violence creates greater wealth by directly limiting wealth destruction, increasing the scope for contracts and long-term relations, and promoting the growth of specialization and division of labor, which enable societies to use their assets and resources more efficiently. This big question is whether to kill the goose that lays golden eggs and eat the goose today, or pamper the goose and enjoy a flow of gold in the future.

Both Bates and Tilly develop models of society with an economic sector with the potential for producing increasing wealth. The economic sector is concentrated in towns and cities but linked to rural agricultural producers and consumers. They also have a political sector whose primary skill is the production and application of coercion. For both Bates and Tilly, urbanization produces wealth and capital. Bates identifies the conditions under which political elites want to promote economic growth in the cities: when military leaders find it in their interests to promote good economic policies so that the leaders can obtain more resources with which to be violent.[19]

Tilly explains how the various patterns of state formation in Europe resulted from the initial distributions of coercion and capital that derive from the distribution and character of political and economic institutions and organizations. In Tilly's model, governments exist to make war, and their behavior is shaped by how best to mobilize, coordinate, and deploy resources to win wars. Tilly employs the same logic as Bates: social and economic development ensue when political or military leaders find it in their interest to provide security to the cities in order to obtain more

---

[18] The appendix to Bates (2008) lays out this logic in clear and nontechnical terms. The basic logic is the same as Olson (1993) or North (1981). For a more sophisticated treatment see Bates, Greif, and Singh (2002).

[19] Bates (2001) discusses a case where a modern developing country leader chose to abandon urban elites and create a power base in the country side, Flight Lieutenant Jerry Rawlings in Ghana (p. 93).

resources with which to fight. In societies where too much power lies on the side of coercion, the possibility for growth-promoting arrangements is limited. In societies where capital possesses too much power, the possibilities for political development are limited. However, in the few societies where the distribution of capital and coercion is appropriately balanced, as in England and France, it is possible to consolidate the military, increase political sophistication, and promote political and economic development simultaneously.

Our simple depiction of Bates and Tilly does not do justice to the power and sophistication of their theoretical and historical insights. Neither Bates nor Tilly would dispute that all states are organizations and that all power is exercised through a coalition of powerful interests. Nonetheless, both begin with the state as a single actor, a problem Tilly explicitly acknowledges.[20] The separation of politics from economics, of the politically powerful from the economically powerless (militarily), follows inevitably and naturally from the single-actor model, even if the single actor is a representative agent of a large group of elites. The characteristic that the single actors share is the use of military power to extract economic wealth.

In natural states, in contrast, economics and politics are not separate but closely intertwined within the dominant coalition. Bates and Tilly assume that the separation of political and economic interests is a natural separation and take it as their point of departure. The separation of military, political, and economic interests and organizations is, in fact, not a natural outcome in human societies but the result of a very special set of conditions. The separation of distinct economic and military interests within the dominant coalition only occurs in a mature natural state with strong elite organizations. It is only when the goose that lays the golden egg is not owned by a helpless peasant or powerless non-elite, but a strong and well-organized economic specialist, that a credible commitment not to use violence can produce sustained commitment to governmental policies that promote economic security. The initial allocations of capital and coercion across European societies that Tilly takes as exogenous are instead the

---

[20] "In the interests of compact presentation, I will likewise resort to metonymy and reification on page after page. Metonymy, in that I will repeatedly speak of 'rulers,' 'kings,' and 'sovereigns' as if they represented a state's decision-making apparatus, thus reducing to a single point a complex, contingent set of social relations. Metonymy, in that cities actually stand for regional networks of production and trade in which the large settlements are focal points. Reification, in that I will time and again impute a unitary interest, rationale, capacity, and action to a state, a ruling class, or the people subject to their joint control. Without a simplifying model employing metonymy and reification, we have no hope of identifying the main connections in the process of state formation" (Tilly, 1992, p. 34).

reflection of deeply endogenous relationships within the dominant coalitions of European societies.

Although Tilly begins his account in 990, the interesting part of the story for us emerges after 1500, a point at which none of the Western European powers had a distinct military advantage. In the late sixteenth and seventeenth centuries, England, France, and the Dutch Republic began to create more sophisticated organizations and state institutions within their basic natural state frameworks, including sophisticated elite organizations outside the direct control of the state. All three countries used quasi-private corporations as vehicles for colonization, whereas the Spanish and Portuguese did not. The British, Dutch, and French created colonial empires by licensing "merchants to organize colonial rule."[21] Corporations were developed for domestic purposes as well. By 1700, the distinctive pattern of support for elite organizations outside the immediate framework of the state characterized the development of mature natural states in all three of the European first movers.

Nonetheless, none of these states had established political control of the military. Britain experienced a civil war and a revolution in the seventeenth century. France underwent the Fronde in the confusing years of the mid-seventeenth century and would undergo a revolution late in the next century. The Dutch federal structure complicated the organization of its navy, which in its mid-seventeenth-century wars with England, was commanded by a confusing coalition of five or more admirals; each Dutch province had its own admiralty and military resources (Rodger, 2004, pp. 9, 64). In contrast, by 1800 all three nations as well as the United States had established consolidated political control of their militaries, although in different ways in each country. We accept Tilly's basic facts – his story about what happened – but replace his model of coercion and capital with our model of the natural state. This allows us to explain the endogenous relationship between capital and coercion that Tilly is forced to take as given.[22]

---

[21] Tilly (1992), p. 92. In the first wave of New World colonization, the Spanish and Portuguese exported basic natural state institutions, while the English, French, and Dutch exported mature natural state institutions.

[22] Tilly's Figure 1.8, p. 27, illustrates how he sees the endogenous structure. The figure contains seven "items": accumulation of coercion, concentration of coercion, accumulation of capital, concentration of capital, growth of states, growth of cities, and form of states. There are eleven arrows connecting the seven elements. The only exogenous elements (the ones from which an arrow leads but to which no arrows point) are the accumulation of capital and coercion. These are the elements of Tilly's story that he takes as exogenous, the endowments of capital and coercion. Everything else is endogenous, but without a clear and specific structure.

All of Europe in 1500 was composed of basic and fragile natural states. Along with more complex economies, mature natural states began developing more quickly in Western than in Eastern Europe. The result was more sophisticated, articulated, and independent elite organizations in Western Europe than in Eastern Europe. The rise of Northwestern European cities reflects the organizational sophistication of their mature natural states, as does their use of corporations to colonize overseas holdings and their burgeoning financial, commercial, and industrial organizations. The separation and specialization of economic, political, and military organizations – the larger presence of cities, of more complex, nonagrarian economies, and of capital – in Northwestern Europe were not exogenous to the political and economic history of Britain, France, and the Dutch Republic. They were a product of the evolution of the natural state structure from basic to mature natural states. Eastern and Southern Europe, with the exception of a few Italian city-states, failed to develop more independent political and economic organizations and institutions. Their capital and coercion remained more closely intertwined.

In 1700, control over the military was dispersed through the dominant coalition in every country in Europe. Tilly describes the changes that occurred after 1700 as *nationalization* and *specialization*:

[N]*ationalization*: a period (especially 1700 to 1850 or so in much of Europe) when states created mass armies and navies drawn increasingly from their own national populations, while sovereigns absorbed armed forces directly into the state's administrative structure, and similarly took over direct operation of the fiscal apparatus, drastically curtailing the involvement of independent contractors.

[S]*pecialization*: an age (from approximately the mid-nineteenth century to the recent past) in which military force grew as a powerful specialized branch of national government, the organizational separation of fiscal from military activity increased, the division of labor between armies and police sharpened, representative institutions came to have significant influence over military expenditures, and states took on a greatly expanded range of distributive, regulatory, compensatory, and adjudicative activities (1992, p. 29).

Tilly describes consolidation of control over the military and growing impersonality in the organizations that the state used to control the military. He begins with a basic natural state structure in which economic and political activities, such as collecting taxes and holding military resources, were dispersed throughout the dominant coalition. After 1700, political control of the military began to be consolidated into the formal organizational structure of the government. A parallel consolidation and specialization occurred in other state functions.

Changes in military technology in the late sixteenth and seventeenth centuries drove at least part of this transformation. The military revolution literature (Parker, 1996) describes the rising scale of military operations in Europe arising first from improvements in fixed-point defense, and then the evolution of more highly trained infantry and improved artillery. Each of these developments increased scale directly in the size of military operations and indirectly by raising the fixed and permanent component of a professional military that had to be maintained to provide the higher levels of sophistication necessary to implement the revolutionary offensive and defensive technologies. Along with the rising scale and greater expense came the need for better fiscal and administrative arrangements within formal governments.

Tilly sees these changes as the inevitable result of an inexorable process of military competition within Europe: "war drove state formation and transformation" (1992, p. 20). States throughout Europe quickly emulated the winners in the competition (Britain, France, and the Dutch). The followers put themselves on the doorstep later in the nineteenth century (for example, Germany and the Scandinavian countries). The military revolution literature argues the same point: when a few countries developed new military technologies, their competitors were forced to adopt the same technologies or succumb. Because the new military technologies developed in Europe after the seventeenth century involved larger armies and unprecedented levels of military expenditure, states had to grow or die.[23]

The importance of scale in the military revolution brings Bates's logic of violence to the forefront. Military leaders who grasped the new technology found themselves in positions where the benefits of increasing revenues had suddenly increased, enabling them to credibly honor agreements to secure the productive capacity of their economies. Changing military technology becomes a causal force driving the change in state formation, as well as an explanation for growing wealth and accumulations of capital. Increasing the economic means available for warfare allowed an increase in the scale of military operations. Increasing military scale created demands for more resources. Better enforcement of property rights for capital and commerce emerged as political elites realized that they could capture more resources from cities in exchange for honoring rights and privileges. The economic success that followed allowed more resources to be devoted to

[23] Parker (1996) summarizes the debate and evidence on the military revolution; see also the essays in Rogers (1995). Roberts (1967) is usually attributed as the origin of the modern literature. McNeill (1982) provides an overview of military technology in history.

the military. This logic describes a reinforcing cycle: greater demand for greater military resources in military competition led countries to protect capital and commerce and, generally, to enhance their abilities to make credible commitments. This cycle led to greater resources and greater military power.

The importance of scale in military technology, however, was nothing new. There were always potential advantages to having a bigger army or navy provided a society had the leadership to make use of the resources. Military competition within Europe had been going on since before the establishment of the Roman Empire; why did military competition transform state organization and institutions after 1700? Elites always had an interest in defining their property rights better to increase their economic productivity and to glean more resources for military adventures that would produce even more resources. This aspect of Bates, Tilly, and Parker's argument applies to all of human history, not just to eighteenth-century Europe. Wealth had risen and fallen with some regularity throughout all of human history. Societies were richer when they figured out how to govern themselves better, subject to various parameters, such as the favorable coincidence of climate, geography, and demography. Even so, rising wealth and military competition had never before produced consolidated political control of the military or rule-of-law protection of property rights and commerce.

Historical problems aside, the argument for the military revolution as a cause for consolidated control of the military and consequent social development not only fails to explain why all states with large militaries did not consolidate political control but also why only a handful of countries with large militaries made the transition to modern open access societies before the end of the nineteenth century. As Tilly himself argues, in most nations of Europe the pressures of military expediency did not produce nation-states capable of modern development. He characterizes three types of societies: coercion intensive, capital intensive, and capitalized coercion.[24]

In the coercive-intensive societies of Eastern and Southern Europe, Russia is the example. The power of agrarian-based, rural political elites prevented the development of urban commercial centers and as a result "states grew up starved for capital" (1992, p. 143). In the capital-intensive societies (the Dutch and Swiss), powerful urban commercial interests were able to

---

[24] The basic argument about capital- and coercion-intensive societies is presented in Tilly (1992), pp. 6–28, then extended on pages 84–91 and 130–7. The examples of each of the three types follow on pp. 143–60.

buy defense when they needed it and so avoided "creating bulky, durable national administrations" (1992, p. 151). These states were economically successful, but too weak to sustain international political independence. Coercion-intensive societies developed governments that were too repressive; capital-intensive societies developed governments that were too weak and poorly coordinated. However, the capitalized coercion societies (Tilly's example is Britain but he includes France as well) became the "state built on a conjunction of capital and coercion that from very early on gave any monarch access to immense means of warmaking, but only at the price of large concessions to the country's merchants and bankers" (1992, p. 159).

The single-actor approach to the state really gets in the way of understanding the developments Tilly is describing and attempting to understand. In order to sustain competent military power married with sustained economic development, capital and coercive interests were required to be somehow balanced. Yet how is this done? Tilly gives us little to go on besides historical accident and contingency: his single-actor monarchy must somehow strike a Batesian deal with the commercial elements, but the ability to do that is not inherent in his conceptual framework as Tilly takes the distribution of capital and coercion as given.

In 1600 and possibly as late as 1700, the dominant coalitions of all European societies were enmeshed in networks of organizations that combined political, economic, and military power. The Dutch, French, and British (along with their colonies) had moved the farthest toward perpetually lived elite organizations, including the governing structures of their colonies. Specialization within the organizations of the dominant coalition notably increased over the course of the eighteenth century in all three countries, although the Dutch lost their ability to operate effectively as an independent military power. Supported by rule of law for elite organizations, specialized economic organizations that were visibly independent of the state provided a counterpoise to political organizations that controlled and funded military organizations. The process was neither easy nor without bumps. As we show in Chapter 6, fear of political and economic organizations played a central role in both the American and French Revolutions and colored British political thought throughout the eighteenth century.

By themselves, bigger armies did not stimulate specialization and separation within the elite. The Spanish Empire, with its enormous army and navy, did not develop specialized elite organizations. It was not for lack of sophistication, as Drelichman and Voth (2008) show that the Spanish

Court possessed the ability to finance King Philip's wars until the military disasters of the 1580s in a manner that "was at least as 'responsible' as the U.S. in the twentieth century or as Britain in the eighteenth century" (2008, p. 29, quotation from the abstract). The Spanish, however, did not finance their army, navy, or borrowing through specialized elite perpetually lived organizations, but through the traditional personalized connections of the court. The Russians were able to build a large army, but as Tilly describes the Russians, "They [Ivan the Great and his successors] needed an army that was dependent as possible upon them, and upon whose loyalty, they themselves could depend. But they lacked money to buy the men and allegiance they required. So they decided to use land" (Tilly, 1992, p. 140, quoting Blum, 1964, pp. 170–1). Just as in feudal England, the Russians financed their large army by granting it direct control of economic assets. In neither Russia nor Spain did specialized and separate elite organizations arise.

By the eighteenth century, their military power allowed the British, French, and the Dutch to overwhelm every other state on the planet. The continuous warfare between them from the late seventeenth through the early nineteenth centuries afforded the context in which political control of the military took place. They developed more sophisticated organizations and institutions that allowed them to outperform all other societies (Schultz and Weingast, 2003; Tilly, 1992). Nevertheless, military competition must be seen in the context of other central changes that made up the doorstep conditions, the ability to support more sophisticated organizations, both within and outside of the state. Not until the eighteenth century did widespread support for perpetually lived organizations both inside and outside of the state become a reality. The emergence of perpetually lived organizations and political control of the military created the conditions for a transition to take place.

5.6 The British Navy and the British State

In the eighteenth-century military struggle of the British and the Dutch against the French, British sea power – *The Command of the Ocean*, to use Rodger's (2004) title – gave Britain the key advantage at several crucial points. We want to understand how the British Navy as an organization evolved from a loose structure of widely dispersed control over military assets and activities to one under central and direct control of the political system; how the navy accomplished this by consciously developing perpetually lived organizations within the state and within a network of large elite firms in direct competition with one another; and how personal relationships among elite individuals were replaced by impersonal relationships among perpetually lived organizations.

In the Seven Years' War (1754–63), also known as the French and Indian War, the British defeated the French in Canada because the British Navy prevented the French Navy from provisioning their forces in Canada. Although the British Navy had a significant numerical superiority over the French, in order to realize its advantage, the British had to keep the French Navy in one place. Once out on the open ocean, the French Navy could obtain local superiority by combining tactical planning with surprise. Corralling and defeating the French Navy on the open ocean was impossible. Success required that the British Navy maintain an effective blockade of French ports and, when the French fleet did come out, to decisively defeat or contain it. To protect its own merchant fleets, provision its armies and allies, and concentrate its superior numbers and weapons, the British Navy had to pin down the French fleet (Rodger, 2004, p. 279). The British Navy's ability to bottle up the French fleet turned the tide of war.

The problem with blockading France, as Rodger explains, is that no navy in 1700 could keep a large fleet of ships at sea for more than a month or so. The low quality of provisions meant that the men and officers on ships became enfeebled and sick in a short time (Rodger, 2004, p. 291). Yet in 1758, Admiral Hawke's fleet stayed at sea continuously for six months. Hawke stayed off the French coast until the French fleet came out of Brest on November 16. Hawke fought the French and confined the French fleet to the harbor at Quiberon Bay, where the French stayed under British blockade for the remainder of the war.

Keeping the fleet at sea required not better sailors, ships, or tactics, but an administrative system to secure high-quality provisions and supplies on a regular basis: "It was precisely in these matters of administration that the British opened a decisive superiority over their enemies, particularly over the French" (Rodger, 2004, p. 291; see also Ch. 19). How did this transformation come about?

The navy had long been organized in a classic natural state form. Individual towns and cities provided ships and officers. The policy goes back to at least the eleventh century and the *scipfyrd* in which military service to the crown was discharged by the supply of a ship, officers, and crew (Rodger, 1997, pp. 26–7). As late as the fourteenth century, less than 10 percent of the ships in the navy were royal ships (Rodger, 1997, p. 118 and Appendix III). The navy was a coalition of ships, captains, and crews. In the sixteenth century, the Tudors began to centralize the navy, but administrative control remained widely dispersed in shipyards, armories, and victuallers. Moreover, the continued importance of patronage networks affected the development of officers and crews. Pursers of individual ships were responsible for provisioning their ships.[25]

In the 1630s, Charles I attempted to increase the size of his navy by levying the infamous "ship money" tax. The tax was laid on individual towns, theoretically in lieu of them actually providing ships (Rodger, 1997, p. 381). Parliamentary debate over ship money became a central issue in the origins of the English Civil War (1642–9). Indeed, this was a constitutional debate: Were the dispersed financial and naval resources of the country to be monetized and tapped by the central authority of the crown, or were they to be consolidated under the control exercised by parliament?

The English Civil War, Restoration (1660), and Glorious Revolution (1688–9) left the British Navy with a deeply divided officer corps, many of whom had fought against one another, and a disorganized administrative structure. When war broke out with France in 1689, a combined Anglo-Dutch fleet was completely unprepared, on the English side, to put effective ships to sea. The situation was so bad that the "House of Commons solved the problem in its own fashion by throwing the entire Victualling Board into the Tower."[26] The low point occurred in the summer of 1693, when the fleet failed to fulfill its charge to escort a convoy to the Western Mediterranean, resulting in the French taking ninety-two merchantmen and selling their prizes for 30 million livres, more than the entire French naval budget for 1692.

The navy was not an easy policy instrument for the state to wield in 1700. The old navy structure reflected the logic of the natural state. Three boards shared the responsibility for building and supplying the navy – the Board of Victualling, the Board of Ordinance, and the Navy Board (including its relationship with independent shipyards) – each closely tied to its own network of elite suppliers and contractors capturing ample economic rents (Rodger, 2004, pp. 189–90).

Before the eighteenth century, naval credit was deeply enmeshed in the system of naval supply. Suppliers held "navy debts" either directly in the form of formal debt instruments or more commonly in the form of invoices for supplies that they had delivered but for which the navy had yet to pay. These invoices and relationships were personal. In 1665, Denis Gauden,

---

[25] Rodger (1986) provides an accessible overview of the structure of the British Navy.

[26] Rodger (2004) p. 193. Chapters 12 and 13 detail the problem of administration and politics in the aftermath of the Glorious Revolution.

the surveyor-general of the Victualling Board, was owed "£425,993 6s 8d, including advances to pack next year's meat over the winter . . . After the war Gauden's accounts were found to be substantially accurate, no better system of victualling could be proposed but to renew his contract with addition of some partners lest he should die in office" (Rodger, 2004, p. 105). Gauden's mode of operation was intensely personal. As with the treasurers in early American states, Gauden personally arranged for credits from suppliers that he used to purchase goods. Gauden then waited to be reimbursed by the government. As long as the debts owed to the suppliers were personally linked to individuals in the navy, such as Gauden, competition among suppliers could not be sustained. Which supplier would be paid first? The answer to that question would determine which supplier survived. Potential suppliers realized that personal credit arrangements would result in one supplier possessing a distinct advantage over the others. As a result, potential suppliers remained potential, not actual suppliers.

The development of an external financial market in government debt, specifically Navy Bills, allowed the finances of the Victualling Board and the Navy Board to be put on a new footing. In anticipation of revenues, the Navy Board was able to issue short-term credit instruments in the form of navy bills, payable "in the course." Contractors were paid with bills, which they could hold until their repayment in course or which they could discount on a secondary market (Carlos, Neal, and Wandscheider, 2009; Rodger, 2004, p. 293). The new credit arrangements were central to new relationships with suppliers. The various naval organizations paid their debts with bills negotiable on a secondary market. The financial markets monitored the creditworthiness of the navy and reflected their beliefs in the interest they paid on navy bills. Suppliers could quickly realize their payments by discounting the bills, removing one source of personal connection between the suppliers and the navy. This process also lowered the risk of repayment to individual suppliers.

Symmetrically, the navy began letting contracts to several suppliers under competitive conditions. The navy encouraged large firms to develop that did not have exclusive contracts but with which the navy could credibly commit to engage in an ongoing business. The firms were large and limited to elite business organizations, so the supply process was not characterized by open entry; the navy encouraged only a few firms to compete for business.[27]

---

[27] Here it would be nice to know the identities of the suppliers, whether they were formal corporations, and their connections with the government. We do not know that, however.

Nonetheless, the elite competition was enough to secure both an increase in quality of the supplies provided and a decrease in the cost of supplies as well. The navy could credibly commit to honor its promises to these firms, because each individual firm could and did take the navy bills with which it was paid to the financial markets and get cash immediately. This eliminated the necessarily personal decisions made under the old system of which debts would be paid first, the impersonal and perpetually lived organizations in the financial markets could also credibly threaten the government and the navy in particular if either was slow in paying their debts, because new debt issues would be at higher interest rates.

The transformation of the system involved the creation of competition in combination with perpetually lived organizations on both sides of the process of naval supply. Rodger describes the overall effect of the Victualling Board development:

Beyond naval operations, the work of the Victualling Board has a wider significance for the agricultural and economic history of Britain. The Board was the largest single purchaser on the London markets for agricultural products, and its policy of managing the markets so as to encourage the growth of large firms, while at the same time promoting competition, was at least influential, and possibly critical, in the growth of a sophisticated and integrated national and eventually international agricultural market (Rodger, 2004, p. 307).

The new system enabled the provision of high-quality food that enabled Hawke to remain on station for six months, chase Conflans into Quiberon Bay, and prevent the provisioning of French troops in Canada and elsewhere around the world. By the 1750s, the British Navy had become a sophisticated organization of organizations; several of its component organizations were independent and had perpetual life – the Admiralty, the Navy Board, the Victualling Board, and the Ordinance Board among them. Developments in the navy were balanced by corresponding developments in perpetually lived elite organizations in the economy. One set of organizations emerged in financial markets that dealt in the various naval debt instruments and provided specialized monitoring of the current and future state of navy finances (tuned to each specific division within the navy structure). Another set of economic organizations developed in the form of elite, but competitive suppliers. Competition among suppliers eliminated the personal and rent-conveying natural state relationships that prevailed for centuries and that precluded significant increases in the quality of naval supplies. Elite competition transformed this system by reducing rents and providing the right incentives, separating the suppliers from their old role as creditors of the navy. To work, these new arrangements required perpetually lived organizations.

The three-cornered interaction of the navy supply boards, the financial markets, and naval suppliers did not develop in a vacuum. England in the seventeenth century had been racked by revolution and conspicuous evidence of a lack of consolidated political control of the military. A lively literature discusses the events leading to the Glorious Revolution of 1688–9, and these need not be retold here.[28] After the Restoration (1660), the English dominant coalition divided into two factions that came to be called the Tories and the Whigs by the end of the century. Tories tended to draw from the traditional countryside and generally supported the king, while the Whigs tended to draw from the commercial trading economy and commercial agriculture and opposed the king (Carswell, 1973, pp. 40–41). Both factions were part of the dominant coalition and represented a narrow portion of English society (Clark, 1985). Charles II (1660–85) and his ministers proved to be effective natural state coalition managers. Although the Whigs raised many grievances about Charles's rule, the king retained sufficient support among the Tories to thrive in power. His brother and successor, King James II (1685–8), however, failed miserably at managing the coalition, turning his brother's erstwhile supporters, the Tories, against him. The nearly united elite opposition ousted James in a coup and sought a new king under new constitutional circumstances.

The new coalition made many constitutional changes, including the basis for a perpetually lived state, a central ingredient in creating perpetually lived public and private organizations. The two factions did so by creating a new consensus in parliament about the rules of government and citizen duty. The Tories and Whigs agreed, among other things, that parliament, as a corporate body with self-constituting membership and perpetual life, possessed the ability to make law that was sacrosanct, above the king. As a corporate body, parliament embodied the sole source of taxation. In the Declaration of Rights, they announced that any king who failed to abide by these rules risked the same fate as James II (Jones, 1972, p. 318). Members

---

[28] Among economic and political historians, see, for example, Jha (2008), North and Weingast (1989), Stasavage (2003), Sussman and Yafeh (2006), and among the vast literature in English history, see, for example, Jones (1972), and Schwoerer (1981). For recent work on the effects of the Glorious Revolution see Quinn (2006), Robinson (2006), and Stasavage (2006).

of parliament declared their willingness to defend their prerogatives against the king's abuse.

Events quickly revealed the effects of parliament's perpetual life, particularly after the creation of the Bank of England in 1694. The personal nature of sovereign debt in a natural state meant that all early modern European sovereigns were credit rationed, and the Stuart kings could not raise much money to finance their governments (North and Weingast, 1989; Veitch, 1986). After the Revolution of 1688, sovereign debt became the impersonal liability of parliament. To issue or alter debt now required a law of parliament. The king could no longer unilaterally alter the terms of debt (e.g., reduce interest payments, fail to pay creditors, or default) without first obtaining a new law from parliament. The new commitment mechanisms greatly increased the creditworthiness of the English state. Debt rose by an order of magnitude in less than a decade, from around 5 percent of estimated Gross National Product to 40 percent (North and Weingast, 1989). The enhanced financial wherewithal of the British gave them and their international coalition partners a critical advantage in their ongoing wars with France.

As the British Navy discussion suggests, the Glorious Revolution is one step among many in a long series of steps of the British transition from a natural state to an open access order. The British victory in 1763 tipped the balance of power within Western Europe toward Britain and set its American colonies on the road to revolution (Anderson, 2000). Financing the Americans put the French monarchy in perilous condition, which provided the spark to a French revolution and led to the Napoleonic Wars in which Britain emerged victorious. At the close of the Napoleonic period, the British – along with the French, the Dutch, and the Americans – were on the verge of creating fully open access orders.

5.7 Time, Order, and Institutional Forms

We have suggested that the three doorstep conditions built on one another. Rule of law for elites helps support perpetually lived organizations for elites, which helps shape conditions that enabled consolidated control of the military. As this chapter makes clear, however, nothing necessitates a particular order of development for these conditions. Elements of different doorstep conditions can arise at different times in different societies. For example, Haber et al. (2008) demonstrate that rule of law for elites is problematic in modern Mexico, even for perpetually lived elite organizations such as banks. The doorstep conditions do not follow an inevitable ordering in time.

Time also plays an important role in the process of institutional change. The first societies to move to the doorstep conditions and then to the transition proper changed forever the conditions facing other societies. All of the institutional forms adopted in Europe as societies moved toward the doorstep conditions in the seventeenth and eighteenth centuries had to be consistent with the logic of the natural state. The institutional forms – for example, courts, corporations, armies, and navies – can therefore be adopted by other natural states. Once these institutions developed in Western Europe, they could be used throughout the world as a legal form of organization. However, adopting Western institutions, such as corporations, does not necessarily produce open access. Nor does it necessarily create perpetually lived organizations: in many fragile and basic natural states, the granting of a corporate charter to an elite group means the existence of the corporation as an organization continues to depend on the goodwill of the government. These corporations are not perpetually lived. Similarly, adopting a European legal code does not guarantee rule of law for elites.

Time also complicates how we interpret the intentionality of elite decisions. Elite groups in eighteenth-century Europe could not have intended to produce a transition to open access because no one knew an open access society was a viable alternative, much less how to construct it. In the modern world, in contrast, intentional decisions by elites to open access, such as those envisioned by Acemoglu and Robinson, are possible. Leaders in natural states can look to the developed world and see how open access produces enough output to make everyone, elite and non-elite, better off. The failure of most societies to make that transition – even when the path to open access is laid out for them by the historical experience of other societies – suggests that the problem lies deeper than the will of elites to share their power.

The three doorstep conditions illuminate the circumstances under which elites in natural states have incentives to create institutions that formalize their relationships, creating impersonal relationships between elites. The central insight is that when elites institutionalize their own impersonal intra-elite relationships, they lower the costs of expanding the size of the coalition covered by these institutions. Extending impersonality also holds the possibility of significantly expanding the size of gains from exchange.

The doorstep conditions are necessary, but not sufficient conditions for a transition from a natural state to an open access order. States attaining the doorstep conditions may have incentives to expand the citizenry covered by rule-of-law institutions, but nothing about the doorstep conditions implies success in the transition. States on the doorstep may well fail to succeed in the transition or may fall back to being a natural state.

SIX

The Transition Proper

6.1 Institutionalizing Open Access

The transition proper begins when elites find a common interest in transforming some elite privileges into impersonal elite rights shared by all members of the elite. The process is by no means inevitable. The natural tendency of powerful groups faced with uncertainty and novel situations is to consolidate privileges, not to expand them to include more elites. The transition proper is the process by which elites open access within the dominant coalition, secure that open access through institutional changes, and then begin to expand access to citizenship rights to a wider share of the population.

In the logic of the transition, elites find it in their interests to protect their privileges by converting them into rights. The biggest threat to elite privileges is other elites, especially factions within the dominant coalition. It was believed that intra-elite competition in mature natural states presented the biggest internal threat to elites. Those ideas formed the core of a crystallizing political theory in the eighteenth century called the *republican tradition* or *civic humanism* by some (with roots stretching back to Greece and Republican Rome). The backward-looking idea that intra-elite competition posed the greatest threat to social order described a natural state, not an open access order. The specific idea that political manipulation of economic privileges posed the greatest threat to a republic was the central hypothesis of Whig or Commonwealth thinking in the eighteenth century in Britain, France, and the United States.

We explore these ideas by focusing on political parties and economic corporations. Parties and corporations are highly visible in the historical record, were the subject of much debate in the eighteenth and nineteenth centuries, and have been studied in the historical literature since then. Not

190

only did these two types of organizations change during the transition proper, but they are fundamentally important to it. Critically, ideas that factions, parties, and corporations were dangerous and needed to be contained by institutional constraints help us understand beliefs held around 1800 in all three countries. However, those ideas alone do not explain the transition. These societies made transitions because they stopped limiting access to political and economic organizations. How did these societies move to institutions that allowed open access for both formally organized political parties and economic corporations by 1880?

The bulk of the chapter is couched in historical terms, both because it is easier to grasp the concepts when they are illustrated and because our concern is to explain the first transitions. The conceptual issues are clear. Once the doorstep conditions enable impersonal relationships among elites to grow, a transition proper can begin when elites transform personal elite privileges into impersonal elite rights. The transformation of privileges into rights occurs when elites in general perceive that their privileges will be more secure from intra-elite competition when those privileges are defined as commonly shared rights rather than personal prerogatives. As long as the ability to form organizations remains a privilege, access is not open. Open access does not require universal access, nor does it require complete elimination of all privileges; but it does require that a sufficiently large portion of the population be able to create political, economic, and other organizations at will. The extension of elite rights to larger groups in the population follows quickly once citizens' rights are defined and enforced. Once the rights of citizens are impersonally defined, the logic of open access suggests that those rights will be easier to sustain under conditions of wider political and economic competition.

Conceptually, a key idea in Western political thought is that the balance of interests in the polity protects rights. Madison famously argued this point in Federalist No. 10. In Britain, the balance of interests among the king, lords, and commons checked one another. For Aristotle, it was the interests of the one, the few, and the many that had to be kept in balance. Limits on access in all natural states create interests, and those political, economic, and military interests are balanced against each other within the dominant coalition. Historically, as late as 1790 parties and corporations were thought to be a threat to republican society in British, French, and American societies because organized interests threatened the balance of interests within the coalition. While the British Whigs, French Republicans, and American founders were trying to create societies with formal and informal checks and balances as a way to protect elite rights, few, if any of them, argued for open access.

The unique feature of the first transitions is that, by the middle of the nineteenth century, the very same parties and corporations that were feared in 1790 came to be seen as important elements in maintaining stability. In the transition proper, societies transform elite privileges based on personal identities to elite rights based on impersonally defined citizenship. Competitive political parties and open access to economic organizations become an inherent part of protecting citizen rights. In later transitions, beliefs in the inherent danger of political parties and corporations would be altered by the example of Britain, France, and the United States, which we call the *first movers* because they were the first to make the transition.

The transformation in thinking about organizations and the institutions that support organizations did not arise from eighteenth-century republican political theories. Earlier theories were based on a sophisticated analysis of natural states, which valued political balance and feared that political factions and the use of economic privilege for political ends would unbalance the constitutional equipoise of forces within society. The new elite ideas and institutions arose from changing experience and a new interpretation of that experience. In an interesting evolution, most of the vocabulary of the older republican theory persisted, particularly the overriding concern with balance, but parties and corporations were transformed into forces that could maintain balance rather than corrupt it. Parties and corporations can only maintain a balance of interests, however, under conditions of open access and competition, a set of conditions that had not existed prior to the nineteenth century and that the eighteenth-century republican theorists could not have observed or foreseen.

As we argued in Chapter 4, open access sustains and protects a much more flexible balance within the polity and the economy. Access, however, does not result from having balanced interests in a society. All natural states have a balance of interests without open access. A new understanding developed in the early nineteenth century that enabling open access could be a way to ensure a balance of interests in the polity and economy. This was often stated in the language of rights – that allowing citizens the right to participate was the best way to ensure the civil and economic rights all citizens enjoyed. The logic of the argument is the logic of open access orders: open access protects and sustains a dynamic balance of interests within society.

By 1880, competitive political parties and open access to corporate forms in many areas of economic and social life were prominent features of all three first movers. Nonetheless, the evolving institutional structure of these countries followed divergent paths. No clear, simple, and unique recipe of specific institutions produced the transition. Britain moved toward a congenial parliamentary sovereignty with few explicit checks or balances. France went through eighty years of constitutional instability ranging from republics with universal male suffrage to monarchies, but also legislative tyranny. The United States developed an election-intensive federal system with a stable national constitution and state governments that continued to experiment with their institutions.

Once the transition proper was underway after 1830, access continued to open, and non-elites began using organizational forms to pursue their own agendas. In contrast to any earlier period in European history, in the late nineteenth century non-elite organizations were neither suppressed nor prohibited in the first movers. Full citizenship involved more than the right to vote; it enabled non-elites to form organizations. Trade unions, socialists, churches, and suffragists all began building bases in economic and social organizations that they used as launching pads for political movements. The commitment to open access held; the growth of new organizations was not suppressed. Political and economic competition grew in scope and intensity.

The extension of citizenship to a wider share of the population was an important element of intensified political competition. Governments began to provide public goods – infrastructure, education, and social insurance – and distribute them on the basis of impersonal criteria, foregoing the manipulation of those public goods for political gains. Impersonal citizenship expanded on the extensive margin as suffrage broadened and more people were included among those who selected governments. Impersonal citizenship also expanded on the intensive margin as government capacity grew and began delivering public goods without regard to faction or party (or, in modern American terms, without respect to sex, race, creed, color, or age).

Our historical emphasis on Britain, France, and the United States in the early nineteenth century opens us up to the charge that our Euro-American focus leads to narrow inferences from historically unique conditions that are inappropriate for other societies. We agree that many of the specific contingent historical paths taken by the three countries will not be duplicated in subsequent transitions, not the least because the experience of the first transitions changed the way we think about the world.

Nonetheless, our focus has compensating virtues. A framework for understanding the transition must be consistent with the experience of the first movers. Examining Britain, France, and the United States addresses that requirement at the cost of ignoring the Dutch and the Swiss. The process of opening access to political and economic organizations, and the ensuing maturation of civil society, is a feature of all developed societies. Even if the specific historical paths the first movers followed to open access were unique, every subsequent transition accomplished the same results with respect to institutions, organizations, and the transformation of elite rights into citizen rights. The increasing sophistication of organizations is often treated as an incident of modernity rather than a fundamental transforming force in its own right. It is therefore of central importance to demonstrate that the first movers deliberately constructed social tools that supported more sophisticated organizations and made those tools available to all elites.

6.2 Fear of Faction

Modern political theory begins with Machiavelli. He was primarily concerned with the problem of faction and how to maintain a balance among competing factions. Competition among elite factions in natural states potentially included all of the possible ways to compete, including violence. As Madison explained in Federalist No. 10: "By a faction, I understand a number of citizens, whether amounting to a majority or minority of the whole, who are united and actuated by some common impulse or passion, or of interest, adverse to the rights of other citizens, or to the permanent and aggregate interests of the community" (Hamilton, Jay, and Madison, n.d.) The threat to stability and order in a natural state usually came from elite factions within the dominant coalition that sought to use violence or coercion to gain control of the political system.

Machiavelli and republican theorists down to Madison sought a political balance of counterpoised factions, classes, and interests. Elite factions would not have incentives to use violence to obtain their ends if violence could not succeed at making them better off because other, equally powerful factions would oppose them. The natural state exhibits such a balance, maintained in part by the threat of violence. Political competition in Machiavelli's world did not occur between well-organized political parties that step down from power when they lose elections. Political competition involved attempts at control and dominance, often using violence and coercion. Under the right social framework, therefore, the interests underlying factions could be used to sustain a stable republic, but only by dissuading interests from using violence. "When accompanied by factions and parties, [divisions of interest] are injurious; but when maintained without them they contribute to prosperity of republics."[1] Fear of faction was not paranoia; rather, it reflected a sophisticated analysis of political stability in a mature natural state.

Beliefs about factions had historical as well as theoretical foundations. Hume's essay "Of Parties in General" (1987[1777]) lists historical cases where conflicts among factions imperiled republics, and Machiavelli's *Discourses on Livy* (1996) analyzes how the Roman Republic harnessed factional conflict to better social ends. The belief that competition among factions was the primary threat to republics and that the liberty of a republic could only be secured if factions could somehow be contained was an empirical observation justified by close historical analysis as well as a causal belief about the structure of human societies. It is not surprising, then, that major contributors to the theory of balance lived in societies governed by mature natural states: Aristotle in Athens, Polybius in Rome, and Machiavelli in Florence.

The canonical example is Rome. The end of the Roman Republic in the first century B.C.E. stemmed directly from civil wars. For example, the breakdown of the triumvirate of Julius Caesar, Pompeii, and Crassus instigated a civil war. The reestablishment of order under a new and formal triumvirate of Octavian (to become Augustus Caesar), Marc Antony, and Lepidus broke down and led to another civil war. Augustus's triumph at Actium in 31 B.C.E. left him in control of the Roman Empire, and the Roman Republic withered away. Faction has always been the heart of this Roman history. When Augustus set down his record in *The Achievements of the Divine Augustus*, he wrote of his struggle to obtain his rights and property as Julius Caesar's heir: "At the age of nineteen on my own responsibility and at my own expense I raised an army, with which I successfully championed the liberty of the republic when it was oppressed by the tyranny of a faction" (as quoted and translated by Wells, 1992, pp. 12–13).

When Alexander Hamilton and James Madison described the evils of faction and argued that the new constitution would "form a barrier against domestic faction and insurrection" (Hamilton) or have a "tendency to break and control the violence of faction" (Madison) through the agency

---

[1] Machiavelli, (1854), *History of Florence*, 7.1 (p. 306), quoted in Wolin (2004), p. 208. Wolin argues that Machiavelli's analysis of interests "not only converted the problem of interest into the central problem of political theory, but that he sought to accompany this with a theory which indicated the salutary effects of socioeconomic conflicts and the techniques by which they might be resolved" (p. 208).

of a confederate republic (Hamilton) or an extended republic (Madison) in Federalist Papers No. 9 and No. 10, they drew on the best political theory of their time. Modern readers have a great deal of difficulty remembering that Hamilton and Madison were not writing about modern politics. Their concern with the essential problem of constraining interest groups from manipulating the political process for their own advantage related to natural states, not open access orders. Hamilton and Madison argued that the mechanisms embodied in the confederate republic – the checks and balances of the U.S. Constitution – would quell the violence of faction. History appears to have vindicated their argument and, as a result, it is hard to imagine that the checks and balances they described were not sufficient to produce the social order of modern republican government and open access societies.

The overarching concern of modern republican theorists for balance in government and fear of faction was grounded in the reality of a natural state. Beginning with Aristotle, continuing through Polybius, Machiavelli, Guicciardini, Harrington, Sidney, Montesquieu, Bolingbroke, Hume, Hamilton, and Madison, the political ideal of the best-designed republic included multiple interests whose presence within the state provided a check on factions, groups, and individuals. These interests were thought to arise naturally from differences in resources, abilities, and inheritance in the population. The main groups were military leaders, large landholders, religious, and commercial leaders.[2] Their deep concern for history could not produce a design for a functioning republic on an open access model because an open access society had never existed. Instead, these theorists sought to improve the natural state. They could only have imagined how a modern open access society worked and, in several key respects, their imagination failed.

The design of institutions that mitigated the divisive and corrupting influence of factions comprised the foundation of the modern concept of balanced or mixed government. Republican political theorists in the eighteenth century made a direct connection between organized political factions, organized economic interests in the form of corporations, and

---

[2] Aristotle's classic groups were the one, the few, and the many; meaning a king, an aristocracy, and the citizens (who were only "many" in relation to the few; the many did not include everyone). Theorists generally took the existence and distribution of interests as a natural phenomenon: for example, Madison's analysis of the origin of interests in *Federalist #10*: "The latent causes of faction are thus sown in the nature of man . . . " Similarly, Marx argued that the material consequences of the technology of production determined interests.

factions.[3] The constitutional structures of Britain, France, and the United States in 1800 did not support open access to political or economic organizations. As Hofstadter (1969) famously noted, the U.S. Constitution of 1787 was a "constitution against party." The paradox of the early nineteenth century is that societies in which people initially believed that political parties and corporations were dangerous, even evil, eventually adopted open access mass political parties and open access to the corporate form for economic, religious, educational, and other social activities. The assertion of most histories of the last two centuries that the growth of competitive political parties and competitive access to economic organizations in the early nineteenth century was a direct outgrowth of eighteenth-century ideas needs to be reexamined. In Britain, France, and the United States the transition proper – the changes in the structure of societies that institutionalized open political and economic access – occurred in the nineteenth, not the eighteenth century.

Fear of faction was rooted in the fear of one elite faction gaining ascendancy over the other factions. If balance among the factions was lost, tyranny and slavery would inevitably follow because one faction would gain ascendancy and overpower the others. Tyranny and slavery characterized any form of government where the governed did not give their consent to the selection and policies of the governors.[4] Tyranny and slavery, in the sense of the governed not giving consent to the governors, characterize most natural states. Republican theorists wanted a special case of the natural state: a society where all of the appropriate individuals who should be citizens could enjoy their privileges with some security. They wanted to guarantee good natural states where all of the significant elements of society participated,

---

[3] Fortunately, understanding how elites secured impersonal rights has been the core enterprise of Western political philosophy and intellectual history over the last three and a half centuries (Skinner, 2002). Considerable attention has been paid to the transition process in Britain, France, and the United States and perhaps the most commonly asked question of Western European political history is "What did they think they were doing?" In the last half of the twentieth century the debate reached some common understandings led by J. G. A. Pocock's *The Machiavellian Moment* (1975) and Bernard Bailyn's *Ideological Origins of the American Revolution* (1967). Gay's *The Enlightenment* (1966, 1969) comes at the same set of issues from a much broader disciplinary approach, focusing on the eighteenth century. Skinner's *Foundations of Modern Political Thought* (1978) covers much the same ground and time period as Pocock, while Van Gelderen and Skinner (2002) gather a recent set of essays connecting developments in republican theory throughout Europe. Wolin's *Politics and Vision* (2004) traces political ideas from ancient Greece to the present and intersects with the republican period throughout much of his book.

[4] See Skinner, *Liberty before Liberalism* (1998), for a discussion of the concepts of tyranny and slavery in the republican context.

the government was, therefore, mixed and no faction eliminated another faction through violence or insurrection.

Language can be confusing here. Prior to 1800 the terms *faction*, *party*, and *interest* were used interchangeably in political debates. Factions were not formally organized. Factions were congeries of individuals with similar interests, often integrated into a patron–client network of a powerful or charismatic leader. The term *party* before 1800 or even 1850 (depending on the country and speaker) did not refer to modern organized political parties. Parties with formal organization only began to form in the early to mid-nineteenth century. By the end of the nineteenth century, parties were not only allowed but encouraged to provide the vehicle for political competition. The process of party formation followed different paths in Britain, France, and the United States, and we discuss those paths later in the chapter. For clarity, from this point forward we use the term *political party* to designate (potentially) competitive political organizations with formal structures and often perpetual life. Permanent organized political parties, so defined, did not exist anywhere until the United States in the 1820s and 1830s.[5]

In contrast, *factions* are groups of individuals with a common purpose or interest and are endemic to all societies. Political parties in most modern societies are organizations made up of multiple factions. Fear of factions in a natural state extended to fear of parties because organized factions were capable of violence. The prevalence of civil war and the unconsolidated nature of military power in a natural state made fear of factions a real and pressing concern. If factions and parties are unchecked, the balance of the political system will be lost, the constitution will be corrupted, and tyranny and slavery will follow. To twenty-first-century readers the words make sense, but they seem to be paranoid exaggerations. The eighteenth-century writers were men who knew what tyranny and slavery were. Many American theorists actually owned slaves – how could they fear that tyranny and slavery lurked just around the corner if the government lost balance?[6]

---

[5] As Duverger (1959, p. xxiii) notes, "In 1850 no country in the world (except the United States) knew political parties in the modern sense of the word. There were trends of opinion, popular clubs, philosophical societies, and parliamentary groups, but no real parties." The widespread adoption of formal political organizations in modern natural states suggests that formal parties are not inconsistent with natural states, as the PRI in Mexico (1930–2000) and Nazi Germany (1933–45) illustrate. Democracy is not defined solely by the presence of parties but requires the presence of competitive political organizations with the property that, when incumbent parties lose elections, they step down peacefully.

[6] "The leaders of the [American] Revolutionary movement were radicals – but they were eighteenth-century radicals concerned, like the eighteenth-century English radicals not

Skinner (1998) explains that the eighteenth-century political theorists used tyranny and slavery to describe a situation in which the governed had not given their consent to be governed. Bailyn goes further in his reading of the pamphlets of the American Revolution:

I began to see new meaning in phrases that I, like most historians, had readily dismissed as mere rhetoric and propaganda: "slavery," "corruption," "conspiracy." These inflammatory words were used so forcefully by pamphleteers of so great a variety of social statuses, political positions, and religious persuasions; they fitted so logically into the pattern of radical and opposition thought; and they reflected so clearly the realities of life in an age in which monarchical autocracy flourished, in which the stability and freedom of England's "mixed" constitution was a recent and remarkable achievement, and in which the fear of conspiracy [faction] against constituted authority was built into the very structure of politics, that I began to suspect that they meant something very real to both the writers and their readers; that these were real fears, real anxieties, a sense of real danger behind these phrases, and not merely the desire to influence by rhetoric and propaganda the inert minds of an otherwise passive populace (Bailyn, 1965, p. ix; see also Bailyn 1967).

In the eighteenth century, Americans and Britons watching the development of British politics feared that a faction, held together by grants of economic privileges, including ownership of stock in the Bank of England and other companies, had gained control of the political process and suborned the independence of the House of Commons. As Bailyn stresses, these people held real fears about what would happen to their societies if a faction was allowed to manipulate the granting of economic privilege to obtain control of the process of political decision making. Grounded in beliefs about the causal structure of their world, these fears played a central role in the Americans' decision to revolt from Britain.

Many political theorists believed they understood the solution, namely, the possibility of controlling factions through mixed government.[7] The increasing importance of a society's constitution, written or unwritten, in mobilizing the inherent interests of monarchs, landed aristocracies, and commercial elites into a structure that neutralized their danger as factions by setting their interests against one another epitomized the structure of a stable mature natural state. Most political thinkers in Britain, America, and

---

with the need to recast the social order nor with the problems of economic inequality and the injustice of stratified societies but with the need to purify a corrupt constitution and fight off the apparent growth of prerogative power" (Bailyn, 1967, p. 283).

[7] The title of Hume's essay, "That Politics May Be Reduced to a Science," reflects the hopes of theorists that a solution to the problem of factions within a natural state could be found in a system of government that balanced conflicting interests against one another.

France thought that the British constitution was the best yet developed in human history.[8] They feared, however, that it was threatened by faction in the eighteenth century.

The major perceived threats to the British constitution and its balanced government were corporations and parties: organized economic and political interests. The rise of a new military/financial complex in eighteenth-century Britain resulted in two developments. First, economic organizations and corporations, such as the Bank of England and the South Sea Company, closely tied to financing of government came to enjoy exclusive privileged positions in the economy. Second, under the terms of the Revolution Settlement reached between parliament and King William, the growth of government revenues and expenditures required parliamentary approval. The result was a much closer cooperation between the king (and eventually his cabinet) and parliament, including the development of a legislative interest responsive to the king's interests. The development of parliamentary interests raised the specter of faction. The systematic use of economic privileges enabled the Whig coalition under Robert Walpole to manage the king's parliamentary interest effectively.[9] Privileges included the distribution of the national debt; the creation of privileged corporations; the manipulation of appointments of members of parliament to offices in the army, navy, and government; and the granting of royal pensions to members of parliament.

Bolingbroke was among the most vocal critics of Walpole and the Whigs. It is a matter of lasting confusion that the term *Whig* was applied to both a parliamentary party as well as to a way of thinking about politics. Bolingbroke was a Tory politician (in the parliamentary sense) and a Whig (or True Whig or Commonwealth) theorist. Although Bolingbroke was an important theorist, he was more important as a publicist for Whig ideas and as a conduit for those ideas to flow into France and the United States. In and out of office in the early eighteenth century, Bolingbroke spent considerable time in France where he befriended Montesquieu and Voltaire, eventually returning to England in the 1720s.[10] Barred from holding office,

---

[8] Montesquieu's *Spirit of the Laws* is a sustained argument in favor of balance in small republics. He regarded the English Constitution as the best approximation to his ideal.

[9] The Whig and Tory Parties were legislative parties, without a permanent structure or organization and little or no presence in the electorate.

[10] Elected to parliament in 1701, Bolingbroke became secretary of war in 1704 at the age of twenty-six, although he and his patron Harley eventually fell out of favor. Returned to office in 1710, he served as secretary of state and, after a split with Harley, was the de facto prime minister at the time of Queen Anne's death in 1714. After George I succeeded Anne, Bolingbroke fell out of favor again and was exiled from England in 1715, having being stripped of his lands and title.

Bolingbroke published a newspaper, *The Craftsman,* and choreographed the opposition to Walpole. Along with Trenchard and Gordon's *Cato's Letters,* Bolingbroke's *Craftsman* was widely read in the United States.

The heart of Bolingbroke's critique revolved around the new role of money in British politics and its corrupting effect on the constitution. The rising expenditures for military action against France created an alliance between financial corporations and the crown. The distribution of the ever-growing national debt to favored political allies or opponents secured the interests of the debt-holders to support the government. The growing size of the military – accompanied by the increasing number of army and navy officers serving in parliament as well as the increasing number of placemen (members of parliament [MP's] with government jobs) and pensioners – gave Walpole and the king's interest a predominant presence in the House of Commons. Bolingbroke accused the king and his ministers of using the money power to suborn parliamentary independence, destroying the balance of the constitution. To maintain their flow of benefits, favors, and privileges, these MPs had to support the crown. The independence of parliament was compromised by the political dependence of MPs on Walpole's patronage. Once the independence of parliament was suborned, tyranny and slavery would follow.[11]

These Whig claims contained a great deal of truth. The British government owed the three monied companies – the Bank of England, the East Indies Company, and the South Sea Company – in the neighborhood of 35 to 40 percent of the national debt in the 1820s.[12] The Bank of England secured a monopoly of note issue in the area around London. The East Indies Company held a monopoly on the lucrative trade with India and Asia. Placemen, pensioners, stockholders in the monied companies, and holders of the national debt held a large number of seats in the House of Commons.[13] It was difficult to obtain charters for incorporated companies. Outside of incorporation by royal patent or parliamentary act, business organizations were required to use partnerships or trusts. Because each of the three monied companies depended on their close connections with

---

[11] Bolingbroke's writings are available in several modern editions. His ideas are treated in Kramnick (1968). Pages 39–83 are particularly relevant to the question of faction and corporations. Similar criticisms of corporations and stock jobbing can be found throughout *Cato's Letters,* published by Trenchard and Gordon (1995), and conveniently collected by the Liberty Fund Press.

[12] Dickson (1967) reports that the government directly owed the three companies £15 out of £40 million in September of 1714, p. 80, and £18 out of £50 million in 1719, p. 93.

[13] See Namier (1966, pp. 224–5), as well as the larger surveys in Namier and Brook (1964).

government for their privileges – and because other organizations could not easily become corporations – the companies, their stockholders, and their representatives were drawn by their interests to support the government. In particular, members of parliament closely connected to these interests could not exercise independent judgment on a range of issues. In this way, the king and the government built a supporting coalition that allowed them to circumvent the normal parliamentary constraints.

Nonetheless, it seemed clear to many that Britain was doing as well as ever. The Revolution Settlement guaranteed the right of parliament to participate fully in government policy decisions. The economy was growing and maturing. Despite fears about their effects, modern financial institutions were developing rapidly. A disconnect between the accomplishments of the age and the dangers ahead, however, permeated public discussion. As Dickson (1967, 32–3) notes:

[W]hile few aspects of the Financial Revolution were of greater political and economic utility than the development of a market in securities in London, none united contemporary opinion more against it. It was denounced as inherently wicked and against the public interest. The phrase 'stock-jobbing,' freely used to denote every kind of activity in the market, had clear overtones of self-interest and corruption. An anthology of comments by contemporaries would be remarkably uniform, indeed monotonous, in its tone, and uninformative about how the market actually worked.

Others expressed similar thoughts.[14] Were conditions in Britain good and getting better, or did the warning signs of faction and corruption portend a return of despotism? Were tyranny and slavery just around the corner?

---

[14] Hume (1987[1777]), pp. 28–9). Hume expressed similar thoughts about the hyperbole of the times in his essay "That Politics may be Reduced to a Science" when he commented on the intense criticism (and defense) of Walpole by Bolingbroke and his critics (and partisans): "But I would fain persuade these-party zealots that there is a flat contradiction both in the accusation and panegyric [of Walpole], and that it were impossible for either of them to run so high, were it not for this contradiction. If our constitution be really that noble fabric, the pride of BRITAIN, the envy of our neighbors, raised by the labor of so many centuries, repaired at the expense of so many millions, and cemented by such a profusion of blood; I say, if our constitution does in any degree deserve these eulogies, it would never have suffered a wicked and weak minister to govern triumphantly for a course of twenty years, when opposed by the great geniuses in the nation, who exercised the utmost liberty of tongue and pen, in parliament, and in their frequent appeals to the people. But if the minister be wicked and weak, to the degree so strenuously insisted on, the constitution must be faulty in its original principles, and he cannot be consistently charged with undermining the best constitution in the world." Hume, nonetheless, worried about the effects of Walpole's administration. "During his time trade has flourished, liberty declined, and learning gone to ruin. As I am a man, I love him; as I am a scholar, I hate him; as I am a BRITON, I calmly wish his fall." Hume's comments were directed at Bolingbroke's *Dissertation on Parties*.

6.3 Events

Looking back from the twenty-first century, eighteenth-century beliefs about the danger of parties and corporations appear to be misplaced. Despite what intellectuals wrote, we can only be sure that elites held those beliefs if we have evidence that they acted on them. Were factions, parties, and economic organizations suppressed, restricted, or discouraged? And if so, how and when?

Rival factions always contend for control in natural states, as they do in open access orders. Natural state and open access orders differ, however, in the cost of losing. When violence breaks out in natural states, losing factions are often killed, exiled, or otherwise eliminated. Bolingbroke provides an example. As secretary of state under Queen Anne (1702–14), Bolingbroke had sought to eliminate the Whig faction: "The view, therefore, of those among us who thought in this manner, was to improve the queen's favor, to break the body of the Whigs, to render their support useless to them, and to fill the employments of the kingdom down to the meanest with Tories."[15] Under Anne, several Whigs were imprisoned, including Walpole. When Anne died and George I turned to the Whigs to form his government, Bolingbroke fled to France in 1715, and Walpole turned the tables on him. Walpole "immediately moved [Bolingbroke's] impeachment, a motion that was carried without a single dissenting vote. Bolingbroke was declared a permanent exile and stripped of his title and estate" (Kramnick, 1968, p. 13). Bolingbroke complicated his position in Britain by associating with James II, deposed in the Glorious Revolution of 1688–9, then in exile in France. Bolingbroke soon repented of his association with James. He ultimately obtained the favor of King George, and returned to Britain in 1725. As late as the 1720s then, indeed perhaps as late as the final Jacobite rising in 1745, losing British factions faced the threat of imprisonment, loss of land and titles, and perhaps death if they were defeated. The British actively restricted factions by the threat of death or exile, until the mid-eighteenth century.[16]

The 1720s produced a crisis – the South Sea Bubble – brought on by the behavior of a corporation. Chartered in 1711, the South Sea Company possessed the *asiento*, the right to carry slaves to Spanish colonies. However,

---

[15] Bolingbroke in a *Letter to Sir William Windham*, quoted in Kramnick (1968, p. 9).

[16] Bailyn's essay on the "Sources of Political Culture" (1968, pp. 3–58) gives a clear explanation of and justification for the active fear of faction in British politics. The last British peer to be attainted was Lord Edward Fitzgerald for leading the Irish Rebellion of 1798. Fitzgerald died in prison of wounds inflicted during his arrest. The bill of attainder confiscating his property was repealed in 1819.

the major purpose of the company was to refinance the large government debts incurred during the War of the Spanish Succession (1701–14). In 1719 and 1720, the company was authorized to increase its capital. Stockholders could purchase new shares of company stock with government bonds. Because South Sea shares were more liquid than government bonds it was possible for investors, the company, and the treasury all to benefit from the conversion of bonds into company shares.[17] The price of South Sea shares rose dramatically early in 1720 as the bond conversion commenced. Later in the year, the bubble burst, and South Sea shares and the entire stock market collapsed.

As negotiations with the government and the company for the bond conversion operation were taking place, parliament also considered what would later come to be known as the Bubble Act. Passed in June of 1720, before the bubble burst, the act created two new insurance companies with a monopoly on marine insurance in London, solidified the position of the monied companies, and provided for penalties against any company that presumed to act as a corporate body without the permission of parliament or the crown.[18] Patterson and Reiffen (1990) argue that the act was intended to protect the fiscal and political interests of the crown and parliament "by restricting corporate status to relatively few firms and preventing competition" (p. 165). Harris (1994) also suggests that, to a large extent, the act was special-interest legislation for the South Sea Company.

Scott's conclusions, reached in 1912, sum up the effects of the act in the circumstances of the eighteenth century:

The true significance of the panic [of 1720], however, is not so much in terminating one epoch, but in beginning and dominating another. To the statesmen of the first quarter of the eighteenth century, it seemed demonstrable that the joint-stock system – "the pernicious art of stock jobbing" – was the sole and sufficient explanation of the miseries of the country. No words were too strong to condemn what was then considered to be a malign perversion of industry, destructive of commercial probity, of a well-ordered social life, even of religion and virtue. In fact the joint-stock type of organization received only a little less abuse than the directors of the South Sea company . . . In short the result of opinion in 1720 and 1721 was

---

[17] Neal (1990, pp. 62–117) describes the bubble, the operations of the South Sea Company, and the Bank of England. Many bonds were annuities issued for the lifetime of a specific person. These bonds were difficult to transfer, because evidence that the original person was still alive had to be produced every year. Consolidating the debt in the South Sea Company simplified the task of administering the debt, lowering the interest on the debt paid by the government, and increased the liquidity of the bond holders.

[18] See Harris (1994, 1997, 2000) and Patterson and Reiffen (1990). Because the act passed before the bubble burst, the act was not a reaction to the stock market crash.

that the rise of the joint-stock system had been the cause of the panic, and therefore it was decided that the Bubble Act should be strictly enforced. As a consequence, no company was safe in beginning business without first obtaining a charter, and such instruments were now only granted after a more searching enquiry than had been usual in the past. Under the existing circumstances, it was fortunate that no more restrictive measures were passed (Scott, 1951[1912], Vol.1, pp. 436–7).

The Bubble Act significantly restricted the number of corporate charters issued over the next hundred years.

Adam Smith's *Wealth of Nations* provides the final piece of evidence about attitudes toward corporations in eighteenth-century Britain. Smith presented the economic case for free and open competition; he charged the government and corporations with the desire to limit entry and create rents. Smith did not absolutely oppose incorporation. He saw some joint-stock companies as legitimate business enterprises.[19] His low opinion of corporations in general reflected less on the economic and organizational aspects of joint-stock businesses than on the natural state's political effects of chartering – the corrosive effects of corporate privileges given to towns, guilds, and monopolies.[20] Although much of the debate about Smith's view of corporations has focused on his view about their efficiency, Smith saw corporations in a traditional Whig manner: grants of economic privilege used to secure political advantage. As late as 1776, the founder of modern economics viewed corporations largely in natural-state terms – as tools for the political manipulation of the economy.

The situation in France in the eighteenth century differed considerably. Political organizations came under even more suspicion than in Britain. The absolute monarchy brooked no serious competitors, and leaders of factions were eradicated or exiled. Administration of the French state involved a well-articulated set of corporations and corporate privileges that were used to govern and administer municipalities, courts, and other aspects of French life. The network of corporations was connected to the system of venal office holding in which offices within the corporation were periodically available for purchase from the king; most offices could be resold in an organized market; and the king and officeholders made a series of regular payments to each other (Doyle, 1996).

---

[19] In particular see Smith (1981[1776], Vol. 2, pp. 731–58), "Of the Publick Works and Institutions which are necessary for facilitating particular Branches of Commerce."

[20] For towns see Smith (1981[1776], Vol. 1, pp. 397–410), "Of the Rise and Progress of Cities and Towns, after the Fall of the Roman Empire" and for apprenticeships and guilds see Vol. 1, pp. 135–59, "Inequalities occasioned by the Policy of Europe."

In France, as in Britain, the term *corporation* included a much wider array of organizations than joint-stock business companies and municipalities. The sale of privilege for cash, the center of the venal office-holding system, led to the development of much more durable and sophisticated forms of organization in France. The value of a specific office was directly related to the privileges it carried, the security of the officeholder, and the conditions under which the office could be transferred to a third party or passed on to an heir. Although perpetually lived in theory, the ability of the king to credibly honor his promises to officeholders often meant that these organizations were not fully perpetually lived in practice. The financial difficulties facing the French crown in the 1770s and 1780s were in part a reflection of the commitments made to officeholders that made negotiating solutions to the state's financial problems difficult. In consequence of the king's strong fiscal incentives to provide institutional support for corporate organizations of many types, including the central organizations of courts, municipalities, and businesses, the French polity and economy had a richer variety of complex organizational structures than the British did circa 1750.

The question of corporate organization and privilege came to a head during the revolution. On the night of August 4, 1789, the National Assembly – in what "is justly remembered as the most radical legislative session of the entire French Revolution" – abolished or condemned many of the central institutions of French society (Doyle, 1996, p. 1). It declared the end of venal offices. Municipalities and their officials were to be retained; offices would no longer be titular, but elected; assemblies no longer by right, but by representation. The old organizational forms ultimately had to go as well. The Chapelier law was passed by the Assembly in June of 1791, which banned many types of economic and social organizations and applied to organizations of workers, professionals, and entrepreneurs (Stewart, 1951, p. 165–6).

The sentiments against organizations were prominently placed in the Constitution of 1791. The Preamble reads:

The National Assembly, wishing to establish the French Constitution upon the principles it has just recognized and declared, abolishes irrevocably the institutions which were injurious to liberty and equality of rights.

Neither nobility, nor peerage, nor hereditary distinctions, nor distinctions of orders, nor feudal regime, nor patrimonial courts, nor any titles, denominations, or prerogatives derived therefrom, nor any order of knighthood, nor any corporations or decorations requiring proofs of nobility or implying distinctions of birth, nor any superiority other than that of public functionaries in the performance of their duties any longer exists.

Neither venality nor inheritance of any public office any longer exists.

Neither privilege nor exception to the law common to all Frenchmen any longer exists for any part of the nation or for any individual.

Neither *jurandes* nor corporations of professions, arts, and crafts any longer exist.

The law no longer recognizes religious vows or any other obligation contrary to natural rights or the Constitution (Stewart, 1951, p. 231).

The French Revolution has always been seen as a revolution against privilege. Missing is the understanding that it was also a revolution against corporations, against the forms of organized privilege that were used to structure the French natural state and the larger French society. This reaction was not part of the revulsion against the aristocracy: most corporate privileges had no connection to the nobility or to ennoblement.

The American case presents a third variation on these themes. Americans shared a long history with the British and had developed during the colonial period a style of politics in their colonial legislatures that stressed united policies and opposition to colonial governors (Hofstadter, 1969, p. 45). We have already drawn on Bailyn's history of Whig ideology in America to illustrate how fear of factions and corporations played a key role in the coming of the American Revolution. Two instances in the 1790s illuminate how these fears arose during the early years of the republic.

First, consider George Washington's farewell address in 1796. After his plea to appreciate the value of the Union and his prediction that geographic divisions could imperil it, he raised the danger of faction:

All obstructions to the execution of the laws, all combinations and associations, under whatever plausible character, with the real design to direct, control, counteract, or awe the regular deliberation and action of the constituted authorities, are destructive of this fundamental principle and of fatal tendency. They serve to organize faction; to give artificial and extraordinary force; to put in the place of the delegated will of the nation the will of a party, often a small but artful and enterprising minority of the community, and, according to the alternate triumphs of different parties, to make the public administration the mirror of the ill-concerted and incongruous projects of faction rather than the organ of consistent and wholesome plans, digested by common counsels and modified by mutual interests.

However combinations or associations of the above description may now and then answer popular ends, they are likely in the course of time and things to become potent engines by which cunning, ambitious, and unprincipled men will be enabled to subvert the power of the people, and to usurp for themselves the reins of government, destroying afterwards the very engines which have lifted them to unjust dominion (Richardson, 1897, Vol. 1, pp. 209–10).

Washington then moved to the dangers of party:

Let me now take a more comprehensive view, and warn you in the most solemn manner against the baneful effects of the spirit of party generally...

The alternate domination of one faction over another, sharpened by the spirit of revenge natural to party dissension, which in different ages and countries has perpetrated the most horrid enormities, is itself a frightful despotism. But this leads at length to a more formal and permanent despotism...

Without looking forward to an extremity of this kind (which nevertheless ought not to be entirely out of sight), the common and continual mischiefs of the spirit of party are sufficient to make it the interest and duty of a wise people to discourage and restrain it (Richardson, 1897, Vol. 1, pp. 210–11).

Washington's warning against the dangers of faction and party was based on his own experience as president with the first economic corporation chartered by the national government. The first challenge facing the new government was financial. The Constitution of 1787 was motivated, in part, by the need to give the national government the power to tax so it could raise revenue to repay debts from the Revolutionary War. When the first Congress met, Treasury Secretary Alexander Hamilton proposed a three-part scheme. All of the existing national and state debts would be consolidated in a new set of bond issues; a national bank would be chartered by the national government and act as the government's financial agent in servicing the new bonds; and a moderate revenue tariff would be established on imports and excise taxes would be levied to supply the national government with revenue. All three elements of Hamilton's plans passed Congress in March of 1791.

Hamilton's arguments for America's new financial system, however, had ominous overtones. In his January 1790 *Report on the Public Credit*, Hamilton proposed, "If all the public creditors receive their dues from one source... their interests will be the same. And having the same interests, they will unite in support of the fiscal arrangements of the government."[21] Hamilton proposed to create precisely the type of factional interest in support of the government – an alliance with the monied interest – that Whigs feared in Britain.

---

[21] "Report on the Public Credit," *American State Papers, Finance*, Vol. I, p. 15. Ferguson (1961) analyzes how constitutional issues and the public debt interacted in Hamilton's thinking.

Opposition to Hamilton's plan arose quickly and focused on the power of the national government to create corporations. While considering whether to sign or veto the bank bill, Washington asked Hamilton, Jefferson (his secretary of state), and Randolph (his attorney general) for their opinions. Hamilton vigorously encouraged Washington to sign the bill. Jefferson and Randolph opposed it. They couched their arguments in constitutional terms: the U.S. Constitution did not explicitly give the national government the power to create corporations; therefore, the national government did not possess the power. Hamilton argued that the powers were implied in the Constitution.[22] This confrontation launched one of the most enduring political debates in American history over the national powers implied by the Constitution.

The debates also discussed the larger issues about the dangers of corporations. James Madison, then a congressional representative from Virginia, feared that chartering corporations would destroy the delicate constitutional balance, risking constitutional failure:

Mr. M. then enlarged on the exact balance or equipoise contemplated by the Constitution, to be observed and maintained between the several branches of Government; and showed, that except this idea was preserved, the advantages of different independent branches would be lost, and their separate deliberations and determinations be entirely useless . . .

The power of granting charters, he observed, is a great and important power, and ought not to be exercised unless we find ourselves expressly authorized to grant them. Here he dilated on the great and extensive influence that incorporated societies had on public affairs in Europe. They are powerful machines which have always been found competent to effect objects on principles in a great measure independent of the people (Annals of Congress, 1st Congress, 3rd Session, pp. 2008–9).

The financial program provoked Whig fears of executive influence distorting the constitutional balance rather than concerns over the economic implications of Hamilton's plan.[23] The debate about the implications of

---

[22] "That every power vested in a government is in its nature *sovereign*, and includes by *force* of the *term*, a right to employ all the *means* requisite and fairly applicable to the attainment of the *ends* of such power, and which are not precluded by restrictions and exceptions specified in the Constitution, or not immoral, or not contrary to the *essential ends* of political society" McKee (1957[1934], 101, emphasis in the original).

[23] "It is hard to imagine how by deliberate intent, Alexander Hamilton's economic program for the new republic could have been better calculated to exacerbate these [commonwealth] fears . . . they inevitably brought to mind the entire system of eighteenth-century English governmental finance, with all the consequences that entailed for minds shaped by British opposition thought" Banning (1978, p. 128).

the financial plan after it was passed in 1791 opened a division within the national government (Banning, 1978; McCoy, 1980). On the Federalist side, the Adamses, joined by Hamilton, praised the British constitution and argued against extending democracy too far. On what became the Republican side, Jefferson and Madison, abetted by Thomas Paine and Phillip Freneau, attacked the Adamses as monarchists and Hamilton as an aspiring Walpole. The Republicans castigated the financial plan as an attempt by Hamilton to use his position as treasury secretary to secure control of the government through systematic corruption. Public acrimony between the participants set in motion the formation of distinct Federalist and Republican factions in national politics. We will consider the factions' organization later. The way in which the conflict was resolved placed corruption in government promotion of economic development at the center of American politics for the next seventy years. Parties were appearing in America, but they were not yet considered legitimate. Corporations remained a threat to republican principles, and the national government would not create another one until 1816.

People in Britain, France, and the United States in the 1790s regarded factions, parties, and corporations as threats to the operation of a sound republic. Constitutions and policies, including limits on the number of corporation charters issued, reflected the fear that a faction would use the political power to manipulate economic privileges to obtain stable, long-term control over the government, eliminate rival factions, and tyrannize its opponents.

6.4 Parties and Corporations

In order to sort out how parties and corporations developed in the nineteenth century, it helps to have a standard vocabulary. Duverger (1959) distinguished four types of early party development. The first two are parliamentary parties and electoral parties. Parliamentary parties develop within legislative bodies. Parliamentary parties are typically loose associations of persons. Whigs and Tories as parties in eighteenth-century Britain were parliamentary parties; they had no organized electoral counterparts (Duverger, 1959, p. xxiii).

Electoral parties develop when the suffrage is wide enough and the voters disorganized enough so that it pays political activists to devote resources to organizing voters and getting the vote out (Duverger, 1959, p. xxvii). Electoral parties develop in a number of different ways. Sometimes they arise around issues of local interest; others organize along geographical interests, and still others through a central leadership.

Recognizable modern political parties, the third type of party, appear when parliamentary and electoral parties merge or arise together (Duverger, 1959, p. xxiii). A modern political party contains a legislative arm coordinating the behavior of legislators, and an elective arm identifying party voters and getting out the vote. Most parties formed in the nineteenth century in the three first movers grew out of parliamentary and electoral parties and their merger.

Duverger calls the fourth type of party "externally created parties" or "extra-parliamentary parties." Rather than emerging from the legislative or electoral process, external parties are "essentially established by a preexisting institution of which the true activities lie outside elections and parliament: it is then accurate to speak of creation from without" (Duverger, 1959, p. xxx). Duverger treats labor and trade unions, socialist and other ideologically motivated groups, churches, philosophical societies, ex-servicemen's associations, and business firms as prominent sources of external party organization.[24] External parties are often organized with the intent of raising awareness of issues and conditions, rather than in the serious hope of winning elections and installing governments. External parties with specific, narrow, factional interests that are allowed to compete in the political arena signal the arrival of open access politics.

Economic organizations also come in a number of distinct forms. The traditional progression of firms emphasizes partnership (or general partnership), limited partnership, and the corporation or joint-stock company.[25] All of these forms of business enterprise are contractual organizations. They rely on the third-party enforcement of the state to structure relationships within the organization and between the organization and other individuals and organizations outside of the enterprise.

General partnerships are agreements reached among individuals without requiring the express consent of the state to form them. The state provides and enforces standardized forms that the partnership relationships can take.[26] A partnership is inherently personal. Each individual partner can act in the name of the others, and all partners are jointly and individually liable

---

[24] Duverger (1959, p. xxxiv) cites E. H. Underhill as showing that the birth of the Canadian Conservative Party in 1854 was influenced by the Bank of Montreal, the Grand Trunk Railway, and by Montreal "big business" generally.

[25] A fourth form, the trust, was important primarily in Britain.

[26] Individuals have the ability to form partnerships at will, but not the form that partnerships will take. This is a subtle distinction of some importance. The state defines what forms of partnership relationships that it will enforce, inside and outside the firm. Individuals can structure whatever form of partnership they want. If, however, the forms turn out not to be incentive-compatible, the partners can only obtain third-party enforcement through the forms enforced by the states. So, for example, partners and their creditors may sign

for debts and obligations incurred by the partnership. The partnership does not possess legal personhood. Actions taken by the partnership are actions taken jointly by the partners as individuals. Upon the death or resignation of one partner, the partnership must be reformed. An extensive law of partnership existed in Britain, France, and the United States throughout the nineteenth century.

Limited partnerships contain two types of partners. In France, the *société en commandite* included limited (sleeping) partners, *commanditaires*, whose liability for the debts and actions of the partnership was limited to their investment. The active partner(s), the *gerant(és)*, ran the business without interference or advice from the *commanditaires*. All partners in a standard partnership or *société générale*, as well as the *gerantés* in a *société en commandite*, were subject to unlimited liability. Only *commanditaires* possessed limited liability. A variant of the *société en commandite* developed in France – the *société en commandite par action*, a limited partnership where the sleeping partners held shares that could be transferred, subject to some conditions.[27]

The third form of business organization was the corporation, joint-stock company, or *société anonyme*. Corporations were perpetually lived organizations with impersonal legal identities. The governance structure of the corporation was determined by its charter. Corporations were headed by a board of directors or governing council.[28] Corporations were typically chartered to provide specific functions or to operate in certain geographic areas. Some corporations possessed monopoly privileges but not invariably. Management was typically selected by the board or by the shareholders. Limited liability was not a generalized feature of corporation charters until the middle of the nineteenth century. Shareholders in a *société anonyme* automatically enjoyed limited liability after 1807, as did most shareholders after the 1840s in the United States and after 1856 in Britain.

---

agreements that the state will not enforce, because the agreements do not conform to the state standard.

[27] Limited partnerships were not allowed in Britain until 1907. Several American states had a form of limited partnership in the nineteenth century, but none supported limited partnership with shares. Limited partnerships enable some separation between ownership and management, a restricted type of limited liability, some aspects of transferability of ownership shares, but not perpetual life. See Lamoreaux and Rosenthal (2004, 2005) for a discussion and comparison of partnership and corporate forms in France and the United States in the nineteenth and twentieth centuries.

[28] For examples of the variety of voting schemes in America see Dunlavy (2004); for France see Freedeman (1979, pp. 43–4); for Britain see Scott (1951[1912], pp. 163, 228, 270, and 340).

Consistent with the logic of the natural state, the institutions governing the formation of corporations of any type required the explicit consent of the state in all three countries. A charter required an explicit grant by the legislature, the crown, or in France, approval of the *Conseil d'État*. Unlike partnerships, corporations could not be created at will by individuals. After the 1780s, as we discuss in the sections that follow, a new institution developed, called *general incorporation*, which allowed the creation of a corporation through an administrative procedure without the explicit approval of a political body. General incorporation developed first in the United States. A statute that creates such a procedure is a general incorporation act.

The remainder of the chapter explores how formally organized, competitive political parties came into existence and how the formerly limited access to corporate forms of business enterprise became open access through general incorporation laws over the course of the nineteenth century.

6.5 The Transition to Open Access in Britain

On the eve of the American Revolution, the British possessed several distinct institutional advantages. They had a long experience with representative legislative institutions through the parliament and elections, although without widespread suffrage. Parliament had developed parliamentary parties, and the idea of a legitimate opposition party gained credence in the eighteenth century (Foord, 1964). The British also had a long experience with corporations, business and otherwise, and a framework of common and equity law to govern partnerships, corporations, and trusts. However, the British had neither competitive electoral parties nor open entry into the corporate form.

Namier's, *The Structure of Politics at the Accession of George III* affords a good starting point: "There were no proper party organizations about 1760, though party names and cant were current; the names and the cant have since supplied the materials for an imaginary superstructure" (1957, p. x). Despite the persistent use of party labels, the parliament of the eighteenth century was not organized by political parties as we know them today. Selection to parliament was not typically the result of a competitive political process but through a localized decision of notable members of the community.

The suffrage requirement for English voters in the counties was a 40-shilling freehold. Each county returned two members. A rough approximation of the number of voters in England was 160,000, an average of 4,000 per county in the forty counties. "This might seem a numerous electorate. But as the voting was open and recorded in poll-books, people in dependent positions could seldom exercise free choice" (Namier, 1957, p. 65). "The electorate in the counties formed an independent and fairly large class; still it would be ludicrous to talk of any kind of 'democracy' in 39 of 40 counties" (Namier, 1957, p. 73).

Of the 203 boroughs, only 11 "potwalloper" boroughs enfranchised all inhabitant households not receiving alms or poor relief. In ninety-two boroughs, the right of voting belonged to all freemen. These boroughs varied in size.

In 1761, of the forty-four boroughs with electorates numbering more than five hundred, only twenty-three held an election. In "the remaining 201 English constituencies only 18 [held elections]; i.e., more than half of the larger boroughs were contested, and about one in ten of the rest of the constituencies." In these noncontested constituencies only two candidates announced, and no election was held.[29] The 148 remaining boroughs were narrow constituencies in which "the ideas of the time closely connected franchise and representation with property, and gradually the vote and the seat themselves tended to become realty, like advowson, sublime in its ultimate significance, beneficial in practice to its owner."[30] As late as 1830, neither political parties nor electoral competition was a constant feature of British politics. The British had few contested elections; most MPs were selected because of their social standing and connections.[31]

The first Reform Act in 1832 dramatically changed the structure of politics and political parties in Britain. The act implemented three changes, the first two intended to reallocate political representation within the elite. The first change wholly or partly disenfranchised eighty-six of the smallest and most rotten of the boroughs. The seats freed were redistributed among urban and industrial constituencies (including Birmingham, Manchester, and Leeds, which had no representation before 1832) and more widely among the counties. The second change was to enfranchise copyholders with property valued at £10 or greater. This change resulted in a small expansion of the suffrage, but did not represent a lowering of the wealth or property requirements to vote. Copyholders had been excluded from voting because of the form of title they held to their land, not because they held

---

[29] The same tendencies would remain after the first Reform Bill redefined the electorate and electoral districts up to 1832. See Cox (1987, pp. 127–32) and Kishlansky (1986) and the discussion of the size of the electorate see Namier (1957, p. 83) for voting in 1761.

[30] Advowson was the right to nominate an ecclesiastical office, a priest, or bishop, Namier (1957, p. 126).

[31] Namier, (1957, p. 2) concludes that "it is hardly astonishing to find . . . how very few among those who desired to enter the House of Commons failed to get a chance."

land and property of less value than freeholders did. The third institutional change implemented by the bill required registration of voters. Because of the change in the property requirements, all voters had to be registered.

The Reform Act represented a new intra-elite bargain, reallocating rights and privileges in the same natural state manner we have seen in earlier chapters. The major intention of the act was to restructure political representation within the elite, to move closer to a situation in which all elites enjoyed the same political rights. The act was not a compromise between elite and non-elites within British society. Nor was it designed to produce modern open access politics with universal suffrage. Despite the significant reform, major elements of the old privileges remained. The industrial towns of the north and London remained underrepresented.[32]

The registration provision of the act, however, had an unintended consequence: the establishment of permanent electoral political parties (Bulmer-Thomas, 1965, p. 66). Registration created a strong incentive at the local level for political organizations to form to police the registration lists and to encourage their compatriots to register. Sir Robert Peel, leader of the Conservative Party, saw the opportunity and began organizing local registration societies. In a letter to a friend on November 8, 1838, he wrote:

The Reform Bill has made a change in the position of parties, and in the practical working of public affairs, which the author of it did not anticipate.

There is a perfectly new element of political power – namely, the registration of voters, a more powerful one than either the Sovereign or the House of Commons.

That party is the strongest in point of fact which has the existing registration in its favour. It is a dormant instrument, but a most powerful one, in its tacit and preventive operation.

The registration will govern the disposal of offices, and determine the policy of party attacks; and the power of this new element will go on increasing as its secret strength becomes better known and is more fully developed. We shall soon have, I have no doubt, a regular systematic organization of it. Where this is to end I know not, but substantial power will be in the Registry Courts, and there the contest will be determined.[33]

---

[32] "Although many constituencies now had competitive elections, proprietary or pocket boroughs, the seats of which were essentially in the gift of certain powerful noblemen and commoners, persisted; and electoral influence, corruption, and violence remained, in the view of many historians, the chief determinants of electoral results" (Cox, 1987, p. 10).

[33] As quoted in Bulmer-Thomas (1953, pp. 13–14). Bulmer-Thomas follows the long quote with a shorter one: "More concisely, in 1841, Peel told his supporters at Tamworth, 'Register, register, register.'"

Because of the advantage provided by electoral organization, Whig-Liberals had to imitate the organization that Peel and the Conservatives had initiated. Modern competitive political parties – impersonal, mass organizations – first appeared in the late 1830s. The change resulted directly from an attempt to create more equal representation within the elite by transforming the old, personal, and idiosyncratic elite privileges into rights, and then institutionalizing those elite rights.

In the 1830s and 1840s, party discipline in the parliament and the electorate became more apparent. Cox (1987) documents how parties simultaneously arose in both the legislature and the electorate, dating the rise of modern parties to the Reform Act of 1832. New, competitive political organizations evolved and transformed the British political landscape. The series of reform acts that followed in 1867, 1883, and 1885 progressively widened the suffrage, extending the vote down the economic and social scale in a way that the reforms of 1832 had not, irreversibly propelling Britain down the path to sustainable political competition through mass political parties.

The economic side of organizations experienced a fundamental change in 1844. The restrictive effects of the Bubble Act in 1720 put a damper on the formation of corporations in general. The act made it much riskier for firms to operate as if they were corporations, as so-called unincorporated joint-stock companies.[34] Unincorporated companies, using modified forms of the partnership and trust, did develop in the eighteenth century, but we do not discuss them at great length.

Before or after the Bubble Act, however, the corporate form was available to anyone who could get parliamentary support. What limited access to charters was competition from existing interests. Parliament had a well-established procedure for establishing charter by act, but relatively few charters were created because of political opposition from existing interests.[35]

---

[34] See the chapter on "Trusts, Partnerships, and the Unincorporated Company" in Harris (2000, pp. 137–67) for a spirited refutation that unincorporated companies were an important part of the economic history of the eighteenth century.

[35] Harris describes the barriers to entry in the following way on p. 135: "The barrier on entry into the corporate world was not created by Parliament intentionally, nor was it to any considerable degree manipulated by Parliament, and it did not benefit the State as such. Parliament and the Committee of the Privy Council (in the case of charters) served only as the arena and set the procedural rules. The arena itself was left open to the active players in this game, the vested interests. And it was the vested interests which created the barriers on entry. In the previous chapter, I exposed the way in which established vested interests in the insurance sectors, and to a lesser degree also older means of transportation, clustered to block newcomers. Examples of the activity of vested interests in other sectors can be found in later chapters. Attempts to form joint-stock companies in sectors controlled by

Applicants for new charters were typically wealthy and powerful interests, often trying to open up the monopoly or limits on banking, insurance, or transportation. Harris wrote, "If a legal framework had not been in existence requiring that each incorporation be granted separately and specifically in an act or a charter, vested interests could obviously not have controlled entry" (2000, p. 135). Negotiations over creation of new charters involved extensive negotiations over the distribution of rents within the existing elite. Charters created rents even when charters did not confer monopolies because the ability to access the corporate form in itself was a substantial advantage to any economic organization.

Over the course of the eighteenth century, the economy grew and began to industrialize, many new economic and political interests formed, and as interests changed, natural states realigned the allocations of their elite privileges and rents. The same occurred in nineteenth-century Britain, but this time with some differences. In the first third of the nineteenth century, new interests successfully challenged the privileges enjoyed by the Bank of England, the East Indies Company, and the marine insurance duopoly created by the Bubble Act. In 1824, the Alliance Insurance Company, which had been created to provide life and fire insurance, and included among its supporters Nathan Rothschild and Alexander Baring, pressed parliament for a charter and was able to overturn the monopoly on marine insurance created in the Bubble Act one hundred years earlier. A group of "country bankers, a few of the London private bankers, and entrepreneurs who aimed at establishing new joint-stock banks in the provinces and in London" was able to convince parliament to loosen the restriction on joint-stock banking that had benefited the Bank of England.[36] Under the original privileges given to the Bank of England, banks in England were limited to at most seven partners, and no corporate banks were allowed. In 1826, a bill passed allowing the formation of corporations and partnerships with any number of shareholders or partners to carry on business as bankers in England. The East Indies Company lost its monopoly on trade with India in 1813 and with China in 1833 (Harris, 2000, pp. 207–15).

---

individuals, such as flour milling and brewing, united all the individual manufactures against the intruder. Slave traders vehemently attacked the bill of the abolitionist Sierra Leone Company. The Bank of England prevented the formation, of joint-stock banks. Many other examples of the same sort can be found." We disagree with Harris's conclusion that Parliament was not active in maintaining the institutions that allowed vested interests to block new charters.

[36] The quote is from Harris (2000, p. 212); the discussion about the marine insurance monopoly and the Bank of England, from pp. 207–15.

However, the reforms did not open the floodgates of incorporation. The economic boom of the 1820s, for example, peaked in 1825. In that year, 624 new companies approached parliament for charters, but only a few were granted. The pressure for new charters resulted from both the boom and a series of judicial decisions that revived active application of the Bubble Act to unincorporated joint-stock companies, adding significant uncertainty to the legal position of unincorporated businesses (Harris, 2000, pp. 230–49). Between 1826 and 1844, 151 new joint-stock banks and 216 railroads were chartered. Many of these projects failed. By 1843, Spackman lists only 720 companies whose shares traded in London.

Agitation for new corporations was intense in the 1820s and 1830s, generated primarily by wealthy individuals already in business who wished to expand their operations under the structure of a corporation. In 1844, parliament passed new legislation, an act Registering, Incorporation, and Regulation of Joint-Stock Companies and an accompanying act for Facilitating the Winding Up of the Affairs of Joint-Stock Companies. The bills were drafted by a committee headed by the young William Gladstone.[37] The registration act established a procedure by which joint-stock companies could be formed by administrative procedure without the consent of the government.[38] The act did more than just keep a registry. In the act of registering the corporation, a deed of incorporation was produced that:

> ... had to include the purpose of the company, the structure of its share capital, the names of the subscribers and the amount of shares they held, and the names of the directors and auditors of the company. Upon complete registration, a company could, among other things, use a registered name, sue and be sued by its registered name, enter into contracts, purchase lands, issue shares, borrow money, hold meetings, and make bylaws. In fact, a company registered by the act enjoyed all the features of incorporation – separate personality, free transferability of shares, and hierarchical managerial structure – with but one exception: limitation of liability (Harris, 2000, p. 283).

The act did not confer limited liability on these joint-stock corporations, a provision that would come in 1856.

Although the historical literature has not focused as much on the Act of 1844 as it has on the debates over the adoption of limited liability in

---

[37] Registration of organizations had a history in England. In 1786, a law establishing a register of ships operating under the Navigation Acts established a procedure for recording information about shareholders and ownership. Early examples of registration are discussed in Harris (2000, p. 275).

[38] The act excluded banks and railroads, which were governed by their own acts also passed in 1844.

1856, two things seem clear about the act. First, the 1844 act opened the gates to incorporation. Within fourteen months of the act's passage, 1,639 joint-stock companies were provisionally registered, more than double the 700 or so in existence in 1843.[39] By 1856, 3,942 companies had provisionally registered and an additional 135 companies were incorporated with limited liability. In the nine years following the introduction of general limited liability in 1855–6, an additional 4,859 limited companies were chartered (Harris, 2000, p. 288). Britain went from seven hundred to ten thousand business corporations in twenty years, open access indeed.

In a significant historical coincidence, Britain used the same word, *registration*, to describe the institutions fostering open access in both political and economic organizations in the mid-nineteenth century. The substantive content of both the electoral registration and company registration created an impersonal administrative process in which individuals were able to obtain the support and services of the state simply by virtue of being citizens. Political citizenship was still defined in economic terms (the 40-shilling freehold and the £10 copyhold restriction), and economic entry was still limited to those with the resources and ability to form a business enterprise. In no sense had the British created universal open access. Instead, British elites in the Reform Act of 1832 and the Registration Act of 1844 created equal rights for themselves. Nevertheless, these steps in elite rule of law and impersonality made later extensions of citizenship to a much wider group easier.

6.6 The Transition to Open Access in France

France ended the eighteenth century with a different set of handicaps and advantages than Britain. For one, France had little experience with representative institutions and elections. Those institutions had to be created after the French Revolution, and it was not easy. Throughout the nineteenth century, the French experimented with different constitutional forms of government and different combinations of executive, legislative, and administrative responsibility. Few were stable in the first half of the century. The extent of suffrage ranged from highly restrictive (e.g., based on wealth or residence) to universal male suffrage in 1848. Political parties formed later in

---

[39] Returns made to parliament in 1846, after the passage of the Registration Act, reported that 947 companies registered under the 1844 law were in existence before 1844. Many of these companies had started as unincorporated joint-stock companies that surfaced when they could become legitimate corporations.

France, in part because of the confusion over the constitutional structure. Yet, with respect to corporate forms, particularly in government, France had a significant endowment of organizational capital. We have already seen how the late eighteenth-century menu of economic organizational forms was richer in France than in Britain or the United States.

The turbulent history of France precludes a straightforward narrative, but it offers valuable opportunities to see the interests of elites in the transition. France had eleven constitutions between 1789 and 1875, and each altered the relationships between the executive and legislative branches and the structure of the legislature. Nonetheless, each contained an electoral and legislative arena. At times unicameral and at times bicameral, the French parliament provided a forum and focus for competition among elite groups. A more or less durable administrative bureaucracy persisted throughout the entire century as well: the *Conseil d'État*, the army, and the various ministries.[40]

Throughout the entire period up to 1877, competition among elite groups over who would and should govern France shaped polity, economy, and society. On the conservative, monarchical side, the royal or Bourbon factions and the Bonapartists were usually allied with the Catholic church, the aristocracy, and large landholders. On the Republican side were numerous groups (often loosely assembled into left, center, and right persuasions) that, like the conservative groups, were focused on individuals and networks of patronage and connections. Although the revolutions of the 1790s raised up many men from many social classes, as with Napoleon himself, successful revolutionary leaders became part of the elite, not a new vanguard for open access.

In the 1830s, Republican politics were just as elite as royalist politics. Algulhon describes what emerged in France in mid-nineteenth century as:

an intermediate stage of 'democratic patronage', and one may distinguish three phases in the process of democratization: voting under the guidance of traditional social authorities; their replacement by a new generation of Republican notables, who sought to take over rather than abolish the traditional means of influence, and whose political position was personal, not party-based; and voting for parties, with the programme and party label mattering more than the individual candidate. The shift from one phase to another could be quite rapid, and associated with specific propaganda campaigns or the influence of local leaders. Many areas were 'converted' to the Republic within a few years in the 1870s (Gambetta's speaking tours

---

[40] "Indeed, there is a French saying that contains much truth: 'We are not governed, but administered.' The administration is, within limits, ready to serve any government, and, in fact, almost any form of government" (Freedeman, 1961, p. 3).

perhaps having a catalytic effect), and the new notables soon established their power after 1877.[41]

Politics were still dangerous and factions were feared. Being on the losing side of a political argument could result in exile or imprisonment. Political victories continued to be, as Tombs had described the Revolution of 1830, "one socio-political faction over one another . . . " (1996, p. 358). Factional conflict within the French polity played out within the natural state framework of personal identity and privilege, but the natural state tendencies of France were subject to other forces as well.

Although elections were held, suffrage was usually quite limited, around one hundred thousand people (the number fluctuated as factions attempted to manipulate suffrage to their advantage). The political nation in France was quite small and limited to elites via tax, residency, or other restrictions. Intra-elite political competition was fierce. Victorious factions used the association laws to limit opposition newspapers and freedom of assembly. No elite faction, however, used the military (or part of the military) to suppress their opponents. A strong norm existed in French politics that the army should be independent of political struggles, although the army itself should be directed ultimately by civilian decisions. When violence broke out in France, as it did periodically, it was not organized interfactional elite violence, but the result of more general discontent with existing economic, political, and military conditions. Mob violence, however directed, played an important role in bringing down governments, particularly governments of royalists whose major claim to govern was their ability to provide stability and order.

Born in a period of popular violence, the Second Republic in 1848 instituted universal male suffrage. The Republicans hoped to secure popular support for their factions by widening the electorate, but the first elections in June of 1848 produced a surprise: "Though all 900 members of the new Constituent Assembly called themselves republicans, fewer than 300 seats were won by moderate '*republicains de la ville.*' The left won only 70–80 seats and nearly 300 seats were won by crypto-royalists" (Tombs, 1996). The election of Louis-Napoleon Bonaparte was another surprising result.[42]

---

[41] From M. Agulhon, *La République au Village* (1970, pp. 480–1) as translated and quoted by Anderson (1977, p. 61).

[42] Bonaparte had attempted twice, in 1836 and 1840, to return to France and seize power. Both times he had failed and been imprisoned and exiled. After his election to the National Assembly in 1848, Bonaparte initially resigned his seat in the face of criticism, but was reelected.

The new National Assembly wrote a new constitution creating the office of president to be elected by the people. In December of 1848, Bonaparte won the presidency decisively, receiving 5.5 million of the more than 7 million votes cast (Tombs, 1996, pp. 381, 385–6). "This was not merely sentimental voting for a famous name, but a peasant revolt against the whole political class and the *notables*" (Tombs, 1996, p. 386). The countryside mobilized voters around existing organizations. Priests led voters to the polls after mass, mayors organized voters, and there were, as yet, no political parties capable of coordinating a national election among any political persuasion.

Bonaparte's election brought a conservative faction, the Party of Order, into government. The conservatives began pushing a conservative agenda, including imposing limits on the press, restoring Catholic influence in the schools, and trimming suffrage by about one-third. Bonaparte's term as president was for four years with no possibility of reelection. He campaigned for a constitutional amendment allowing him to serve a second term. A majority in the Assembly was willing to support the amendment, but the republican minority and an Orleanist group led by Thiers blocked it by preventing the required three-fourths supermajority. In 1851, Bonaparte publicly asked the Assembly to repeal the voting law of May 1850 and restore universal suffrage. The National Assembly refused, weakening its republican credentials.

On December 2, Bonaparte staged a coup – Operation Rubicon – in which Thiers and other key deputies were arrested in their beds, the National Assembly occupied, and deputies turned away. Those who resisted were imprisoned. Bonaparte's coup was initially limited to Paris, but it soon spread to the countryside. The rural uprising was confused. Some took up arms to defend the Republic, others to defend the "people's Napoleon" from his enemies, and some undoubtedly thought the two causes were the same. Although the violence was sporadic and unorganized, the government responded dramatically, arresting twenty-seven thousand and transporting ten thousand to Algeria and Cayenne (Tombs, 1996, p. 393). Politics remained a dangerous business in France into the 1850s. Intrafactional competition could result in exile or imprisonment for the losers.

Democracy proved unstable in the face of a strong leader like Bonaparte. After the coup, Bonaparte held a plebiscite on December 21, 1851, which successfully confirmed the legality of his actions; a new constitution was written and elections to the *Corp Législatif* were held in February 1852; and on November 21, 1852, a second plebiscite was held to confirm the restoration of the empire under Napoleon III. Bonaparte thus earned the unique distinction of being the first elected president of France as well as the last monarch. Although universal suffrage was restored in 1852, the Bonapartists manipulated the electoral process by designating official candidates to ensure control of the legislature.

Bonaparte's actions reflected the reality of French politics since the French Revolution: intense infighting continued among elite factions, with the winning faction using the association laws to harry the opposition and altering electoral and constitutional institutions to prevent the losers from regaining power. However, this was not a process that one faction could permanently dominate. Today's winners could not dismantle all of the institutional and organizational supports for the opposition. France doggedly stuck to the institutions of a mature natural state, particularly the idea of a representative legislature in which elites granted consent to or influence over governmental policy and support for elite organizations outside the framework of the state. Bonaparte's Second Empire began to bring about conditions that institutionalized open access. To understand why elites moved toward economic open access, we need to follow the changes in economic organization that occurred in and after the revolution and to see how elites were increasingly frustrated by their inability to obtain special economic privileges.

The strict revolutionary antagonism to corporations began to ease in 1795 when the Directory allowed for the formation of joint-stock companies. A commission was appointed in 1801 to consider a new commercial code. Part of the commission's work was initially modeled on the Ordinance of 1673, which provided the legal framework for the *société générale* and the *société en commandite* (Freedeman, 1979, p. 4). French monarchs before the revolution had chartered *société anonymes* directly at will. The new *Code de Commerce* went into effect on January 1, 1808, and recognized three types of firms: the *société en nom collectif* (the old *société générale*), the *société en commandite* (both in its simple form and as a *commandite par actions*), and the *société anonyme*. General and limited partnerships could be formed at will. Formation of a *société anonyme*, a true limited liability corporation, required the approval of the *Conseil d'État* (Freedeman, 1979, pp. 10–16).

The development of the corporate form in France followed similar developments in Britain with the major difference being that French firms had a third legal option of forming limited partnerships with or without shares. As in Britain, the number of corporations created was limited. Freedeman (1979) lists only 642 *société anonymes* created between 1808 and 1867. Formation of all types of firms was linked to the business cycle, with waves of new promotions coming in boom years. The booms created pressure to liberalize the procedures for creating new corporations; the busts emphasized the danger of allowing entrepreneurs to take advantage of easy credit and naive investors in booms and created pressures to tighten the procedures.

As in Britain, the groups in France petitioning the *Conseil d'État* for new corporate charters represented some of the most powerful and well-organized interests. The slow rate of corporate formation created tensions within the elite:

The size and diversity of *anonymes* grew during the 1850s. This very success and the growing dependence upon the joint-stock form made the existence of a two-tiered system separating *anonymes* and *commandites*, privileged and underprivileged, all the more intolerable. Even the favored complained about the inflexible molds, created by the *Conseil d'État*, to which they had to conform. Demands for reform burgeoned, and none were louder than those from the growing number who had been denied the fruits of governmental favor (Freedeman, 1979, p. 99).

Again, as in Britain, demands for reforms came from elites, particularly from elites unable to crack the existing privileges of vested interests.

Although the *société en commandite* (with or without tradable shares – *par actions*) was a more flexible business form unavailable to British or American entrepreneurs, the form suffered some of the same problems that unincorporated joint-stock firms did in Britain. Sleeping investors in a *société en commandite* were denied any connection with management, which was left solely in the hands of the *gerant(és)*. The complete separation of ownership and control worked for some businesses, but for many it raised considerable difficulties, particularly when investors attempted to use *société en commandites* to coordinate larger business enterprises. The danger arose if a sleeping investor was found to have had a role in management. He then became an active partner subject to unlimited liability and put the firm at risk to possible legal actions. The use of *société en commandite par actions* complicated the difficulty. Holders of "bearer" shares in a *par actions* possessed anonymity, but could potentially be named as active partners if they were involved in management decisions. The *société anonyme* did not suffer from these problems.

A *société en commandite* also offered numerous opportunities for deception and fraud on the part of the *gerant*. Particularly in boom times, *gerantes* could float proposals for a business, raise capital, and then operate the business in ways that were difficult if not impossible for sleeping partners and shareholders to monitor. In 1856, the government passed a bill, ostensibly to repress these fraudulent practices. The number of new such firms fell thereafter (Freedeman, 1979, pp. 100–14). The increasing costs of forming a *société en commandite par actions* raised the pressure on the government to liberalize the *société anonyme*, just as increasing the costs of forming unincorporated joint-stock companies in Britain in the 1820s led to the Registration Act in 1844.

International economic competition between Britain and France also affected the movement toward open access. With the liberalization of British incorporation law in 1856, limited liability corporations were available in Britain through a simple registration process. Prior to 1856, British firms occasionally formed as French *société en commandites* in order to enjoy the advantages of limited partnership. After 1856, the flow reversed; French firms began registering in Britain as limited liability corporations. In response, in 1863 the French government proposed a bill that created a new business form, the *société a responsabilité limitée*:

The character of the *société a responsabilité limitée* (SARL), the French translation of the English "limited liability company," was described in the committee's reports as follows: "It is, in reality, a *société anonyme* without the authorization of the government and in which the inherent guarantees of authorization are replaced by a set of requirements destined to protect shareholders and third parties. . . . This new form offers all the features of security that can be found in a regular *société anonyme* and at the same time avoids the slowness and difficulties of government authorization" (Freedeman, 1979, p. 136).

The SARL moved halfway toward open access. SARLs were still subject to the restrictive regulations of the 1856 *société en commandite* bill, making it difficult for firms to establish themselves. Continued pressure for reform led to the passage of a law in July 1867, allowing the formation of *société anonymes* at will, with a registration process: "The initial result was an immediate rise in the creation of [*société anonymes*] from an annual average of 14 for the period 1842–1866 to an average of 219 per year for the period 1868–1878" (Freedeman, 1993, p. 9). In the ten years after the free entry into corporate forms was allowed, more than two thousand corporations were created. Elite access to economic organizations had been transformed from a privilege to a right. Open access to economic organizations had finally come to France.

The century-long political conflicts in France did not end in 1867; intra-elite competition for control of the government continued under Napoleon III. Winning elite factions continued to use the instruments of government to exclude the losers when in power. When the Germans captured Napoleon III at Sedan in 1870, the empire fell, and the Third Republic was declared. France faced the same set of problems it had faced since 1814, but was now in an even worse situation because the Germans occupied roughly half of France and threatened Paris. An Assembly was elected in February of 1871 to meet in Bordeaux. An agreement within the

Assembly – the Bordeaux Pact reached in February of 1871 – gave the new government headed by Thiers time to negotiate with the Germans for peace and German withdrawal, restore state finances, and rebuild the army. Parisians, however, were not part of the Bordeaux Pact and were angry at the terms reached by Thiers. The government moved back to Paris, but only to Versailles. On March 18, Thiers sent the army into Paris to remove several hundred cannons that had been seized by the National Guard Federation. After a period of waiting, army troops entered Paris in May. In the ensuing fighting, twenty thousand people were killed. The resistance of the Paris commune discredited the left within French politics. The conservative majority in the Assembly moved to repress the socialists, passing a law in 1872 prohibiting membership in L'Internationale, the International Working Men's Association.

The conservative royalists, however, were unable to capitalize on their opportunity. As divided among themselves as from the Republicans, Thiers' government fell in 1873. The Republicans gained steadily in the elections of 1873, and in 1875 the Assembly passed the constitutional laws of 1875, creating a president and senate, as well as a chamber of deputies. In elections in 1876, the Republicans held 340 seats to the Royalists' 153, of which 75 were Bonapartists (Anderson, 1977, p. 10). The conservative President MacMahon, however, refused to put a Republican government in place. In May of 1877, MacMahon dissolved parliament, but the Republicans returned a solid majority in the new elections, 54.5 percent of the vote and 60.5 percent of the seats in the Assembly (Campbell, 1958, p. 74).

The Republican victory over MacMahon:

> . . . was of considerable constitutional importance. MacMahon was the last president to use the weapon of dissolution, and the last to see his powers as the foundation of an executive independent of Parliament. Against the intentions of the makers of the constitution, the Republic became a regime of pure parliamentary sovereignty. The crisis was also politically significant, as the last attempt by the old governing class to hold back the progress of democracy. They had pushed the constitution to its limits, but kept within it – some of MacMahon's advisers wanted him to continue resistance even after the 1877 election, but such an enterprise was fraught with the danger of civil war. In the last resort, the French "notables" submitted to the decision of universal suffrage, and gave up power peacefully. They had seemed to hold many cards in 1871, but had lost the struggle through their disunity . . . (Anderson, 1977, pp. 10–11).

The Republicans gained control of the government in 1879, and then instituted major changes in French politics. Although conservatives were removed from government posts, the Republicans did not use their powers to harry conservative or radical organizations, to close conservative or radical newspapers, or to enforce the laws of association to prevent opposition groups from organizing. The government permitted the opposition to remain active. In 1881, laws guaranteeing freedoms of the press and the right of public meetings were passed; in 1884 trade unions were legalized and local governments were reorganized (Anderson, 1977, p. 12).

A debate exists about the date when France developed open, competitive, and modern political parties. Hanley (2002) argues for the 1870s, Kreuzer (2001, p. 27) for the 1880s, Anderson (1977, pp. 65–70) sees seeds in the 1870s and 1880s but suggests that full-blown modern parties developed in the 1900s. Important evidence exists in the society at large that helps date the process to the late 1870s and early 1880s. The Republicans gained control of the government through the electoral process and in coordination with different conservative factions in 1877. Although socialism had been suppressed and membership in the L'Internationale was illegal as late as 1872, active repression of radical groups began to ease later in the decade. The first 'workers' congress' was sponsored by the Gambrettist Republicans in 1876 and was attended by representatives of eighty-eight unions. A third congress at Marseille was a turning point, leading to the creation of a Socialist Party: the *Fédération du Paris des Travailleurs Socialistes de France* (FPTSP). The FPTSP later split, with a group of Marxists led by Guesde forming the *Parti ouvrier* (Anderson, 1977, p. 123, Appendix 2). These were external parties in Duverger's terms, organized for ideological, economic, and political reasons other than gaining office. In the 1880s, radical parties like the FPTSP were not suppressed.

Political access had truly opened in France. Crises nonetheless lay ahead, the Boulanger and the Dreyfus Affair for example. More stable political arrangements did not produce more stable governments: France had forty-four governments in the thirty-five years between 1879 and 1914. Rather than having a set of institutionalized checks and balances, the French, like the British, ended up with a system of parliamentary sovereignty. However, the Third Republic persisted, capable of accommodating entry and political competition in a way that France never had before. Unlike the two-party systems in Britain and the United States, France developed a multiparty system. The fifteen-fold increase in the rate at which corporations were created each year following the legislation of 1867 is the concrete expression of opening economic access. The multitude of political parties, particularly of socialist parties that would have been suppressed as late as 1872, is concrete expression of opening political access.

6.7 The Transition to Open Access in the United States

Democracy, political competition, secure property rights, and open entry economic competition are hallmarks of the American founding myth. The myth holds that the national constitution written in 1787 produced balanced government and brought about sustained economic growth. Government was limited by a set of checks and balances, both within the national government and between the national and state governments. Individual rights and property rights were protected by political balance, and political mechanisms maintained balance. Secure rights promoted investment in physical and human capital, resulting in economic growth.

Americans adopted their constitution and form of government because of their belief that the British constitution, the best in the world, had been corrupted in the eighteenth century by the influence of political factions and economic interests. The Americans set out to capture the best of the British constitution in a system that limited the dangers of faction and concentrated economic power.[43]

We have two problems with the myth. First, Americans believe it in part because of what the Founding Fathers wrote, including their intentions and hopes fulfilled through the experience of the national government. The Founders wanted to create a free society, they intended to do it, they promised it would happen, and it did. What more is there to explain? As Bailyn summarizes:

The Founders of the American nation were one of the most creative groups in modern history...

Since we inherit and build on their achievements, we now know what the established world of the eighteenth century flatly denied but which they broke through convention to propose – that absolute power need not be indivisible but can be shared among states within a state and among branches of government, and that the sharing of power and the balancing of forces can create not anarchy but freedom.

We know for certain what they could only experimentally and prayerfully propose – that formal, written constitutions, upheld by judicial bodies, can effectively constrain the tyrannies of both executive force and populist majorities.

We know, because they had the imagination to perceive it, that there is a sense, mysterious as it may be, in which human rights can be seen to exist independent of

---

[43] Gordon Wood's *Creation of the American Republic* (1969) beautifully explains the influence of republican ideas on the writing of the American Constitution.

privileges, gifts, and donations of the powerful, and that these rights can somehow be defined and protected by the force of law.

We casually assume, because they were somehow able to imagine, that the exercise of power is no natural birthright but must be a gift of those who are subject to it (Bailyn, 2004, pp. 4–5).

Bailyn's operative word is because: because the Constitution and the institutions of government created in the 1770s and 1780s solved these problems, our world is the way it is today. Just as in Britain and France, however, key institutional changes occurred after the 1780s that were neither envisioned nor intended by the founders. Elections alone were not enough to make democracy work; Americans had to figure out how to integrate economics and politics in a way that sustained open access and competition between all parties. Further, as they would have phrased it in the early nineteenth century, they had to prevent factions from manipulating the economy to corrupt the polity.

The second problem with the American founding myth is the double assumption that everything of importance in the constitutional development of American society happened at the national level and that the Constitution itself provided the roadmap for economic and political development. Yet, once established, both Constitution and the national government were insufficient to ensure economic or political openness, to guarantee the full range of economic or political rights, or to provide the physical infrastructure to unite the nation and sustain economic development. Instead, federalism allowed creative state governments to solve the problem of opening access and general incorporation; state governments wrestled with the problem of sustainable, open access political parties (with some help from the national level); and state governments figured out how to provide physical and financial infrastructure that united the national economy. Much of American history, however, treats state government development as a sideshow, thereby missing crucial elements in the transition to open access in the United States. In the histories of Britain and France, institutionalizing open access by defining and securing elite rights occurred at the national level. In the United States, most of the institutionalization occurred at the state level.

Focusing on the national government also leads to the erroneous conclusion that laissez-faire government policies promoted economic development. The conclusion depends on the inaction of the national government (laissez faire by default rather than by design) and on ignoring state governments that were not laissez faire but that actively promoted both democracy and economic growth.[44]

Finally, a national-level focus places inordinate weight on the Constitutional Convention in Philadelphia in 1787 and the speculative ideas of the Founders. The Founders did not intend for political parties to play a central role in government. As Hofstadter notes, the U.S. Constitution was a "Constitution against parties" in which balance in government is explicitly thought to reside in the Constitution, not in political competition per se:

> The necessity of checks on power is a theme struck over and over. But it is important that for the Fathers these checks had to be *built into the constitutional structure itself.* They were not content – and still less were the people they had to persuade – to rest their hopes on those checks that might arise in the political process alone, and this is one reason why they put no faith in party competition. Their hopes were pinned on a formal, written system of internal checks and balances, the precise enumeration of limited powers, and the explicit statement of constitutional guarantees, such as the opponents of the Constitution insisted on adding to it. Such informal forces in politics as the temper of the public, the process of opposition, the institutionalization of party structures, which to us seem so vital in democracy, seemed to them too slender a reliance, too inadequate a substitute for explicit constitutional specifications (Hofstadter, 1969, p. 50, emphasis in the original).

However, by the 1820s and 1830s, organized parties emerged as central to American politics and government. The Founders were wrong about parties. As we have emphasized throughout this book, open access in either economics or politics can be sustained only by the double balance of open access in both systems, and open access requires that a large share of individuals be able to form organizations at will. The federal constitutional structure alone was insufficient to sustain that competition. The constitutional changes that institutionalized open access in the United States occurred primarily at the state level, and it is to the states that we must turn.

---

[44] The first, and still one of the most articulate, treatments of state activism in the late eighteenth and early nineteenth century is Callender (1902). In the 1950s, the Economic History Association launched a research project designed to discover whether government policy in the early republic really was laissez faire. Research monographs were commissioned by the Committee on Research in Economic History. The answer came back a resounding NO: state governments actively promoted economic development and fiddled with and participated in economic activity. The series of books produced are sometimes referred to as the "commonwealth" tradition: Handlin and Handlin on Massachusetts (1969); Hartz on Pennsylvania (1948); Benson on New York (1961); Primm on Missouri (1954); Heath on Georgia (1954); Goodrich on canals and railroads (1960). See the retrospective essay on the CREH in Cole (1970) and the review article by Lively (1955).

The new American political order was election intensive. Although there were national government elections, all elections were administered by state and local governments and regulated by state governments.[45] States and state governments were the arena in which decisions about the creation of economic privileges and the relationship of those privileges to politics, and particularly to democratic elections, played themselves out. Unlike Britain and France, where the coming of general incorporation stemmed from frustrations within the elite over access to the corporate form, in the United States open access to corporate forms evolved out of fears that the political process and parties would manipulate economic access to the advantage of factions. As a result, the interrelated aspects of political and economic access are starker and easier to see in the United States.

Political balance in Britain and France in the eighteenth century rested on the interaction of elite groups. The lack of hereditary elites, either royal or aristocratic, and the strong presumption against creating a new nobility expressed in the state and national constitutions forced the Americans to provide balance in government through institutional checks and balances and through elections. At both the state and national level, direct popular elections were common for the lower house of the legislature, but indirect elections or selection by the legislature was more common for the upper house and the executive. Senators were chosen by state legislatures and the president through the electoral college. Most states selected governors through the legislatures rather than popular vote; initially only New York and Massachusetts had direct election of governors.[46] A majority of states initially chose national presidential electors through the state legislature rather than by popular election (Aldrich, 1995, p. 106). Suffrage in every state was limited by tax-paying or property-holding requirements, although the percentage of free white males voting was probably on the order of 50 percent or higher in most states (Keyssar, 2000; Lutz, 1988).

---

[45] After a brief interference with state control over election procedures during Reconstruction, the national government removed itself from the election process until the civil rights era with the passage of the Voting Rights Act (1965), which made the national government a major regulator of election procedures.

[46] See Adams (1980, pp. 266–71). There has been a long-running debate over the relative distribution of power between legislatures and the executive: Wood (1969, pp. 162–3) and elsewhere; Adams (1980, pp. 271–5); Kruman (1997, 35–59). Wood echoes James Madison and argues that excessive powers given to the legislatures in the state constitutions were a major reason why the national constitution needed to be rewritten in 1787. Kruman convincingly shows that states were as much concerned with legislative tyranny as executive tyranny and sought to constrain both branches of government.

Unlike the national government, which after the Bill of Rights was rat-
ified in 1795 amended the Constitution only twice before the Civil War,
states amended and replaced their constitutions frequently in the early
nineteenth century.[47] Competition among the states resulted in a steady
movement toward universal free white male suffrage and popular direct
election of lower and upper houses of the legislature and the governor
(Engerman and Sokoloff, 2005). States continued to experiment with the
constitutional forms of their governments. These constitutional changes
placed more reliance on political competition to ensure balance and a corresponding reduction in the formal structure of political mechanisms and
the guidance of wise and experienced individuals.

Political historians often divide the nineteenth-century development of
American political parties into three systems. The first party system, roughly
1790 to 1815, grew out of competition between the Federalists and the
Republicans. The second party system, roughly 1835 to 1854, grew out
of competition between the Democrats and the Whigs. The third party
system, in place sometime after 1854, grew out of the demise of the Whig
Party and the new alignments associated with competition between the
Democrats and the newly formed Republican Party.[48] Political historians
identify these as national party systems because partisans sought to carry
national elections in the Congress and the presidency.

Both the first and second party systems had their origins in debates
about economic organizations and economic policy at the national level.
The division between Federalists and Republicans arose over Hamilton's
financial plans in the 1790s. The Republican reaction was motivated by
Whig fears that a Bank of the United States modeled on the Bank of England
would result in corruption, tyranny, and the use of economic privileges for
political gain. Those fears were more pressing when the hopes expressed by
both Madison and Hamilton in the *Federalist Papers* that the structure of the
national government would prevent a political faction from seizing control

---

[47] The Eleventh Amendment limited federal judicial authority over the states and the Twelfth
Amendment straightened out the flaw in the election procedure for the president. Seven
of the sixteen states in existence in 1800 had written two or more constitutions. While the
twelve states added to the Union by 1840 all wrote their first constitutions, six existing
states wrote new constitutions in the 1820s to 1830s, and twelve new constitutions replaced
existing constitutions in the 1840s and 1850s (Tarr, 1998, pp. 61, 96). See Wallis (2009),
NBER/Maryland Constitution project for amendments to individual constitutions.

[48] Not all political historians agree with this periodization; see Silbey (1991) and Keller
(2007).

of the government did not bear fruit. By the early 1790s, the Federalists controlled all three branches of the national government.[49]

Madison, Jefferson, and the other Republicans opposed the Federalist majorities by forming a political party to pursue the presidency (Ferejohn, Rakove, and Riley, 2001, p. 7). However, the formation of an overt opposition political party carried an explicit danger. The incumbent Federalists, with Washington at their head, could plausibly claim that their administration was nonpartisan. Because parties and factions were inherently and systematically corrupt, for the Republicans to contest for control of the government as an organized party exposed them to the charge of per se corruption in the 1790s.[50] Jefferson and Madison organized a party as quietly as possible, denying, as all good democrats do, the negative political implications of the Republicans' existence as an organized party by stressing the rightness of their cause. The Republicans argued that, if their cause were truly right, it was not a partisan but a righteous one, and when the country came to see the wisdom of their position there would no longer be a need for competing parties.[51] The Republican triumph in the election of 1800 led to an era of Republican dominance in national politics. With the decline of the Federalists as a political force, the need for a well-organized political party diminished at the national level.

The need to organize and coordinate electoral competition did not diminish at the state level, however, nor did the fear that factions would corrupt politics. The creation of economic privileges for political gain posed more pressing problems at the state level than at the national level. After the creation of the first national corporation in 1791, the national government did not charter another corporation until the Second Bank of the United States in 1816. Despite several attempts to involve the national government in financing transportation and financial infrastructure, including Jefferson's suggestion in his second inaugural address contemplating a national system of transportation improvements, competition in Congress among

[49] "The success of the Federalist Party in gaining control of all three branches of the national government called into question the fundamental premise of the Madisonian federalism of 1787–8: that durable factious majorities would be far less likely to coalesce at the national level of politics. . . . " (Ferejohn, Rakove, and Riley, 2001, p. 3).

[50] In particular see Hofstadter (1969, pp. 80–6), and the third chapter, "The Jeffersonians in Opposition." Madison, in a series of articles published in the *National Gazette* in the early 1790s, attempted to provide an intellectual justification for parties (Rutland et al., 1983, Vol. 14, pp. 157–69). See Sheehan (1992) and Leonard (2002) for a discussion of early thinking about parties.

[51] John Taylor, *A Definition of Parties*, p. 2; cited in Hofstadter (1969, p. 100).

states and regions prevented the national government from mounting a serious investment program.[52] States, however, began chartering banks, bridge companies, and toll roads in the 1790s and eventually canals and railroads, in increasing numbers in the early nineteenth century as well as providing financial assistance to key projects. Indeed, between 1790 and 1860, states outspent the national government in infrastructure investment by nearly an order of magnitude (Wallis and Weingast, 2005).

The dynamic interaction between political and economic organizations took a different path at this point in American history than in British and French history. The difference was not the kind of corporations the Americans chartered: banks, insurance companies, and transportation ventures dominated chartering in all three countries. Ostensibly, public permission was required to ensure that a public purpose was served, but Americans were no less willing to create charter privileges that ensured a small group had economic control over valuable markets and activities. Where the Americans diverged from the Europeans was in the options open to elite groups frustrated in their attempts to obtain a charter.

In France, charters were granted by the *Conseil d'État,* a bureaucratic entity largely beyond the immediate influence of election results. In Britain up to 1844, parliament granted charters by act, but obtaining a majority in parliament by electing a majority was much less efficient than simply bribing or influencing existing members. In the United States, however, elections to lower and upper houses occurred regularly, and obtaining a legislative majority to support the granting of a charter was feasible for a well-organized faction. State legislatures in the 1790s were biased against issuing charters in principle, but not so much in practice, and the rate of chartering increased with each succeeding decade.[53]

Because of conflicting regional interests, the national government was unable to pursue charters or investments in finance and transportation. Similar forces were at work in the states. Corporations and projects were typically opposed by geographic or economic interests that bore costs through

---

[52] See Wallis and Weingast (2005). The classic history of transportation investments is Goodrich (1960) supplemented by Larson (2001). Both Goodrich and Larson, however, treat state investments as a result of the failure of the national government to make investments, rather than seeing the complicated politics involved at the state level.

[53] Maier summarizes the anticharter sentiments in state legislatures (Maier, 1993, pp. 73–4). Statistics on the number of charters issued can be found in Evans (1948) and the ongoing research of Sylla and Wright, reported in Wright (2008). In addition to the sources cited here, for the larger history of corporations in the United States, see Dodd (1954), Hurst (1964), Lamoreaux (2004), and Seavoy (1982).

taxes and received no benefits from the bank, canal, or bridge. Very often banks or transportation projects were supported by the creation of a charter with specific privileges. The fact that corporate privileges generated economic rents could be tapped for political purposes. The promoters of proposed banks, in particular, offered to purchase their charters from the legislature by paying substantial fees or charter bonuses, sometimes by gifting shares of stock to the state. Charter fees and dividends on stock could be used to lower taxes on everyone, thereby mollifying legislators and voters who would otherwise oppose the formation of a privileged corporation. Revenues from corporations made up a substantial portion of state revenues in early nineteenth-century America. In several states, corporate fees and taxes made up more than 20 percent and as much as half of all state revenues.[54]

Granting of charters for revenue was common in Britain and France as well. What set the Americans apart was the formation of political coalitions that used organized electoral tactics to pursue their goals. In several states, bank parties or canal parties were important in legislative politics.[55] State politics in the 1790s followed the traditional pattern of patronage networks and individual leadership. However, a charter for a bank or canal, or a chance to influence the physical location of a turnpike or transportation improvement, provided sufficient economic incentive to sustain a more durable political organization. Once created for a specific purpose, organized political interests provided the structure capable of pursuing other political goals.

At this point, Whig political theory and democratic realities came into conflict. Political organizations formed to exploit grants of economic privilege to secure their political position: this was corruption in both Whig theory and pure natural state politics. Nothing inherent in the politics of American democratic constitutions resisted this phenomenon, particularly if privileges could be secured from a popularly elected legislature through

---

[54] Sylla, Legler, and Wallis (1987) and Wallis, Sylla, and Legler (1994). The French system of creating and selling corporate offices produced much the same result, but the eighteenth-century French system was crown rather than legislative based.

[55] Both banks and canals played an important role in New York; Miller (1962), Benson (1961), and Gunn (1988). Canal parties were also important in Indiana, Illinois, and Ohio; Esarey (1918), Scheiber (1969), and Ford (1946). Indiana and Missouri had monopoly state banks, which played an integral role in their politics. In Arkansas, ownership in the two state-chartered banks was dominated by a political faction (Worley, 1949, 1950). Brantley (1961) shows how bank parties affected politics in Alabama. New Jersey granted a monopoly on northeast/southwest rail routes (connecting New York and Philadelphia) to the Camden and Amboy railroad (Cadman, 1949).

promises that revenues from the sale of privilege would reduce taxes for everyone. The possibility of taxless finance – the provision of a valued public service without cost to the taxpayers – was an offer too good for democratically elected legislatures to refuse.[56]

In New York, for example, a political faction led by Martin Van Buren initially called the Bucktails but ultimately known as the Albany Regency constructed a political machine to control New York politics through the 1820s and 1830s. Finances for electoral machinations came from donations gladly pledged by the recipients of bank charters. Van Buren and his colleagues changed the state constitution in 1821 to require a two-thirds majority vote of the state legislature to approve a bank charter. Because only the Bucktails had the possibility of obtaining a two-thirds majority, they were able to limit new bank charters and renewals of old bank charters to their political friends (Benson, 1961; Bodenhorn, 2006). Rather than selling bank charters for revenues, they used the chartering of banks to create and finance a political organization.

The Bucktails eventually became Democrats, and Van Buren became vice president and then president of the United States, but the party origins in New York were not unique. As McCormick relates, "Especially in allocating the economic resources and privileges whose distribution formed the State's most characteristic activity, partisan legislators genuinely excelled" (McCormick, 1986, p. 3). Parties that used the manipulation of economic privileges to secure the basis of a political organization developed at the state level throughout the country in the 1820s and 1830s.

When Andrew Jackson was denied the presidency in the election of 1824 because of the "corrupt bargain" between Henry Clay and John Quincy Adams, he immediately began campaigning for the presidential election of 1828. Jackson accused Adams and Clay of corruption, the manipulation of the political process by a party faction. Jackson and his supporters organized a successful national party by bringing together the existing state parties and in the process constructed the first modern political party in world history, the Democratic Party, which still exists in America today. The Democratic Party was a complicated coalition of state-level parties throughout the country. For the first time under Jackson, these separate entities were wielded into a coordinated set of organizations. After winning the election of 1828, Jackson's party did not disband.

---

[56] Wallis (2005) develops the concept of taxless finance and the options facing state legislatures.

Just as in the 1790s, the critical issue that cemented the Democratic Party as a political organization was the formation of economic organizations by the national government. The Second Bank of the United States was chartered in 1816, after the charter of the First Bank of the United States was allowed to expire in 1811. The national government struggled to finance the War of 1812 without a national bank. Madison, then president, reversed his earlier opposition to a national bank and supported a new bank in the last year of his administration. The Second Bank of the United States' charter ran for twenty years. Four years before its expiration, Nicholas Biddle, the Second Bank's president, and Henry Clay, Jackson's political opponent and champion of the Bank, successfully convinced Congress to renew the Second Bank's charter in the summer of 1832. Jackson's party platform excoriated banks as instruments of aristocratic factions and a monied conspiracy in terms that Bolingbroke would have found congenial. By forcing Jackson to veto or sign the Bank bill, Biddle and Clay hoped to make the Bank an issue that they could use in the upcoming election.

Not only did Jackson continue to press his classic Whig arguments against the Bank as a monster of corruption and the instrument of a political faction intent on obtaining control of the government, but Jackson used his veto of the Bank bill and the congressional vote to override the veto to strengthen his party. Jackson forced pro-Bank Democrats, who were numerous enough to secure passage of the original bill, to vote against overriding his veto on a straight party line vote. Jackson exerted his power as a party leader in 1832 in a way that no president had ever done before. The so-called bank war continued for four more years.[57] In order to compete with the Democrats, the Whigs had to organize as well. Biddle, Clay, and the pro-Bank forces provided the base around which the Whig Party was built (Holt, 1999). Whigs and Democrats both wrapped themselves in the republican tradition. Each claimed that the other was corrupt, that the other was creating a political faction, and that the other was using manipulation of economic privilege to gain and secure political power.

When we focus on Jackson, Clay, Biddle, and the gripping story of national politics, it is easy to forget that the issue of chartering banks was not salient in American politics because of the presidential election of 1832. The issue

---

[57] Remini (1981, pp. 331–74; 1967) argues that Jackson's role in the struggle over the Bank was a turning point in the rising power of the presidency. Jackson's claim as the representative of the public interest by virtue of his selection in the only national election was immediately opposed by the Whigs as a usurpation of executive power that could only lead to tyranny.

was salient in the presidential election because it was currently a subject of heated debate and controversy in most states and in most state legislatures. States had already chartered six hundred banks by 1832, and in many cases, those banks possessed economic privileges.[58] Jackson merely capitalized on a century of republican rhetoric to paint the Second Bank as a monster of corruption and exploit an issue alive in state politics. New political historians have long argued that traditional historians have overemphasized the importance of national politics and underappreciated the importance of state governments, state economic policy, and state politics (Holt, 1978, 1999; Silbey, 1967, 1985, 1991).

Unlike the national government, state governments struggled with the problem of promoting economic development through the creation of public and private corporations. Corporate economic organizations played critical roles in the financial and transportation sectors, particularly important to the movement of agricultural goods from the rapidly developing western states to the settled eastern seaboard and across the Atlantic. Privileged corporations served valuable public purposes, but privileged corporations also threatened republican values because of their effect on politics. Individual citizens wanted banks, canals, and railroads to raise the value of their lands, help get their crops to market, and more closely integrate them into the American economy and society. They feared that those corporations would undermine and ultimately destroy the democratic political process they also valued. The solution hit upon by the Americans was not to eliminate corporations but to eliminate privileges by opening entry into the corporate form to anyone who wanted to form a corporation.[59]

The 1830s witnessed an economic boom, complete with new state investments in banks, canals, and railroads financed with money borrowed by states. In the settled East, states expanded their canal networks, whereas frontier states in the West and South made their first forays into state investment in internal improvements. The economic downturn in 1839 resulted in the largest public debt crisis in the nation's history. By 1842, eight states and the territory of Florida were in default on their bonds. In the recovery from the crisis in the 1840s, states asked how and why they had gotten themselves into such trouble. The answer came in traditional republican terms:

---

[58] The largest number of banks was in New England. Massachusetts adopted de facto free entry into banking in the 1810s. The Massachusetts system continued in Maine after it became a state, and was copied by Connecticut and Rhode Island. Banks elsewhere in the country tended to be larger and more closely connected to state politics. Indiana and Missouri had official state bank monopolies. See Wallis, Sylla, and Legler (1994).

[59] The argument of this paragraph and the evidence are based on Wallis (2005, 2006).

narrow interest groups had sought economic privileges from states in the form of corporate charters and public bond issues to support banks, canals, and railroads. Voters were promised that taxes would not be necessary to repay debts issued on behalf of the companies. The promises turned out to be too good to be true. The way to prevent this from happening again was to take the possibility of making such promises off the political table. First, corporation charters would be available to everyone through general incorporation acts. Opening entry to corporate forms would eliminate the rents associated with special privileges that drove the quest for special incorporation in the first place. Second, in order for states to issue bonds in the future, voters would have to approve bond referenda that raised taxes before bonds could be authorized. Between 1842 and 1851, twelve states wrote new constitutions. Eleven states incorporated procedural debt restrictions and eight states mandated general incorporation laws.

Remarkably, as states and the nation were coming to accept the existence of permanent political parties, as Martin Van Buren was writing his autobiography justifying party competition as a way to secure the public good rather than to sacrifice the common good to private interests, advocates of general incorporation articulated the idea that general incorporation (and what was known as "free banking" in banks) would take the process of incorporation out of the political process altogether, and thus eliminate the pressure of special interests on the legislature.[60] The issue was free entry and open access: removing discretionary power from the legislature to limit entry into a particular line of business to one or a few firms. William Leggett, a New York newspaper columnist, wrote extensively about general incorporation in the 1830s:

Nothing can be more absurd than to suppose that the advocacy of these sentiments [supporting general incorporation] implies opposition to any of the great undertakings for which special legislative authority and immunities are usually sought. We are opposed only to a violation of the great democratic principle of our government; that principle which stands at the head of the Declaration of Independence; and that which most of the states have repeated, with equal explicitness, in their separate constitutions. A general partnership law, making the peculiar advantages of a corporation available to any set of men who might choose to associate, for any lawful purpose whatsoever, would wholly obviate the objections which we urge. Such a law would confer no exclusive or special privileges; such a law would be in strict accordance with the great maxim of man's political equality; such a law would

---

[60] The paths by which Americans convinced themselves intellectually that parties were a bulwark rather than a threat to democracy are investigated by Hofstader (1969), Wallace (1968), and Leonard (2002).

embrace the whole community in its bound, leaving capital to flow in its natural channels, and enterprise to regulate its own pursuits.[61]

Advocates of mandatory general incorporation hammered away at the political costs of special legislation. E. P. Hurlbut, a New York lawyer, wrote in 1845 that general incorporation would annihilate "the lobby, or third house, that embodiment of selfishness and gross corruption. The halls of legislation would be cleansed, and the representatives of the people would breathe a purer and freer atmosphere. All 'logrolling' . . . would cease."[62] In the end, it was the political arguments that carried the day. In 1846, New York wrote a new constitution that mandated general incorporation laws.

The adoption of general incorporation laws was an economic solution to a political problem. Instead of creating corporate privileges for a few groups, general incorporation allowed everyone access to this form of valuable organization. Open access eliminated the corruption and rent-creation aspect associated with the corporate form. By the early 1850s, open access to political and economic organizations had been institutionalized in the United States.

6.8 Institutionalizing Open Access: Why the West?

The transition from limited to open access orders occurs in two steps, and each step must be consistent with elite self-interest. The transition does not require a discontinuous leap of faith on the part of elites, a radical change of circumstances, or a deliberate and conscious attempt to transform a limited access society into an open access one. The two steps are different, however, particularly in historical and chronological terms. Reaching the doorstep conditions involved several centuries of technological, intellectual, and institutional change in Western European society. The transition proper occurred over a period of decades.

If the transition involves a two-step process, then answering why the West went first divides into two components: first, how did the West come to meet the doorstep conditions and in the process come to dominate the world militarily; and second, why did the transition proper first occur in the West? Previous attempts to tackle this issue have not kept the component

---

[61] Leggett, *Democratick Editorials* (1984, p. 342). The column appeared in the *Plaindealer*, December 3, 1836.

[62] Hurlbut, *Essays on Human Rights*, pp. 11–15, as quoted in Gunn (1988, p. 231). Wallis (2006) describes how the influence of republican ideas created fears for democracy that eventually led to the growth of open access in the United States.

parts of the answer separate. The strong tendency has been to emphasize the preconditions for the transition at the expense of understanding the transition itself.

6.8.1 Creating the Doorstep Conditions and the West's Dominance of the World

We have provided an alternative hypothesis about the transition to the military revolution thesis advanced by Bates (2001), Parker (1996), Tilly (1992), and others. Tilly argues that long-term military competition drove state formation in early modern Europe. Bates asks why did early modern Europe develop when modern Africa has not; his answer is persistent military competition. These arguments hold that, as states adopted newer and more expensive military technologies, they forced others to adapt as well – or succumb to those that had. The rising expense of war meant all states had to grow; that is, had to devise new institutions for administering and financing war. Similarly, Schultz and Weingast (2003), building on North and Weingast (1989), argue that liberal states had an advantage: credible commitments allowed them to foster growing economies and to borrow funds to finance larger and longer wars with lower deadweight costs to the economy.

We do not dispute the facts of this literature, but provide a new interpretation. The problem with this approach is that it begins by assuming elements that were actually end products of the process. The monopoly on violence enjoyed by modern open access orders is the result of a long evolution of state-building to create the doorstep conditions; it did not hold for the competing states of early modern Europe in 1700. Instead, the major Western European states were natural states with dispersed access to violence. All these states had major internal wars in this period. Although the king in seventeenth-century England had official control of the state, the opposition – capital in Tilly's terms – had sufficient access to military resources to defeat the king in the mid-century civil war. Similarly, French nobles had sufficient military resources to fight against the revolutionary state during the revolution. These illustrations show that we cannot view the process of state-building during this period as representing a deal among capital and coercion. In the fragile and basic natural states of early modern Europe, access to violence was widely dispersed. These states failed to meet the Weberian assumption of a monopoly on violence.

Where the military revolution thesis emphasizes war, our approach emphasizes organizations, institutions, and the internal dynamics of the dominant coalition in combination with war. Where models of the military revolution thesis (Bates, 2001; Tilly, 1992) begin with the assumption that the state has a monopoly on violence, we begin with the assumption of dispersed violence and argue that these states attain a monopoly on violence only at the end of the process of completing the doorstep conditions in the late eighteenth and early nineteenth centuries. What distinguished early modern Western Europe was the rise of independent organizations and the movement from basic natural states to mature ones and from mature natural states to the doorstep conditions. In particular, organizations distinguish the Western European competition from military competition in the rest of the world, explaining why European competition produced different results.

The increasing Western European ability to project military force required more than larger militaries, new financial institutions, and bigger systems of taxation. It required the attainment of the doorstep conditions: rule of law for elites, perpetual life for both organizations and the state, and consolidated control over the military. We illustrated these developments with the evolution of British naval victualling. Even though the British Navy was significantly larger than the French Navy in 1756, it could not take "command of the ocean." The changes in ship supply during the Seven Years' War enabled the navy to keep the blockade fleet at sea for six months, giving it a distinct military advantage. In part, the changes reflect the pressure of war, but they also illuminate in fine detail the transition from personal elite relationships in a natural state to impersonal elite relationships of the doorstep conditions.

The changes in the process of supply involved, first, fostering a small number of large organizations that competed for contracts. Although the new system retained some personalistic characteristics – there were still a small number of elite firms – it had significant advantages over the old system. Intra-elite competition helped drive down prices and gave firms incentives to innovate, creating better systems of administration and supply. Second, the system transformed government organizations, such as Victualling and Ordinance Boards, into perpetually lived public organizations. This transformation enabled the third change, the new system of credit involving the creation of impersonal financial instruments for paying suppliers. These instruments allowed suppliers to sell them and obtain cash, significantly lowering the risk of participating in the supply system. The instruments also created a dispersed set of interests in maintaining this system. Importantly, the development of an impersonal market for navy bills created a means of punishing the government if it failed to honor the bills: the cost of future financing would rise.

Although war played an obvious role in the transformation of Western Europe, it was not the sole or even the most important force propelling the doorstep conditions in the West's transition. A great many steps in attaining these conditions were taken for wholly internal reasons. They include the major institutional changes throughout seventeenth-century England, including Charles I's innovations, those following both the English Civil War and Restoration, and those of the Glorious Revolution and Revolution Settlement. Although the Glorious Revolution allowed the British to finance much larger wars against France, these changes did not result from war, but from the English attempts to solve the domestic political and constitutional problems of the previous century (North and Weingast, 1989). The same point holds for many of the institutional changes in France, notably those fostering the rise of Louis XIV as a far more powerful monarch in the mid-seventeenth century and many of those following the revolution in the late eighteenth century. A great many of the institutional and organizational changes propelling these countries to the doorstep followed from domestic politics.

6.8.2 The Transition Proper

In the conceptual framework, getting to the doorstep conditions and establishing impersonal relations among elites are necessary conditions for institutionalizing open access. Yet, the historical developments that bring a particular society to the doorstep may not be sufficient to propel it to complete the transition, nor will the same historical developments necessarily bring another society to the doorstep. Differences in how societies get to the doorstep conditions are likely to be magnified in later transitions. After the first societies succeed in making a transition, beliefs about how the world works will change in other societies, therefore altering the process they will follow to the doorstep. These caveats apply *a fortiori* to the transition proper.

The critical period for the transition proper in the West was the nineteenth century when open access occurred in the structure of access to political and economic organizations and the transformation of Western societies. Nonetheless, analysis of why the West developed usually ignores the nineteenth century, focusing instead on the long period from the sixteenth to the eighteenth century and the buildup of nation-states, military prowess, technological innovation, global colonial domination, financial markets, and institutional change generally conceived. In other words, pre-vious explanations focus on what got the West to the doorstep rather than what pushed through the transition.

The long historical view provides many insights. One narrative about the rise of modern societies in Britain, France, and the United States focuses on the intellectual cultivation of the Enlightenment and the eventual transfer of those ideas into concrete political institutions, a process lasting centuries. By the late eighteenth century, elites in Britain, France, and the United States had articulated a set of rights that all citizens should enjoy. Yet, not even all elites enjoyed the rights in equal measure in 1800. Access to economic and political organizations was not open even within the elite, and enlightened political thinking of the time regarded parties and organized economic interests as the greatest threats to elite rights.

Much of the intellectual, political, and economic history of modernity identifies the preconditions for the emergence of the institutions of the new Western proto-democracies. Peter Gay's history of the Enlightenment ends with an essay on the *Federalist Papers* and quotes approvingly George Washington's circular to the state governors after the victory in 1783:

"The foundation of our empire was not laid in the gloomy age of Ignorance and Superstition, but at an Epocha when the rights of mankind were better understood and more clearly defined than at any former period; the researches of the human mind after social happiness, have been carried to a great extent, the treasurers of knowledge, acquired by the labours of Philosophers, Sages, and Legislators, through a long succession of years, are laid open for our use, and their collected wisdom may be happily applied in the Establishment of our forms of Government" (Gay, 1969, p. 560).

[The Federalist papers] achieved and fully deserved, immortality as a classic in the art of politics. It is also a classic work of the Enlightenment, a worthy successor to Montesquieu's *De l'esprit des lois* and a worthy companion to Rousseau's *Social Contract* (Gay, 1969, p. 563).

Similarly, Bernard Bailyn captured the impetus given to social change by these Enlightenment ideas in the title of his book, *To Begin the World Anew: The Genius and Ambiguities of the American Founders* (2004).

The long historical precedents are important. Yet claims that the modern world owes its development to the British Whigs, the French Republicans, and the American founding generation, that their ability to begin the world anew created the modern world, present us with a profound historical problem. Although the founding generations took important steps in the transition, their ideas did not take their countries through the transition proper. Their ideas were backward-looking; they tried to make sense of the world and history that they experienced. To the extent that they looked on a new world, it was because they believed they had figured out solutions to the problems of the seventeenth and eighteenth centuries. They identified the historical source of weakness in republics as the dangers of faction, party, and concentrated economic power. They hoped to minimize and contain these dangers by the construction of balanced governments with separation of powers and checks and balances. They faced an unknown world and could not envision an open access society that had yet to exist. What they saw as dangers – political parties and corporations – turned out to be the solutions to making an open access republic sustainable.

The republican history ends too soon to understand the transition proper. The struggles to create open access continued well into the middle of the nineteenth century and required considerable conceptual, organizational, and institutional innovation that went well beyond republican ideas. In the critical areas of political parties and economic organizations, republican ideas had to be dramatically transformed. Resolving intra-elite conflicts and ensuring that elite rights were secure from conflict ultimately led to institutionalizing open access in economics and politics. Attributing the mid-nineteenth-century innovations in open access economic and political organization to the inevitable playing out of Enlightenment ideas hinders our ability to understand these nineteenth-century changes. In America, the Constitution of 1787 and the *Federalist Papers* were insufficient to produce the modern world; they did not produce the transition to an open access order.

Another explanatory narrative of the transition hinges on the masses threatening or forcing elites to give up privileges and share power. Acemoglu and Robinson (2006) are the most recent and theoretically sophisticated proponents of non-elite assertion. They argue that, to forestall a worse outcome, elites create democracy as a durable method of redistribution that allows them both to redistribute wealth today and to commit to do so in the future. As we have emphasized, the formation of rights in England and, after the Act of Union in 1707, Britain resulted from the process of converting elite privileges into rights and was the product of intra-elite politics, a process assumed away in the Acemoglu and Robinson framework where elites act as a unified group. The first reform act in 1832 was largely an intra-elite bargain, reallocating political representation among different elite groups, not a power-sharing agreement with the masses. The internal dynamism of natural states leads to the regular reallocation of rights and privileges as individuals and groups become more or less powerful. The first reform act reallocated political representation in part to reflect the new political realities after many decades of industrialization, finally enfranchising the new industrial urban centers of Birmingham, Leeds, and Manchester at the expense of the weakest of the traditional elite rotten boroughs. This act also enfranchised copyholders with at least £10 of property. Finally, this reform provided for registration, which had the unintended consequence of helping parliamentary parties organize their electoral counterparts. The reforms of 1832 undoubtedly set in motion forces that mobilized the masses as a political force; and furthermore, those forces were an important factor in the later reforms, as Acemoglu and Robinson suggest. However, intra-elite politics was also important in these reforms, including the incentives facing elite politicians and their new political parties to extend the franchise to the masses to gain electoral advantages, as Peel suggested.

Other histories, as we have noted, revolve around the role of military and production technology in changing conditions over the long term. The military revolution literature focuses on events that antedate the problems of the transition in the nineteenth century. We examined in Chapter 5 the idea that changing military technology forced governments to become larger and more sophisticated. The scale of militaries in Western Europe increased after the seventeenth century, and sovereign states grew to finance and administer those armies. Larger militaries required bigger budgets; but they also required bigger, better, and more complex organizations. Societies well along the road to developing those organizations possessed real advantages. Similarly, Britain and France, by virtue of their military power, possessed global empires by the eighteenth century, including sophisticated institutions and organizations necessary to administer a global empire. However, it is far from clear that the global dimensions of their power and wealth played an important role in the institutional developments of the nineteenth century at issue in this chapter. The same changes proceeded in the United States without the spur of global competition.

A long tradition in economic history emphasizes production technologies and control of nature. This approach embeds the rapid economic development of Western economies after 1850 in technological developments stretching back long before. The beginning of the Industrial Revolution is usually dated to the late eighteenth century in Britain, but a main strand of economic history acknowledges the many precedents to earlier European technological changes (Mokyr, 1990, 2002). Improvements in financial institutions go back to the Italians of the sixteenth and seventeenth centuries, the

Dutch of the seventeenth and eighteenth centuries, and the British financial revolution of the late seventeenth and early eighteenth centuries. European colonial expansion originates with the late fifteenth-century Spanish and Portuguese, joined by the Dutch, French, and British after 1600, long before 1800.[63] Long-term comparisons of Europe and China (Jones, 1981; Pomeranz, 2000) emphasize the importance of "ghost acres," the ability of Europeans to draw on the acreage of colonial holdings around the globe to lessen resource constraints and avoid Malthusian dynamics. Mokyr (2009) and McCloskey (2006) emphasize the long intellectual developments in Europe, culminating in the Enlightenment that not only produced a scientific revolution and the idea that humankind could be improved through conscious and rational effort but also an increasing faith in the ability of competitive markets to allocate resources. These histories typically conclude in the early nineteenth century; few consider periods later than 1850 (the economic history of late nineteenth-century Britain grapples with relative economic decline, not relative development).

Economic historians have therefore not explained events in the mid- and late nineteenth century. Although no decisive year or decade exists of when growth began to accelerate, nonetheless the onset of modern economic growth rates, per capita income growth in the neighborhood of 1 to 1.5 percent per year, does not occur in any of the countries until after 1840.[64] After the 1850s, and with modest ups and downs, this steady growth occurred until the present day, with the exceptions of wars and the depressions of the 1920s and 1930s.

Economic historians have directed an enormous amount of effort to measuring the standard of living of workers in agriculture and industry from 1750 to 1850. The evidence shows that standards of living for most workers did not begin rising in an indisputable and quantitatively clear way until after 1850.[65] Not only did wages begin rising in all three first movers, but in

---

[63] Moreover, by the early nineteenth century, Europeans had found that they could also lose their colonies, as occurred with British North America and the Spanish colonies in Latin America.

[64] Rostow's (1960) hypothesis about the "take-off" into sustained economic growth in the nineteenth century has been much abused by economic historians, but the basic fact of an increasing rate of economic growth after the middle of the nineteenth century has never been disputed. For evidence on the performance of aggregate economies and national income statistics for Britain see Crafts (1998), for the United States see Weiss (1992), and for France see Hoffman and Rosenthal (2000).

[65] For example, the great debate about the standard of living of workers in Britain has both proponents of elevation and immiseration of workers, but neither side disputes that living standards began rising significantly, and to date, almost irreversibly over the long term

rough terms, labor productivity in agriculture rose commensurately with labor productivity in manufacturing over the second half of the nineteenth century. Moreover, labor shifted among sectors efficiently to take advantage of new opportunities, so that agriculture did not fall behind in any meaningful sense other than a declining share of the labor force. Open access in all sectors of the society and for a large share of the population enabled resources and individuals to shift toward more profitable and efficient uses. The result was modern economic development and growth.

Historical origins, preconditions, culture, and intellectual development for the transition in Britain, France, and the United States were all important for the rise of the West. So too were military technology, scale, trade, urbanization, demography, climate, and relative prices. Yet, these factors were insufficient to generate the transition of the mid-nineteenth-century Europe and America that altered their history. Nor were the doorstep conditions sufficient to produce a transition to open access. To understand the transition proper, we have to study what happened in the early and mid-nineteenth century.

We have emphasized that institutions work differently in different contexts. Britain, France, and the United States did not come to open access along the same path or using the same institutions. Furthermore, although Germany and Spain adopted forms of general incorporation in the 1870s and 1880s, they remained limited access societies in other ways (Harris, 2000, p. 289). The transition proper is about institutionalizing open access, not simply adopting specific policies, institutions, or reforms. The success of formal party organization and corporation law in the first movers led other countries to adopt the institutional forms. However, formally organized parties do not necessarily imply competitive politics, nor do formal definitions of corporations imply open access to economic organizations and activities.

The logic of the transition – both attaining the doorstep conditions and the transition proper – allows us to return to an issue raised at the end of Chapter 2 and again in Chapters 3 and 5: how to constrain a ruler who is above the law. As we have seen, societies in the West wrestled with this problem for two millennia. Part of the difficulty in understanding the answer to this question is that it has been asked in the wrong way: the solution involves more than simply placing the ruler under the laws, it

---

after the 1850s. Feinstein (1998) summarizes the debate and the most recent data. For the United States see Gallman and Wallis (1992) and Margo (2000). For France see Hoffman and Rosenthal (2000).

involves a fundamental change in the relationship among individuals and organizations throughout the society.

Rulers head the dominant coalition and are only powerful to the extent that they command the respect and cooperation of other elites. We have emphasized the inadequacy of the single-actor approach to the state. Placing the ruler under the law requires that the identity of the ruler be transformed into a perpetually lived organization; it is not simply the ruler that must be brought under the law but the state itself. Rule of law that limits the state results from the entire dominant coalition devising credible and enforceable rules for intra-elite relationships. Natural states, in which the dominant coalition constantly adjusts rents and privileges as circumstances change, cannot attain credible rule of law.

In each of the two parts of the transition – the doorstep conditions and the transition proper – institutions develop that transform the ability of elites to form organizations inside and outside of the state. These new institutions and organizations supply the tools that allow elites to credibly commit to respect fundamental elite rights, which all elites share. The transformation of elite privileges into rights marks the steps in the transition from natural states to open access orders. Institutions create a perpetually lived state and allow it to sustain perpetually lived organizations throughout society. These organizations and institutions transform the identity of the ruler from a powerful individual with a unique social persona into an impersonal office. Because they are perpetually lived, these institutions and organizations are also binding on tomorrow's leaders and coalitions. The social identity of the ruler becomes embedded in the larger identity of the state as a perpetually lived organization. It is the state that comes under the rule of law. That we continue to identify the state with the ruler is understandable, but it is a convenience that causes enormous confusion.

The birth of the nation-state did not occur with the apotheosis of the ruler, but by subsuming the personal identity of all rulers in a durable and perpetual corporate organization of the state.[66] Perpetually lived organizations and institutions with veto powers, such as parliaments and independent judiciaries, become an integral part of the state. Consolidated control of the military concentrates military power and involves limits that constrain its use against the citizenry.

---

[66] The literature on the rise of the nation-state is enormous. For considerations on the rise of the nation-state, particularly with respect to identity, see Anderson [2006[1983]]), Gellner (1983), and Tilly (1992, 1996, 2005a, and 2005b). Recent political theory studies of the rise of the nation-state include Ertman (1997) and Spruyt (1994).

Most importantly, however, the institutions of the transition proper ensure open access in the polity and economy. Open access competition is the fundamental constraint on states, actuated in the polity through organized political parties and in the economy through organized business entities. The building of state capacity associated with the doorstep and the transition are therefore central to constraining the state to be bound by the law.

SEVEN

A New Research Agenda for the Social Sciences

7.1 The Framing Problems

We have built our framework on the rich literature in history, political science, economics, anthropology, and the social sciences. Our story is set in the context of the growth in the stock of human knowledge, which is the deep underlying source of the improving human material well-being. We have taken as given the changing patterns of technology, fertility, mortality, migration, and general demographics undergirding our account. Our focus has been on the changing structure of human interaction and its implications for the human condition.

A full account of human behavior would begin by asking how the mind deals with the process of change. A necessary preliminary is to understand how the brain interprets signals received by the senses and how the mind structures the result into coherent beliefs. Although some progress has been made in cognitive science, a pressing concern for future research is to understand the origin of conflicting belief systems, their flexibility, and their interaction with organizations and institutions. Many of the changes in the environment are novel, without precedent. The theories we have in the social sciences, however, are predicated on the notion of an ergodic, repeated, and predictable world in which the same problems recur and individuals can fashion solutions to them. How do we think about social processes when individuals, at best, have a limited understanding of what is happening to them as they continue to confront new experiences and novel situations that require an awareness of the dynamic nature of the process of change in which they are participants? How do we deal with the new and novel problems that emerge as humans reshape the human environment in ways that have no historical precedent? We do not have an answer to these questions, although we acknowledge their importance.

We have made progress in understanding how societies deal with the unending and dynamic process of change that goes on in every society. To be clear, a dynamic theory of change is not necessarily a theory that implies growth or development. The response to changing conditions often produces change without progress. Historical experience suggests that neither societies nor social scientists deal very well with the problem of persistent change and endless novelty. Natural states possess some social resources to deal with change, but the long-run history of human societies before the last several centuries paints a dim picture of the ability of societies to overcome all the changes and problems they face. Recorded human history is largely a history of rises and declines of civilizations. Gregory Clark (2007b) recently reiterated what economic historians have long known: over the long period of time stretching from the discovery of agriculture to the beginning of the nineteenth century, the long-run rate of economic growth per capita has been extremely low, almost zero. For every episode of economic growth, there has been a corresponding episode of economic decline. As Table 1.2 in Chapter 1 showed, poorer societies in the modern world are not poor because they suffer from low growth rates when they grow, but because the share of years when they experience negative growth and the intensity of the negative growth experience are so much greater than in the developed world. Over the last two centuries, sustained economic growth results from the reduction of negative shocks to social output rather than a marked increase in the rate of growth in years when output is growing.

The world has always been an uncertain place. The radical transformation of some societies over the last two centuries lends credence to the idea that open access societies are better at constructing effective responses to novel problems. We have tried to explicate why open access societies enjoy a greater degree of adaptive efficiency: an institutional framework that encourages trial and error so that in the face of Knightian uncertainty successful adaptations remain while failures tend to disappear. Although never unerring in their response to an uncertain world, the history of open access societies is replete with experimentation leading eventually to solutions. Creative political and economic destruction is the norm in open access societies. Such experimentation is precisely in the spirit of Hayek's (1952) optimistic views on the consequences of entry and competition. Adaptive efficiency entails the creation of institutions and organizations that encourage experimentation, reward successful innovation, and, equally important, eliminate failures. There is clearly no guarantee that humans will find solutions to the new and novel problems that we will confront in the future, but some sets of social institutions and organizations make it more likely we will do so.

We have learned enough about institutions to realize that they are imperfect vehicles to solve problems (Eggertsson, 2005). Human societies never manage to solve the problem of violence completely, although some have developed more effective ways of constraining it than others. The emergence of natural states beginning ten thousand years ago dramatically expanded the range of institutions and organizations that societies could support. The use of rent-creation to constrain the use of violence enabled the creation of much larger societies capable of supporting larger populations, urban agglomerations, and significant technological change. Natural states, however, have inherent limits to the type of social arrangements that can be supported: anything that threatens rent-creation may eventually threaten the provision of order. Rent-creation and limited access place limits on the long-term economic growth of natural states, limits that became glaringly apparent over the last two centuries in comparison to open access societies.

Open access orders appear to be better at coping with change over the long run. Decision makers in an open access society are widely decentralized and include leaders in economic and political organizations. They reach decentralized decisions within the organizations they represent. Open access increases the possibility of stumbling onto better policies that solve or mitigate problems. Creative destruction in both the economic and political realm appears to be a necessary requirement for adaptive efficiency. Schumpeter's failure to imagine creative political destruction led him to conclude that capitalism was ultimately doomed to failure. Perhaps he will ultimately be proved right: open access social orders may turn out not to be sustainable in the same way that natural states have been sustainable for ten thousand years. Nonetheless, the durability of the open access society in the face of ubiquitous efforts to create rents is testimony to the crucial role of adaptive efficiency.

Natural states cannot rely on adaptive efficiency as a bulwark to deal with change. In a dynamic world, decision makers in limited access societies are constrained in their ability to exploit new opportunities and develop solutions to new problems by the desire of elites to protect their privileges and the dangers that reducing rents pose to the stability of the dominant coalition and society at large. Limits on competition in both economics and politics reduce innovation, creative destruction, and the ability to replace losers and discard bad ideas. It is not that natural states are incapable of progress; it is that they are as likely to move back toward personal arrangements and more limited access as they are toward impersonal arrangements. Even when societies perceive the benefits of open access, natural state coalition members perceive that simply adopting open access institutions would not only destroy their rents but would also fail to produce the desired outcome of sustained economic development.

We recognize that we have grappled incompletely with the need to comprehend the sources of beliefs, the origin of institutions, and the nature of human organizations that comprise the different social orders. However, our story does have profound implications for the incentives to increase the stock of human knowledge and everything to say about the degree to which societies could exploit that knowledge both to improve the human condition and to deal with the potential increase in the deadliness of violence.

7.2 The Conceptual Framework

In the foraging order, exchange occurs mainly through face-to-face repeated interaction; all relationships are personal. The typical size unit of human interaction is the band of about twenty-five people, with larger groups forming temporarily and sporadically. The foraging order deals with violence imperfectly through the formation of groups in which personal interaction occurs among individuals who know each other well and interact repeatedly. The level of violence within and between groups can be very high.

The natural state builds on the personal relationships of the foraging order and is able to expand beyond the scale of simpler societies. Personal relationships in natural states build on traditional face-to-face interaction, but hierarchies of elites form personal relationships that extend the control of the dominant coalition. Limited access orders provide a solution to violence by embedding powerful members of society in a coalition of military, political, religious, and economic elites. Elites possess privileged access to valuable resources or valuable activities and the ability to form organizations sanctioned by the larger society. Unique elite identities are closely tied to the privileged organizations that elites head or participate in. Because elite rents are reduced if violence breaks out, rent-creation enables elites to credibly commit to each other to limit violence. However, because peace depends on the balance of interests within the dominant coalition, limited access orders are sensitive to changes that alter elite interests and capabilities. The limited access order is stable as a social order, but each natural state is subject to constant change; and because natural states rely on an interlocking system of elite interests, they are not always robust to changing circumstances. In well-developed natural states, elite privileges include control over powerful social organizations, such as the church, governments, courts, and military units.

The open access order builds on the organizational achievements of the natural state but extends impersonal citizenship to an ever-growing proportion of the population. All citizens are able to form economic, political, religious, or social organizations to pursue any number of functions. All open access orders proscribe the use of violence by organizations other than the military or police. Unlike the natural state, which actively manipulates the interests of elites and non-elites to ensure social order, the open access order allows individuals to pursue their own interests through organizations. Individuals continue to be motivated by economic rents in both political and economic markets, but the presence of open entry induces competition, which tends to make such rents temporary. Social order is maintained through the interaction of competition, institutions, and beliefs. Control of the military is concentrated in government, and control over the government is subject to both political and economic competition and institutional constraints. Attempts to use government to coerce citizens either directly through the use of military force or indirectly through the manipulation of economic interests result in the activation of existing organizations or creation of new organizations to mobilize economic and social resources to bid for control of the political system. Maintaining open access is critical to sustaining the social order.

Both limited and open access orders are dynamic and subject to continuous and often unexpected change. This dynamism is not progressive; no teleological movement pushes societies to become more complex, more stable, or more developed. The dynamism is change, constant change. In the simplest terms, what distinguishes the dynamics of limited access from open access orders is the way the social orders use access to limit violence and provide order. Natural states respond to change by manipulating access and reallocating rents within the dominant coalition. In contrast, the greater stability of open access orders does not stem from greater rigidity in social arrangements but from the opposite, from more fluid social arrangements that respond more flexibly to changing conditions. Open access orders are more robust to changes because their internal institutional and organizational structures are freer to adjust to and accommodate change within a much wider range because rent creation is not actively used to limit violence. Both social orders are dynamic, but the internal logic of their dynamism differs.

How is the transition made from one social order to another? In the previous chapter, we outlined the transition to open access orders in Britain,

France, and the United States. While the transition in each society depended on specific features of that society, there are common features to the transition. The doorstep conditions made it possible for elites to deal with each other impersonally, to reduce the incidence of disruptive violence, and ultimately to create and sustain impersonal elite rights. In each case, elites faced incentives to transform privileges into impersonal rights. The creation of a few elite rights under the doorstep conditions opened an opportunity to extend elite rights in a way that was credibly sustained by the entire elite. The privilege of owning shares in a joint-stock company, for example, may begin as a unique privilege. However, if that privilege becomes widespread and shares are transferable, then an elite interest in supporting impersonal exchange of shares may grow. Impersonal exchange in shares, in turn, may create an interest in impersonal formation of companies, forces that clearly came to the fore in all three countries in the nineteenth century. Open access to corporate forms becomes credible when large numbers of the elite benefit directly. In a similar way, open access to political organizations can be sustained when powerful groups in the polity find it in their interests to support political parties.

The transition is about institutionalizing open access via impersonal relationships, not about adopting specific institutions, such as a bill of rights or the universal franchise. Institutions matter because they structure the incentives and constraints facing individuals. However, as we have demonstrated, the same institutions work differently in different circumstances, particularly in the absence or presence of open access. Elections and corporations, for example, work differently in natural states than in open access orders.

This way of thinking about the transition process results in a new interpretation of the economic and political history of the birth of modern open access societies at the end of the eighteenth and the beginning of the nineteenth centuries. Our economic history emphasizes the concern about the development of powerful new forms of elite economic organizations and the "corrupting" effect of these organizations on politics that led to the acceptance of open access in the mid-nineteenth century. Our political history emphasizes modifications to natural state institutions in the eighteenth century that led to concerns among elites that intra-elite political competition would inevitably lead to consolidated political control by a faction that maintained control through manipulation of the economy. Ultimately, elites moved to protect their privileges by converting them into rights through institutions that guaranteed open economic and political competition by allowing the formation of economic and political organizations at will, something the world had never seen before. The transforming effects of open access in the mid-nineteenth century are manifest in the political and economic developments of the late nineteenth century and twentieth century, including fostering more favorable circumstances for technological progress.

The historical details and specific institutional mechanisms that developed in each specific society were critically important in that society, but neither the specific details nor the specific institutions were the same across societies. The transition was secured in the middle of the nineteenth century by institutionalizing open access for a growing number of citizens who enjoyed impersonally defined rights and were embedded in a set of social arrangements that sustained impersonal relationships. The operation of existing natural state institutions, even institutions with long histories such as the British Parliament, began changing as access opened. Elected assemblies produced different outcomes in the presence of competitive political parties. Economic corporations produced different outcomes in the presence of competitive entry.

The adoption of similar institutions in other societies later in the nineteenth century did not immediately foster transitions in those societies. For example, Latin American countries that adopted constitutions similar to the U.S. Constitution in the nineteenth century and the adoption of general incorporation laws elsewhere in Europe were insufficient in themselves to induce transitions. Elite interests in limiting access societies can easily be served in the presence of elections, representative assemblies, and more sophisticated corporate and other types of organizations. Adopting the institutions of Britain, France, or the United States without securing open political and economic access is insufficient to produce the transition. History shows that adopting better institutions enables the adopting societies to function better as natural states, but transitions do not occur without opening access.

7.3 A New Approach to the Social Sciences: Violence, Institutions, Organizations, and Beliefs

The conceptual framework is more than another political or economic model; it is a fundamentally new approach to social science analysis. It is concerned with the process of change through time. Just how much have we learned about the process of societal change? We can illustrate our contributions through the concepts that have provided the structure of this study: violence, institutions, organizations, and beliefs.

We began with the idea that the systematic creation of rents can induce powerful individuals and groups to refrain from violence. When combined with the simple and powerful idea that the most valuable form of rent-creation in most societies is the ability to form organizations sanctioned and supported by the society, we were a few steps away from the implication that the structure of all social institutions is deeply conditioned by the methods used to address the problem of violence. Because causal beliefs about the behavior of other people depend on the nature of organizations within which individuals act, we can draw important implications about the nature of beliefs in personal or impersonal relations. When societies can support impersonal organizations, they create the possibility of impersonal elite relationships, sustaining a transition to open access, and creating widespread causal beliefs that social relationships can be impersonally based. And when perpetually lived and impersonal economic organizations come into being alongside the consolidation of the military, the society eliminates the need for personal identification with networks of patronage and protection. With all their myriad and sometimes offsetting costs and benefits, open access societies depend for their operation on impersonal identity and the associated beliefs in equality and fairness.

Violence must be near the heart of any explanation of how societies behave. The necessary prerequisite for forming durable large social groups is a way to control violence. Natural states do not deal with violence by consolidating control over it. Instead, utilizing the dispersion of violence in the population, they create a pattern of interlocking economic, religious, political, and social interests that provide powerful individuals with incentives not to use violence. All states are organizations of organizations. Rent-creation combines with the internal structure of organizations with the dominant coalition to limit violence in a natural state.

Approaches to violence that begin with the Weberian assumption that the state is an entity with a monopoly on the legitimate use of violence start in the wrong place. By assuming away the most fundamental problem societies face – managing violence – these approaches misunderstand how most human societies function. In natural states, military assets are dispersed throughout the dominant coalition. To be stable, natural states must give those powerful individuals credible incentives not to use violence but to cooperate. Assuming the state is a single entity eliminates our ability to understand how natural states – and thus most societies in history – contain violence.

Consolidation of the military into one organization can occur only if other nonmilitary elements in the dominant coalition are confident that they can credibly discipline the military organization if it attempts to abuse its military power. Consolidation of the military must be accompanied by a set of developments in economic and political organizations and institutions that allow economic and political actors to control the military. Mature natural states must maintain a double balance between military and nonmilitary organizations. For a natural state to create consolidated control of the military, it must simultaneously develop powerful forms of economic and political organizations. In the absence of such organizations, the military organization and those who lead it have the power to subvert the privileges of other members of the dominant coalition. This conclusion holds whether or not the administration is nominally civilian. Violence and organizations are intimately connected.

Whether discussing historical or modern developing societies, we must not assume that the state is a single coercive individual with a monopoly on violence. Rather than starting with a specialist in violence and reasoning from there, we have tackled the problem of increasing specialization in violence as an outcome of the structure of the institutions, organizations, and beliefs within the larger society. In short, to understand the control of violence, we must begin with a group of powerful individuals, constrained by a set of self-enforcing arrangements, who manage to increase the degree of specialization within their coalition organization by allowing some members to specialize in violence, some in economic activities, and some in political activities.

Institutions are the rules of the game, the patterns of interaction that govern and constrain the relationships of individuals. Institutions include formal rules, written laws, formal social conventions, and informal norms of behavior. Institutions must also include the means by which rules and norms are enforced. We focus on institutions and emphasize the implication that the same institution works differently in different circumstances. This insight plays a pivotal role in our explanation of the transition process. Institutions that make impersonal elite relationships possible can be created in mature natural states and then used by open access orders, but they will produce different results in the open access order than in the natural state. We have been particularly concerned with how institutions – such as elections, representative legislative bodies, corporations, and political parties – operate differently in the presence of open or limited entry and access.

Greif's (2006) concept of institutions includes institutions, organizations, and beliefs as institutional elements. We deliberately chose not to adopt such an inclusive definition of institutions, not because we disagree with Greif's insights, but because unpacking Greif's logical structure into its component elements is both inevitable and necessary if we want to think about the process of social change. Greif shows how rules and norms, by themselves, are not self-sustaining; they must be embedded in a larger structure of organizations and beliefs. People's causal beliefs must be consistent with the actual behavior of individuals under the institutions and organizations they deal with. We want to stress the importance of organizations and beliefs in understanding how institutions work and to follow how the institutions that govern the formation of organizations change across social orders and over time. Understanding social change in actual historical events requires separating institutions, organizations, and beliefs, as well as violence, in order to track their interrelated development over time. Social development, historically and in the contemporary world, is not simply a matter of changing institutions, adopting the appropriate governance structures, or constructing systems of property rights.

Organizations are made up of individuals who act in a coordinated manner to pursue common as well as individual goals. An *adherent* organization consists of individuals whose individual interests, at every point in time, enable the organization to secure voluntary cooperation. *Contractual* organizations, in contrast, utilize third parties to enforce agreements within the organization and between the organization and outsiders. Because they have additional tools to foster cooperation, contractual organizations are more powerful than adherent organizations.

Our framework builds on three insights about organizations:

1. The structure, extent, and number of organizations in any society are intimately tied to the way that society controls violence.
2. The social technology of structuring organizations depends on personality and the identity of the individuals within the organization. The creation of impersonally defined, perpetually lived organizations whose identity is independent of the identity of their members is difficult to accomplish. But where it occurs, it fundamentally changes the possibility for relationships among individuals.
3. The existence of organizations with impersonal identities, in both the public and private sphere, is a necessary condition for the existence of impersonal relationships in the larger society.

The vast literature on organizations in economics, sociology, and political science has largely overlooked changes in social support for organizations in the first movers during the nineteenth century. Social scientists explain social structures. We do so largely in terms of the intentional actions of individuals, abstracting from the social tools at their disposal. The organizational tools available to individuals not only improved as better legal forms arose for both organizations and their contractual relations but the distribution of those tools throughout society also increased dramatically. Many histories attribute the spread of impersonal rights through the population as the result of changes in large social institutions, such as democracy, and processes, such as economic growth. We have identified how open access to organizational forms can make social institutions such as democracy work much better by sustaining economic and political creative destruction; we have also identified why open access to organizational forms failed to spread through all human societies before the nineteenth century. A challenge for all the social sciences is to redirect their consideration of organizations to the fundamental changes in organizational tools that occurred in the nineteenth century.

The number and scope of new organizations explode when a society undergoes transition. This explosion is not just an incident to the main action of increasing citizen rights, new institutions, or economic growth. Nor does the explosion simply follow from the natural human tendency to truck, barter, and exchange. Instead, the transition provides citizens with new tools, fewer restrictions, and greater scope for impersonal relations, all of which dramatically increase the gains from specialization and exchange while reducing the risk of expropriation. These changes in turn foster the growth of new organizations to exploit new opportunities. The explosion in organizations is thus a direct consequence of the transition.

We documented the emergence of perpetually lived public, private, and religious organizations in Western Europe from 1400 to 1800. These organizations exhibited the logic of the natural state through the creation of elite privileges. The creation of these organizations in natural states was an integral part of the emergence and success of mature natural states at that time. Organizational sophistication lay at the root of late medieval and early modern economic growth in Europe, and it enabled the creation of much more clearly articulated state structures capable of consolidating control of the military after 1600 and exploiting the gains from exchange.

Without a perpetually lived state and impersonal organizations, institutional mechanisms – such as checks and balances between king and parliament or president and congress – cannot operate effectively. Similarly, consolidated control of the military is possible only if perpetually lived, and therefore impersonal organizations in the public and private sphere can be utilized to check the military, as we illustrated with the case of provisioning the British Navy in the mid-eighteenth century. The newly developed, rich network of impersonal organizations was able to sustain impersonally defined rights for elites. Only then did it become possible for notions of equality to support beliefs about how the real world operated rather than ideas, ideologies, or theologies about how the world should work.

Beliefs about equality cannot be sustained by experience in a natural state; equality can only be an ideal. One of the basic features of an open access order is the prevalence of impersonal relationships that sustain beliefs in freedom and equality. The key is understanding how open access both supports and requires impersonal relationships. Open access is not universal access, but it does require impersonal identity.

We do not have a general theory of belief formation and human cognition, but we have tried to come to grips with two aspects of beliefs. First, beliefs about causal relationships in the world intimately affect people's decisions. Second, the cultural environment – the political, economic, social context – fundamentally influences beliefs. Social structures that create fundamental inequalities among participants are reflected in the belief system and in forms of social relationships exchange – specifically personal versus impersonal exchange and the forms, types, and access to organizations that the society supports. These organizations range from the family to the church to political, economic, and educational organizations. In large part, beliefs in impersonal identity derive from the structure of organizations and institutions that a society supports and people live within.

Because limited and open access orders control violence and structure organizations in different ways, the two social orders produce differences in the beliefs held by their populations. Controlling violence through rent-creation results in a society based on personal identities and privilege. We emphasize the importance of open access for sustaining beliefs about equality and impersonality. In particular, perpetually lived organizations embody the reality of impersonal identity. Beliefs that impersonal identities can be sustained lie at the heart of beliefs in equality. Equality depends on impersonal identity; for citizens to be equal before the law, for example, the law must treat citizens impersonally. Beliefs that citizens really are equal in some dimensions therefore cannot be maintained unless societies create impersonal identities along those dimensions. Implementing equality in a society requires that the society be able to create and sustain impersonal categories – such as citizens – and then to treat everyone in the same category alike.

The principal reason for superior rule of law in open access orders is that institutions support impersonality and perpetual life. Indeed, these concepts are at the heart of the rule of law. Institutions supporting impersonality allow open access orders to sustain rights for all citizens rather than just privileges for elites. Without perpetually lived public organizations, new coalitions and governments are able to alter institutions and rights, including dismantling those that support impersonality. The inability of natural state governments to provide benefits on an impersonal basis fundamentally hinders their ability to provide both the rule of law and basic public goods, including the social insurance programs so essential to modern open access orders.

7.4 A New Approach to the Social Sciences: Development and Democracy

We have used historical examples to illustrate the conceptual framework rather than testing detailed hypotheses. More systematic evidence awaits future studies. We have not attempted statistical analyses because no straightforward measures of our concepts exist. We believe that our concepts can be operationalized, but the concepts of limited and open access in both economics and politics are subtle and multidimensional.[1] Putting them into practice will require serious effort that is beyond the scope of this study. We value and encourage this effort.[2]

The current state of empirical investigation into the determinants of development illustrates the difficulty of explaining complex social phenomena with a few unidimensional variables. It is nothing new to say that development is a complex problem. Recent experience has shown that development is not simply a matter of adding more capital or grafting onto a society the right institutions, such as democracy, property rights, markets, or the rule of law. Nor does it simply involve providing the right mix of public goods, such as social insurance or education. Proponents of a traditional economic approach to development advice face a paradox: Why do so many developing countries fail to choose policies that economists argue

---

[1] In his comments about this project, James Robinson has suggested an intriguing possibility of distinguishing between natural states and open access orders using event studies to investigate the effect of leadership turnover. Because individuals matter far less in the impersonal and perpetual open access orders, surprise changes in the prospects of leaders should have a much smaller impact in open access orders than in natural states. Consistent with this idea, Fisman's (2001) study of Suharto's health shows a dramatic effect on assets.

[2] Meisel and Ould Aoudia (2008) did a quantitative study that explores cross-country economic performance and relates to some of our ideas. Khan (2005, 2006) also examines quantitative evidence that relates to some measures of access and rent-creation across countries.

are Pareto improving, when all members of the society can be better off from the advice? Something must be fundamentally wrong with the advice.

Development policy has been based on the institutions, policies, organizations, and beliefs essential to the open access order's success. The logic of the natural state enables us to see why open access policies and institutions directly threaten the stability of the natural state. Economists typically conclude that natural states suffer from too much market intervention, laws fostering monopolies and other rent-creating privileges, inadequate property rights, ineffective public goods provision, and incomplete markets. All this is true. The economists' natural prescription is to suggest that a country introduce reform, that it should systematically adopt policies that mimic those in open access orders: easier entry by firms, less regulatory control, reduction of monopolies, more secure property rights, improved public goods provision such as education, and more complete markets. Until societies are at least on the doorstep of a transition to opening access, however, transplanting these institutions and policies cannot produce economic development in natural states.

The economists' approach fails because it ignores the logic underlying natural states: natural states implement limited access policies address the problem of violence by giving individuals and groups with access to violence an incentive to cooperate, they are not intended simply to maximize the incomes of the ruling elite. Policies from open access orders – universal, impersonal rights and rule of law; open access to markets; and greater political freedoms – reduce the natural state's ability to control violence. These changes therefore threaten to make people worse off, not better off. Modern economics implicitly adopts the Weberian assumption that the state has a monopoly on violence and will not use it to exploit citizens, and so economics fails to understand the basic problem of development because it assumes the problem of violence away.

The framework suggests that two development problems exist. The first is development within the natural state and the second is the transition from limited to open access social orders. In effect, most development advice attempts to induce a transition. The relevant dynamics of social change for developing countries, however, lie in the logic of the natural state, not in the logic of open access orders. With few exceptions, most developing countries today do not meet the doorstep conditions. They are not in a position where elites can credibly deal with others through impersonal relationships in critical matters of economic and political interactions, so advice that suggests they undertake elements of the transition is misplaced. The establishment of well-defined elite rights is not sustainable under such conditions. The transplanting of institutions from open access orders to natural states cannot, in and of itself, produce political and economic development. Indeed, to the extent that these institutions are forced onto societies by international or domestic pressure but do not conform to existing beliefs about economic, political, social, and cultural systems, the new institutions are likely to work less well than the ones they replace. Worse, if these institutions undermine the political arrangements maintaining political stability, these new institutions may unleash disorder, making the society significantly worse off.

The economists are not alone in bringing open access ideas to the problem of development; political scientists share the same tendency. The lesson that the same institution works differently under limited as opposed to open access applies with particular force to the transfer of democratic institutions into natural states. Elections work differently in natural states than in open access orders. This view contrasts with the dominant view in the literature that, following Przeworski et al. (2000) and including the lion's share of empirical political science studies, defines democracy by whether a country sustains competitive elections with partisan turnover. The popular press commonly identifies democracy with elections, often using them interchangeably. This approach to democracy lumps together elections in limited access orders with open access orders.

Just as with economic development policy, we take a different view.[3] Although elections are central to democracy, democracy is not solely about elections, as Dahl (1971) argued in his classic work, *Polyarchy*. As an institution in an open access order, democracy provides citizen control over political officials, generating responsiveness to their interests with limits on corruption. For democracy to work, elections must be embedded in an institutional and competitive environment that allows political competition to convey information to and constrain politicians. Elections in natural states typically do not provide these functions or do so incompletely. Indeed, a host of differences distinguish elections in limited from open access orders; these differences suggest that democracy, in the sense of citizen control of governments and officials, can only be sustained in open access orders.

Because open access orders are capable of supporting perpetually lived, impersonal public organizations, they have the ability to deliver policies on an impersonal basis to citizens. This allows them to provide a wide range of public goods and social insurance programs missing from natural states. Poverty-reduction programs can be targeted to the poor as measured

---

[3] We expand on these views about democracy in North, Wallis and Weingast (2009).

by impersonal and observable characteristics; education can be delivered to all citizens; drivers' licenses can be given to everyone who meets an age requirement and passes a competency test; unemployment insurance is available to everyone who has contributed to the system and meets the impersonal requirements for being unemployed.

The ability to provide impersonal public services works to enhance open access. If public goods are provided impersonally, it is much easier for voters to evaluate the provision of the services and discipline governments that do not deliver the goods. If public goods are provided on a personal and discretionary rather than an impersonal basis, governments are able to use the threat of withdrawal of valued public goods and services as a means of forcing citizens to support the incumbents rather than exercise choice. Personal provision of public goods becomes a way for governments to discipline citizens rather than to respond to citizen interests. Elections under these circumstances are a means of manipulating citizens rather than the exercise of citizen choice. Open access orders limit this type of threat by delivering policies impersonally, not subject to manipulation based on political criteria.

Impersonal and credible delivery of public goods has another important implication for democracy. The logic of a median voter model suggests that widening the suffrage in a democracy to include more low-income voters will likely result in populism and other forms of zero- or negative-sum redistributive politics emphasized by Meltzer and Richard (1981). If the median voter makes less than the average income, it is in his or her interest to transfer income from rich to poor people. Such an analysis, however, ignores the incentives for redistribution that exist if the government is able to deliver redistribution impersonally. As Lindert (2004) shows, the social costs of redistribution create incentives for the poor and rich to redistribute in ways that have the least negative effects on society as a whole. They create strong incentives to redistribute opportunity to poor individuals through the provision of education, public health, and public services rather than strictly cash. When public goods enhance human capital, the ability to provide impersonal policies allows open access orders to respond to citizens in ways that complement markets rather than undermine them. In this way, open access orders sustain democracy as a positive-sum game. Of course, if the government cannot credibly deliver impersonal public services, then the poor have every incentive to use their votes to transfer cash now and are susceptible to populist appeals from factional leaders. This is the dark side of democracy, a side often visible in natural states.

Open access supports an effective opposition and competitive electoral process. It supports a rich civil society, fostering a wide range of economic, political, and social groups that can mobilize interests and help constrain democratic policymaking. Schumpeterian competition constantly produces new interests and groups. Widespread access to organizations makes it difficult for public officials to manipulate economic interests in support of the regime. In contrast, most natural states inhibit or compromise electoral competition, including limits on citizen organization, on the opposition's ability to compete, and on the free press.

Open access orders support the rule of law, including a judicial system relatively free of corruption. An important, if little recognized, consequence is that rule-of-law courts allow the legislative branch to write legislation detailing impersonal rules of policy distribution and to enforce those rules through the courts. In contrast, legislators in natural states with corrupt courts have little ability to implement such constraints because the courts cannot or will not enforce them. The absence of rule-of-law courts limits public good provision and limits the ability of the legislature to serve as a check on the executive. Natural states exhibit far more executive dominance regardless of the nominal constitutional system of checks and balances.

Open access orders limit the stakes of politics through perpetually lived institutions and credible commitments that place checks and balances on political officials. These limits lower the incidence of coups and violence. Elections in open access orders are therefore more stable, and these societies are less subject to dramatic changes in policy. In natural states, coups and other forms of instability alter the competitive process. They prevent parties from becoming perpetually lived organizations, and the threat of regime change means that, even if it is legal to compete today, a party official may be thrown in jail tomorrow.

Taken together, these differences show that elections differ under limited as against open access. Elections in open access orders implement the democratic ideals of citizen expression and control over political officials in ways that elections simply cannot in natural states. Elections alone are insufficient to effectively constrain political officials, especially the executive. Open access limits the stakes of power, creates perpetual institutions that survive crises and partisan turnover, allows a wider range of groups to form and mobilize, allows more effective competition for office, and allows the provision of public goods and services. In sum, many mature natural states sustain elections, but they are not the same as elections in open access orders and they do not come close to meeting the ideals of democracy.

7.5 Toward a Theory of the State

We have ducked the problem of defining the state in part because it is a difficult problem, but also because it did not make sense to grapple with the definition of the state until the framework was fully described. We begin with two requirements: a theory of politics should explain the distribution and use of power, violence, and coercion within a society, and a theory of government should explain both the structure of governments and the behavior of political officials and employees of the government. A theory of the state should encompass a theory of politics and a theory of government.

In natural states, power, violence, and coercion reside in the dominant coalition. The dominant coalition depends on the threat of violence to maintain balance among elites, and thus dispersed control of violence is a general characteristic of the coalition structure. Therefore, the formal structure of the government rarely contains consolidated control of the military. As a result, the state contains much more than the formal structure of government in limited access orders. Powerful actors with power over violence and coercion are not identified with the formal government.

An immediate implication of acknowledging the difference between the state and the government concerns efforts to promote good governance. In many natural states where power, violence, and coercion lay outside the control of government, attempts to affect the incentives of government actors are likely to result in a lack of political will to implement the goals the incentives were designed to further. The levers that move powerful individuals are not all in the hands of the government. In situations like this, it is not surprising that external actors who come into a natural state, like foreign governments, international donors, and nongovernmental organizations, may find it in their interest to strengthen one faction within the dominant coalition in order to create a partner to deal with. These interventions reconfigure relationships within the dominant coalition and may destabilize long-term relationships within the coalition. When the external actor withdraws, the configuration of the state will change again, perhaps returning to its former configuration. In few cases will foreign manipulation of incentives within a natural state permanently alter the structure of the state unless the foreign intervention continues indefinitely.

Accepting that the state, however defined, differs from the formal government does not produce an adequate theory of the state, but it does indicate that such a theory must come to grips with the close interrelationship between economics and politics in limited access orders. This invalidates a basic assumption of modern social science, whose dominant paradigm separates political and economic actors into distinct, well-defined spheres. The most advanced economics and political science scholarship studies the developed world: where the operation of markets and the operation of democratic institutions are seemingly independent. Both disciplines have produced sophisticated theories that generate a wide range of insights into the operation of markets and democratic institutions in open access orders. Yet both disciplines have failed to produce a theory explaining why markets and democratic institutions can be sustained only under some circumstances and have failed to explain or disentangle the intimate connection between the historic development of markets and democracy.

The seeming independence of economic and political systems in open access societies has deceived modern social science. In natural states, all big economic organizations are necessarily also political ones. In open access orders, big economic organizations typically concentrate far more on markets and are only tangentially involved in politics. The ability of firms in open access orders to concentrate on economics produces the seeming independence of markets and democracy. This seeming independence has allowed both economists and political scientists to study their respective domains while holding the other constant. The seeming independence of the economic and political systems on the surface is apparent, not real. In fact, these systems are deeply intertwined.

We emphasize the importance of a much more closely integrated political economy. We are not the first to argue for this integration, and the recent literature on political economy is exploding with new and exciting work on this important frontier.[4] However, our approach does provide new insights, the most important of which can be summed up in the phrase, "Natural states are not sick." Natural states have their own logic; they are not dysfunctional. Although they are less robust to shocks than open access orders, they generate internal forces that provide for two of the basic tasks of all societies: stability and order. Natural states may appear to be corrupt according to the norms and values of open access orders, but that corruption is an inherent part of the operation of the social order. Failure to understand how the much more visible and direct connections among political, economic, religious, and military privileges are integral to the social order is a major impediment to a better development policy and better social science history. This also suggests that an adequate theory of the state applied to limited

---

[4] To name just a few: Acemoglu and Robinson (2006), Bates (2001), Greif (2006), Haber et al. (2003), North (1981, 1990), Persson and Tabellini (2000). Roland (2000), Spiller and Tommasi (2007), and Stein and Tommasi (2006).

access orders must acknowledge and explain the close interaction of politics and economics; it cannot be just a theory of government.

Most theories of the state take the existence of a formally identified leader or ruler as a given. Barzel (2001, Bueno de Mesquita et al. (2003), Levi (1988), Myerson (2006), North (1981, Ch. 3), and Olson (1993) all assume the state is a single actor with a monopoly on violence and study its behavior.[5] This approach is fundamentally flawed. It assumes the separation and specialization of politics and economics that are so crucial to the transition process. The monopoly of violence possessed by all open access governments is a modern phenomenon and reflects the logic of the doorstep conditions and of open access orders, which does create consolidated – and, yes, monopoly – control over violence. Viewing the natural state as a solution to the problem of violence causes us to think differently about these states.

We do not provide a coherent and well-integrated theory of the state. Instead of a monopoly on violence, we suggest that the governance structures of societies can be described in terms of organizational sophistication. The progression from less to more complex exhibits no teleology, and nothing compels societies to more complex organizations; many societies move forward and backward. Organizational complexity occurs over multiple dimensions. We add violence to these considerations by labeling three types of natural states: fragile, basic, and mature. We adopted these terms for convenience; we do not propose a stage theory of development within the limited access orders.

Nonetheless, the range of internal structures does differ across societies in predictable ways. The key feature of development within the natural states is the coevolution of institutional supports for organizations inside and outside the formal structure of the government. Fragile societies are able to secure more order through the proliferation of public organizations. These organizations need institutions to support and protect them and their flow of goods and services from opportunism. Similarly, the range of sustainable private organizations is linked to institutions that provide services to these organizations – such as contract enforcement – but also that provide credible commitments by the state not to expropriate the value created by the organizations. Public and private organizations develop in parallel and connected ways.

Political scientists have never had an adequate definition of political development, let alone one that mirrors the consensus surrounding the economists' notions of economic development. We suggest a new way of

---

[5] Haber's (2006) study of the launching organizations that support different types of authoritarian regimes is an exception.

thinking about political development that involves increasing state capacity to support complex and specialized organizations, create impersonality, sustain a perpetually lived state, and control the dispersion and use of violence in society. Each of these elements of state capacity is necessary for the transition from a natural state to an open access order.

7.6 Violence and Social Orders: The Way Ahead

If the foregoing analysis has merit, it suggests a new approach to social science research. The existing body of knowledge in social science can be transformed by a new conceptual framework that changes the way we think about traditional problems in economics, political science, sociology, anthropology, and history that result from an explicit consideration of the role violence plays in shaping social orders, institutions, and organizations and their development over time. Our recommendations for new research entail an in-depth understanding of violence, institutions, organizations, and beliefs in the natural state that we do not currently possess.

We have come some distance in our understanding of institutions and organizations but we have a way to go in understanding the polity in natural states and the interconnections of institutions and organizations in both the natural state and open access societies that undergird each social order. In addition, we still are some distance from a deeper comprehension of the interaction of formal rules, informal norms, and enforcement character-istics that together determine the performance of the overall institutional framework.

Every society evolves in unique ways, so that a deep understanding of change must go beyond broad generalizations to a specific understanding of the cultural heritage of that particular society. The paths and policies that created open access in the Western world cannot be indiscriminately applied to foster the transition among today's limited access orders.[6] The world constantly changes, and our ideas about how societies function are constantly being made obsolete by new developments and changes. The world we are creating today is like no other that has ever existed. Can we prepare ourselves to comprehend and deal with it? We can do better if we are self-conscious about the limitations of human understanding and stand ready to maintain institutions that will encourage adaptive efficiency.

---

[6] The idea that Western institutions cannot simply be transferred to developing countries is hardly a new insight, see Rodrik (2007), but the reason why the dynamics of natural states resist or transform open access institutions is new.

Those limits apply to the conceptual framework we have laid out in this book, already made obsolete by the onward press of events. However, it is time to reevaluate the accumulated experience of the last two hundred years; it is time to acknowledge that open access societies are not just modestly improved versions of the societies that preceded them. Whereas the origins of the transition in the Western world lay in the eighteenth century and earlier, the events that transformed those societies and produced a new social order with a fundamentally different logic occurred in the mid-nineteenth century. Since then a relatively small number of societies and a small percentage of the world's population have made the transition to open access. The development of an open access society has not only enabled societies to achieve a world of plenty but has also created efficient institutions and organizations that make violence more efficient. Focusing on the complex interaction of beliefs, institutions, and organizations should open the door to serious research on the underlying sources of violence. A clearer vision of the two social orders, where we have been and where we are now, is a necessary element in understanding where we are headed. That is the challenge of the future.

References

Acemoglu, D., Johnson, S., & Robinson, J. A. (2001). The colonial origins of comparative development: An empirical investigation. *American Economic Review, 91*(5), 1369–1401.

Acemoglu, D., Johnson, S., & Robinson, J. A. (2002). Reversal of fortune: Geography and institutions in the making of the modern world income distribution. *Quarterly Journal of Economics, 117*(4), 1231–1294.

Acemoglu, D., Johnson, S., & Robinson, J. A. (2005). Institutions as the fundamental cause of long-run growth. In P. Aghion & S. Durlauf (Eds.), *Handbook of economic growth* (pp. 385–472). New York: North Holland.

Acemoglu, D., Johnson, S., Robinson, J. A., & Yared, Pierre. (2007, August). Reevaluating the modernization hypothesis. NBER Working Paper No. 13334.

Acemoglu, D., & Robinson, J. A. (2000). Why did the West extend the franchise? Democracy, inequality, and growth in historical perspective. *Quarterly Journal of Economics, 115*(4), 1167–1199.

Acemoglu, D., & Robinson, J. A. (2006). *Economic origins of dictatorship and democracy.* New York: Cambridge University Press.

Adams, Willi Paul. (1980). *The First American constitutions.* (Rita Kimber & Robert Kimber, Trans.). Chapel Hill: University of North Carolina Press.

Aldrich, John H. (1995). *Why parties: The origin and transformation of political parties in America.* Chicago: University of Chicago Press.

Alesina, Alberto, & Spolaore, Enrico. (2003). *The size of nations.* Cambridge, MA: MIT Press.

Allen, Robert C. (1992). *Enclosure and the yeoman.* New York: Oxford University Press.

Alston, Lee J., & Ferrie, Joseph. (1985). Labor costs, paternalism, and loyalty in southern agriculture: A constraint on the growth of the welfare state. *Journal of Economic History, XLV*(1), 95–117.

Anderson, Benedict. (2006[1983]). *Imagined communities: Reflections on the origin and spread of nationalism.* New York: Verso Books.

Anderson, Fred. (2000). *Crucible of war.* New York: Vintage Books.

Anderson, R. D. (1977). *France 1870–1914: Politics and society.* London: Routledge & Kegan Paul.

Annals of Congress. (1834). Published as *The debates and proceedings in the Congress of the United States with an appendix.* Washington: Gales and Seaton. From Library of

Congress collection *A century of lawmaking: Annals of Congress.* http://lcweb2.loc.gov/ammem/amlaw/lwaclink.html.

Bailyn, Bernard. (1965). *Pamphlets of the American Revolution.* Cambridge, MA: Harvard University Press.

Bailyn, Bernard. (1967). *The ideological origins of the American Revolution.* Cambridge, MA: Harvard University Press.

Bailyn, Bernard. (1968). *The origins of American politics.* New York: Vintage Books.

Bailyn, Bernard. (2004). *To begin the world anew: The genius and ambiguities of the American founders.* New York: Vintage Books.

Ballard, A. (1913). *British borough charters, 1042–1216.* Cambridge: Cambridge University Press.

Ballard, A., & Tait, J. (1923). *British borough charters, 1216–1307.* Cambridge: Cambridge University Press.

Baloyra, Enrique A. (1986). Public opinion and support for the regime: 1973–83. In John D. Martz and David J. Myers (Eds.), *Venezuela: The democratic experience,* rev. ed. New York: Praeger.

Bandy, Matthew S. (2004). Fissioning, scalar stress, and social evolution in early village societies. *American Anthropologist, 106*(2), 322–333.

Banning, Lance. (1978). *The Jeffersonian persuasion.* Ithaca: Cornell University Press.

Barro, Robert J. (1979). On the determination of the public debt. *Journal of Political Economy, 87*(5), 940–971.

Barro, Robert J. (1996). Democracy and growth. *Journal of Economic Growth, 1*(1), 1–27.

Barro, Robert J. (1999). Determinants of democracy. *Journal of Political Economy, 107*(6 part 2): S158–83.

Barzel, Yoram. (2001). *A theory of the state.* New York: Cambridge University Press.

Bates, Robert H. (2001). *Prosperity and violence: The political economy of development.* New York: W. W. Norton.

Bates, Robert H. (2008). *When things fell apart: State failure in late century Africa.* Cambridge: Cambridge University Press.

Bates, Robert H., Greif, Avner, & Singh, Smita. (2002). Organizing violence. *Journal of Conflict Resolution, 46*(5), 599–628.

Baumol, William J. (2002). *The free-market innovation machine: Analyzing the growth miracle of capitalism.* Princeton: Princeton University Press.

Bean, J. M. W. (1989). *From lord to patron: Lordship in late medieval England.* Philadelphia: University of Pennsylvania Press.

Bean, Richard. 1973. War and the birth of the nation state. *Journal of Economic History, 33*(1): 203–221.

Bell, H. E. (1953). *An introduction to the history and records of the court of wards & liveries.* Cambridge: Cambridge University Press.

Bellamy, J. G. (1973). *Crime and public order in England in the later Middle Ages.* Toronto: University of Toronto Press.

Bellamy, J. G. (1989). *Bastard feudalism and the law.* Portland, OR: Areopagitica Press.

Benson, Lee. (1961). *The concept of Jacksonian democracy: New York as a test case.* Princeton: Princeton University Press.

Berdan, Frances. (1982). *The Aztecs of central Mexico: An imperial society.* San Francisco: Holt, Reinhardt, and Wilson.

Berdan, Frances. (1985). Markets in the economy of Aztec Mexico. In Stuart Plattner (Ed.), *Markets and marketing*. Lanham, MD: University Press of America.

Berdan, Frances. (1987). The economics of Aztec luxury trade and tribute. In Elizabeth Hill Boone (Ed.), *The Aztec templo mayor*. Washington, DC: Dumbarton Oaks Research Library and Collection.

Berdan, Frances. (1996). The tributary provinces. In Michael E. Smith & Frances F. Berdan (Eds.), *Aztec imperial strategies* (pp. 47–84). Washington, DC: Dumbarton Oaks Research Library and Collection.

Berdan, Frances F., Blanton, Richard E., Boone, Elizabeth H., Hodge, Mary G., Smith, Michael E., & Umberger, Emily. (1996). *Aztec imperial strategies*. Washington, DC: Dumbarton Oaks Research Library and Collection.

Berman, Harold J. (1983). *Law and revolution: The formation of the Western legal tradition*. Cambridge, MA: Harvard University Press.

Berman, Sheri. (2006). *The primacy of politics: Social democracy and the making of Europe's twentieth century*. New York: Cambridge University Press.

Bernard, G. W. (1985). *The power of the early Tudor nobility: A study of the Fourth and Fifth Earls of Shrewsbury*. Brighton: Harvester Press.

Bertrand, Marianne, Djankov, Simeon, Hanna, Rema, & Mullainathan, Sendhil. (2007). Obtaining a driving license in India: An experimental approach to studying corruption. *Quarterly Journal of Economics, 122*(4), 1639–1676.

Bhagwati, Jagdish N. (1982). Directly unproductive profit-seeking (DUP) activities. *Journal of Political Economy, 90*(5): 988–1002.

Blanton, Richard E. (1996). The basin of Mexico market system and the growth of empire. In Michael E. Smith & Frances F. Berdan (Eds.), *Aztec imperial strategies* (pp. 47–84). Washington, DC: Dumbarton Oaks Research Library and Collection.

Blanton, Richard E., & Fargher, Lane F. (2008). *Collective action in the formation of premodern states*. New York: Springer.

Bloch, Marc. (1961). *Feudal society, 2 volumes*. (L. A. Manyon, Trans.). Chicago: University of Chicago Press.

Blum, Jerome. (1964). *Lord and peasant in Russia from the ninth to the nineteenth century*. New York: Atheneum.

Bodenhorn, Howard. (2006). Bank chartering and political corruption in ante-bellum New York: Free banking as reform. In Edward Glaeser & Claudia Goldin (Eds.), *Corruption and reform*. Chicago: University of Chicago Press.

Boehm, Christopher. (1999). *Hierarchy in the forest: The evolution of egalitarian behavior*. Cambridge, MA: Harvard University Press.

Bogart, Dan. (2005a). Did turnpike trusts increase transport investment in eighteenth-century England? *Journal of Economic History, 65*(2), 439–468.

Bogart, Dan. (2005b). Turnpike trusts and the transportation revolution in eighteenth-century England. *Explorations in Economic History, 42*(4), 479–508.

Boix, Carles. (2003). *Democracy and redistribution*. Cambridge: Cambridge University Press.

Bonney, Richard. (1981). *The king's debts: Finance and politics in France, 1589–1661*. New York: Oxford University Press.

Bossenga, Gail. (1991). *The politics of privilege: Old regime and revolution in Lille*. New York: Cambridge University Press.

Brantley, William H. (1961). *Banking in Alabama, 1816–1860, 2 volumes.* Birmingham: Birmingham Printing Co.

Brennan, Geoffrey, and Buchanan, James M. (1980). *The power to tax: Analytical foundations of a fiscal constitution.* New York: Cambridge University Press.

Brumfiel, Elizabeth. (1987). Elite and utilitarian crafts in the Aztec state. In Elizabeth Brumfiel & Timothy Earle (Eds.), *Specialization, exchange, and complex societies* (pp. 102–118). Cambridge: Cambridge University Press.

Brundage, Burr Cartwright. (1972). *A rain of darts: The Mexica Aztecs.* Austin: University of Texas Press.

Buchanan, James M., Tollison, Robert D., & Tullock, Gordon. (1980). *Toward a theory of the rent-seeking society.* College Station: Texas A&M University.

Bueno de Mesquita, Bruce, Smith, Alastair, Siverson, Randolph M., & Morrow, James D. (2003). *The logic of political survival.* Cambridge, MA: MIT Press.

Bulmer-Thomas, Ivor. (1953). *The party system in Great Britain.* London: Phoenix House.

Bulmer-Thomas, Ivor. (1965). *The growth of the British party system.* London: John Baker.

Burton, Michael, Gunther, Richard, & Higley, John. (1992). Introduction: Elite transformations and democratic regimes. In John Higley & Richard Gunther (Eds.), *Elites and democratic consolidation in Latin America and Southern Europe.* Cambridge: Cambridge University Press.

Butterfield, Herbert. (1965[1931]). *The Whig interpretation of history.* New York: W. W. Norton.

Cadman, John W. (1949). *The corporation in New Jersey: Business and politics, 1791–1875.* Cambridge: Harvard University Press.

Callender, Guy Stevens. (1902). The early transportation and banking enterprises of the states in relation to the growth of corporations. *Quarterly Journal of Economics, 17*(1), 111–162.

Campbell, Bruce M. S. (2000). *English seigniorial agriculture, 1250–1450.* Cambridge: Cambridge University Press.

Campbell, Peter. (1958). *French electoral systems and elections since 1789.* Hamden, CT: Archon Books.

Carlos, Ann, Neal, Larry, & Wandscheider, Kirsten. (2009). The origins of the national debt: The financing and re-financing of the War of Spanish Succession. Working Paper.

Carrasco, Pedro. (1999). *The Tenochca empire of ancient Mexico: The triple alliance of Tenochtitlan, Tetzcoco, and Tlacopan.* Norman: University of Oklahoma Press.

Caso, Alfonso. (1958). *The Aztecs: People of the sun.* Norman: University of Oklahoma Press.

Chang, Kwang-chih. (1983). *Art, myth, and ritual: The path to political authority in China.* Cambridge, MA: Harvard University Press.

Clanchy, M. T. (1965). *The treatise on the laws and customs of the realm of England commonly called Glanvill.* (G. D. G. Hall, Trans. & Ed.). London: Nelson.

Clark, Gregory. (2005). The condition of the working-class in England, 1209–2004. *Journal of Political Economy, 113*(6), 1307–1340.

Clark, Gregory. (2007a). The long march of history: Farm wages, population growth, and economic growth, England 1209–1869. *Economic History Review, 60*(1), 97–136.

Clark, Gregory. (2007b). *A farewell to alms: A brief economic history of the world.* Princeton: Princeton University Press.

Clark, Gregory. (2007c). A review of Avner Grief's *Institutions and the path to the modern economy: Lessons from medieval trade. Journal of Economic Literature, XLV*(3), 727–743.

Clark, J. C. D. (1985). *English society 1688–1832.* Cambridge: Cambridge University Press.

Coates, Dennis, Heckelman, Jac C., & Wilson, Bonnie. (2007). The determinants of interests group formation. *Public Choice, 133,* 377–391.

Cole, Arthur H. (1970). The committee on research in economic history: An historical sketch. *Journal of Economic History, 20*(4), 723–741.

Coleman, James S. (1974). *Power and the structure of society.* New York: W. W. Norton.

Coleman, James S. (1990). *Foundations of social theory.* Cambridge, MA: Harvard University Press.

Collins, James B. (1995). *The state in early modern France.* New York: Cambridge University Press.

Conrad, Geoffrey W., & Demarest, Arthur A. (1984). *Religion and empire: The dynamics of Aztec and Inca expansionism.* New York: Cambridge University Press.

Coss, P. R. (1989). Bastard feudalism revisited. *Past and Present, 125,* 27–64.

Cooper, J. P. (1983). *Land, men, and beliefs: Studies in early modern history.* (G. E. Aylmer & J. S. Morrill, Eds.). London: Hambledon Press.

Cox, Gary. (1987). *The efficient secret: The cabinet and the development of political parties in Victorian England.* New York: Cambridge University Press.

Cox, Gary. (1997). *Making votes count: Strategic coordination in the world's electoral systems.* New York: Cambridge University Press.

Crafts, N. F. R. (1998). Forging ahead and falling behind: The rise and relative decline of the first industrial nation. *Journal of Economic Perspectives, 12*(2), 193–210.

Creighton, Andrew L. (1990). *The emergence of incorporation as a legal form for organizations.* Unpublished doctoral dissertation, Stanford University.

Dahl, Robert A. (1962). *Who governs?* New Haven, CT: Yale University Press.

Dahl, Robert A. (1971). *Polyarchy: Participation and opposition.* New Haven, CT: Yale University Press.

Davis, John P. (1961). *Corporations: A study of the development of the origin and development of great business combinations and their relation to the authority of the state.* New York: Capricorn.

Davis, Joseph Stancliffe. (1917). *Essays in the earlier history of American corporations.* Cambridge, MA: Harvard University Press.

Davis, Lance, Easterlin, Richard A., & Parker, William N., et al. (1972). *American economic growth: An economist's history of the United States.* New York: Harper & Row.

De Soto, Hernando. (1989). *The other path: The economic answer to terrorism.* New York: Harper & Row.

De Soto, Hernando. (2000). *The mystery of capital: Why capitalism succeeds in the West and fails everywhere else.* New York: Basic Books.

de Vries, Jan, & Van DerWoude, Ad. (1997). *The first modern economy.* New York: Cambridge University Press.

Dickson, P. G. M. (1967). *The financial revolution in England: A study in the development of public credit, 1688–1756.* London: Macmillan.

Dietz, Frederick C. (1964). *English public finance, 1485–1641.* New York: Barnes & Noble.

Digby, Kenelm Edward. (1897). *An introduction to the history of the law of real property.* Oxford: Clarendon Press.

Dodd, Edwin Merrick. (1954). *American business corporations until 1860; with special reference to Massachusetts.* Cambridge, MA: Harvard University Press.

Doyle, William. (1996). *Venality: The sale of offices in eighteenth-century France.* New York: Oxford University Press.

Drelichman, Mauricio, & Voth, Hans-Joachim. (2008). The sustainable debts of Philip II: A reconstruction of Spain's fiscal position, 1560–1598. University of British Columbia Working Paper.

Drew, Katherine Fisher. (1991). *The laws of the Salian Franks.* Philadelphia: University of Pennsylvania Press.

Duff, P. W. (1938). *Personality in private law.* Cambridge: Cambridge University Press.

Dunbar, Robin. (1996). *Grooming, gossip, and the evolution of language.* Cambridge, MA: Harvard University Press.

Dunlavy, Colleen A. (2004). From citizens to plutocrats: Nineteenth-century shareholder voting rights and theories of the corporation. In Kenneth Lipartito & David B. Sicilia (Eds.), *Constructing corporate America: History, politics, and culture.* New York: Oxford University Press.

Duverger, Maurice. (1959). *Political parties: Their organization and activity in the modern state.* (Barbara & Robert North, Trans.). London: Methuen.

Earle, Timothy. (1997). *How chiefs come to power.* Stanford: Stanford University Press.

Earle, Timothy. (2003). *Bronze Age economics: The beginnings of political economies.* Boulder, CO: Westview Press.

Eggertsson, Thráinn. (2005). *Imperfect institutions: Possibilities and limits of reform.* Ann Arbor: University of Michigan Press.

Elton, G. R. (1977). *Reform and reformation: England 1509–1558.* Cambridge, MA: Harvard University Press.

Elton, G. R. (1991). *England under the Tudors.* New York: Routledge.

Engerman, Stanley E., & Sokoloff, Kenneth L. (2005). Colonialism, inequality, and long-run paths of development. NBER Working Paper 11057.

Ertman, Thomas. (1997). *Birth of the leviathan: Building states and regimes in early modern Europe.* New York: Cambridge University Press.

Esarey, Logan. (1918). *A history of Indiana: From its exploration to 1860.* Indianapolis: B. F. Bowen and Company.

Estevez-Abe, Margarita, Iversen, Torben, & Soskice, David. (2001). Social protection and the formation of skills: A reinterpretation of the welfare state. In Peter A. Hall & David Soskice (Eds.), *Varieties of capitalism: The institutional foundations of comparative advantage.* Oxford: Oxford University Press.

Evans, George Heberton. (1948). *Business incorporations in the United States, 1800–1943.* New York: NBER.

Evans-Pritchard, E. E. (1940). *The Nuer.* Princeton: Princeton University Press.

Fargher, Lane F., & Blanton, Richard E. (2007). Revenue, voice, and public goods in three premodern states. *Comparative Studies in Society and History, 49*(4), 848–882.

Fearon, James D. (2006). Self-enforcing democracy. Working Paper, Stanford University.

Feinman, Gary M., & Marcus, Joyce. (1998). *Archaic states.* Santa Fe, NM: School of American Research Press.

Feinstein, Charles H. (1998). Pessimism perpetuated: Real wages and the standard of living in Britain during and after the Industrial Revolution. *Journal of Economic History, 58*(3), 625–658.

Ferejohn, John, Rakove, Jack N., & Riley, Jonathan. (2001). *Constitutional culture and democratic rule.* New York: Cambridge University Press.

Ferguson, E. James. (1961). *The power of the purse.* Chapel Hill: University of North Carolina Press.

Ferguson, Niall. (2002). *The cash nexus: Money and power in the modern world.* New York: Basic Books.

Figgis, John Neville. (1923). *Studies of political thought from Gerson to Grotius 1414–1625, second edition.* Cambridge: Cambridge University Press.

Figgis, John Neville. (1960). *Political thought from Gerson to Grotius: 1414–1625.* New York: Harper and Brothers.

Fishback, Price V., & Kantor, Shawn Everett. (2000). *A prelude to the welfare state: The origins of workers' compensation.* Chicago: University of Chicago Press.

Fogel, Robert William. (2004). *The escape from hunger and premature death, 1700–2100: Europe, America, and the third world.* New York: Cambridge University Press.

Foord, Archibald S. (1964). *His majesty's opposition: 1714–1830.* Oxford: Clarendon Press.

Ford, Thomas. (1946). *A history of Illinois from its commencement as a state in 1818 to 1847. Vol. II.* Chicago: Lakeside Press.

Fortescue, Sir John. (1885). *The governance of England* (C. Plummer, Ed.). Oxford: Clarendon Press.

Freedeman, Charles E. (1961). *The Conseil d'État in modern France.* New York: Columbia University Press.

Freedeman, Charles E. (1979). *Joint-stock enterprise in France, 1807–1867: From privileged company to modern corporation.* Chapel Hill: University of North Carolina Press.

Freedeman, Charles E. (1993). *The triumph of corporate capitalism in France, 1867–1914.* Rochester: University of Rochester Press.

Freid, Morton H. (1967). *The evolution of political society: An essay in political anthropology.* New York: Random House.

Fukuyama, Francis. (1995). *Trust: The social virtues and the creation of prosperity.* New York: Free Press.

Galbraith, John Kenneth. (1956). *American capitalism.* New York: Houghton Mifflin.

Gallman, Robert E., & Wallis, John Joseph. (Eds.). (1992). *American economic growth and standards of living before the Civil War.* Chicago: NBER/University of Chicago Press.

Ganshof, Francois Louis. (1968). *Frankish institutions under Charlemagne.* (Bryce & Mary Lyon, Trans.). Providence: Brown University Press.

Garrett, Geoffrey. (1998). *Partisan politics in the global economy.* Cambridge: Cambridge University Press.

Gay, Peter. (1966). *The Enlightenment.* Volume 1: *The rise of modern paganism.* New York: W. W. Norton.

Gay, Peter. (1969). *The Enlightenment*. Volume 2: *The science of freedom*. New York: W. W. Norton.

Geary, Patrick J. (1988). *Before France and Germany: The creation and transformation of the Merovingian world*. New York: Oxford University Press.

Gellner, Ernest. (1983). *Nations and nationalism*. Ithaca: Cornell University Press.

Gellner, Ernest. (1994). *Conditions of liberty: Civil society and its rivals*. New York: Penguin Press.

Gierke, Otto. (1958[1900]). *Political theories of the Middle Age*. (F. W. Maitland. Trans.). Boston: Beacon Press. (Originally published by Cambridge University Press.)

Glaeser, Edward, LaPorta, Rafael, Lopes-de-Silanes, Florencio, & Shleifer, Andrei. (2004). Do institutions cause growth? *Journal of Economic Growth, 9*(3), 271–303.

Glaeser, Edward, & Shleifer, Andre. (2002). Legal origins. *Quarterly Journal of Economics, 117*, 1193–1230.

Goldman, Marshall. (2008). *Petrostate: Putin, power, and the New Russia*. Oxford: Oxford University Press.

Goodrich, Carter. (1960). *Government promotion of American canals and railroads*. New York: Columbia University Press.

Gray, Charles Montgomery. (1963). *Copyhold, equity, and the common law*. Cambridge, MA: Harvard University Press.

Gray, H. L. (1934). Incomes from land in England in 1436. *English Historical Review, 49*(196), 607–639.

Greif, Avner. (2006). *Institutions and the path to the modern economy*. New York: Cambridge University Press.

Guinnane, Timothy W., Harris, Ron, Lamoreaux, Naomi R., & Rosenthal, Jean-Laurent. (2007). Putting the corporation in its place. *Enterprise and Society, 8*(3), 687–729.

Gunn, L. Ray. (1988). *The decline of authority: Public economic policy and political development in New York, 1800–1860*. Ithaca: Cornell University Press.

Habakkuk, H. J. (1958). The market for monastic property, 1539–1603. *Economic History Review*, New Series, *10*(3), 362–380.

Habakkuk, H. J. (1965). Landowners and the Civil War. *Economic History Review*, New Series, *18*(1), 130–151.

Haber, Stephen H. (2006). Authoritarian government. In Barry R. Weingast & Donald Wittman (Eds.) *Handbook of political economy*. New York: Oxford University Press.

Haber, Stephen H., Klein, Herbert S., Maurer, Noel, & Middlebrook, Kevin J. (2008). *Mexico since 1980*. Cambridge: Cambridge University Press.

Haber, Stephen H., Razo, Armando, & Maurer, Noel. (2003). *The politics of property rights: Political instability, credible commitments, and economic growth in Mexico, 1976–1929*. Cambridge: Cambridge University Press.

Haggard, Stephan, & Kaufman, Robert. (1995). *The political economy of democratic transitions*. Princeton: Princeton University Press.

Hamilton, Alexander, Jay, John, and Madison, James. (n.d.[1787–88]). *The Federalist*. New York: Modern Library.

Handlin, Oscar, & Handlin, Mary Flug. (1969). *Commonwealth: A study of the role of government in the American economy: Massachusetts, 1774–1861*. Cambridge, MA: Belknap Press.

Hanley, David. (2002). *Party, society, and government: Republican democracy in France.* New York: Berghahn Books.

Harris, Ron. (1994). The Bubble Act: Its passage and effect on business organization. *Journal of Economic History, 54*(3), 610–627.

Harris, Ron. (1997). Political economy, interest groups, legal institutions, and the repeal of the Bubble Act in 1825. *Economic History Review, 50*(4), 675–696.

Harris, Ron. (2000). *Industrializing English law.* New York: Cambridge University Press.

Hartz, Louis. (1948). *Economic policy and democratic thought: Pennsylvania, 1776–1860.* Chicago: Quadrangle Books.

Hassig, Ross. (1988). *Aztec warfare: Imperial expansion and political control.* Norman: University of Oklahoma Press.

Hayek, Friedrich A. (1952). *The sensory order.* Chicago: University of Chicago Press.

Hayek, Friedrich A. (1960). *The constitution of liberty.* Chicago: University of Chicago Press.

Heath, Milton S. (1954). *Constructive liberalism: The role of the state in economic development in Georgia to 1860,* Cambridge, MA: Harvard University Press.

Heather, Peter. (1996). *The Goths.* Oxford: Blackwell Publishing.

Heather, Peter. (2006). *The fall of the Roman Empire.* New York: Oxford University Press.

Heckleman, Jac C., & Wallis, John Joseph. (1997). Railroads and property taxes. *Explorations in Economic History, 34*(1), 77–99.

Hegel, G. W. F. (1991[1820]). *Elements of the philosophy of right.* New York: Cambridge University Press.

Heston, Alan, Summers, Robert, & Aten, Bettina. (2006, September). *Penn world table version 6.2.* Philadelphia: Center for International Comparisons of Production, Income, and Prices at the University of Pennsylvania.

Hicks, Michael. (1995). *Bastard feudalism.* New York: Longman.

Historical statistics of the United States. (2006). Richard Sutch & Susan Carter (Eds.). New York: Cambridge University Press.

Hodge, Mary G. (1996). Political organization of the central provinces. In Michael E. Smith & Frances F. Berdan (Eds.), *Aztec imperial strategies* (pp. 13–46). Washington, DC: Dumbarton Oaks Research Library and Collection, 1996.

Hodges, Richard. (1989). *Dark age economics: The origins of town and trade A.D. 600–1000.* London: Gerald Duckworth & Company.

Hodges, Richard, & Whitehouse, David. (1983). *Mohammed, Charlemagne, & the origins of Europe: Archeology and the Pirenne hypothesis.* Ithaca: Cornell University Press.

Hoffman, Philip T., & Rosenthal, Jean-Laurent. (2000). New work in French economic history. *French Historical Studies, 23*(3), 439–453.

Hofstadter, Richard. (1969). *The idea of a party system.* Berkeley: University of California Press.

Holmes, George. (1957). *The estates of the higher nobility in fourteenth-century England.* Cambridge: Cambridge University Press.

Holt, Michael F. (1978). *The political crisis of the 1850s.* New York: John Wiley and Sons.

Holt, Michael F. (1999). *The rise and fall of the American Whig party: Jacksonian politics and the onset of the Civil War.* New York: Oxford University Press.

Hoyle, R. W. (Ed.). (1992). *The estates of the English crown, 1558–1640.* New York: Cambridge University Press.

Hughes, J. R. T. (1976). *Social control in the colonial economy.* Charlottesville: University of Virginia Press.

Hughes, J. R. T. (1977). What difference did the beginning make? *American Economic Review, 67*(1), 15–20.

Hume, David. (1987[1777]). *Essays: Moral, political, and literary.* Indianapolis: Liberty Fund.

Hurst, James Willard. (1964). *Law and the conditions of freedom in the nineteenth-century United States.* Madison: University of Wisconsin Press.

Hurst, James Willard. (1980). *The legitimacy of the business corporation.* Charlottesville: University of Virginia Press.

Hurstfield, Joel. (1949). Lord Burghley as master of the court of wards, 1561–1598. *Transactions of the Royal Historical Society,* Fourth Series, *31,* 95–114.

Hurstfield, Joel. (1953). Corruption and reform under Edward VI and Mary: The example of wardship. *English Historical Review, 68*(266), 22–36.

Hurstfield, Joel. (1955). The profits of fiscal feudalism, 1541–1602. *Economic History Review,* New Series, *8*(1), 53–61.

Iversen, Torben. (2005). *Capitalism, democracy, and welfare.* Cambridge: Cambridge University Press.

Iversen, Torben, and Soskice, David. (2001). An asset theory of social policy preferences. *American Political Science Review, 95*(4): 875–893.

Jha, Saumitra. (2008, August), "Shares, coalition formation and political development: evidence from 17th century England," Stanford GSB Research Paper No. 2005.

John, Eric. (1960). *Land tenure in early England: A discussion of some problems.* Welwyn Garden City: Leicester University Press.

Johnson, Allen W., & Earle, Timothy. (2000). *The evolution of human societies,* 2nd edition. Stanford: Stanford University Press.

Johnson, Gregory A. (1982). Organizational structure and scalar stress. In Colin Renfrew, Michael J. Rowlands, & Barbara Abbott Segraves (Eds.), *Theory and explanation in archaeology.* New York: Academic Press.

Jones, Eric. (1981). *The European miracle.* New York: Cambridge University Press.

Jones, J. R. (1972). *The revolution of 1688 in England.* New York: W. W. Norton.

Kantorowicz, Ernst H. (1997[1957]). *The king's two bodies: A study in mediaeval political theology.* Princeton: Princeton University Press.

Katzenstein, Peter. (1985). *Small states in world markets: Industrial policy in Europe.* Ithaca: Cornell University Press.

Keefer, Philip. (2004). Democratization and clientelism: Why are young democracies badly governed? Development Research Group, World Bank Working Paper Series No. 3594.

Keefer, Philip, & Vlaicu, Razvan. (2005, January). Democracy, credibility and clientelism. World Bank Working Paper 3472.

Keely, Lawrence H. (1996). *War before civilization.* New York: Oxford University Press.

Keller, Morton. (2007). *America's three regimes: A new political history.* Oxford: Oxford University Press.

Kelly, Robert L. (1995). *The foraging spectrum: Diversity in hunter-gatherer lifeways.* Washington, DC: Smithsonian Institution Press.

Kennedy, David M. (1999). *Freedom from fear: The American people in depression and war, 1929–1945.* New York: Oxford University Press.

Kettering, Sharon. (1986). *Patrons, brokers, and clients in seventeenth-century France.* New York: Oxford University Press.

Keyssar, Alexander. (2000). *The right to vote: The contested history of democracy in America.* New York: Basic Books.

Khan, Mushtaq. (2004). State failure in developing countries and institutional reform strategies. *Annual World Bank Conference on Development Economics – Europe 2003.* Washington, DC: International Bank for Reconstruction and Development/World Bank.

Khan, Mushtaq. (2005). Markets, states, and democracy: Patron–client networks and the case for democracy in developing countries. *Democratization, 12*(5), 704–724.

Khan, Mushtaq. (2006, November 11–12). Governance and development. Paper presented at the Workshop on Government and Development, World Bank, Dhaka.

Khan, Mushtaq, & Jomo, KS. (2000). *Rents, rent-seeking, and economic development.* New York: Cambridge University Press.

Kishlansky, Mark A. (1986). *Parliamentary selection: social and political choice in early modern England.* New York: Cambridge University Press.

Klerman, Daniel. (2007). Jurisdictional competition and the evolution of the common law. *University of Chicago Law Review, 74*(Fall), 1179–1226.

Knack, Steven, & Keefer, Philip. (1995). Institutions and economic performance: Cross-country tests using alternative measures. *Economics and Politics, 7*(3), 207–227.

Knack, Steven, & Keefer, Philip. (1997). Does social capital have an economic payoff: A cross-country investigation. *Quarterly Journal of Economics, 112*(4), 1251–1288.

Kosminsky, E. (1931). The hundred rolls of 1279–80 as a source for English agrarian history. *Economic History Review, 3*(1), 16–44.

Kramer, Gerald H. (1971). Short-term fluctuations in U.S. voting behavior. *American Political Science Review, 65*(1), 131–143.

Kramnick, Isaac. (1968). *Bolingbroke and his circle: The politics of nostalgia in the age of Walpole.* Cambridge, MA: Harvard University Press.

Kreuzer, Marcus. (2001). *Institutions and innovation: Voters, parties, and interest groups in the consolidation of democracy – France and Germany, 1870–1939.* Ann Arbor: University of Michigan Press.

Krueger, Anne O. (1990). The political economy of controls: American sugar. In M. Scott & D. Lal (Eds.), *Public choice and economic development: Essays in honor of Ian Little.* Oxford: Clarendon Press.

Kruman, Marc W. (1997). *Between authority and liberty: State constitution making in revolutionary America.* Chapel Hill: University of North Carolina Press.

Kurov, Andrey. (2008). Anatomy of crisis: Political aspects of macroeconomic policies and reforms in Russia, 1994–2004. Unpublished doctoral dissertation, Department of Political Science, Stanford University.

Kwass, Michael. (2000). *Privilege and the politics of taxation in eighteenth-century France.* New York: Cambridge University Press.

Lamoreaux, Naomi. (2004). Partnerships, corporations, and the limits on contractual freedom in U.S. history: An essay in economics, law, and culture. In Kenneth Lipartito & David B. Sicilia (Eds.), *Constructing corporate America: History, politics, and culture.* New York: Oxford University Press.

Lamoreaux, Naomi, & Rosenthal, Jean-Laurent. (2004, February). Legal regime and business's organizational choice. NBER Working Paper No. 10288.

Lamoreaux, Naomi R., & Rosenthal, Jean-Laurent. (2005). Legal regime and contractual flexibility: A comparison of business's organizational choices in France and the United States during the era of industrialization. *American Law and Economics Review, 7*(1), 28–61.

Landau, Martin. (1969). Redundancy, rationality, and the problem of duplication and overlap. *Public Administration Review, 29*(4), 346–358.

Landes, David. (1999). *The wealth and poverty of nations.* New York: W. W. Norton.

La Porta, Rafael, Lopes-de-Silanes, F., Shleifer, Andre, & Vishny, Robert. (1998). Law and finance. *Journal of Political Economy, 106*(6), 1113–1155.

Larson, John Lauritz. (2001). *Internal improvement: National public works and the promise of popular government in the early United States.* Chapel Hill: University of North Carolina Press.

Lebergott, Stanley. (1984). *The Americans: An economic record.* New York: W. W. Norton.

LeBlanc, Steven A. (2003). *Constant battles: The myth of the peaceful, noble savage.* New York: St. Martin's Press.

Leggett, William. (1984). *Democratick editorials: Essays in Jacksonian political economy.* Indianapolis: Liberty Press.

Leon-Portilla, Miguel. (1963). *Aztec thought and culture.* (Jack Emory Davis, Trans.). Norman: University of Oklahoma Press.

Leonard, Gerald. (2002). *The invention of party politics: Federalism, popular sovereignty, and constitutional development in Jacksonian Illinois.* Chapel Hill: University of North Carolina Press.

Levi, Margaret. (1988). *Of rule and revenue.* Berkeley: University of California Press.

Levi, Margaret. (1997). *Consent, dissent, and patriotism.* New York: Cambridge University Press.

Levitt, Steven D., & Dubner, Stephen J. (2005). *Freakonomics: A rogue economist explains the hidden side of everything.* New York: William Morrow.

Lindert, Peter H. (2004). *Growing public: Social spending and economic growth since the eighteenth century.* Cambridge: Cambridge University Press.

Lipset, Seymour Martin. (1959). Some social requisites of democracy: Economic development and political legitimacy. *American Political Science Review, 53*(1), 69–105.

Lipset, Seymour Martin. (1963). *Political man: The social bases of politics.* Garden City: Anchor Books.

Lively, Robert A. (1955). The American system: A review article. *Business History Review, 29*(1), 81–96.

Livy. (1998). *The rise of Rome, Books 1–5.* New York: Oxford University Press.

Lockhart, James. (1992). *The Nahuas after the conquest: A social and cultural history of the Indians of Central Mexico.* Stanford: Stanford University Press.

Londregan, John B., & Poole, Keith. (1990). Poverty, the coup trap, and the seizure of executive power. *World Politics, 42*(2), 151–183.

Lutz, Donald S. (1988). *The origins of American constitutionalism.* Baton Rouge: Louisiana State University Press.

Machiavelli, Niccolo. (1854). *The History of Florence.* London: Bohn.

Machiavelli, Niccolo. (1988). *The prince.* (Quentin Skinner & Russell Price, Eds.). New York: Cambridge University Press.

Machiavelli, Niccolo. (1996). *Discourses on Livy.* (Harvey C. Mansfield & Nathan Tarcov, Trans.). Chicago: University of Chicago Press.

Maier, Pauline. (1993). The revolutionary origins of the American corporation. *William and Mary Quarterly,* Third Series, *50*(1), 51–84.

Maitland, F. W. (1963[1908]). *The constitutional history of England.* Cambridge: Cambridge University Press.

Maitland, F. W. (1968[1909]). *The forms of action at common law.* In A. J. Chaytor & W. J. Whittaker (Eds.), *Medieval sourcebook.* Cambridge: Cambridge University Press.

Maitland, F. W. (2003). *State, trust, and corporation.* (David Runciman & Magnus Ryan, Eds.). New York: Cambridge University Press.

Mares, Isabela. (2003). *The politics of social risk: Business and welfare state development.* Cambridge: Cambridge University Press.

Margo, Robert A. (2000). *Wages and labor in the United States, 1820 to 1860.* Chicago: University of Chicago Press.

Marshall, Monty G., & Jaggers, Keith. (2005). *Polity IV project: Political regime characteristics and transitions, 1800–2004.* Arlington, VA: Center for Global Policy.

Mathias, Peter, & O'Brien, Patrick K. (1976). Taxation in Britain and France, 1715–1810: A comparison of the social and economic incidence of taxes collected for the central governments. *Journal of European Economic History, 5*(3), 601–650.

McCloskey, Dierdre N. (2006). *The bourgeois virtues: Ethics for an age of commerce.* Chicago: University of Chicago Press.

McCormick, Michael. (2001). *Origins of the European economy: Communications and commerce A.D. 300–900.* New York: Cambridge University Press.

McCormick, Richard L. (1986). *The party period and public policy: American politics from the age of Jackson to the progressive era.* New York: Oxford University Press.

McCoy, Drew R. (1980). *Elusive republic: Political economy in Jeffersonian America.* Chapel Hill: University of North Carolina Press.

McFarlane, K. B. (1973). *The nobility of later medieval England.* Oxford: Clarendon Press.

McFarlane, K. B. (1981). *England in the fifteenth century.* London: Hambledon Press.

McKee, Samuel. (1957[1934]). *Alexander Hamilton's papers on public credit commerce and finance.* New York: Liberal Arts Press (reprint of original Columbia University Press).

McNeill, William H. (1982). *The pursuit of power: Technology, armed force, and society since A.D. 1000.* Chicago: University of Chicago Press.

Meisel, Nicolas, & Ould Aoudia, Jacques. (2008, January). Is 'good governance' good development strategy? Working Paper No. 58, Agence Francaise de Dèvelopment.

Meltzer, Allan H., & Richard, Scott F. (1981). A rational theory of the size of government. *Journal of Political Economy, 89*(5), 914–927.

Meyer, John W. (1994). Rationalized environments. In W. Richard Scott & John W. Meyer (Eds.), *Institutionalized environments and organizations.* New York: Sage Publications.

Meyer, John W., Boli, John, & Thomas, George M. (1987). Ontology and rationalization in the western cultural account. In G. Thomas, J. Meyer, F. Ramirez, & J. Boli (Eds.), *Institutional structure: Constituting state, society, and the individual.* New York: Sage Publications.

Milgrom, Paul, & Roberts, John. (1992). *Economics, organization, and management.* Englewood Cliffs, NJ: Prentice-Hall.

Miller, Nathan. (1962). *The enterprise of a free people: Aspects of economic development in New York State during the canal period, 1792–1838.* Ithaca: Cornell University Press.

Milsom, S. F. C. (1969). *Historical foundations of the common law.* London: Butterworths.

Milsom, S. F. C. (1976). *The legal framework of English feudalism.* Cambridge: Cambridge University Press.

Milsom, S. F. C. (2003). *Natural history of the common law.* New York: Columbia University Press.

Mital, Sonia. (2008). A necessary precaution: The separation of powers and political stability in America. Unpublished Working Paper, Department of Political Science, Stanford University.

Mobarak, Ahmed Mushfiq. (2005). Democracy, volatility, and development. *Review of Economics and Statistics, 87*(2), 348–361.

Mokyr, Joel. (1990). *The lever of riches: Technological creativity and economic progress.* Oxford: Oxford University Press.

Mokyr, Joel. (2002). *The gifts of Athena: The historical origins of the knowledge economy.* Princeton: Princeton University Press.

Mokyr, Joel. (2009). *The enlightened economy: An economic history of Britain, 1700–1850.* New Haven, CT: Yale University Press.

Munro, J. (1977). Industrial protectionism in medieval Flanders: Urban or national? In H. A. Miskimin, D. Herlihy, & A. L. Udovitch (Eds.), *The medieval city.* New Haven CT: Yale University Press.

Munro, J. (1990). Urban regulation and monopolistic competition in the textile industries of the late-medieval low countries. In E. Aerts, & J. Munro (Eds.), *Textiles of the low countries in European economic history.* Studies in Social and Economic History, vol. 19. Leuven: Leuven University Press, pp. 41–52.

Myerson, Roger B. (2008). The autocrat's credibility problem and foundations of the constitutional state. *American Political Science Review, 102*(01), 125–139.

Namier, Lewis. (1957). *The structure of politics and the accession of George III (second edition).* New York: St. Martin's Press.

Namier, Lewis. (1966). *England in the age of the American revolution (second edition).* New York: St. Martin's Press.

Namier, Lewis, & Brooke, John. (1964). *The House of Commons, 1754–1790.* London: History of the Parliament Trust.

Neal, Larry. (1990). *The rise of financial capitalism: International capital markets in the Age of Reason.* Cambridge: Cambridge University Press.

North, Douglass C. (1961). *The economic growth of the United States: 1790–1860.* New York: W. W. Norton.

North, Douglass C. (1981). *Structure and change in economic history.* New York: W. W. Norton.

North, Douglass C. (1988). Institutions and economic growth: An historical introduction. In Michael A. Walker (Ed.), *Freedom, democracy, and economic welfare.* Canada: Fraser Institute.

North, Douglass C. (1990). *Institutions, institutional change, and economic performance.* New York: Cambridge University Press.

North, Douglass C. (2005). *Understanding the process of economic change.* Princeton: Princeton University Press.

North, Douglass C., Summerhill, William, & Weingast, Barry R. (2000). Order, disorder, and economic change: Latin America vs. North America. In Bruce Bueno de Mesquita & Hilton Root (Eds.), *Governing for prosperity,* New Haven: Yale University Press.

North, Douglass C., Wallis, John Joseph, Webb, Stephen B., & Weingast, Barry R. (2007) Limited access orders in the developing world: A new approach to the problems of development. World Bank Policy Research Working Paper 4359.

North, Douglass C., Wallis, John Joseph, and Weingast, Barry R. (2009). Violence, natural states, and open access orders *Journal of Democracy 20*(1), forthcoming.

North, Douglass C., & Weingast, Barry R. (1989). Constitutions and commitment: The evolution of institutions governing public choice in 17th century England. *Journal of Economic History, 49*(4), 803–832.

Oates, Wallace. (1972). *Fiscal federalism.* New York: Harcourt Brace Jovanovich.

Ober, Josiah. (2008). *Democracy and knowledge: Innovation and learning in classical Athens.* Princeton: Princeton University Press.

O'Brien, Patrick K. (1988). The political economy of British taxation, 1660–1815. *The Economic History Review,* New Series, *41*(1), 1–32.

O'Donnell, Guillermo, & Schmitter, Philippe C. (1986). *Transitions from authoritarian rule: Tentative conclusion about uncertain democracies.* Baltimore: Johns Hopkins University Press.

Olson, Mancur. (1965). *Logic of collective action.* Cambridge, MA: Harvard University Press.

Olson, Mancur. (1982). *The rise and decline of nations.* New Haven, CT: Yale University Press.

Olson, Mancur. (1993). Democracy, dictatorship, and development. *American Political Science Review, 87*(3), 567–575.

Parker, Geoffrey. (1996). *The military revolution: Military innovation and the rise of the west, 2nd edition.* New York: Cambridge University Press.

Patterson, Margaret, & Reiffen, David. (1990). The effect of the Bubble Act on the market for joint-stock shares. *Journal of Economic History, 50*(1), 163–171.

Pederson, Jesper Strandgaard, & Dobbin, Frank. (1997). The social invention of collective actors: On the rise of organizations. *American Behavioral Scientist, 40*(4), 431–443.

Perrow, Charles. (2002). *Organizing America: Wealth, power, and the origins of corporate capitalism.* Princeton: Princeton University Press.

Persson, Torsten, & Tabellini, Guido. (2000). *Political economics: Explaining economic policy.* Cambridge, MA: MIT Press.

Pirenne, Henri. (2001[1954]). *Mohammed and Charlemagne.* Mineola, NY: Dover Press. (F. Vercauteren, Trans.). Originally published in English by George Allen and Unwin.

Pocock, J. G. A. (1975). *The Machiavellian moment: Florentine political thought and the Atlantic republican tradition.* Princeton: Princeton University Press.

Pollard, A. J. (1988). *The Wars of the Roses.* New York: St. Martin's Press.

Pollock, Frederick, & Maitland, Frederic William. (1899). *The history of English law before the time of Edward I, second edition, 2 volumes.* Cambridge: Cambridge University Press.

Pomeranz, Kenneth. (2000). *The great divergence: China, Europe, and the making of the modern world economy.* Princeton: Princeton University Press.

Prasad, Monica. (2006). *The politics of free markets: The rise of neoliberal economic policies in Britain, France, Germany and the United States.* Chicago: University of Chicago Press.

Primm, James N. (1954). *Economic policy in the development of a western state: Missouri, 1820–1860.* Cambridge, MA: Harvard University Press.

Przeworski, Adam. (1991). *Democracy and the market.* Cambridge: Cambridge University Press.

Przeworski, Adam, Alvarez, Michael E., Cheibub, Jose Antonio, & Limongi, Fernando. (2000). *Democracy and development: Political institutions and well-being in the world, 1950–1990.* Cambridge: Cambridge University Press.

Putnam, Robert. (1993). *Making democracy work.* Princeton: Princeton University Press.

Putnam, Robert. (2000). *Bowling alone: The collapse and revival of American community.* New York: Simon & Schuster.

Quinn, Stephen. (October 21, 2006). Securitization of sovereign debt: Corporations as a sovereign debt restructuring mechanism in Britain, 1688–1750. Paper delivered at the Conference on Financial History, UCLA.

Ramey, Garey, & Ramey, Valerie A. (1995). Cross-country evidence on the link between volatility and growth. *American Economic Review, 85*(5), 1138–1151.

Rappaport, Roy A. (1968). *Pigs for the ancestors: Ritual in the ecology of a New Guinea people.* New Haven, CT: Yale University Press.

Remini, Robert V. (1967). *Andrew Jackson and the bank war: A study in the growth of presidential power.* New York: W.W. Norton.

Remini, Robert V. (1981). *Andrew Jackson: Vol. 2. The course of American freedom.* Baltimore: Johns Hopkins University Press.

Richardson, Gary. (2001). A tale of two theories: Monopolies and craft guilds in medieval England and modern imagination. *Journal of History of Economic Thought, 23*(2), 217–242.

Richardson, Gary. (2004). Guilds, laws, and markets for manufactured merchandise in late medieval England. *Explorations in Economic History, 41*(1), 1–25.

Richardson, James D. (1897). *A compilation of the messages and papers of the presidents.* Washington, DC: National Bureau of Literature.

Riesenberg, Peter N. (1956). *Inalienability of sovereignty in medieval political thought.* New York: Columbia University Press.

Riker, William H. (1982a). *Liberalism against populism.* San Francisco: W. H. Freeman.

Riker, William H. (1982b). The two party system and Duverger's law: An essay in the history of political science. *American Political Science Review, 76*(4), 753–766.

Rivers, Theodore John. (1986). *The laws of the Salic and Ripuarian Franks.* New York: AMS Press.

Robinson, James. (October 21, 2006). Debt repudiation and risk premia: The North-Weingast thesis revisited. Paper delivered at the Conference on Financial History, UCLA.

Roberts, Michael. (1967). *Essays in Swedish history.* Minneapolis: University of Minnesota Press.

Rodger, N. A. M. (1986). *The wooden world: An anatomy of the Georgian Navy.* New York: W. W. Norton.

Rodger, N. A. M. (1997). *The safeguard of the sea: A naval history of Britain, 660–1649.* New York: W. W. Norton.

Rodger, N. A. M. (2004). *The command of the ocean: A naval history of Britain, 660–1649.* New York: W. W. Norton.

Rodrik, Dani. (1999). Where did all the growth go? External shocks, social conflict and growth collapses. *Journal of Economic Growth, 4*(4), 385–412.

Rodrik, Dani. (2007). *One economics, many recipes: Globalization, institutions, and economic growth.* Princeton: Princeton University Press.

Rodrik, Dani, Subramanian, A., & Trebbi, F. (2004). Institutions rule: The primacy of institutions over geography and integration in economic development. *Journal of Economic Growth, 9*(2), 131–165.

Rogers, Clifford. (1995). *The military revolution debate.* Boulder, CO: Westfield Press.

Rogowski, Ronald. (1987). Trade and the variety of democratic institutions. *International Organization, 41*(2), 203–223.

Rogowski, Ronald. (1989). *Commerce and coalitions.* Princeton: Princeton University Press.

Root, Hilton. (1994). *The fountain of privilege: Political foundations of economic markets in old regime France and England.* Berkeley: University of California Press.

Rosenberg, Nathan, & Birdzell, L. E. (1986). *How the West grew rich.* New York: Basic Books.

Rosenblum, Nancy L. (1998). *Membership and morals: The personal uses of pluralism in America.* Princeton: Princeton University Press.

Rostow, Walt Whitman. (1960). *The stages of economic growth: A non-communist manifesto.* Cambridge: Cambridge University Press.

Roy, William G. (1997). *Socializing capital: The rise of the large industrial corporation in America.* Princeton: Princeton University Press.

Rutland, Robert A. et al., (Eds.). (1983). *The papers of James Madison, vol. 14: 6 April 1791–16 March 1793,* Charlottesville, Va.: University of Virginia Press, pp. 157–169.

Scheiber, Harry N. (1969). *Ohio canal era: A case study of government and the economy, 1820–1861.* Athens, Ohio: The Ohio State University Press.

Schelling, Thomas C. (1960). *Strategy of conflict.* Cambridge, MA: Harvard University Press.

Schultz, Kenneth A., & Weingast, Barry R. (2003). The democratic advantage: The institutional sources of state power in international competition. *International Organization, 57,* 3–42.

Schumpeter, Joseph A. (1942). *Capitalism, socialism, and democracy.* New York: Harper Colophon.

Schwoerer, Lois. (1981). *The declaration of rights, 1689.* Baltimore: Johns Hopkins University Press.

Scott, J. (1917). Limitations of guild monopoly. *American Historical Review, 22*(April), 586–589.

Scott, James C. (1972). *Comparative political corruption.* Englewood Cliffs, NJ: Prentice-Hall.

Scott, James C. (1987). *Weapons of the weak.* New Haven, CT: Yale University Press.

Scott, W. Richard. (2001). *Institutions and organizations, second edition.* New York: Sage Publications.

Scott, William Robert. (1951[1912]). *The constitution and finance of English, Scottish and Irish joint-stock companies to 1720: 3 volumes.* New York: Peter Smith. (Reprinted from the Cambridge University Press original).

Seavoy, Ronald E. (1982). *The origins of the American business corporation, 1784–1855.* Westport: Greenwood Press.

Service, Elman R. (1971). *Primitive social organization: An evolutionary perspective,* second edition. New York: Random House.

Service, Elman R. (1975). *Origins of the state and civilization: The process of cultural evolution.* New York: W.W. Norton.

Sheehan, Colleen A. (1992). The politics of public opinion: James Madison's "Notes on government." *The William and Mary Quarterly,* Third Series, *49*(4), 609–627.

Shin, Doh Chull. 2000. The evolution of popular support for democracy during Kim Young Sam's government. In Larry Diamond & Doh Chull Shin (Eds.), *Institutional reform and democratic consolidation in Korea.* Stanford, CA: Hoover Institution Press.

Silbey, Joel H. (1967). *The transformation of American politics, 1840–1960.* Englewood Cliffs, NJ: Prentice-Hall.

Silbey, Joel H. (1985). *The partisan imperative: The dynamics of American politics before the Civil War.* New York: Oxford University Press.

Silbey, Joel H. (1991). *The American political nation.* Stanford: Stanford University Press.

Simpson, A. W. B. (1986). *A history of the land law, second edition.* Oxford: Clarendon Press.

Skinner, Quentin. (1978). *Foundations of modern political thought, 2 volumes.* New York: Cambridge University Press.

Skinner, Quentin. (1998). *Liberty before liberalism.* New York: Cambridge University Press.

Skinner, Quentin. (2002). *Visions of politics.* Cambridge: Cambridge University Press.

Smith, Adam. (1981[1776]). *The wealth of nations.* Indianapolis: Liberty Fund.

Smith, Michael E. (2001). The Aztec empire and the Mesoamerican world system. In Susan E. Alcock, Terence N. D'Altroy, Kathleen D. Morrison, & Carla M. Sinopoli (Eds.), *Empires: Perspectives from archaeology and history* (pp. 128–154). New York: Cambridge University Press.

Smith, Michael E. (2003). *The Aztecs, second edition.* Oxford: Blackwell Publishers.

Smith, Michael E. (2004). The archaeology of ancient state economies. *Annual Review of Anthropology, 33,* 73–102.

Smith, Michael E., & Montiel, Lisa. (2001). The archaeological study of empires and imperialism in pre-Hispanic Central Mexico. *Journal of Anthropological Archaeology, 20*(3), 245–284.

Spiller, Pablo T., & Tommasi, Mariano. (2007). *The institutional foundations of public policy in Argentina.* Cambridge: Cambridge University Press.

Spruyt, Hendrik. (1994). *The sovereign state and its competitors.* Princeton: Princeton University Press.

Stasavage, David. (2003). *Public debt and the birth of the democratic state: France and Great Britain, 1688–1789.* Cambridge: Cambridge University Press.

Stasavage, David. (2006, October 21). Cites, constitutions, and sovereign borrowing in Europe, 1274–1785. Paper delivered at the Conference on Financial History, UCLA.

Steckel, Richard H., & Rose, Jerome C. (2002). *The backbone of history: Health and nutrition in the western hemisphere.* New York: Cambridge University Press.

Steckel, Richard H., & Wallis, John. (2006). Stones, bones, and states. Working Paper.

Stein, Ernesto and Tommasi, Pablo (Eds.). (2006). *The politics of policies: Economic and social progress in Latin America.* Washington, DC: Inter-American Development Bank.

Stenton, F. M. (1963[1932]). *The first century of English feudalism 1066–1166.* Oxford: Clarendon Press.

Stepan, Alfred. (2004). Toward a new comparative politics of federalism, multinationalism, and democracy: Beyond Rikerian federalism. In Edward L. Gibson (Ed.), *Federalism and democracy in Latin America.* Baltimore: Johns Hopkins University Press.

Stewart, John Hall. (1951). *A documentary survey of the French Revolution.* New York: Macmillan Company.

Stone, Lawrence. (1965). *The crisis of the aristocracy 1558–1641.* Oxford: Clarendon Press.

Stone, Lawrence. (2002). *Causes of the English Revolution, 1529–1642.* New York: Routledge.

Sussman, Nathan, & Yafeh, Yishay. (2006). Institutional reforms, financial development, and sovereign debt: Britain, 1690–1790. *Journal of Economic History, 66*(4), 906–935.

Swanson, H. (1988). The illusion of economic structure: Craft guilds in late medieval English towns. *Past and Present, 121*(1), 29–48.

Swanson, H. (1989). *Medieval artisans: An urban class in late medieval England.* Oxford: Oxford University Press.

Swanson, H. (1999). *Medieval British towns.* New York: St. Martin's Press.

Swensen, Peter. (2002). *Employers against markets.* Cambridge: Cambridge University Press.

Sylla, Richard, Legler, John B., & Wallis, John Joseph. (1987). Banks and state public finance in the new republic. *Journal of Economic History, 47*(2), 391–403.

Syme, Ronald. (1939). *The Roman revolution.* Oxford: Oxford University Press.

Tarr, G. Alan. (1998). *Understanding state constitutions.* Princeton: Princeton University Press.

Tawney, R. H. (1941). The rise of the gentry, 1558–1640. *Economic History Review, 11*(1), 1–38.

Taylor, George Rogers. (1951). *The transportation revolution, 1815–1860.* New York: Holt, Rinehart, and Winston.

Thomas, David. (1977). Leases in reversion on the Crown's lands, 1558–1603. *Economic History Review,* New Series, *30*(1), 67–72.

Thompson, F. M. L. (1966) The social distribution of landed property in England since the sixteenth century. *Economic History Review,* Second series *19,* 505–517.

Thorne, S. E. (1959). English feudalism and estates in land. *Cambridge Law Journal,* 193–209.

Thrupp, S. (1948). *The merchant class of medieval London 1300–1500.* Chicago: University of Chicago Press.

Tiebout, Charles. (1956). A pure theory of local expenditures. *Journal of Political Economy, 64*(5), 416–24.

Tierney, Brian. (1955[1968]). *Foundations of the conciliar theory.* New York: Cambridge University Press.

Tilly, Charles. (1992). *Coercion, capital, and European states: 990–1992.* Malden, MA: Blackwell Publishing.

Tilly, Charles. (1996). *Citizenship, identity, and social history.* New York: Cambridge University Press.

Tilly, Charles. (2005a). *Trust and rule.* New York: Cambridge University Press.

Tilly, Charles. (2005b). *Identities, boundaries, and social ties.* Boulder, CO: Paradigm Publishers.

de Tocqueville, Alexis. (1969[1835]). *Democracy in America.* New York: Doubleday Anchor.

Tombs, Robert. (1996). *France 1814–1914.* New York: Longman.

Trenchard, John, & Gordon, Thomas. (1995). *Cato's letters.* (Ronald Hamowry, Ed.). Indianapolis: Liberty Fund.

Trigger, Bruce G. (2003). *Understanding early civilizations.* Cambridge: Cambridge University Press.

Truman, David. (1952). *The governmental process.* New York: Alfred Knopf.

Tsebelis, George. (2002). *Veto players: How political institutions work.* Princeton: Princeton University Press.

Tufte, Edward R. (1978). *Political control over the economy.* Princeton: Princeton University Press.

Ullman, Walter. (1969). *The Carolingian renaissance and the idea of kingship.* London: Methuen & Co.

Ullman, Walter. (1972a[1938]). *The origins of the great schism.* Hamden, CT: Archon Books.

Ullman, Walter. (1972b). *A short history of the papacy in the Middle Ages.* New York: Routledge.

Ullman, Walter. (1975). *Law and politics in the Middle Ages.* Ithaca: Cornell University Press.

Van Gelderen, Martin, & Skinner, Quentin. (2002). *Republicanism: A shared European heritage, 2 volumes.* New York: Cambridge University Press.

Veitch, John M. (1986). Repudiations and confiscations by the medieval state. *Journal of Economic History, 46*(1): 31–36.

Vinogradoff, Paul. (1905). *The growth of the manor.* London: Swan Sonnenschein & Co.

Vinogradoff, Paul. (1908). *English society in the eleventh century: Essays in medieval history.* Oxford: Clarendon Press.

Vinogradoff, Paul. (1923). *Villainage in England: Essays in medieval history.* New York: Russell & Russell.

Wallace, Michael. (1968). Changing concepts of party in the United States, 1815–1828. *American Historical Review, 74*(2), 453–491.

Wallis, John Joseph. (2003). Market augmenting government? The state and the corporation in 19th century America. In Omar Azfar & Charles Cadwell (Eds.), *Market-augmenting government: The institutional foundations for prosperity.* Ann Arbor: University of Michigan Press.

Wallis, John Joseph. (2005). Constitutions, corporations, and corruption: American states and constitutional change, 1842 to 1852. *Journal of Economic History, 65*(1), 211–256.

Wallis, John Joseph. (2006). The concept of systematic corruption in American economic and political history. In Edward Glaeser & Claudia Goldin (Eds.), *Corruption and reform.* Chicago: University of Chicago Press.

Wallis, John Joseph. (2009). NBER/Maryland Constitution Project. http:// www. stateconstitutions.umd.edu.

Wallis, John Joseph, Sylla, Richard, & Legler, John. (1994). The interaction of taxation and regulation in nineteenth century banking. In Claudia Goldin & Gary Libecap (Eds.), *The regulated economy: An historical approach to political economy* (pp. 121–144). Chicago: NBER/University of Chicago Press.

Wallis, John Joseph, & Weingast, Barry. (2005). Equilibrium federal impotence: Why the states and not the American national government financed infrastructure investment in the antebellum era. NBER Working Paper No. 11397.

Wallis, John Joseph, & Weingast, Barry. (2008). Dysfunctional or optimal institutions?: State debt limitations, the structure of state and local governments, and the finance of American infrastructure. In Elizabeth Garret, Elizabeth Graddy, & Howell Jackson (Eds.), *Fiscal challenges.* New York: Cambridge University Press.

Wallis, John Joseph, Weingast, Barry R., & North, Douglass C. (2006, September). The corporate origins of individual rights. Paper presented at the Economic History Association Meeting.

Waugh, Scott L. (1986). Tenure to contract: Lordship and clientage in thirteenth-century England. *English Historical Review, 101*(401), 811–839.

Webb, Sidney, & Webb, Beatrice Potter. (1908). *English local government from the revolution to the Municipal Corporations Act.* New York: Longmans, Green, 1908.

Weber, Max. (1947). *The theory of social and economic organization.* New York: Free Press.

Weingast, Barry R. (1995). The economic role of political institutions: Market-preserving federalism and economic development. *Journal of Law, Economics, and Organization, 11*, 1–31.

Weingast, Barry R. (1997). The political foundations of democracy and the rule of law. *American Political Science Review, 91*(2), 245–263.

Weingast, Barry R. (1998). Political stability and civil war: Institutions, commitment, and American democracy. In Robert Bates, Avner Greif, Margaret Levi, Jean-Laurent Rosenthal, & Barry R. Weingast (Eds.), *Analytic narratives.* Princeton: Princeton University Press.

Weingast, Barry R. (2002). Rational choice institutionalism. In Ira Katznelson & Helen V. Milner (Eds.), *Political science, state of the discipline: Reconsidering power, choice, and the state.* New York: Norton.

Weingast, Barry R. (November, 2006a). Self-enforcing constitutions: With an application to democratic stability in America's first century. Working Paper, Hoover Institution.

Weingast, Barry R. (November, 2006b). Second-generation fiscal federalism: Implications for decentralized democratic governance and economic development. Working Paper, Hoover Institution.

Weiss, Thomas. (1992). U.S. labor force estimates and economic growth, 1800 to 1860. In Robert E. Gallman & John Joseph Wallis (Eds.), *American economic growth and standards of living before the Civil War.* Chicago: NBER/University of Chicago Press.

Wells, Colin. (1992). *The Roman Empire, second edition.* Cambridge, MA: Harvard University Press.

Widner, Jennifer A. (2001). *Building the rule of law.* New York: W. W. Norton.

Williamson, Oliver O. (1985). *The economic institutions of capitalism.* New York: Free Press.

Wintrobe, Ronald. (1998). *The political economy of dictatorship.* Cambridge: Cambridge University Press.

Wolin, Sheldon. (2004). *Politics and vision (expanded edition).* Princeton: Princeton University Press.

Wood, Gordon. (1969). *Creation of the American republic.* Chapel Hill: University of North Carolina Press.

Worley, Ted R. (1949). Arkansas and the money crisis of 1836–1837. *Journal of Southern History, 15*(2), 178–191.

Worley, Ted R. (1950). The control of the real estate bank of the state of Arkansas, 1836–1855. *Mississippi Valley Historical Review, 37*(3), 403–426.

Wren, Anne. (2006). Comparative perspectives on the role of the state in the economy. In Barry R. Weingast & Donald Wittman (Eds.), *Handbook of political economy.* Oxford: Oxford University Press.

Wright, Robert. (2008). Corporate entrepreneurship and economic growth in America, 1790–1860. Paper presented at the Economic History Association meetings, New Haven.

Yoffee, Norman. (2005). *The myth of the archaic state: Evolution of the earliest cities, states, and civilizations.* New York: Cambridge University Press.

Zorita, Alonso de. (1963[1570]). *Life and labor in ancient Mexico.* (Benjamin Keen, Trans.). New Brunswick: Rutgers University Press.

Index

access limitation. *See* natural state (limited access order)

Acemoglu, Daron
democracy/nondemocracy, 149
elite/non-elite framework, 149
income redistribution, 143
modernization hypothesis, 12–13
non-elite assertion, 245–246
open access orders, 188

Adams, John, 210

Adams, John Quincy, 236

Adams, Samuel, 210

adaptive efficiency, 133–136, 144–147, 252–254

adherent organizations, 16, 20, 36, 151–152, 260–262. *See also* organizations

Agulhon, M., 220–221

alienation/alienability. *See also* land law
of Church property, 67, 161–162
kings' right to, 162–164
in medieval England, 82
nature of, 89–90
and subinfeudation, 82

American Constitution, 114–115, 195–196, 197

American Revolution, 198–199, 207

Anderson, R. D., 227

archbishops. *See* bishops/archbishops

aristocracy. *See also* land law
as dominant coalition, 94
"extinctions" of peerages, 93–94
gentry, vs. nobility, 92
and influence, 95
land ownership of, 92–93
as limited access order, 95
the Mexica (Aztec Empire), 56–57

mobility within, 94
nobility, role of, 91–92
and patron-client networks, 94–95

Aristotle, 191–192, 196

authoritarian states, 131

Aztec empire
as basic natural state, 55
economic system, 57–58
education, 57
land distribution, 56
and mature natural states, 62
religion, 56–57
societies/city-states, 55–56

Bailyn, Bernard
Enlightenment, influence of, 244
factions, fear of, 199, 207
on Founding Fathers, 228–229

balance, double. *See* double balance

barriers to entry, 216–217

Barzel, Yoram, 270

basic natural state. *See also* Aztec empire;
Carolingian empire; natural state
(limited access order)
emergence of, 105–106, 155
fragile natural state, movement from, 55
military, consolidated control of, 177
organization/institution structures, 21, 43, 46
organizational complexity, 74
and rule of law, 74
violence suppression, 173–174

bastard feudalism. *See also* land law
courts/juries, 97–99
Crown land/revenue reduction, 102–104